James

Coban..

Manchester

REDUNDANCY

The Law and Practice

THIRD EDITION

REDUNDANCY

The Law and Practice

THIRD EDITION

By

JOHN MCMULLEN

MA, PhD (Cantab), FCIPD, FRSA;
Director of Employment Law, Wrigleys Solicitors LLP;
Visiting Professor of Law, Durham University

OXFORD
UNIVERSITY PRESS

OXFORD
UNIVERSITY PRESS

Great Clarendon Street, Oxford ox2 6DP

Oxford University Press is a department of the University of Oxford.
It furthers the University's objective of excellence in research, scholarship,
and education by publishing worldwide in

Oxford New York

Auckland Cape Town Dar es Salaam Hong Kong Karachi
Kuala Lumpur Madrid Melbourne Mexico City Nairobi
New Delhi Shanghai Taipei Toronto

With offices in

Argentina Austria Brazil Chile Czech Republic France Greece
Guatemala Hungary Italy Japan Poland Portugal Singapore
South Korea Switzerland Thailand Turkey Ukraine Vietnam

Oxford is a registered trade mark of Oxford University Press
in the UK and in certain other countries

Published in the United States
by Oxford University Press Inc., New York

First published 2011

British Library Cataloguing-in-Publication Data
Data available

Library of Congress Cataloging in Publication Data
Library of Congress Control Number: 2011922688

Typeset by Glyph International, Bangalore, India
Printed in Great Britain
on acid-free paper by
CPI Antony Rowe, Chippenham, Wiltshire

ISBN 978-0-19-954417-2

1 3 5 7 9 10 8 6 4 2

PREFACE

This book is intended to be a comprehensive view of redundancy law, ranging from individual entitlement to a redundancy payment, employment protection rights associated with redundancy, unfair dismissal law in relation to redundancy, information and consultation obligations relating to multiple redundancies and contractual redundancy payments. European and Equality law developments are noted at appropriate junctures.

The book is published at a time coincident with one of the worst recessions in modern history. We have therefore drawn on recent case law in the field of redundancy law, particularly unfair dismissal and information and consultation which has arisen due to the increased level of litigation over redundancy dismissals.

The book has its origins in editions published by other publishers. I am pleased to have had the support of Oxford University Press in producing the present book. I owe a debt to a number of colleagues including Martin Brewer, Helen Rice-Birchall, Helen Milgate, and Jon Fisher, who have allowed me to draw to a greater or lesser extent on contributions to previous incarnations of the book. Eleanor Wild has been very helpful and made major contributions to Chapters 1 and 10. I also thank the anonymous reviewers of earlier drafts of certain chapters of the book, and I express my gratitude to my publishers, in particular Roxanne Selby, Faye Judges, Eleanor Walter and Bethan Cousins at Oxford University Press.

John McMullen
March 2011

v

CONTENTS

List of Abbreviations   xi
Table of Cases   xiii
Table of Legislation   xxvii
Table of Statutory Instruments   xxxiii
Table of European Instruments   xxxv

I REDUNDANCY PAYMENTS

Introduction   3

1. Qualifying Factors   11
    A. Eligibility for a Statutory Redundancy Payment   11
    B. Employment Relationship: Introduction   12
    C. Employment Relationship: Historical Context   15
    D. Employment Status: Multi-factor Approach   16
    E. Illegality of Contract   42
    F. Continuous Employment Under a Contract of Employment   44
    G. Employees Excluded From Claiming a Statutory Redundancy Payment   48

2. The Requirement of Dismissal   50
    A. Termination of Employment Law by Operation of Law   51
    B. Other Cases   52

3. The Definition of Redundancy   59
    A. General   59
    B. The Presumption of Redundancy   60
    C. The Definition Analysed   61
    D. The Contract Test Versus the Job Function Test   77
    E. Bumped Redundancies   81
    F. Bumping—A Different View   82
    G. Summary   84

4. Re-employment   85
    A. General   85
    B. Scope of Sections 138 and 141   86
    C. The Distinction Between Renewal and Re-engagement   87
    D. The Offer of Re-employment   88

 E. Acceptance of an Offer of Re-employment   92

 F. Unreasonable Refusal of Re-employment   99

5. **Death of an Employer or Employee**   106

 A. General   106

 B. Death of an Employer   106

 C. Death of an Employee   107

6. **Lay-off and Short-time Working**   108

 A. General   108

 B. Common Law Rules   109

 C. Express Contractual Terms   109

 D. Implied Contractual Terms   110

 E. The Statutory Scheme   112

7. **Misconduct and Strikes**   116

 A. The Overall View   116

 B. Misconduct: The General Scheme   116

 C. Misconduct and Strike Action   117

 D. Strike Action: Treatment of Entitlement to a Redundancy Payment   119

 E. Appendix to *Simmons v Hoover Ltd*   120

8. **Claiming and Calculating**   122

 A. Time Limits   122

 B. The 'Relevant Date'   123

 C. Amount, Seniority Issues, and the Equality Act 2010   124

 D. Failure or Inability to Pay: The National Insurance Fund, the Old Redundancy Fund, and the (Defunct) Redundancy Rebate   130

II EMPLOYMENT PROTECTION RIGHTS ASSOCIATED WITH REDUNDANCY

9. **Guarantee Payments and Time Off to Look for Work or Training**   133

 A. Guarantee Payments   133

 B. Time Off to Look for Work or Training   138

III UNFAIR DISMISSAL

10. **Redundancy and Unfair Dismissal**   145

 A. General   145

 B. The Standard of Reasonableness Expected of Employers   153

C. The Warning and Consultation Process 163

D. The Selection Process 172

E. Alternative Employment 185

F. Remedies 188

G. Automatically Unfair Dismissal 200

IV INFORMATION AND CONSULTATION

11. **Information and Consultation on Multiple Redundancies** **211**

A. Introduction 211

B. General Scope 212

C. The Impact of European Law on Information/
Consultation Obligations 214

D. Special Circumstances 228

V CONTRACTUAL SCHEMES

12. **Contractual Redundancy Schemes** **239**

A. General 239

B. Enforceability 255

C. Contractual Redundancy Schemes and Age Discrimination 260

D. Unfair Dismissal Law: Proceduralism Revisited 265

Appendices

Appendix 1: Redundancy Payment Ready Reckoner 269

Appendix 2: Redundancy Selection Matrix 271

Appendix 3: Specimen Letter: Informing Trade Unions and/or Employee
Representatives and Initiating Consultation on Collective
Redundancies Pursuant to TULRCA 1992, section 188 272

Appendix 4: Specimen Letter: To Affected Employees Inviting Them to Elect
Representatives 273

Appendix 5: Specimen Letter/Notice: Informing all Employees of
Redundancy Proposals 275

Appendix 6: Specimen Letter: Informing Individual Employee of Proposed
Selection for Redundancy 276

Appendix 7: Specimen Letter: To Individual Employee Informing
Him of Final Selection for Redundancy 277

Appendix 8: Form HR1 (Advance Notification of Redundancies) 278

Appendix 9: Form RP1 (Redundancy Payments: Claims from the
National Insurance Fund) 280

Index 285

LIST OF ABBREVIATIONS

ACAS	Advisory, Conciliation and Arbitration Service
All ER (D)	All England Law Reports
ALR	Australian Law Reports
BBC	British Broadcasting Corporation
BERR	The Department for Business, Enterprise and Regulatory Reform (now BIS)
BIS	Department for Business Innovation and Skills
BRB	British Railway Board
BT	British Telecom
Ch	Cinancery Division
CIPD	The Chartered Institute of Personnel and Development
COIT	Central Office of Industrial Tribunals
CSOH	Court of Session, Outer House
DDA 1995	Disability Discrimination Act 1995
DSO	Direct Service Organisation
DTI	Department of Trade and Industry
EA 2010	Equality Act 2010
EAT	Employment Appeal Tribunal
EC	European Community
ECJ	European Court of Justice
EEC	European Economic Community
EOR	Equal Opportunities Review
EPCA	Employment Protection (Consolidation) Act 1978
ERA 1996	Employment Rights Act 1996
EU	European Union
HC	House of Commons
HL	House of Lords
HMRC	HM Revenue and Customs
HON	Home Office notice
HR	Human Resources
ICR	Industrial Case Reports
ILJ	Industrial Law Journal
IRLB	Industrial Relations Law Bulletin
IRLR	Industrial Relations Law Reports
ITR	Industrial Tribunal Reports
KIR	Knights Industrial Cases
LIFO	Last in, first out
MLR	Modern Law Review
NHS	National Health Service
NIRC	The National Industrial Relations Court
NMWA	National Minimum Wage Act 1998
PIDA	Public Interest Disclosure Act 1998
RPI	Retail Prices Index
SLPQ	Scottish Law and Practice Quarterly

STC	Simon's Tax Cases
TFEU	The Treaty of the Functioning of the European Union
TLR	Times Law Reports
TSS	Teachers Superannuation Scheme
TULR(C)A 1992	Trade Union and Labour Relations (Consolidation) Act 1992
TUPE 2006	Transfer of Undertakings (Protection of Employment) Regulations 2006
TURERA	Trade Union Reform and Employment Rights Act 1993
UK	United Kingdom
UK SC	UK Supreme Court
USA	United States of America
WLR	Weekly Law Reports

TABLE OF CASES

102 Social Club and Institute Ltd v Bickerton [1977] ICR 911 . . . . 1.124
A Dakri & Co Limited v Tiffen [1981] IRLR 57 . . . . 6.05, 6.06
Abbey National Plc v Chagger [2009] IRLR 86, EAT, [2010] IRLR 47, CA. 10.144
Abbotts and Standley v Wesson-Glynwed Steels Ltd [1982] IRLR 51 . . . . 10.165, 10.217
Aerospace Plc v Green and Another [1996] IRLR 199 . . . . 10.170
Ahsan v Westmead Business Group Limited, UKEAT/0480/10. . . . . 1.24
Air Canada v Lee [1978] ICR 1202. . . . . 4.54
Airfix Footwear Ltd v Cope [1978] IRLR 396 . . . . 1.49
Akavan Erityisalojen Keskusliddo AEK ry v Fujitsu Siemens Computers
      Oy [2009] IRLR 944 . . . . 11.18, 11.20, 11.47, 11.61
Akzo Coatings Plc v Thompson, UKEAT/0117/94 . . . . 10.184
Albion Automotive Ltd v Walker [2002] EWCA Civ 946 . . . . 12.45, 12.48
Alboni v Ind Coope Retail Ltd [1998] IRLR 131 . . . . 10.35
Alexander v Brigden Enterprises Limited [2006] IRLR 422 . . . . 10.114, 12.23
Alexander v Standard Telephones and Cables Ltd (No. 1) and (No. 2)
      [1990] IRLR 55 . . . . 12.20, 12.21, 12.22,
                                                                                           12.27, 12.54, 12.55, 12.58
Allinson v Drew Simmons Engineering Ltd [1985] ICR 488. . . . . 6.21
Allsop v North Tyneside Metropolitan Borough Council [1992] ICR 639 . . . . 12.67, 12.68
Alvis Vickers Limited v Lloyd, UKEAT/0785/04 . . . . 3.96
Amalgamated Society of Boilermakers, Shipwrights, Blacksmiths and Structual
      Workers v George Wimpey ME & Co Ltd [1977] IRLR 95 . . . . 11.37
Amos v Max-Arc Ltd [1973] ICR 46. . . . . 3.57
Anderson v David Winter & Sons Ltd [1966] 1 ITR 326 . . . . 4.27
Anderson v Pringle of Scotland Ltd [1998] IRLR 64 . . . . 12.30, 12.55
Anglia Regional Co-operative Society v O'Donnell, UKEAT/655/91 . . . . 3.13
Aparau v Iceland Frozen Foods Plc [1996] IRLR 119 . . . . 3.15, 3.20
Argos Electronics Ltd v Walsh, UKEAT/184/89, 7 March 1990 . . . . 10.83
Armour (Hamish) v Association of Scientific, Technical and Managerial
      Staffs [1979] IRLR 24, EAT 11.68
Armstrong Whitworth Rolls Ltd v Mustard [1971] 1 All ER 598. . . . . 8.18
Arora v Coopers & Lybrand [1998], unreported 10.110
Ashby v Monterry Designs Limited, UKEAT/0226/08 . . . . 1.134
Association of Pattern Makers and Allied Craftsmen v Kirvin Ltd [1978] IRLR 318, EAT 11.68
Association of University Teachers v University of Newcastle upon Tyne [1987] ICR 317 . . . . . . 3.49
Athinaiki Chartopoliia AE v Panagiotidis [2007] IRLR 284 . . . . 11.28
Atlantic Power & Gas Ltd v More, UKEAT/1125/97 . . . . 10.76
Augustin v Total Quality Staff Limited, UKEAT/0343/07. . . . . 1.47
Autoclenz Limited v Belcher & Ors [2009] EWCA Civ 1046 . . . . 1.106
Aylward v Glamorgan Holiday Home Ltd t/a Glamorgan Holiday Hotel, UKEAT/167/02 . . . . . . 3.45
Ayse Süzen v Zehnacker Gebäudereinigung GmbH Krankenhausservice [1997] IRLR 255 . . . . . . 3.43

Babar Indian Restaurant v Rawat [1985] IRLR 57. . . . . 10.132
Bailey v Whitehead Bros (Wolverhampton) Limited, COIT 1265/232 . . . . 4.44
Bainbridge v Westinghouse Brake and Signal Company Ltd [1966] 1 ITR 89 . . . . 4.77
Baker v Gill [1970] 6 ITR 61, DC 4.38
Ball v Balfour Kilpatrick Ltd [1997] ICR 740 . . . . 12.81
Bansi v Alpha Flight Services, UKEAT/0652/03 . . . . 10.139
Barley v Amey Roadstone Corp Ltd [1977] ICR 546, [1977] IRLR 299, EAT. 11.22
Barnes v Gilmartin Associates, UKEAT/825/97, 29 July 1998. . . . . 3.65, 3.67

xiii

Barratt Construction Ltd v Dalrymple [1984] IRLR 385 . . . . 3.96, 10.178
Barratt Developments (Bradford) v Union of Construction, Allied Trades and
    Technicians [1978] ICR 319, [1977] IRLR 403, EAT. 11.22
Barry v Midland Bank Plc [1991] ICR 859 . . . . 8.16
Bartholomew v The Mayor & Burgess of the London Borough of Haringey,
    UKEAT/627/90. . . . . 10.163
Bass Leisure Ltd v Thomas [1994] IRLR 104. . . . . 3.30, 3.31, 4.67
Beckmann v Dynamco Whicheloe MacFarlane Ltd [2002] IRLR 578 . . . . .12.61, 12.66
Benton v Sanderson Kayser Ltd [1989] ICR 136. . . . . 4.40
Beynton v Saurus General Engineering Limited, unreported, 1999 . . . . 10.156
Birch v University of Liverpool [1985] ICR 470, [1985] IRLR 165, CA 2.20, 10.19
Birch and Humber v University of Liverpool [1985] IRLR 165 . . . . 11.08
BL Cars Ltd v Lewis [1983] IRLR 58 . . . . 10.167
Blatchford Solicitors v Burger, UKEAT/207/00 . . . . 10.138
Booth and Others v United States of America [1999] IRLR 16 . . . . 1.152, 1.157, 1.158
Boots Co Plc v Lees-Collier [1986] IRLR 485. . . . . 10.199
Boulton and Paul Ltd v Arnold [1994] IRLR 532 . . . . 10.218
Boxfoldia Ltd v National Graphical Association (1982) [1988] ICR 752. . . . . 7.06
Boyo v Lambeth London Borough Council [1994] ICR 72. . . . . 12.58
Breakspear v Colonial Financial Services (UK) Ltd [2002] EWHC 1456. . . . . 12.08
Briggs v Oates [1990] IRC 473 . . . . 1.135
Bristol Channel Ship Repairers Ltd v (1) O'Keefe and Others and (2) G N Lewis
    [1977] IRLR 13 . . . . 10.122
British Broadcasting Corporation v Farnworth [1998] ICR 116 . . . . 3.62
British Coal Corporation v Cheesbrough [1990] IRLR 148. . . . . 8.23
British Gas v McCarrick [1991] IRLR 305 . . . . 10.59
British Home Stores v Burchell [1978] IRLR 379 . . . . 10.61
British Leyland (UK) Ltd v McQuilken [1978] IRLR 245. . . . . 12.15, 12.18
British Leyland (UK) Ltd v Swift [1981] IRLR 91. 10.46, 10.59, 10.64
British Shoe Machinery Co Ltd v Clarke [1977] IRLR 297 . . . . 10.178
British Sugar Plc v Kirker [1998] IRLR 624 . . . . 10.155, 10.156
Britool Ltd v Roberts [1993] IRLR 481 . . . . 10.222
Brook Street Bureau (UK) Limited v Dacas [2004]
    EWCA Civ 217 . . . . 1.08, 1.70, 1.75, 1.77, 1.78
Bryan v George Wimpey & Co [1968] 3 ITR 28. . . . . 4.75
Buchan and Ivey v Secretary of State for Employment [1997] IRLR 80 . . . . 1.129
Burgess v Stevedoring Services [2002] IRLR 810. . . . . 7.08
Burne v Arvin Meritor LVS (UK) Ltd, UKEAT/239/02 . . . . 3.96
Burroughs Machines Ltd v Timmoney [1977] IRLR 404 . . . . 12.35
Burton Allton and Johnson Ltd v Peck [1975] ICR 193, [1973] IRLR 87 . . . . .2.19, 10.18
Burton Group Ltd v Smith [1977] IRLR 351, EAT. 2.10
Byrne v Arvin Meritor LVS (UK) Limited, UKEAT/239/02 . . . . 10.140
Byrne v Castrol (UK) Ltd, UKEAT/429/96 . . . . 10.163

C F Brooke v London Borough of Haringey [1992] IRLR 478 . . . . 10.155
Cable & Wireless Plc v Muscat [2006] EWCA Civ 220. . . . . .1.75, 1.78
Cambridge & District Co-operative Society Ltd v Ruse [1993] IRLR 156. . . . . 4.61
Camden Exhibition and Display Ltd v Lynott [1966] 1 QB 555 . . . . 12.15
Camelo v Sheerlyn Productions Limited [1976] ICR 531, EAT. 4.07
Cameron v Digital Equipment Co Ltd [2001] EWCA Civ 1751 . . . . 12.08
Campbell and Others v Dunoon & Cowal Housing Association Ltd
    [1993] IRLR 496 . . . . 10.104, 10.219
Camps Mount Farm Estate v Kozyra, UKEAT/499/85 . . . . 3.73
Canadian Imperial Bank of Commerce v Beck, UKEAT/0141/10. . . . . .8.25, 11.74
Candy v The London Borough of Lewisham, UKEAT/1367/97, 26 November 1998 . . . . 10.78
Cann v Fairfield Rowan Limited (1966) 1 KIR 510. . . . . 4.21

Carmichael v National Power Plc [1998] IRLR 301, CA, [2000] IRLR 43, HL 1.08, 1.28, 1.29,
                                                                    1.35, 1.48, 1.51, 1.115
Carrington v Harwich Dock Co Limited [1998] IRLR 567 . . . . 1.147
Carron Company v Robertson [1967] 2 ITR 484 . . . . 4.61, 4.73
Carry All Motors Ltd v Pennington [1980] ICR 806 . . . . 3.38
Carter v Ludwig Institute Limited [2007] EWHC 1456 . . . . 12.08
Cartwright v G Clancey Ltd [1983] IRLR 355 . . . . 9.21
Catamaran Cruisers Ltd v Williams [1994] IRLR 386, EAT 11.06
Catherall v Michelin Tyre Plc [2005] ICR 28, EAT 2.25
Chagger v Abbey National Plc [2010] IRLR 47, CA, [2009] IRLR 86, EAT 10.159, 10.220
Chapman v Goonvean and Rostowrack China Clay Company Ltd
    [1973] 2 All ER 1063 . . . . 3.51, 3.64
Christopher Neame Ltd v White, UKEAT/451/79 . . . . 9.11
Church v West Lancashire NHS Trust (No. 2) [1998] IRLR 492 . . . . 3.06, 3.99, 3.102, 3.106
City and East London FHS Authority v Duncan, EAT, unreported 1.32
Claes and Others v Landsbanki Luxembourg SA, In Liquidation,
    combined cases C-235 to C-239/10 . . . . 11.70
Clark v Oxfordshire Health Authority [1998] IRLR 125 . . . . 1.32
Clarke v Wolsey Limited [1975] IRLR 154 . . . . 4.35
Clarkes of Hove Ltd v Bakers' Union [1979] 1 All ER 152,
    [1978] ICR 1076 (CA) 11.22, 11.59, 11.67, 11.68
Clarkson International Tools Ltd v Short [1973] IRLR 90 . . . . 10.211
Clarkson v Pensher Security Doors Limited, UKEAT/0107/09 . . . . 1.13
Clearsprings Management Limited v Ankers, UKEAT/0054/08 . . . . 3.43
Clemens v Peter Richards Ltd [1977] IRLR 332 . . . . 9.12
Clews v Liverpool City Council, UKEAT/463/93, 4 May 1994 . . . . 10.105
Cold Drawn Tubes Ltd v Middleton [1992] IRLR 160 . . . . 10.199
Cole v London Borough of Hackney, UKEAT/973/99 . . . . 2.25, 10.184
Collin v Flexiform Ltd (1966) 1 ITR 253 . . . . 8.30
Collins v Secretary of State for Trade and Industry [2001] All ER (D) 286 . . . . 2.08
Collison v BBC [1999] IRLR 238 . . . . 1.145
Colne Valley Spinning Ltd v Yates, UKEAT/1091/02 . . . . 8.18
Commission of the EC v United Kingdom [1994] IRLR 412 . . . . 3.03
Commission for Healthcare Audit & Inspection v Ward,
    UKEAT/0579/07 . . . . 4.60, 4.61, 4.62, 4.72
Constantine v McGregor Cory Limited, UKEAT/236/99 . . . . 10.189
Construction Industry Training Board v Labour Force Ltd [1970] 3 All ER 220 . . . . 1.55
Continental Tyre Group Limited v Mrs I Holman, 1997, unreported 10.217
Corby v Morrison [1980] IRLR 218 . . . . 1.140
Cornwall County Council v Prater [2006] EWCA Civ 102 . . . . 1.42, 1.47, 1.114
Corus & Regal Hotels Plc v Wilkinson, UKEAT/0102/03 . . . . 3.70, 3.74
Costain Building and Civil Engineering Limited v (1) Mr DR Smith and
    (2) Chanton Group Plc [2000] ICR 215 . . . . 1.61, 1.125
Courtaulds Northern Spinning Ltd v Sibson [1988] ICR 451 . . . . 3.18
Cowell v Quilter Goodison Company Ltd and QC Management Services Ltd
    [1989] IRLR 392, CA 1.135
Cowen v Haden Carriers Ltd [1982] IRLR 314 . . . . 10.124, 10.125, 10.126
Cowley v Manson Timber Ltd, UKEAT/0115/92, unreported, 1994 . . . . 10.188, 10.189
CPS Recruitment Ltd v Bowen [1982] IRLR 54 . . . . 2.15
Crehan v Courage Ltd, unreported 1.138
Cummings v Siemens Communications Ltd, ET/3500013/10 . . . . 10.39
Curling v Securicor Ltd [1992] IRLR 549 . . . . 3.23, 3.24, 3.25, 3.27, 3.106, 4.76

Davies v Farnborough College of Technology [2008] IRLR 14 . . . . 10.115
Davies v Presbyterian Church of Wales [1986] IRLR 194 . . . . 1.41
De Grasse v Stockwell Tools Ltd [1992] IRLR 269 . . . . 10.75, 10.102

Delanair Ltd v Mead [1976] ICR 522 . . . . 3.48
Denton v Neepsend Ltd [1976] IRLR 164 . . . . 3.56, 4.81
Devon County Council v Cook [1977] IRLR 188 . . . . 2.10
Devonald v Rosser & Sons [1906] 2 KB 728 . . . . 6.07
Dietman v Brent London Borough Council [1988] ICR 842 . . . . 12.58
Digital Equipment Co Limited v Clements (No. 2) [1998] ICR 258 . . . . 10.221
Dita Danosa v LKB Lizings SIA (Case C-232/09), [2010] All ER (D) 178 . . . . 1.134
Dixon v Automobile Association Ltd, UKEAT/0874/03 . . . . 3.96
Drake International Systems Limited t/a Drake Distribution Services v O'Hare,
    UKEAT/0384/03 . . . . 10.138
Driver v Cleveland Structucal Engineering Co Ltd [1994] IRLR 636 . . . . 10.26
Duffin v Secretary of State for Employment [1983] ICR 766 . . . . 8.01
Duffy v Yeomans & Partners Ltd [1994] IRLR 642 . . . . 10.98
Duke v Reliance Systems Ltd [1982] IRLR 347 . . . . 12.35, 12.39, 12.47
Dundon v GPT Ltd [1995] IRLR 403 . . . . 10.236
Dunnachie v Kingston-upon-Hull City Council [2004] UKHL 36 . . . . 10.226
Dutton v Hawker Siddeley Aviation Ltd [1978] IRLR 390 . . . . 9.32

E & J Davies Transport Limited v Chattaway [1972] ICR 267 . . . . 4.84
E Green & Sons (Castings) Ltd v Association of Scientific, Technical and
    Managerial Staffs [1984] ICR 352, [1984] IRLR 135, EAT 11.22, 11.85
East Suffolk Local Health Services NHS Trust v Palmer [1997] ICR 425 . . . . 4.54
Eaton Ltd v King [1995] IRLR 75 . . . . 10.170
EBAC Limited v Wymer [1995] ICR 466, EAT 4.06
EC Commission v United Kingdom [1994] ICR 664, [1994] IRLR 412 . . . . 11.13
Edinburgh Council v Brown [1999] IRLR 208 . . . . 12.09, 12.31
Edwards v Chesterfield Royal Hospital NHS Trust [2010] EWCA Civ 571 . . . . 12.58
Edwards v Skyways Ltd [1964] 1 All ER 494 . . . . 12.14
Egg Stores (Stamford Hill) Ltd v Leibovici [1977] ICR 260 . . . . 2.08, 5.01
Elkouil v Coney Island Limited [2001] UKEAT/0520/00 . . . . 10.87
Eltringham v Sunderland Co-operative Society Ltd [1971] 6 ITR 121 . . . . 4.66
Euroguard Ltd v Ryecroft, UKEAT/842/92 . . . . 10.180, 10.183
Eversheds LLP v De Belin, TET Case No. 1804069/09 . . . . 10.157
Executors of Everest v Cox [1980] 1 ICR 415 . . . . 4.62, 4.72
Express and Echo Publications Ltd v Tanton [1999] IRLR 367 . . . . 1.25, 1.91, 1.94, 1.95, 1.96

Fabar Construction Ltd v Race [1979] ICR 529 . . . . 6.22
Faccini Dori v Recreb Srl (Case C-91/92) [1994] ECR I-3325 . . . . 10.05
Farrow v Wilson [1869] LR 4 CP 744 . . . . 5.01
Farthing v Midland Household Stores Ltd [1974] IRLR 354 . . . . 10.164
FC Shepherd & Co Ltd v Jerrom [1986] ICR 802 . . . . 2.08, 5.01
Ferguson v Prestwick Circuits [1992] IRLR 268 . . . . 10.103
Fisher v Hooper Finance Ltd, UKEAT/0043/05 . . . . 4.75
Fisher v Hooper Finance Ltd, UKEAT/0166/07 . . . . 10.184
Fleming v Secretary of State for Trade and Industry [1997] IRLR 62 . . . . 1.129
Fletcher v Federal Mogul Aftermarket UK Limited, ET, unreported, 1999 . . . . 10.155
Flett v Matheson [2006] IRLR 277 . . . . 1.121
Foley v Post Office [2000] ICR 1283 . . . . 10.66
Ford v Warwickshire County Council [1983] IRLR 126 . . . . 1.151
Forman Construction Ltd v R Kelly [1977] IRLR 468 . . . . 10.161
Forth Estuary Engineering Ltd v Litster [1986] IRLR 59 . . . . 10.222
Four Seasons Healthcare Ltd v Maughan [2005] IRLR 324 . . . . 2.09
Frame It v Brown, UKEAT/177/193 . . . . 3.40
Framptons Ltd v Badger, UKEAT/0138/06 . . . . 12.16
Frankling v BPS Public Sector Ltd [1999] IRLR 212 . . . . 12.60
Freemans Plc v Flynn [1984] IRLR 486 . . . . 10.199

Freud v Bentalls Ltd [1982] IRLR 443, [1983] ICR 77 . . . . 10.90, 12.19
Fulcrum Pharma (Europe) Limited v Bonaserra, UKEAT/0198/10 . . . . 10.138, 10.140

Gallagher v Post Office [1970] 3 All ER 712 . . . . 12.15
Galloway v Export Packing Services Ltd [1975] IRLR 306 . . . . 8.30
Galt v National Starch and Chemical Limited, ET/2101804/07 . . . . 12.75, 12.77
Gardiner v London Borough of Merton [1980] IRLR 472, CA 4.21
Gardner v (1) Haydn Davies Catering Equipment (1988) Ltd (In Liquidation)
       (2) ABE Catering Equipment Ltd, UKEAT, 9 January 1992 . . . . 1.150
Garricks v Nolan [1980] IRLR 259. . . . . 10.176
Gascol Conversions Ltd v Mercer [1974] ICR 420 . . . . 12.14
Gateshead Metropolitan Borough Council v Mills, UKEAT/610/92. . . . . 2.21, 10.21
GD Systems Ltd v Woods, UKEAT/470/09 . . . . 4.82
GEC Ferranti Defence Systems Ltd v MSF [1993] IRLR 101, EAT. 11.55
General and Municipal Workers' Union (Managerial, Administrative, Technical and
       Supervisory Association Section) v British Uralic Ltd [1979] IRLR 413. . . . . 11.85
Gibbons v Associated British Ports [1985] IRLR 113 . . . . 12.33
Gilham and Others v Kent County Council (No. 2) [1985] ICR 233 . . . . 10.54, 10.55, 10.64
Gimber and Sons Ltd v Spurrett [1967] 2 ITR 308 . . . . 3.98, 3.99
Gisda Cyf v Barratt [2010] UKSC 41 . . . . 2.05
GKN Sankey Ltd v National Society of Metal Mechanics [1980] ICR 148,
       [1980] IRLR 8, EAT. 11.85
Glasgow City Council v MacFarlane and Skivington, UKEAT/1277/99, unreported. 1.94, 1.95
GMB v MAN Truck & Bus Ltd [2000] IRLR 636. . . . . 11.06
GMB v Rankin and Harrison [1992] IRLR 514, EAT. 11.69
Gotch & Partners v Guest [1966] 1 ITR 65. . . . . 4.68
Governing Body of Thomas Mills High School v Rice, UKEAT, 17 February 1998 . . . . 3.39
Graff Diamonds Ltd v Boutwright (EAT/0148/10). 11.09
Graham v ABF [1986] IRLR 90 . . . . 10.108, 12.19
Granger v White, Brighton Tribunal, 1 March 1985, COIT 1631/134 . . . . 4.71, 4.83
Green v A & I Fraser (Wholesale Fish Merchants) Ltd [1985] IRLR 55 . . . . 3.96, 10.121, 10.132
Greenaway Harrison Ltd v Wiles [1994] IRLR 380, EAT 2.11
Greenwich Health Authority v Skinner and Ward [1989] ICR 220, EAT. 8.02
Gregory v Philip Morris Ltd (90) ALR 455 . . . . 12.58
Greig v Sir Alfred McAlpine & Son (Northern) Ltd [1979] IRLR 372 . . . . 10.120, 10.123
Grundy (Teddington) Limited v Plummer [1983] ICR 367 . . . . 11.91
Gryf-Lowczowski v Hinchingbrooke Healthcare NHS Trust [2005]
       EWHC 2407 (QB), [2006] ICR 425, [2006] IRLR 100 . . . . 2.08
Gunton v London Borough of Richmond upon Thames [1980] ICR 755,
       [1981] 1 Ch 448. . . . . 4.53, 12.58

Hachette Filipacchi UK Ltd v Johnson, UKEAT/0452/05. . . . . 3.106
Haddon v Vandenbergh Foods Limited [1999] IRLR 672. 10.49, 10.60,
                                                                              10.61, 10.62, 10.64
Haden v Cowen Ltd [1983] ICR 1 . . . . 3.82, 3.87, 3.93
Hair Colour Consultants Limited v Mena [1984] ICR 671, [1984] IRLR 386, EAT 4.21
Halfords v Roache, UKEAT/ 1 May 1989. . . . . 3.50
Hall v Farrington Data Processing Ltd [1969] 4 ITR 230 . . . . 3.55
Hall v Shorts Missile Systems Limited, EOR 72, 1997 . . . . 10.147
Hall v Woolston Hall Leisure Limited [2000] IRLR 578. . . . . 1.138, 11.91
Hall (Inspector of Taxes) v Lorimer [1992] STC 599, [1994] 1 WLR 209. . . . . 1.26, 1.116
Hammonds LLP v Mwitta, UKEAT/0026/10. . . . . 10.69, 10.160
Hancill v Marcon Engineering Limited [1990] ICR 103, [1990] IRLR 51. . . . . 4.21
Handford v Nationwide Building Society [2000] All ER (D) 2018 . . . . 3.71
Hanson v Wood (Abington Processing Gravers) [1986] 3 ITR 46 . . . . 3.44
Hardy v Tourism South East [2005] IRLR 242 . . . . 11.09

Harford v Swiftrim Limited [1987] ICR 429, [1987] IRLR 360, EAT. 4.21
Harlow v Artemis International Corporation Limited [2008] EWHC 1126 . . . . 12.08
Harris v E Turner & Sons (Joinery) Ltd [1973] ICR 31 . . . . 4.65
Hart v CE Payne & Sons Limited, 7 March 1985 . . . . 4.31
Hartlebury Printers Ltd (In Liquidation), Re [1992] ICR 559, [1992] IRLR 516 . . . . 11.69, 11.71
Haseltine Lake & Co Ltd v Dowler [1981] ICF 222, [1981] IRLR 25, EAT 2.10
Hasler v Tourell Precision Engineers Ltd, UKEAT/1426/103 . . . . 9.33, 9.37
Hatton Logistics Ltd v Waller, UKEAT/0298/06 . . . . 2.09
Helen McMullen v Hayes Manor School [1999], unreported 10.117
Hempell v WH Smith & Sons Limited [1986] IRLR 95, [1986] ICR 365 . . . . 4.06
Hendy Banks City Print Limited v Fairbrother, UKEAT/0691/04. 10.136
Henry v London General Transport Services Ltd [2002] IRLR 472 . . . . 12.14
Herbert v Air UK Engineering, UKEAT/575/97. . . . . 10.232, 10.240
Hereford and Worcester County Council v Neale [1986] IRLR 168 . . . . 10.49
Heron v Citylink-Nottingham [1993] IRLR 372 . . . . 10.99
Hetherington v Dependable Products Limited (1971) 6 ITR 1 . . . . 8.01
High Table Ltd v Horst [1997] IRLR 513 . . . . 3.09, 3.32, 3.100, 3.104
Highland Fish Farmers Ltd v Thoburn, UKEAT/1094/94, 9 March 1995 . . . . 10.133
Holden v Bradville Ltd [1985] IRLR 483 . . . . 12.19
Hollister v National Farmers' Union [1979] ICR 542 . . . . 10.28, 11.06, 11.91
Home Office v Evans [2008] IRLR 59 . . . . 3.24, 3.106
Horton v Farnell Electronic Services Ltd, UKEAT/755/95 . . . . 3.84
Hough v Leyland DAF Limited [1991] ICR 696. . . . . 11.14, 11.91
Hough and APEX v Leyland DAF Ltd [1991] IRLR 194. . . . . 10.69
Howard v Siemens Energy Services, ET/2324423/2008 . . . . 10.144
Huddersfield Parcels v Sykes [1981] IRLR 115 . . . . 12.19
Hudson v George Harrison Ltd, UKEAT/0571/02. . . . . 4.62, 4.72
Hunt v (1) Storm Communications Limited (2) Wild Card Public Relations Limited
    (3) Brown Brothers Wine (Europe) Limited, UKEAT/2702456/06. . . . . 3.43
Hyde v Britvic, COIT 2055/134, unreported 10.32

Iceland Frozen Foods Ltd v Jones [1982] IRLR 439. . . . . 10.48, 10.59, 10.64, 10.171
Inchcape Retail Limited v Large, UKEAT/0500/03. . . . . 4.61
Inchcape Retail Limited v Symonds, UKEAT/0316/09. . . . . 10.174
Ingeniorforeningen i Danmark v Region Syddanmark (Case C-499/08)
    [2010] All ER (D) 99 . . . . 12.79
Ingersoll-Dresser Pumps (UK) Ltd v Taylor, UKEAT/391/94 . . . . 2.10
International Computers v Kennedy [1981] IRLR 28, EAT 2.10
Ironmonger v Movefield Ltd [1988] IRLR 461 . . . . 1.55

J C King Ltd v Valencia [1966] 1 ITR 67 . . . . 1.137
James v London Borough of Greenwich [2008] EWCA Civ 35 . . . . 1.76
James v Redcats (Brands) Limited [2007] IRLR 296 . . . . 1.96
James W Cook & Co (Wivenhoe) Ltd v Tipper [1990] ICR 716. . . . . 10.28
Jeffries v Powerhouse Retail Ltd, UKEAT/1328/95. . . . . 12.44, 12.59
Jewell v Neptune Concrete Limited [1975] IRLR 147. . . . . 6.03, 6.04
John Brown Engineering Limited v Brown [1997] IRLR 90 . . . . 10.112
John Fowler (Don Foundry) Limited v Parkin [1975] IRLR 89. . . . . 4.84
Johnson v Nottinghamshire Combined Police Authority [1974] 1 All ER 1082,
    [1974] ICR 170 . . . . 3.65, 3.67, 3.68
Johnson v Peabody Trust [1996] IRLR 387. . . . . 3.86
Johnson v Ryan [2000] ICR 236. . . . . 1.123, 1.125
Jones v Associated Tunnelling Co Ltd [1981] IRLR 477 . . . . 3.19
Jones v Aston Cabinet Co Limited [1973] ICR 292, NIRC. 4.60
Jones v Governing Body of Burdett Coutts School [1997] ICR 390, EAT 4.06

Jones v Mid Glamorgan County Council [1997] IRLR 685 . . . . 2.22
Junk v Kühnel [2005] IRLR 310 . . . . 11.16, 11.43, 11.44, 11.46, 11.90

Kaine v Raine [1974] ICR 300 (NIRC) 4.31
Kaur v MG Rover Group Ltd [2005] IRLR 40 . . . . 12.26
Kaur v PKG Manufacturing Limited, ET/2504584/97 . . . . 10.155
Kaye v Cooke's (Finsbury) Limited [1973] 3 All ER 434 . . . . 4.28
Keeley v Fosroc International Ltd [2006] EWCA Civ 1277 . . . . 12.06
Kenneth McRae & Co Limited v Dawson [1984] IRLR 5 . . . . 6.06
Kent County Council v Mingo [2000] IRLR 90 . . . . 4.15, 10.155
Kentish Bus & Coach Company Ltd v Quarry, UKEAT/287/92 . . . . 4.55
Kerry Foods Ltd v Lynch [2005] IRLR 680, EAT 2.11
KGB Micros Ltd v Lewis, UKEAT/573/90, 25 March 1991 . . . . 10.103, 10.109
Kilgallon v Pilkington United Kingdom Limited, UKEAT/0771/03 . . . . 10.184
Kimberley Group Housing Limited v Hamberley [2008] IRLR 682 . . . . 3.43
King and Others v Eaton Limited [1996] IRLR 116 . . . . 10.110, 10.113
Kingwell v Elizabeth Bradley Designs Ltd, UKEAT/0661/02 . . . . 3.36, 3.63, 3.68
Kitching v Ward [1967] 2 ITR 464 . . . . 4.60
Kraft Foods UK Limited v Hastie, UKEAT/0024/10 . . . . 12.78
Kuncharalingham v Word by Word Translations Ltd, UKEAT/0269/10 . . . . 1.97, 1.98
Kvaerner Oil and Gas Limited v Parker, UKEAT/0444/02 . . . . 10.130
Kykot v Smith Hartley Ltd [1975] IRLR 372 . . . . 4.69

Ladbroke Courage Holidays Ltd v Asten [1981] IRLR 59 . . . . 10.28, 11.91
Lancaster University v The University and College Union, UKEAT/0278/10 . . . . 11.10, 11.84
Land v West Yorkshire Metropolitan County Council [1979] ICR 452,
    rvs'd [1981] ICR 334 CA 12.14
Lang v Briton Ferry Working Mens Club and Institute [1967] 2 ITR 35 . . . . 3.42
Langston v Cranfield University [1998] IRLR 172 . . . . 12.19
Lassman and Others v (1) Secretary of State for Trade and Industry (2) Pan Graphics
    Industries Limited (In Receivership), CA, unreported 1.150
Lee v Chung and Shun Shing Construction and Engineering Company Ltd
    [1990] IRLR 236, [1990] ICR 409, PC 1.19
Lee v GEC Plessey Telecommunications [1993] IRLR 383 . . . . 12.14, 12.31, 12.33
Lee v Nottinghamshire County Council [1980] IRLR 284 . . . . 3.76
Leicestershire County Council v UNISON [2005] IRLR 920 EAT,
    [2006] IRLR 810 (CA) 11.21
Leighton v Michael [1995] ICR 1091 . . . . 1.138
Lenting v Bristow Helicopters Limited, [1998], unreported 10.135
Lesney Products & Co Ltd v Nolan [1974] 1 All ER 1082 . . . . 3.66
Leventhal Limited v North, UKEAT/0265/04 . . . . 3.96
Lifeguard Assurance Co Ltd v Zadrozny [1977] IRLR 56 . . . . 10.211
Lightfoot v D & J Sporting Ltd [1996] IRLR 64 . . . . 1.142
Lignacite Products Ltd v Krollman [1979] IRLR 22 . . . . 7.13
Lincoln & Lowth NHS Trust v Cowan, UKEAT/395/99 . . . . 4.63
Lionel Leventhal Limited v North, UKEAT/0265/04 . . . . 10.140
Litster v Forth Dry Dock & Engineering Co Ltd [1989] 1 All ER 1134 . . . . 11.14
Little v Charterhouse Magna Assurance Co Ltd [1980] IRLR 19 . . . . 3.22
Lloyd v Taylor Woodrow Construction [1999] IRLR 782 . . . . 10.94
Logan Salton v Durham County Council [1989] IRLR 99, EAT 2.21
London Transport Executive v Clarke [1990] ICR 532 . . . . 10.188
Lonmet Engineering Limited v Green [1972] 7 ITR 286 . . . . 4.28
Lotus Cars Ltd v Sucliffe and Stratton [1982] IRLR 381 . . . . 8.18
Loxley v BAE Systems (Munitions & Ordinance) Limited [2008] IRLR 853 . . . . .12.76,
                                                                            12.78, 12.79

Loy v Abbey National Financial and Investment Services Plc
    [2005] CSOH 47 . . . . 3.58
LRG (Enfield) Ltd v Smith, UKEAT/344/97 . . . . 12.43, 12.59
LTI Ltd v Radford, UKEAT/164/00 . . . . 12.24
Lucas v Henry Johnson (Packers and Shippers) Limited [1986] ICR 384, EAT 4.21

Mabiritzi v National Hospital for Nervous Diseases [1990] IRLR 133 . . . . 10.199,
                                                                                        10.228, 10.229
McAlwane v Boughton Estates Ltd [1973] ICR 470 . . . . 2.12
McAndrew v Prestwick Circuits Ltd [1988] IRLR 514 . . . . 3.22
McCrea v Cullen and Davison Ltd [1988] IRLR 130 . . . . 3.39
McCreadie v Thomson and MacIntyre (Patternmakers) Ltd [1971] 2 All ER 1135 . . . . 4.25
MacCulloch v Imperial Chemical Industries Plc [2008] IRLR 846 . . . . 12.72
MacGregor v William Tawse Ltd [1967] 2 ITR 198 . . . . 4.78
McGuigan v T G Baynes & Sons, EAT, unreported, 1999 . . . . 10.155
McKindley v William Hill (Scotland) Limited [1985] IRLR 492, EAT 4.41
McLeod v Hellyer Brothers Ltd [1987] IRLR 232 . . . . 1.33
McMeechan v Secretary of State for Employment [1997] IRLR 353 . . . . 1.34, 1.56,
                                                                                        1.59, 1.60, 1.114
McNulty v T Bridges & Company Ltd [1966] 1 ITR 367 . . . . 4.74, 4.75
Mafunanya v (1) Richmond Fellowship (2) Mr A Hanley, UKEAT/0449/03 . . . . 10.96
Mailway (Southern) Ltd v Willsher [1978] IRLR 322 . . . . 9.11
Mairs v Haughey [1994] 1 AC 303 . . . . 12.78
Makro Self Service Wholesalers Ltd v Union Shop, Distributive and Allied Workers,
    UKEAT/828/93 . . . . 11.36
Malone v British Airways Plc [2010] EWCA Civ 1225 . . . . 12.28
Managers (Holborn) Ltd v Hohne [1977] IRLR 230 . . . . 3.21
Manchester College of Arts and Technology v Smith, UKEAT/0460/06 . . . . 10.33
Mann v Secretary of State for Employment [1991] IRLR 566 . . . . 8.16
Marche v John Lewis Plc [1997], unreported 10.117
Mark Insulations Limited v Bunker, UKEAT/0331/05 . . . . 1.157
Market Investigations Ltd v Minister of Social Security [1969] 2 QB 173 . . . . 1.18
Marley v Forward Trust Group Ltd [1986] ICR 891 . . . . 12.33
Marriott v Oxford & District Co-operative Society (No. 2) [1970] 1 QB 186 . . . . 4.53
Marshall v Harland and Wolff Ltd (No. 2) [1972] ICR 97 . . . . 2.08, 5.01
Marshall v Southampton and South West Hampshire Area Health Authority
    [1986] ICR 140 . . . . 10.05
Marsland v Shropshire Mental Health NHS Trust, UKEAT/764/96 . . . . 12.44
Martin v South Bank University (Case C-4/01) [2004] IRLR 74 . . . . 12.65
Martland v Co-operative Insurance Society Limited, UKEAT/0200/07 . . . . 3.72, 3.75
Massey v Crown Life Insurance Co [1978] ICR 580 . . . . 1.25
Matthews v Pearl Assurance Plc, UKEAT/0552/97, 2 March 1998, unreported 2.25
Matthewson v R B Wilson Dental Laboratories Ltd [1988] IRLR 512 . . . . 10.49
Maxwell v Walter Howard Designs Ltd [1975] IRLR 77 . . . . 4.25
MDH Ltd v Sussex [1986] IRLR 123 . . . . 10.179
Meade-Hill and National Union of Civil and Public Servants v British Council
    [1995] IRLR 478 . . . . 3.15
Meadows v Faithfull Overalls Ltd [1977] IRLR 330 . . . . 9.18
Meek v (1) J Allen Rubber Co Ltd and (2) Secretary of State for Employment
    [1980] ICR 24, EAT 4.49
Merseyside v Taylor [1975] IRLR 60 . . . . 10.176
Metropolitan Resources Limited v Churchill Dulwich (In Liquidation) [2009] IRLR 700 . . . . 3.43
Michaelson v Arthur Henriques Plc, Manchester Tribunal, 27 August 1985,
    COIT 1680/214 . . . . 4.71, 4.83
Middlesborough Borough Council v TGWU [2002] IRLR 332 . . . . 11.50, 11.57, 11.59

Midland Bank Plc v Mr J Madden, 7 March 2000, UKEAT/1107/98,
    unreported 10.60, 10.62, 10.65, 10.66
Midland Foot Comfort Centre Ltd v Moppett [1973] IRLR 141. . . . . 3.07
Millat Housing Association v Nijhar, UKEAT, 11 February 1999 . . . . 3.39
Miller v Hanworthy Engineering Ltd [1986] IRLR 461 . . . . 6.12, 6.14
Miller v Harry Thornton (Lollies) Ltd [1978] IRLR 430 . . . . 9.08, 9.11
Mining Supplies (Longwall) v Baker [1988] IRLR 417 . . . . 10.217, 10.218
Mirror Group Newspapers v Gunning [1985] ICR 145. . . . . 1.09
Modern Injection Moulds Ltd v Price [1976] IRLR 72 . . . . 4.75
Mono Car Styling SA v Dervis Odemis (Case C-12/08) [2009] 3 CMLR 1589 . . . . 11.65
Monteresso Shipping Co Ltd v International Transport Workers' Federation
    [1982] ICR 675 . . . . 12.11
Montgomery v Johnson Underwood Ltd and O & K Orenstein & Kopple Ltd,
    UKEAT/509/98, UKEAT/716/98 . . . . 1.58, 1.113, 1.114
Moon v Homeworthy Furniture (Northern) Ltd [1976] IRLR 298 . . . . 10.28
Moore v President of the Methodist Conference (EAT/0219/10). 1.126
Moore v Simoco Europe Ltd, UKEAT/0725/02 . . . . 12.50
Morgan v Davies Bros (Pecander) Ltd, UKEAT, 23 March 1999 . . . . 3.34
Morgan v Electrolux Ltd [1991] IRLR 89 . . . . 10.49
Morgan v Fry [1968] 2 QB 710 . . . . 7.06
Morgan v Welsh Rugby Union [2011] IRLR 376 . . . . 10.71
Morley v CT Morley Ltd [1985] ICR 499, EAT 2.19, 10.19
Morris v Bailey [1969] 2 Lloyd's Rep 215 . . . . 12.33
Morris v Walsh Western UK Limited [1997] IRLR 562. . . . . 1.156
Morton Sundour Fabrics Ltd v Shaw [1967] 2 ITR 84 . . . . 2.10, 4.47, 12.18
Motherwell Railway Club v McQueen [1989] ICR 418 . . . . 10.229
MSF v GEC Ferranti (Defence Systems) Ltd (No. 2) [1994] IRLR 113 . . . . 11.55
MSF v Refuge Assurance Plc [2002] IRLR 324 . . . . 11.17
Mugford v Midland Bank [1997] IRLR 208 . . . . 10.69, 10.78, 10.111
Murphy v Epsom College [1985] ICR 80 . . . . 3.54, 3.70
Murray v Foyle Meats Ltd [1999] IRLR 562, [1999] ICR 827. . . . . 3.58, 3.104, 3.106, 10.125
Muschett v HM Prison Service [2010] EWCA Civ 25 . . . . 1.80

N C Watling & Co v Richardson [1978] ICR 1049. . . . . 10.63
National Coal Board v Galley [1958] 1 All ER 91 . . . . 12.14
National Coal Board v National Union of Mineworkers [1986] IRLR 439 . . . . 12.15, 12.22
National and Local Government Officers' Association v London Borough of
    Bromley, UKEAT/671/91. . . . . 11.55
National Union of Gold, Silver and Allied Trades v Albery Bros Ltd [1978] ICR 62,
    [1977] IRLR 173, EAT, aff'd [1979] ICR 84, [1978] IRLR 504, CA 11.37
National Union of Tailors and Garment Workers v Charles Ingram & Co Ltd
    [1978] 1 All ER 1271, [1977] ICR 530, [1977] IRLR 147, EAT. 11.37, 11.38
National Union of Teachers v Avon County Council [1978] ICR 626, [1978]
    IRLR 55, EAT 11.85
Nelson v BBC (No. 1) [1977] ICR 649. . . . . 3.80, 3.81, 3.82, 3.83, 3.93, 3.99, 10.125
Nelson v BBC (No. 2) [1980] ICR 110. . . . . 3.81, 10.125, 10.126
Nesbitt and Nesbitt v Secretary of State for Trade & Industry (EAT/0091/07) 1.134
Nethermere (St Neots) Ltd v Gardiner and Taverna [1984] IRLR 240 . . . . 1.31, 1.33, 1.50, 1.51
New Testament Church of God v Stewart [2008] ICR 282 . . . . 1.126
Newbrooks and Sweet v Saigal, UKEAT/29695/77. . . . . 9.08, 9.16
Newland v Simons and Willer (Hairdressers) Ltd [1981] IRLR 359. . . . . 1.143
Nicholson v Heaven and Earth Gallery Pty Ltd (126) ALR 233. . . . . 12.58
Noble v David Gold & Son Ltd [1980] IRLR 252. . . . . 10.80
Nolan v United States of America [2009] IRLR 923 . . . . 11.64
North v Pavleigh Ltd [1977] IRLR 461. . . . . 9.08, 9.11

North East Coast Ship Repairers Ltd v Secretary of State for Employment
[1978] IRLR 149 . . . . 1.119
North Wales Probation Area v Edwards, UKEAT/0468/07 . . . . 1.47
Northern Ireland Hotel and Catering College (Governing Body) and North Eastern
Education and Library Board v National Association of Teachers in Further and
Higher Education [1995] IRLR 83, NI CA. 11.36
Northern Ltd v Watson [1990] IRLR 500, EAT 2.13
Northgate HR Limited v Mercy [2008] IRLR 222 . . . . .10.172, 11.65
Norton Tool Co Ltd v Tewson [1973] 1 All ER 183. . . . . .10.225, 10.226
Notcutt v Universal Equipment Co (London) Ltd [1986] ICR 414. . . . . .2.08, 5.01

O'Brien v Associated Fire Alarms Ltd (1968) 3 ITR 182 . . . . 3.20
OCS Group UK Limited v Jones, UKEAT/0038/09 . . . . 3.43
O'Dea v ISC Chemicals Ltd t/a Rhone-Poulenc Chemicals [1995] IRLR 599 . . . . 10.230
O'Donoghue v Redcar & Cleveland Borough Council [2001] IRLR 615 . . . . 10.223
O'Kelly v Trusthouse Forte Plc [1983] IRLR 369 . . . . 1.25, 1.30, 1.51
Optare Group Ltd v Transport and General Workers Union [2007]
All ER (D) 135. . . . . 2.19, 10.23, 11.08
Optical Express Ltd v Williams [2007] IRLR 936 . . . . 4.41, 4.46
Ovidio Rodriguez Mayor and Others v Herencia Yacentre de Rafael de las
heras Dávila, Case C-323/08, 10 December 2009 . . . . 5.06

Paine and Moore v Grundy (Teddington) Ltd [1981] IRLR 267 . . . . 10.163
Palfrey v Transco Plc [2004] IRLR 916 . . . . 2.13
Parkinson v March Consulting Limited [1997] IRLR 308. . . . . 10.35
Parry v Holst & Co Ltd (1968) 3 ITR 317 . . . . 3.15
Pendragon Plc v Pellowe, UKEAT, 15 July 1999 . . . . 12.42
Perceval-Price v Department of Economic Development, The Times, 28 April 2000 . . . . 1.123
Percy v Church of Scotland Board of National Mission [2006] ICR 282 . . . . 1.126
Peries v Wirefast Ltd, UKEAT/0245/06 . . . . 12.08
Pfaffinger v City of Liverpool Community College [1996] IRLR 508 . . . . 1.152, 3.76
Pillinger v Manchester Area Health Authority [1979] IRLR 430 . . . . 3.61, 3.62
Pinewood Repro Ltd t/a County Print v Page, UKEAT/0028/10. . . . . 10.116, 10.168, 10.170
Pink v White and White and Co (Earls Bartion) Ltd [1985] IRLR 489 . . . . 3.84
Pinkney v Sandpiper Drilling Limited [1989] IRLR 425. . . . . 4.21
Pirelli General Cable Works Ltd v Murray [1979] IRLR 130. . . . . .10.187, 10.188
Polkey v A E Dayton Services Ltd [1987] IRLR 503 . . . . 10.70, 10.72, 10.86,
10.94, 10.97, 10.98, 10.217, 10.218, 12.19
Polyflor Ltd v Old, UKEAT/0482/02 . . . . 3.41
Port of London Authority v Payne [1994] IRLR 9. . . . . 10.198
Powermarque Limited v Sykes, UKEAT/0954/03 . . . . 12.56
Powers and Villiers v A Clarke & Co (Smethwick) Ltd [1981] IRLR 483. . . . . 10.131
Price v Salycae Systems Limited, ET/1302205/98. . . . . 10.155
Pritchard-Rhodes Ltd v Boon and Milton [1979] IRLR 19, EAT. 2.10, 2.15
Protectacoat Firthglow Ltd v Szilagyi [2009] EWCA Civ 98 . . . . 1.101, 1.105
Protective Services (Contracts) Ltd v Livingstone, UKEAT/269/91, 18 October 1991. . . . . . . 10.168
Purdy v Willowbrook International Ltd [1977] IRLR 388. . . . . 9.17
Puttick v John Wright & Sons Limited [1972] ICR 457 . . . . 6.10

Quinn v Calder Industrial Materials Ltd [1996] IRLR 126 . . . . 12.36, 12.40, 12.42, 12.47,
12.48, 12.50, 12.56, 12.59
Quinton Hazell Ltd v Earl [1976] IRLR 296. . . . . 10.178

R v British Coal Corporation, ex parte Vardy [1993] IRLR 104. . . . . 10.95, 11.14,
11.17, 11.50, 11.51
R v Gwent County Council, ex parte Bryant [1988], unreported. 10.95

R v Secretary of State of Employees, ex parte Seymour Smith Percy
  [2000] IRLR 263 . . . . .1.145, 10.13
R v Secretary of State for Employment, ex parte EOC [1994] 1 All ER 910 . . . . 1.147
R v Secretary of State for Employment, ex parte Seymour-Smith
  [1995 IRLR 464, [1995] ICR 889, CA 10.04, 10.05, 10.16
R v Secretary of State for Employment, ex parte Seymour-Smith (Case C-167/96)
  [1999] ICR 447, [1999] IRLR 253 . . . . 10.07
Ralph Martindale and Co Limited v Harris, UKEAT/0166/07 . . . . 10.184
Rank Xerox Ltd v Churchill [1988] IRLR 280 . . . . 3.15
Rao v Civil Aviation Authority [1994] ICR 495 . . . . 10.199, 10.200
Ready Case Ltd v Jackson [1981] IRLR 312, EAT. 2.16
Ready Mixed Concrete (South East) Ltd v Minister of Pensions and National
  Insurance [1968] 2 QB 497 . . . . .1.21, 1.23, 1.24, 1.59, 1.93, 1.94, 1.113
Reality (White Arrow Express) Ltd v O'Hara, UKEAT/0447/03 . . . . .4.41, 4.47
Renato Collino and Louisa Chiappero v Telecom Italia SpA (Case C-343/98)
  [2000] IRLR 788 . . . . 12.69
Renfrew District Council v Lornie, Court of Session, 23 June 1995. . . . . .2.21, 10.21
Reynolds v London Borough of Haringey, UKEAT, 10 January 2000 . . . . 12.44
Rice v Mr & Mrs T Walker t/a Kitchen Shop, UKEAT/0498/05 . . . . 4.60
Richmond Engineering Ltd v Pearce [1985] IRLR 179, EAT. 11.06
Roach v CSB (Moulds) Limited [1991] IRLR 200 . . . . 1.147
Robertson v British Gas Corporation [1983] ICR 351 . . . . 12.16
Robertson v Magnet Ltd (Retail Division) [1993] IRLR 512. . . . . 10.104
Robinson v British Island Airways Ltd [1977] IRLR 477, [1978] ICR 304 . . . . 3.53, 3.73
Robinson v Claxton and Garland (Teeside) Ltd [1997] IRLR 159 . . . . 9.08
Robinson v Ulster Carpet Mills Ltd [1991] IRLR 348. . . . . 10.175
Rockfon A/S v Specialarbejderforbundet i Danmark [1996] ICR 163,
  [1996] IRLR 168 . . . . 11.23, 11.27, 11.30
Rolls-Royce Motors Ltd v Dewhurst [1985] IRLR 184 . . . . 10.69
Rolls-Royce v Price and Others [1993] IRLR 203 . . . . 10.104
Rolls-Royce v Unite the Union [2009] EWCA Civ 387 . . . . 10.151
Rolls-Royce v Walpole [1980] IRLR 343. . . . . 10.63
Rose v Henry Trickett & Sons Limited (No. 2) [1971] 6 ITR 211, DC 4.38
Rose v Shelley & Partners Ltd [1966] 1 ITR 169 . . . . 4.79
Rowan v Machinery Installations (South Wales) Ltd [1981] ICR 386 . . . . 1.150
Rowell v Hubbard Group Services Limited [1995] IRLR 195 . . . . 10.85
Rowse-Piper v Anglian Windows Ltd [2010] EWCA Civ 428 . . . . 10.160
RS Components Ltd v Irwin [1973] ICR 535, [1973] IRLR 239, NIRC, [1974]
  1 All ER 41. . . . . 11.06
RSA Consulting Ltd v Evans [2010] EWCA Civ 866 . . . . 1.13
Russell v London Borough of Haringey, UKEAT, 8 February 1999 . . . . 3.99

S & U Stores Limited v Wilkes [1974] IRLR 283 . . . . 8.25
Safeway Stores Plc v Burrell [1997] IRLR 200 . . . . 3.88, 3.98,
                                         3.99, 3.100, 3.104, 3.106, 10.125, 10.126,
St John of God (Care Services) Ltd v Brookes [1992] ICR 715, [1992] IRLR 546 . . . . 11.06
Salvesen v Simons [1994] IRLR 52 . . . . 1.141
Sandhu v Jan de Rijk Transport Ltd [2007] IRLR 519 (CA) 2.26
Scattalon v Ministerio dell' Università e della Ricerca (Case C-108/10) 12.69
Scotch Premier Meat Limited v Burns [2000] IRLR 639 . . . . 11.08
Scott v Coalite Fuels and Chemicals Ltd [1988] ICR 355,
  [1988] IRLR 131, EAT. 2.12, 2.21, 10.21
Scottish Courage Brewing Limited v Berry, UKEAT/0079/04. . . . . 12.15
Secretary for Business, Enterprise and Regulatory Reform v Neufeld and
  Howe [2009] EWCA Civ 280. . . . . 1.132, 1.133, 1.134
Secretary of State for Employment v Aslef (No. 2) [1972] 2 QB 455 . . . . 7.07

Secretary of State for Employment v Chapman [1989] ICR 771 . . . . 4.21
Secretary of State for Employment v Greenfield, UKEAT/147/89, 18 May 1990 . . . . 2.10, 10.81
Secretary of State for Employment v John Woodrow & Sons (Builders) Limited
    [1983] IRLR 11 . . . . 8.25
Secretary of State for Employment v Newbold [1981] IRLR 305, EAT 4.21
Secretary of State for Employment v Stafford County Council [1987] ICR 956,
    [1988] IRLR 3, [1989] ICR 664. . . . . 8.10
Secretary of State for Trade & Industry v Bottrill [1999] ICR 592 . . . . 1.130, 1.132
Secretary of State for Trade & Industry, ex parte Price [1994] IRLR 72 . . . . 10.95
Secretary of State for Trade & Industry v Smith [2000] IRLR 6 . . . . 1.130
Securicor Omega Express Ltd v GmbH [2004] IRLR 9. . . . . 11.50, 11.58
Seldon v Kendall Company (UK) Ltd, UKEAT/1669/22 . . . . 9.34, 9.38
Selfridges v Wayne, IRLB, December 1995. . . . . 11.06
Semple Fraser LLP v Daly, UKEAT/0045/09 . . . . 10.66, 10.171
Senior Heat Treatment v Bell [1997] IRLR 614. . . . . 1.150
Shanahan Engineering Ltd v UNITE the Union, UKEAT/0411/09 . . . . 11.67
Shawkat v Nottingham City Hospital Trust [1999] IRLR 340, [1999] ICR 780,
    aff'd (No. 2) [2001] IRLR 555 . . . . 3.06, 3.69, 3.103
Sheehan v Post Office Counters Limited [1999] ICR 734 . . . . 1.09
Sheet Metal Components Ltd v Plumridge [1974] IRLR 86 . . . . 4.56
Sheffield v Oxford Controls Co Ltd [1979] IRLR 133, [1979] ICR 396, EAT. 2.21, 2.23, 2.24
Sheffield Health and Social Care NHS Foundation Trust v Crabtree,
    UKEAT/0331/09. . . . . 10.66
Shrewsbury v Telford Hospitals NHS Trust v Lairik Yengbam, UKEAT/0499/08 . . . . 3.70
SI (Systems and Instruments) Ltd v Grist and Riley [1983] IRLR 391, EAT 4.12
Simmons v Hoover Ltd [1977] 1 QB 284 . . . . 7.01, 7.06, 7.11, 7.15
Simon v David Altman & Co, ET/2202664/98 . . . . 10.155
Simpson v Dickinson [1972] ICR 474 . . . . 4.26
Singh v British Steel Corporation [1974] IRLR 131 . . . . 12.14
Smith v Adwest Engineering Ltd [1994] 508 IRLB 14. . . . . 10.218
Smith v Brown Bayley Steels Ltd [1973] 8 ITR 606. . . . . 4.24
Smith v The Chairman and Other Councillors of Hayle Town Council
    [1978] IRLR 413 . . . . 10.25
Smith (1) Moore (2) v Cherry Lewis Ltd (In Receivership) [2004] ICR 893. . . . . 11.78, 11.79,
    11.81, 11.82
Smiths Industries Aerospace and Defence Systems v Rawlings [1996] IRLR 656 . . . . 10.231
Snook v London & West Riding Investments Ltd [1967] 23 QB 786 . . . . 1.100
Software 2000 Limited v Andrews [2007] IRLR 568. . . . . 10.222
Solectron Scotland Ltd v Roper [2004] IRLR 4. . . . . 12.51
Souter v Henry Balfour & Company Ltd [1966] 1 ITR 383 . . . . 4.64, 4.70
South West Laundrettes Limited v Laidler [1986] ICR 455, [1986] IRLR 305, CA 4.21
Sovereign Distribution Services Ltd v Transport and General Workers Union
    [1989] IRLR 334, EAT, [1990] ICR 31 . . . . 11.72
Spillers-French (Holdings) Ltd v Union of Shop, Distributive and Allied Workers
    [1980] ICR 31, [1979] IRLR 339, EAT 11.55
Spinpress Limited v Turner [1986] ICR 433 . . . . 6.19
Staffordshire Sentinel Newspapers Ltd v Potter [2004] IRLR 752 . . . . 1.95
Stamkovich v Westminster City Council, UKEAT, 17 October 2001. . . . . 3.104
Stanco Exhibition Plc v Wright, UKEAT/0291/07 . . . . 10.176
Steel Stockholders (Birmingham) Ltd v Kirkwood [1993] IRLR 515. . . . . 10.218
Steikel v Ellice [1973] 1 WLR 191 . . . . 1.135
Stena Houlder Ltd v Keenan, UKEAT/272/93 . . . . 10.196
Stevenson v Teeside Bridge and Engineering Ltd [1971] 1 All ER 296 . . . . 3.17
Stevenson, Jordan and Harrison Ltd v MacDonald and Evans [1952] 1 TLR 101, CA 1.16
Strathclyde Buses Limited v Leonard, UKEAT/507/97 . . . . 3.01

Strudwick v Iszatt Bros Limited [1988] ICR 796, [1988] IRLR 457, EAT 4.21
Suflex Ltd v Thomas [1987] IRLR 435 . . . . 10.146
Susie Radin Ltd v GMB [2004] EWCA Civ 180, [2004] IRLR 400. . . . . 11.76, 11.78, 11.79,
                               11.81, 11.82, 11.83, 11.84
Sutcliffe v Hawker Siddeley Aviation Ltd [1973] ICR 560. . . . . 3.11
Sutton v Revlon Overseas Corporation Ltd [1973] IRLR 173 . . . . 3.37
Sweeney v J&S Henderson (Concessions) Limited [1999] IRLR 306. . . . . 1.147
Sweetin v Coral Racing Ltd [2006] IRLR 252. . . . . 11.83
Sykes v Hereford and Worcester County Council [1989] ICR 800 . . . . 12.19

Tadd v Eastwood and Daily Telegraph Ltd [1983] ICR 320, aff'd [1985] ICR 132. . . . . 12.15
Tarmac Roadstone Holdings Ltd v Peacock [1973] 2 All ER 485 . . . . 8.18
Taskforce (Finishing and Handling) Ltd v Love, UKEAT/0001/05 . . . . 10.175
Taylor v Kent County Council [1969] 2 QB 560 . . . . 4.65
TBA Industrial Products Ltd v Morland [1982] ICR 686, [1982] IRLR 331, CA 2.14
Temple Grove School v Gorst, UKEAT, 15 October 1998. . . . . 3.44
The Burton Group v Smith [1977] IRLR 351 . . . . 4.47
The Earl of Bradford v Jowett [1978] IRLR 16 . . . . 10.161
Thomas & Betts Manufacturing Ltd v Harding [1980] IRLR 255 . . . . 10.128, 10.131
Thompson v Akzo Coatings Plc, UKEAT/1037/95. . . . . 10.183
Thompson v Priest Lindley Ltd [1978] IRLR 99 . . . . 9.15
Tice v Cartwright [1999] ICR 769 . . . . 4.21
Tiffin v Lester Aldridge LLP, UKEAT/0255/10. . . . . 1.136
Tilson v Alstom Transport [2010] EWCA Civ 1308; [2011] IRLR 169 . . . . 1.81
Timex Corporation v Thompson [1981] IRLR 522. . . . . 10.30
Timex Corporation v Thompson [1991] IRLR 522. . . . . 10.199
Toach (1) Hayto (2) v British United Shoe Machinery, UKEAT, 18 May 1998. . . . . 12.31
Todd v Strain, UKEAT/0057/09. . . . . 11.83
Tomczynski v JK Millar Ltd [1976] ICR 127, EAT 4.25
Tootle v Kew Park Hire Limited, ET/2100203/98 . . . . 10.155
Trafalgar House Services Limited v Carder, UKEAT/306/96. . . . . 4.06
Transport and General Workers' Union v Dyer [1977] IRLR 93, EAT. 11.37
Transport and General Workers' Union v Ledbury Preserves (1928) Ltd
   [1986] ICR 855, [1986] IRLR 492. . . . . 11.85
Transport and General Workers' Union v Nationwide Haulage Ltd
   [1978] IRLR 143 . . . . 11.31, 11.33
Transport and General Workers' Union v R A Lister & Co Ltd (1986)
   IRLIB 21 May 1989 . . . . 11.85
Trebor Bassett Ltd v (1) Saxby (2) Boorman, UKEAT/658/91. . . . . 11.06
Turvey v CW Cheyney & Sons Ltd [1979] ICR 341 . . . . 4.55

UK Coal Mining Ltd v National Union of Mine Workers (Northumberland Area)
   [2008] IRLR 4 . . . . 11.17, 11.47, 11.51, 11.52, 11.53
Umar v Pliastar Ltd [1981] ICR 727 . . . . 4.21
Union of Shop, Distributive and Allied Workers v Leancut Bacon Ltd
   [1981] IRLR 295, EAT. 11.68
Union of Textile Workers v FA Morris Ltd (In Liquidation), UKEAT/484/91 . . . . 11.71
United Bank Ltd v Akhtar [1989] IRLR 507. . . . . 3.22
United Kingdom Atomic Energy Authority v Claydon [1974] ICR 128 . . . . 3.10
United States of America v Nolan [2010] EWCA Civ 1223. . . . . 11.20, 11.47, 11.52, 11.53
United States v Silk, 331 US 704 (1946). 1.18

Vaux & Associated Breweries Ltd v Ward (No. 2) [1970] 5 ITR 62 . . . . 3.60
Vokes Ltd v Bear [1973] IRLR 363. . . . . 10.177, 10.179, 10.183
Von Colson and Kamann v Land Nordrhein-Westfalen [1984] ECR 1891. . . . . 11.86

W Devis & Sons Ltd v Atkins [1977] IRLR 314 . . . . 10.213
Waine v R Oliver (Plant Hire) Limited [1977] IRLR 434 . . . . 6.11
Walker v Cotswold Chine Holme School (1977) 12 ITR 342, EAT. 2.16
Wallace v CA Roofing Services Ltd [1996] IRLR 435 . . . . 1.119
Walley v Morgan [1969] 4 ITR 122 . . . . 10.20
Walls Meat Co Ltd v Selby [1989] ICR 601 . . . . 12.19
Walmsley v C & R Ferguson Limited [1989] IRLR 112 . . . . 6.24
Ward Hadaway Solicitors v Love, UKEAT/0471/09 . . . . 3.43
Warman International Ltd v Wilson, UKEAT/1383/00 . . . . 12.49
Washington Arts Association v Forster [1983] ICR 346. . . . . 4.21
Weevsmay Ltd v Kings [1977] ICR 244 . . . . 8.25
West Kent College v Richardson [1998] ICR 511 . . . . 10.34
Westland Helicopters Ltd v Nott, UKEAT/342/88, 11 October 1989. . . . . 10.146
Wheeler v Philip Morris Ltd [1997] ALR 282. . . . . 12.58
Whiffen v Milham Girls School [2001] IRLR 468, CA 10.156
Whitbread Plc t/a Whitbread Berni Inns v Flattery, UKEAT/287/94. . . . . 3.08
White v Reflecting Roadstuds Ltd [1991] ICR 733. . . . . 3.22
Whitewater Leisure Management Ltd v Franklin, UKEAT/964/98 . . . . 12.67
Wickens v Champion Employment [1984] ICR 365. . . . . 1.54
Wilkinson v Corus and Regal Hotels Plc [2004] All ER (D) 370 . . . . 3.104
Willcox v Hastings [1987] IRLR 298 . . . . 3.03
William B Morrison & Son Limited v Sarah Jane Healey, ET, unreported, 1999 . . . . 10.155
William Pentland Stenhouse v First Edinburgh Ltd, UKEAT/0017/04 . . . . 12.53
Williams v Compair Maxam Ltd [1982] IRLR 83. . . . . 10.67, 10.69, 10.71, 10.119,
                10.120, 10.138, 10.142, 10.143, 10.167, 10.183, 10.184, 11.91, 12.19
Williamson v National Coal Board [1970] 5 ITR 43. . . . . 4.80
Wilson v Pimlico Village Housing Cooperative, ET/2300490/98 . . . . 10.155
Wood Group Heavy Industrial Turbines Limited v Crossan [1998] IRLR 680. . . . . 10.201, 10.203
Woodcock v Cumbria Primary Care Trust, UKEAT/0489/09 . . . . 12.78

X v Y Limited [1969] 4 ITR 204. . . . . 7.05

Young v Canadian Northern Railway Co [1931] AC 83 . . . . 12.15

Zaman v Kozee Sleep Products Limited t/a Dorlux Beds UK, UKEAT/0312/10 . . . . 11.74
Zarb and Samuels v British and Brazilian Produce Company (Sales) Ltd
    [1978] IRLR 78, EAT. 4.21

TABLE OF LEGISLATION

Apprenticeship, Skills, Children and
  Learning Act 2009
  s 35 . . . . 1.122
Deregulation and Contracting
  Out Act 1994 . . . . 10.150, 12.81
Disability Discrimination Act 1995 . . . . . . 4.15
  s 68 . . . . 1.09
Education and Skills Act 2008
  s 27 . . . . 10.232
  s 28 . . . . 10.232
Employment Act 1989 . . . . 8.32
  s 17 . . . . 8.32
Employment Act 1990
  s 13 . . . . 8.33
Employment Act 2002 . . . . 10.37
Employment Act 2008 . . . . 1.90,
                                10.37, 10.225
Employment Agencies Act 1973 . . . . 1.90
Employment Protection Act 1975
  s 99 . . . . 3.03, 11.02,
                                  11.11, 11.27
Employment Protection (Consolidation)
  Act 1978
  s 1(1) 1.35
  s 57(1) 10.31
  s 57(3) 10.48, 10.70
  s 59(1)(b) 10.131, 10.150, 12.81
  s 84 . . . . 4.06
  s 104 . . . . 8.32
Employment Relations Act 1999 . . . . . . 1.161,
                                10.227, 10.247
  s 23 . . . . 1.01, 1.12
  s 28(3)(a) 9.09
  s 28(4) 9.09
  s 31(4) 9.20
  s 31(5) 9.20
  s 31(7) 9.19
  s 34 . . . . 8.16
  s 35 . . . . 9.19
Employment Rights Act 1996 . . . . 1.06,
                          1.25, 1.67, 1.114,
                          1.123, 1.125, 3.10,
                          3.49, 8.14, 8.16,
                          10.03, 11.05
  Pt II 6.14, 9.02, 12.57
  Pt III 9.01
  Pt IVA 10.232
  Pt IX, Chap. 11.74
  Pt X 10.01, 10.241,
                              10.251, 10.252

Pt XI 3.06, 4.06
Pt XIV 1.146
s 1 . . . . 1.35, 1.115,
                                4.27, 4.41
s 27(2)(d) 12.57
s 28 . . . . 9.40
s 28(1) 9.07, 9.10
s 28(1)(b) 9.07
s 28(5) 9.09
s 29 . . . . 9.14
s 29(1) 9.05
s 29(3) 9.14, 9.15
s 29(4) 9.16
s 29(4)(a) 9.16
s 29(4)(b) 9.16
s 29(5)(b) 9.17
s 30(1) 9.06, 9.19
s 30(2) 9.19
s 30(3) 9.19
s 30(4) 9.19
s 31(2) 9.20
s 31(3) 9.20
s 32(2) 9.21
s 34(1) 9.23
s 34(3) 9.23
s 35 . . . . 9.21, 9.40
s 35(1) 9.40
s 43K 1.11
s 45 . . . . 12.61
s 46 . . . . 12.61
s 50(5) 9.12
s 50(11) 9.28
s 52 . . . . 9.24, 9.25, 9.35
s 52(1) 9.27, 9.28
s 52(2) 9.26
s 53 . . . . 9.24, 9.25, 9.35
s 53(1) 9.28
s 53(2) 9.28
s 53(3) 9.28
s 53(5) 9.27, 9.37
s 53(7) 9.38
s 54(1) 9.29
s 54(2) 9.30
s 54(3) 9.35
s 54(4) 9.37
s 57A 10.253
s 63D 10.231
s 63J(1)(b) 11.74
s 66(2) 10.253
s 80I(1)(b) 11.74

Employment Rights Act 1996 (*cont.*)

s 86 . . . . 2, 16, 2.15, 8.10,
8.11, 8.29, 10.231
s 86(1) 8.08
s 86(3) 8.10
s 95 . . . . 10.17
s 95(1) 10.18
ss 95(1)(a)–(c) 10.17
s 97(4) 8.09
s 98 . . . . 10.24
s 98(1) 3.06, 10.31
s 98(1)(b) 3.80, 11.06
s 98(2) 3.79
s 98(4) 4.62, 10.37, 10.48,
10.54, 10.55, 10.67,
10.70, 10.102, 10.106,
10.128, 10.130,
10.177, 12.82
s 98(4)(a) 10.73
ss 98(4)(a)–(b) 10.39
s 98A 10.159, 10.224
s 98A(2) 10.222
s 100(1)(a) 10.207,
10.208, 10.231
s 100(1)(b) 1.63, 10.207,
10.208, 10.231
s 100(1)(ba) 10.231
s 100(1)(c) 10.231
s 100(1)(d) 10.231
s 100(1)(e) 10.231
s 100A(a) 10.231
ss 100A(b)–(d) 10.231
s 100B 10.231
s 101 . . . . 10.231
s 101A(d) 10.207, 10.208
s 102(1) 10.207, 10.208, 10.231
s 103 . . . . 10.207, 10.208
s 103(1) 10.231
s 103(2) 10.231
s 104(1)(a) 10.231, 10.232
s 104(1)(b) 10.231, 10.232
s 104(1)(c) 10.231
s 104(2)(a) 10.232
s 104(2)(b) 10.232
s 104(3) 10.232
s 104(4) 10.232
ss 104(4)(a)–(c) 10.231
s 104A(1)(a) 10.231
s 104B(a)(i) 10.231
s 104B(b) 10.231
s 104B(c) 10.231
s 104C 10.231
s 104D 10.231
s 104E 10.231
s 104F 10.231

s 105(7C) 10.244
ss 105(a)–(b) 10.230
s 112 . . . . 10.186, 10.187,
10.188, 10.189, 10.200
s 112(5) 11.74
s 113 . . . . 10.186, 10.200
s 115(1) 10.193
ss 115(2)(a)–(f) 10.195
s 116(1) 10.200
ss 116(1)(i)–(ii) 10.192
s 116(1)(iii) 10.192
s 116(2) 10.200
ss 116(3)(i)–(iv) 10.194
s 116(4) 10.196
s 116(5) 10.197
s 117 . . . . 10.200, 10.227
s 120(1) 10.207
s 121 . . . . 10.207
s 122(1) 10.208
s 122(2) 10.208
s 122(3) 10.208
s 122(4)(b) 10.208
s 123 . . . . 10.212, 10.213, 10.226
s 123(1) 10.221
s 123(7) 10.221
s 135(1) 1.01
s 136 . . . . 2.01, 2.18, 2.19
s 136(1)(a) 2.01, 2.02
s 136(1)(b) 2.01, 4.57
s 136(1)(c) 2.01
s 136(3) 8.06
s 136(4) 2.15
s 136(5) 2.08, 5.02
s 138 . . . . 4.01, 4.04, 4.05,
4.06, 4.07, 4.09,
4.11, 4.13, 4.16,
4.28, 4.36, 4.37,
4.42, 8.05, 10.207
s 138(1) 4.01, 4.02, 4.06,
4.11, 4.12, 4.14,
4.17, 4.22, 4.33,
4.34, 4.35, 4.41
s 138(1)(b) 4.08
s 138(2) 4.03, 4.07, 4.38, 4.46
s 138(2)(b)(i) 4.42, 4.46
s 138(3) 4.39, 4.46
s 138(3)(b)(ii) 4.41
s 138(4) 4.06
s 138(6) 4.41, 4.47
s 139 . . . . 3.01, 3.100
s 139(1) 3.01, 3.03,
3.04, 3.35, 3.58
ss 139(1)(a)(i)–(ii) 3.01
s 139(1)(b) 3.74, 3.87,
3.100, 3.104

s 139(1)(b)(i) 3.103
ss 139(1)(b)(i)–(ii) 3.01
s 139(2) 3.04
s 140 . . . . .7.03, 7.09, 7.11, 7.12
s 140(1) 7.03, 7.04, 7.05,
7.06, 7.11, 7.15
s 140(2) 7.09
ss 140(2)–(4) .7.15
s 140(3) 7.09
s 140(4) 7.09
s 141 . . . . .4.01, 4.03, 4.04,
4.05, 4.06, 4.13,
4.14, 4.15, 4.16,
4.22, 4.28, 4.36,
4.37, 4.58, 4.59
s 141(1) 4.17, 10.207
s 141(2) 4.62, 10.207
s 141(3) .10.207
s 141(4) 4.42
s 142 . . . . 2.15, 2.16
s 142(1) 2.17
s 142(1)(a) 2.15
s 142(2) 2.17
s 142(3) 2.17
s 142(4) 2.17
s 143 . . . . .7.13
s 143(1) 7.14
s 143(2) 7.14
s 143(5) 7.15
s 143(6) 7.15
s 144(1) 7.15
ss 145(2)(a)–(c) 8.04
s 145(3) 8.06
s 145(4) 8.05
s 145(4)(a) 4.48
s 145(5) 1.150, 8.08, 8.09,
8.10, 8.11, 8.29
s 145A 10.232
s 145B 10.232
s 146 . . . . .10.232
s 146(2) 4.28
s 147 . . . . 3.01, 6.16
s 147(1) 6.17
s 147(2) 6.18
s 148 . . . . .6.16, 6.20, 7.12
s 148(1) 6.20
s 148(1)(a) 8.07
s 148(1)(b) 8.07
s 148(2)(a) 6.21
s 148(2)(b) 6.21
s 149 . . . . 6.22, 6.23
s 150(2) 6.24
s 152(1) 6.22
s 152(2) 6.22
s 153 . . . . .8.07

s 154 . . . . .6.26
s 155 .1.01, 1.145,
1.150, 8.08
s 157(2) 1.160
s 157(3) 1.160
s 158 . . . . .8.31
s 159 . . . . .1.160
s 160 . . . . .1.160
s 161 . . . . .1.160
s 162 . . . . 1.150, 8.12
s 162(1) 8.08
ss 162(1)–(3) 12.70
s 162(4) 8.12
s 162(5) 8.12
s 163(2) 3.05, 7.04
s 164 . . . . .8.01
ss 165(1)–(3) .8.30
s 166 . . . . 1.128, 8.33
s 166(1) 8.33
s 167 . . . . 1.150, 8.33
s 167(1) 8.33
s 168 . . . . .10.231
s 168A 10.231
s 169 . . . . .10.231
s 170 . . . . 8.02, 10.231
s 170(2) 8.33
s 170(3) 8.33
s 171 . . . . 1.127, 1.163
s 171(3) 8.02
s 172 . . . . 1.127, 1.164
s 174 . . . . .5.03
ss 174–176 . . . . .5.06
s 174(2) 1.150
s 174(3) 1.150
s 176(1) 5.05, 8.11
s 176(2) 8.11
s 176(3) 5.05
s 176(4) 5.05
s 182 . . . . 1.128, 1.133
s 191 . . . . .1.160
s 191(2) 9.04
s 191(6) 1.160
s 192(2) 9.03
s 194 . . . . .1.160
s 194(2) 9.04
s 195 . . . . .1.160
s 195(2) 9.04
s 196 . . . . .9.04
s 196(6) 1.161
s 197 . . . . .1.160
s 199(2) 1.160, 9.03, 9.25
s 199(4) 9.25
s 200(1) 9.03, 9.25
s 203 . . . . .9.39
s 210(4) 1.149

Employment Rights Act 1996 (*cont.*)
s 210(5) 1.146
s 211(1) 1.146
s 211(3) 1.150
s 212 ....1.46
s 212(1) 1.147, 1.148,
  1.149, 1.150, 1.158
s 212(1)(a) 1.150
s 212(1)(b) 1.150
s 212(1)(c) 1.150
s 212(2) 1.150
s 212(3) 1.150, 1.152
s 212(3)(b) 1.43
s 212(3)(c) 1.154
s 212(4) 1.150
s 212(5) 1.150
s 212(6) 1.150
s 212(7) 1.150
s 212(8) 1.150
s 212(9) 1.150
s 212(10) 1.150
s 213(2) 1.150, 4.36
s 213(3) 1.150
s 213(3)(c) 1.158
s 214 ....1.150
s 214(4) 1.150
s 215 ....1.161
s 215(2) 1.150
s 215(3) 1.150
s 216 ....1.150
s 216(2) 1.150
s 218(6) 1.150
ss 220–229 ....8.16, 8.17, 11.74
s 221 ....8.18, 8.21
s 221(1) 8.18
s 221(2) 8.19
s 221(3) 8.20
s 222 ....8.21
ss 222(1)–(4) 8.26
s 223 ....8.18, 8.21
s 223(3) 8.23
s 224(2) 8.27
s 224(3) 8.28
s 225(2) 9.37
s 226 ....9.26
s 227 ....11.74
s 227(1) 11.74
s 227(3) 8.16
s 227(4) 8.08
s 230 ....1.136
s 230(1) 1.07, 1.136
s 230(2) 1.07, 1.119
s 230(3) 1.10, 1.12, 1.112
s 230(6) 1.11
s 231 ....4.20, 4.21

s 235 ....7.10
s 235(1) 1.147, 4.08,
  9.20, 10.231
s 235(4) 6.27
ss 235(4)(a)–(c) 6.27
s 235(5) 6.27
ss 235(5)(a)–(b) 6.27, 7.10
s 241 ....9.40
Sch 2, Pt. 2, para 1–4 ....9.40
Employment Tribunals Act 1996
s 18(1)(d) 8.01
ss 18–19 ....9.39
Equality Act 2010 ....1.138,
  8.12, 10.155
s 5 ....12.70
s 6 ....4.15
s 13(2) 10.151, 12.71, 12.72
s 19 ....4.15, 10.14
Sch 9 ....12.74
  para 5(a) 12.71
  para 5(b) 12.71
  para 6 ....12.71
  para 10 ....10.151, 10.154
  para 13 ....8.15, 12.70
Sch 13 ....12.72
Sch 22, para 1(1) 8.14
Income Tax (Earnings and Pensions) Act 2003
Ch. 9 ....1.09
Industrial Relations Act 1971 .....12.12
Industrial Tribunals Act 1996
ss 18–19 ....9.39
Limited Liability Partnerships Act 2000
s 4(4) 1.136
National Insurance Act 1965 ....1.21
National Minimum Wage Act 1998 ....1.10, 1.11
s 31 ....10.232
s 54 ....1.10
Partnership Act 1890
s 1(1) 1.136
Pensions Schemes Act 1993 ....12.60
Public Interest Disclosure Act 1998 ....1.10, 1.11
s 1 ....1.11
s 5 ....10.231
s 15(1) 1.11
s 18(2) 1.11, 10.231
Race Relations Act 1976
s 78 ....1.09
Redundancy Payments Act 1963
s 3 ....4.06
Redundancy Payments Act 1965 ......8.16
s 2(2) 7.15
s 10 ....7.15

Sex Discrimination Act 1975 .... 1.123, 1.138
   s 1(1)(b) 10.14
   s 82 .... 1.09
Tax Credits Act 2002
   s 25 .... 10.231
Trade Union and Labour
   Relations (Consolidation)
   Act 1992 .... 1.12, 8.16,
                 10.78, 10.232, 10.241,
                 11.13, 11.22, 11.47,
                 11.54, 11.71
   Chap. II 11.02
   Pt. IV 11.46
   s 68 .... 10.231
   s 145A 10.233
   s 145B 10.233
   s 152 .... 10.233
   s 152(1)(a) 10.233
   s 152(1)(b) 10.34, 10.233, 10.238
   s 152(1)(ba) 10.233
   s 152(1)(bb) 10.233
   s 152(1)(c) 10.233
   s 153 .... 10.230, 10.233,
                 10.235, 10.238
   s 154 .... 10.25, 10.235
   s 157 .... 10.207
   s 178 .... 12.09
   s 178(2) 11.38
   s 178(3) 11.38
   s 179 .... 12.11
   s 179(2) 12.12
   s 188 .... 2.06, 2.19, 3.05, 3.49,
                 10.22, 10.44, 10.69, 11.02,
                 11.14, 11.21, 11.27, 11.35,
                 11.37, 11.39, 11.46, 11.50,
                 11.52, 11.60, 11.62, 11.63,
                 11.64, 11.70, 11.72, 11.75,
                 11.76, 11.77, 11.78, 11.83,
                 11.84, 11.91, 11.92
   s 188(1A) 11.68
   s 188(1B) 11.34, 11.39
   s 188(2) 11.04, 11.51, 11.56,
                 11.58, 11.59, 11.68
   s 188(2)(a) 11.59
   s 188(2)(b) 11.59
   s 188(2)(c) 11.59
   s 188(3) 11.31, 11.32
   s 188(4) 11.04, 11.54, 11.61, 11.68
   s 188(5) 11.55

   s 188(6) 11.56
   s 188(7) 11.53, 11.59, 11.61
   s 188(7A) 11.60
   s 188(7B) 11.60
   s 188A 11.62
   s 188A(1) 11.35, 11.39
   s 188A(2) 11.40
   s 189 .... 11.81, 11.86
   ss 189–192 .... 10.69
   s 189(1) 11.62
   s 189(1A) 11.63
   s 189(1B) 11.63
   s 189(3) 11.72
   s 189(4) 11.72
   s 190 .... 11.74, 11.86
   s 190(3) 11.86
   s 190(5) 11.74
   s 191(1)(a) 11.87
   s 191(1)(b) 11.87
   s 191(2) 11.87
   ss 191(3)–(7) 11.87
   s 192 .... 11.88
   s 193 .... 11.89, 11.90
   s 193(1) 11.90
   s 193(2) 11.90
   s 193(6) 11.90
   s 193(7) 11.90
   s 194 .... 11.90
   s 195 .... 3.03, 3.49, 11.06
   s 195(1) 3.02, 3.03, 3.04, 11.05
   s 195(2) 3.05
   s 207A 10.38, 10.39
   s 238A(2) 10.244, 10.245
   Sch A1 .... 11.13
      para 161(2) 10.241,
                 10.242, 10.243
      para 161(3) 10.243
      para 162 .... 10.241
Trade Union Reform and Employment
   Rights Act 1993 .... 11.13, 11.56,
                 11.58, 11.71,
                 11.86, 11.90
   s 33 .... 11.54
   s 34(1) 3.03, 11.61
   s 34(2)(c) 11.62
   s 34(5) 3.03
Wages Act 1986 .... 8.32
Work and Families Act 2006
   s 14 .... 8.16

TABLE OF STATUTORY INSTRUMENTS

Agency Workers Regulations 2010,
    (SI 2010/93). 1.88
Collective Redundancies
    (Amendment) Regulations 2006,
    (SI 2006/2387). 11.90
    reg 3 . . . . 11.46
Cross-Border Railway Services
    (Working Time) Regulations 2008,
    (SI 2008/1660). 10.231
Collective Redundancies and Transfer of
    Undertakings (Protection of Employment)
    (Amendment) Regulations 1995,
    (SI 1995/2587). 11.02, 11.13,
                             11.27, 11.41
Collective Redundancies and Transfer of
    Undertakings (Protection of Employment)
    (Amendment) Regulations 1999,
    (SI 1999/2402). 11.02, 11.13, 11.72
Employment Equality (Age)
    Regulations 2006,
    (SI 2006/2408). 1.162, 8.12,
                       8.13, 8.31, 12.70
    reg 3(1). 10.151
    reg 27 . . . . 8.14
    reg 32 . . . . 10.154
    Sch 8
        para 31 . . . . 8.31
        para 32 . . . . 8.12
Employment Protection (Continuity of
    Employment) Regulations 1996,
    (SI 1996/3147)
    reg 4 . . . . 1.150
Employment Protection
    (Part-time Employees)
    Regulations 1995, (SI 1995/31) 1.147
Employment Relations Act 1999
    (Blacklists) Regulations 2010,
    (SI 2010/493). 10.231
Employment Rights (Increase of Limits)
    Order 1999, (SI 1999/3375). 8.16
Employment Rights (Increase of Limits)
    Order 2010, (SI 2010/2926). 8.16
Employment Tribunals Extension of
    Jursidiction (England and Wales)
    Order 1994, (SI 1994/1623). 12.56
Employment Tribunals Extension of
    Jurisdiction (Scotland) Order 1994,
    (SI 1994/1624). 12.56
Fixed Term Employees
    (Prevention of Less Favourable

Treatment) Regulations 2002,
    (SI 2002/2034). 10.156
Guarantee Payments (Exemption) (No. 1)
    Order 1977, (SI 1977/156). 9.40
Guarantee Payments (Exemption) (No. 2)
    Order 1977, (SI 1977/157). 9.40
Guarantee Payments (Exemption) (No. 5)
    Order 1977, (SI 1977/902). 9.40
Guarantee Payments (Exemption) (No. 6)
    Order 1977, (SI 1977/1096). 9.40
Guarantee Payments (Exemption) (No. 7)
    Order 1977, (SI 1977/1158). 9.40
Guarantee Payments (Exemption) (No. 8)
    Order 1977, (SI 1977/1322). 9.40
Guarantee Payments (Exemption) (No. 9)
    Order 1977, (SI 1977/1349). 9.40
Guarantee Payments (Exemption) (No. 10)
    Order 1977, (SI 1977/1522). 9.40
Guarantee Payments (Exemption) (No. 11)
    Order 1977, (SI 1977/1523). 9.40
Guarantee Payments (Exemption) (No. 12)
    Order 1977, (SI 1977/1583). 9.40
Guarantee Payments (Exemption) (No. 13)
    Order 1977, (SI 1977/1601). 9.40
Guarantee Payments (Exemption) (No. 14)
    Order 1977, (SI 1977/2032). 9.40
Guarantee Payments (Exemption) (No. 15)
    Order 1978, (SI 1978/153). 9.40
Guarantee Payments (Exemption) (No. 16)
    Order 1978, (SI 1978/429). 9.40
Guarantee Payments (Exemption) (No. 17)
    Order 1978, (SI 1978/737). 9.40
Guarantee Payments (Exemption) (No. 18)
    Order 1978, (SI 1978/826). 9.40
Guarantee Payments (Exemption) (No. 19)
    Order 1979, (SI 1979/1403). 9.40
Guarantee Payments (Exemption) (No. 21)
    Order 1981, (SI 1981/6). 9.40
Guarantee Payments (Exemption) (No. 23)
    Order 1987, (SI 1987/1757). 9.40
Guarantee Payments (Exemption) (No. 24)
    Order 1989, (SI 1989/1326). 9.40
Guarantee Payments (Exemption) (No. 25)
    Order 1989, (SI 1989/1575). 9.40
Guarantee Payments (Exemption) (No. 26)
    Order 1989, (SI 1989/2163). 9.40
Guarantee Payments (Exemption) (No. 27)
    Order 1990, (SI 1990/927). 9.40
Guarantee Payments (Exemption) (No. 28)
    Order 1990, (SI 1990/2330). 9.40

Guarantee Payments (Exemption) (No. 30)
   Order 1996, (SI 1996/2132). 9.40
Health and Safety (Consultation with
   Employees) Regulations 1996,
   (SI 1996/1513). 10.231
Industrial Relations (Northern Ireland)
   Order 1976, (SI 1976/1043)
   art 2(7). 3.104
   art 22(1). 3.105
   art 49(1). 11.36
Information and Consultation of
   Employees (ICE) Regulations 2004,
   (SI 2004/3426)
   reg 20(5). 11.92
Local Government (Compensation for
   Redundancy and Premature Retirement)
   Regulations 1984, (SI 1984/740)
   reg 5. . . . . 12.68
Maternity and Parental
   Leave, etc. Regulations 1999,
   (SI 1999/3312). 10.247
   reg 10. . . . . 4.15, 10.248,
                                    10.251, 10.254
   reg 10(2). 10.248
   reg 10(3). 10.248, 10.250,
                                    10.252, 10.253
   reg 12(A) 10.253
   reg 20(2). 10.252
   reg 20(3)(b). 10.254
Part-time Workers (Prevention of Less
   Favourable Treatment) Regulations 2000,
   (SI 2000/1551). 1.10, 10.156
   reg 1(2). 1.10
Redundancy Payments (Continuity of
   Employment in Local Government, etc)
   (Modification) Order 1999,
   (SI 1999/2277). 4.21
   reg 1. . . . . 1.150
Redundancy Payments (National Health
   Service) (Modification) Order 1993,
   (SI 1993/3167). 1.150, 4.21
Redundancy Payments Office
   Holders Regulations 1965,
   (SI 1965/2007). 1.163
Redundancy Payments Pensions Regulations
   1965, (SI 1965/1932). 8.31

Redundancy Payments Termination of
   Employment Regulations 1965,
   (SI 1965/2022). 1.164
Redundancy Rebate Regulations 1984,
   (SI 1984/1066). 11.89
Safety Representatives and Safety
   Committees Regulations 1977,
   (SI 1977/500). 1.68
Sea Fishing Vessels (Working Time:
   Sea-fisherman) Regulations 2004,
   (SI 2004/1713). 10.231
Sea Merchant Shipping (Working Time:
   Inland Waterway) Regulations 2003,
   (SI 2003/3049). 10.231
Trade Union Reform and
   Employment Rights Act 1993,
   (Commencement No. 1 and
   Transitional Provisions) Order 1993,
   (SI 1993/1908). 3.03
Transfer of Undertakings (Protection of
   Employment) Regulations 1981,
   (SI 1981/1794). 3.43,
                                    10.231, 12.59
Transfer of Undertakings (Protection
   of Employment) Regulations 2006,
   (SI 2006/246). 11.74, 12.42,
                                    12.51, 12.59
   reg 3(1)(b) 3.43
   reg 4. 12.59, 12.60
   reg 5. . . . . 12.60
   reg 10. . . . . 12.60, 12.61
   reg 13. . . . . 11.83
   reg 15. . . . . 11.83
   reg 16(4). 11.74
Unfair Dismissal and Statement of
   Reasons for Dismissal (Variation of
   Qualifying Period) Order 1999,
   (SI 1999/436). 10.04
Work and Families (Increase of
   Maximum Amount) Order 2009,
   (SI 2009/1903). 8.16
Working Time Regulations 1998,
   (SI 1998/1833). 1.10, 1.29,
                                    10.207, 10.231
   reg 2(1). 1.10
   Sch 1 . . . . 10.231

TABLE OF EUROPEAN INSTRUMENTS

Directives

75/129/EC, Collective Redundancies
     Directive 3.03, 11.01,
                        11.12, 11.41
76/207/EC, Equal Treatment
     Directive 1.147, 8.12, 8.13,
                 10.04, 10.06, 10.07
77/187/EEC, Acquired Rights Directive
     Art 3. . . . . 12.65, 12.69
     Art 3(1) 12.65
     Art 3(2) 12.65
     Art 3(3) 12.65
92/85/EEC, Pregnant Workers
     Directive 1.135
97/81/EC, Part-time Workers Directive . . . 1.10
98/59/EC, Collective Redundancies
     Directive 3.03, 5.06, 11.01,
              11.14, 11.22, 11.29, 11.30
     Art 1(1)(a) 11.05, 11.25, 11.26

2001/23/EC, Acquired Rights
     Directive 11.26, 12.60
2002/14/EC, Information and
     Consultation of Employees
     Directive 11.92
2007/78/EC, Equal Treatment
     Directive 12.79
2008/104/EC, Temporary Agency
     Workers' Directive 1.88

Treaties and Conventions

Treaty on the Functioning of the
     European Union
     Art 157. . . . . 1.147, 8.16,
                      10.05, 10.06,
                      10.07, 10.14

Part I

REDUNDANCY PAYMENTS

INTRODUCTION

> Few would deny that redundancy represents one of the most pressing and recurring issues of contemporary industrial relations in Great Britain.
>
> *Robert H Fryer*[1]

This book is concerned with the legal regulation of redundancy in the United Kingdom. Redundancy is generally regarded to be an important factor in the methodology of cultural change and the re-engineering of business structures. Its relevance in the current economic crisis is also obvious. Whilst it is appropriate to commence our study with a reminder that there are economic and social imperatives behind the legal regulation of redundancy, it should be remembered, however, that redundancy carries with it legal implications in terms of individual employment law rights arising from redundancy dismissals and collective labour law rights in connection with information and consultation. Euphemisms such as 'downsizing', 'rightsizing' and other expressions should not delude the reader into thinking that redundancy does not carry with it important employment law implications. Employment law has responded to the effect of redundancy on the individual through the law of unfair dismissal and information and consultation obligations. And this is right.

It is also right that it must be remembered that the legal structure in relation to redundancy dismissals must also be complemented by a successful human resources management strategy. It is well documented that downsizing has a significant effect on the morale of employees.[2] A study in *The Lancet*[3] found that there was a significant association between downsizing and medically certified sick leave and concluded that downsizing was a risk to the health of employees. Not to be forgotten, too, is the effect of redundancy on those who are not displaced. A concept originated in the United States of America (USA), that of survivor's syndrome (although sometimes described as a 'management myth'), is well documented.[4]

---

[1] 'The Myths of the Redundancy Payments Act' (1973) 2 ILJ 1.
[2] See 'Down size but don't demoralise' *Estates Gazette*, 7 March 1998; J Vaherta, M Kivimäki, J Pentt, 'The effect of organisational down sizing on health of employees' *The Lancet*, 28 October 1997.
[3] Ibid.
[4] 'Act now to prevent survivor syndrome' *People Management,* 12 February 2009; 'Survivor syndrome among staff is hindering employers' *Personnel Today,* 10 June 2009; A Travaglione and B Cross, 'Diminishing the social network in organisations: does there need to be such a phenomenon as "survivor syndrome" after downsizing?' (2006) *Strategic Change* 1–13; K Sahder, '"Survivors" reactions to downsizing: the importance of contextual factors' (2003) Human Resources Management J 56–74; G Vinten and DA Lane, 'Counselling remaining employees in redundancy situations' (2002) *Career Development Intl* 430–437; L Worrall, F Campbell, and C Cooper, 'Surviving redundancy: the perceptions of UK managers' (2000) *J of Managerial Psychology* 460–476; T Baruch and P Hind, '"Survivor syndrome'–a management myth?' (2000) *J of Managerial Psychology* 29–45; M Armstrong-Stasson (1993) 'Survivors' reactions to a workforce reduction: a comparison of blue collar workers and their supervisors' (1993) *10 Canadian J of Administrative Sciences* 334–343; J Brockner, M Conovsky, R Cooper-Schneider, R Folger, C Martin, and R Bies, 'Interactive effects of procedural justice and outcome negativity of victims and survivors of job loss' (1994) *37 Academy of Management J* 397–409; W Bridges, 'Surviving the survivor syndrome', (1998) William Bridges and Associates pamphlet; J Brockner, 'Managing the effects of lay offs on others' (1992) *California Management Review* 9–27. (The above references are gratefully taken from TA Hickok, 'Downsizing and Organisational Culture' at (1998) *Journal of Public Administration*

Voluntary redundancy is often suggested as the panacea in this regard. But this is only a partial solution. Often the most talented and mobile staff and, on the other hand, some of the more experienced members of staff looking towards retirement, are attracted to early retirement packages. Voluntary redundancy is not therefore a solution on its own. Those who volunteer are sometimes those who should be kept.[5] As is observed in later chapters, there are other alternatives to redundancy, such as short-time working, sabbaticals, recruitment freezes, and salary sacrifices that may avoid compulsory redundancy.

As to the original individual's legal right on redundancy—the statutory redundancy payment—it is 45 years since the Redundancy Payments Act 1965 (now Pt XI of the Employment Rights Act 1996) created the right for every qualifying employee to be made a redundancy payment upon dismissal by reason of redundancy. The aims of this redundancy legislation are complex and multi-layered.[6] There are differing objectives put forward for the basis of redundancy payments legislation, some less relevant now than they were. Early commentators were taken with two aspects of the scheme in that it both encouraged job mobility and gave a worker a right of 'property' in the job. GR Bretten[7] considered as follows:

> It will be clear that two distinct policy considerations underly the Redundancy Payments Act 1965. First, it is recognised that the economic interest of the nation demands that its man-power shall be efficiently utilised. The overmanning of particular industries impairs productivity and it is necessary to create industrial conditions in which the mobility of labour is encouraged. Secondly, it is deemed desirable to accord to the worker in relation to his job a higher status than he has formerly enjoyed. It is now recognised that a worker has some 'rights' in his job just as his employer has certain 'rights' in his property. In the long term analysis the introduction in our labour law of the principle that a worker has some 'property' interest in his job may be the most significant effect of the Act.[8]

Lawrence S Root commented:

> . . . the Act established the idea that an employee gains the equivalent of *property rights* to his or her job by virtue of years of service with the company. Those rights include the privileges and security associated with seniority as well as rights to the job itself. In his introduction of the Bill for its critical second reading in Parliament, the Minister for Labour equated the rights of an employee to a job with those of an owner:
>
> '. . . if a man is deprived of those rights by economic circumstances outside his control, he ought to be compensated. Industry has long recognised the justice of this for higher management

---

and Management.) The need to take into consideration survivors is, to a small extent, taken into account by the amendment to s 188 of the TULR(C)A 1992 by the 1999 Regulations in so far as consultation about dismissals with employee representatives has to take place not only in relation to employees who may be proposed to be dismissed (as was previously the case) but also all those who may be affected by the proposed dismissals or who may be affected by measures taken in connection with those dismissals.

[5] *Management Today*, March 1997, 8. For an example of a voluntary redundancy programme in practice see 'Natural selection: BT's programme of voluntary redundancy' *IRS Employment Trends* 533, at 11. See also M Clarke, 'Choices and constraints: individual perceptions of the voluntary redundancy experience' (2007) *Human Resource Management J* 76–93; M Clarke, 'The voluntary redundancy option: carrot or stick?' (2005) *Human Resource Management J* 245–251.

[6] See RH Fryer, 'The myths of the Redundancy Payments Act' (1973) *2 ILJ* 1; Parker, Thomas-Ellis, and McCarthy, *Effects of the Redundancy Payments Act* (HMSO, 1981); Lewis, '20 Years of Statutory Redundancy Payments in Great Britain' (University of Leeds and Nottingham, 1985). See also the discussion in Chapter 8.

[7] GR Bretten, 'Termination of employment and the British redundancy Payment Scheme (1969) *American Business L J* 139–151.

[8] (1987) *Monthly Labor Review*, 18–23.

and I believe the House would agree that it is high time to extend it to all workers (*Hansard, April 26, 1965 column 35)*'.[9]

The right to property in one's job was famously first aired, in 1964, by Frederic Meyers[10] but Meyers percipiently observed that the concept of ownership of one's job has its flaws. Given that a true property right connotes undisturbed possession, Meyers accurately observes that any 'right' of property in one's job can only be 'property like'. An expression such as the 'right to work' is categorised by Meyers as being value laden and perhaps redolent of times when the closed shop operated, thus preventing an individual's ability to work if a non-member of a trade union. Writing before the Redundancy Payments Act 1965, however, Meyers observed that the Contracts of Employment Act 1963 providing, for the first time, a statutory employment notice based on length of service, was a real step forward. He also observed that security agreements i.e. collective agreements concerning the manner of redundancies and payments were a valuable mechanism for the protection of employee rights. This is something we pursue in Chapter 12.

The whole area of the concept of property at work was helpfully reviewed by Wanjiru Njoya, writing in 2007, and one of his conclusions was that one of the chief components of any property right in one's job is the 'freedom from arbitrary dismissal'. This is comprised in modern employment law in the right not to be unfairly dismissed and the right not to be discriminated against on grounds of any protected characteristic under the Equality Act 2010.[11]

Robert H Fryer[12] considered the mythology of the 1965 Act to be much more complex.

> The myths of the Redundancy Payments Act to be considered here are sixfold: namely, that the legislation provides employment security; that it gives some sort of job 'property rights' to workers; that by regulating redundancy, it restricts managerial discretion; that it compensates workers for their loss of job; that the Redundancy Payments Act was a disincentive to find alternative work; and that, irrespective of other advantages or disadvantages, it at least affords minimum cover to all who lose their job because of redundancy. Taken together, these six myths add up to a belief that what the Webbs[13] called the 'method of legal enactment' has done something, even too much, to redress the gross imbalance between capital and labour.

Judicial comment, whilst not uniform, stresses the compensatory nature of the redundancy payment. In *Lloyd v Brassey*,[14] Lord Denning MR considered that redundancy payment was 'in a real sense, compensation for long service'.

In *Mairs v Haughey*,[15] a case concerned with the taxation of a contractual redundancy payment, Lord Woolf stated:

> Redundancy, whether statutory or non statutory involves an employee finding himself without a job through circumstances over which he has no control . . . The redundancy legislation reflects an appreciation that an employee who has remained in his employment for the minimum time has a stake in his employment which justifies his receiving compensation if he loses that stake. . . . It is also unlike a deferred payment of wages entitlement in that a redundancy

---

[9] LS Root, 'Redundancy payments in Britain: a view from abroad' (1986) *Policy Studies* 30–51.

[10] F Meyers, *Ownership of jobs: a Comparative Study* (University of California) 1096.

[11] W Njoya, *Property in Work: The Employment Relationship in the Anglo-American Firm* (Ashgate Publishing Limited, 2007).

[12] RH Fryer, 'The myths of the Redundancy Payments Act' (1973) *ILJ* 1.

[13] S Webb and B Webb, *History of Trade Unionism* (1898) printed by the authors for the Amalgamated Society of Engineers; *Industrial Democracy* (1897); 9th edn 1926.

[14] [1969] ITR 100.

[15] [1994] 1 AC 303.

payment is never more than a contingent entitlement, which no doubt both the employer and the employee normally hope, will never accrue.

In *Kraft Foods UK Limited v Hastie*,[16] the EAT considered:

> It is in our view self evident that the object of the scheme was indeed to compensate employees who took voluntary redundancy under it for the loss of earnings that they had a legitimate expectation of receiving if their employment had continued.

The EAT approved the following paragraph from *Harvey on Industrial Relations and Employment Law*:[17]

> The British view of a redundancy payment is that it is in the nature of compensation to the employee for loss of his job: that is to say, for the loss of his expectation of continued employment. It is, so to speak, the price he receives for the compulsory purchase of his existing employment.

Nevertheless, the value of statutory redundancy payments has decreased over the years: the current maximum redundancy payment is just £12,000,[18] and the value of this in real terms has been eroded due to inflation. The basis of calculation of a redundancy payment is a combination of variables of age, length of service, and the amount of a week's pay.[19] But the amount of a week's pay which may be called into account is fixed by statute and currently stands at £400 only.[20] Over the years, governmental unwillingness to increase the level of the maximum allowable amount of a week's pay to bring redundancy payments (and indeed other statutory employment protection payments dependent on a week's pay[21]) into line with inflation was continually criticised.[22] Commenting as long ago as 1973, Fryer[23] considered that the scheme needed improving from the perspective of workers' entitlements. Following on from the Blair Government's Fairness at Work White Paper,[24] the unfair dismissal compensatory award maximum, also a victim of inflation over the years, was increased from £12,000 to £50,000 by virtue of s 34(4) of the Employment Relations Act 1999. This seems a significant hike but in fact all this increase did was to restore the value of an unfair dismissal award to its 1972 value. (It is still only £68,400, at the time of writing.) On this basis, the amount of a week's pay for redundancy payments purposes should have undergone a similar, spectacular, increase. But, curiously, it did not. Section 34 of the Employment Relations Act 1999, however, did institutionalise an annual increase of compensation awards, including the amount of a week's pay in accordance with the retail prices index.[25]

---

[16] EAT/0024/10/ZT.

[17] Para BE [9].

[18] See the Employment Rights Act 1996 (ERA 1996), ss 162, 227(1); SI 2010/2926.

[19] See Chapter 8 and also Appendix 1 for a 'ready reckoner'.

[20] See ERA 1996, s 227(1) and SI 2010/2926.

[21] ERA 1996, s 227(1).

[22] See, e.g. Marsh, *Law Society Gazette*, 15 December 1985.

[23] Ibid.

[24] Published in May 1998 (Cm 3968).

[25] The relevant part of s 34 of the ERA 1999, regarding indexation of the relevant amount reads:

> (2) If the retail prices index for September of a year is higher or lower than the index for the previous September, the Secretary of State shall as soon as is practicable, make an order in relation to each sum mentioned in sub-section (1)—
> (a) increasing each sum, if the new index is higher, or
> (b) decreasing each sum, if the new index is lower, by the same percentage as the amount of the increase or decrease of the index.

The previous maximum of £380 (raised from its previous level of £350) was made on an extraordinary basis by the Work and Families (Increase of Maximum Amount) Order 2009 pursuant to the power in s 14 of the Work and Families Act 2006, given the financial crisis and concerns of business and unions. But the Government rejected the option of increasing the limit to £450 (the then average weekly earnings and further froze the next increase until 2011, thus missing out the February 2010 review). This is not to say, however, that the importance of the concept of redundancy for individual employment law is confined to this relatively modest monetary scheme. First, many employees have, these days, the benefit of a contractual redundancy pay scheme that, although independently enforceable under the law of contract, frequently has as its basic structure the rules of the statutory redundancy payment scheme.[26] A study of the redundancy payments legislation is therefore important in this regard too. Enhanced redundancy schemes may directly or indirectly discriminate against workers on account of age unless the exception in Sch 9, para 13 of the Equality Act 2010 applies (see Chapters 8 and 12). If so, the disparate treatment will need to be justified. The question of what are the proportionate means of achieving a legitimate aim is producing a rich vein of case law (see Chapter 12). Second, the concept of redundancy is highly relevant in other areas of employment protection law. One area is unfair dismissal law,[27] which allows dismissal of an employee on various permitted grounds, one of which is redundancy.[28] The definition of redundancy in s 139(1) of the ERA 1996 is therefore important for the purposes of determining whether the employer has a permitted reason for dismissal in an unfair dismissal case. Indeed, some of the best known case law that we examine in relation to redundancy payments law concerns the definition of redundancy in the context of unfair dismissal claims.[29]

A second area is where redundancy triggers information and consultation obligations in favour of employee representatives.[30]

In 1975, the then European Community (EC) enacted the Collective Redundancies Directive,[31] which for the first time imposed on an employer proposing to dismiss as redundant a number of employees an obligation to inform, and thereafter consult with, employee representatives. This obligation was first enacted in the United Kingdom (UK) by the Employment Protection Act 1975 (EPA 1975). But some controversial features of the UK statute included the limitation of the right in favour of recognised trade union representatives, an absence of duty to inform and consult with a view to reaching agreement, a restricted definition of the meaning of redundancy (confining it only to cases where a definition of redundancy was satisfied for the purposes of redundancy payments liability[32]), and a regime of sanctions which allowed the employer to set off against any awards made in favour of employees sums payable under the contract of employment or payments in lieu of notice—thereby reducing liability in many cases to a manageable level and so raising the question of whether the sanction was 'effective'.

In the case of the amount of a week's pay, when making the calculation the result is rounded up to the nearest £10.

[26] For a discussion of some issues in that area see Chapter 12.
[27] See Chapter 10.
[28] ERA 1996, s 98(2).
[29] See Chapter 3.
[30] See below and Chapter 11.
[31] Council Directive (EC) 75/129. For an early commentary, see MF Freedland, 'Employment protection: redundancy procedures and the EEC' (1975) *ILJ* 24–34.
[32] See Chapters 3 and 4.

From 1993, the law in this area shifted gear. First, the EC Council enacted in 1992 an amending Directive[33] with additional obligations on employers in the context of multiple-redundancy handling. As a result of this and pressure by the EC Commission on the UK to amend its legislation to bring it in line with the Collective Redundancies Directive 75/129, a number of significant and far-reaching changes were made by the Trade Union Reform and Employment Rights Act 1993 (TURERA 1993) to what was by then the Trade Union and Labour Relations (Consolidation) Act 1992 (TULR(C)A 1992).

The principal changes effected by the TURERA 1993 were: to require consultation about ways of avoiding dismissals; reducing the number of employees to be dismissed and mitigating the consequences of dismissals; and to require consultation, in each case, to be with a view to reaching agreement. The set-off provisions under the protective award were abolished. It became no longer possible for an employer controlled by another company to plead an excuse for non-compliance with the provisions owing to the fact that the controlling undertaking had not given information to the employer to enable it to comply with the information requirements. And, finally, a new subsection (195(1)) of the TULR(C)A 1992 enlarged the definition of redundancy to include dismissals 'for a reason not related to the individual concerned or for a number of reasons all of which are not so related'. The latter change means that the redundancy consultation obligations bite not only when there is a redundancy viewed in traditional terms of downsizing but also where there are dismissals through reorganisation. The best example of this is large-scale termination on account of an employer's desire to change terms and conditions, and this expanded definition of redundancy continues to have a significant impact on UK industrial relations law.

By enacting the TURERA 1993, the Government had in part pre-empted the Commission's complaints about the UK's defective transposition of the Collective Redundancies Directive 75/129. Those complaints were, as mentioned: defining redundancy in a narrower form than had been contemplated by Directive 75/129; omitting to require consultation with a view to reaching agreement; creating a regime of ineffective sanctions contrary to European law; and, finally, confining the duties to inform and consult to a limited category of employee representatives, i.e. recognised trade union representatives. It will be seen above that the UK corrected three out of the four complaints by virtue of the TURERA 1993. But it stood firm on the question of designation of employee representatives for the purposes of the Directive.

Since 1975 the accepted channel of communication with employee representatives had been, in UK employment legislation, through a recognised trade union representative. Thus, in a non-unionised workplace the employment protection rights in favour of employee representatives simply did not apply. Such rights included information and consultation on collective redundancies, as well as information and consultation on business transfers, time off for trade union representatives, disclosure of information for collective bargaining purposes, and health and safety representational rights. The UK approach was in a sense justifiable while there existed a regime under which unions might force the employer's hand to recognise the union, where a sufficient number of employees were in favour of recognition. This right existed in the EPA 1975 but was repealed by the Employment Act 1980.

---

[33] Council Directive (EC) 92/56. This and Directive 75/129 have now been consolidated into Directive 98/59.

Turning to the present day, the Employment Relations Act 1999 introduced a new Schedule A1 to the Trade Union and Labour Relations (Consolidation) Act 1992, providing a mechanism for compulsory trade union recognition in the absence of voluntary agreement. But in the years between 1980 and the present day, there was no mechanism at all to impose recognition on an employer, and indeed the statistics over that period show that recognition was on the wane. In short, there were (and still are) a large number of workplaces without a recognised trade union and an employer wishing to avoid statutory employment protection rights granted through recognised trade unions could simply refuse to recognise or, in some cases, de-recognise the relevant union(s). In that sense, compliance with Community obligations to inform and consult employee representatives was voluntary. Nonetheless, in the face of this, the Government of the day still continued to maintain that the Directive, which states that 'workers' representatives' means 'workers representatives provided by the laws or practices of the Member States'[34] justified that stance.

Ultimately, this argument did not convince the European Court and in *Commission of the EC v UK*[35] the Court ruled that the UK was in breach of the Directive in respect of all four complaints including, of course, the question of designation of employee representatives.

As a result, the Government enacted the Collective Redundancies and Transfer of Undertakings (Protection of Employment) Regulations 1995[36] in a minimalistic attempt to correct the outstanding defect concerning designation of employee representatives, both in relation to multiple redundancies and transfers of undertakings. This regime was in some ways curious. In short, the employer was, by the 1995 Regulations, rather left to his own devices, but he now had a choice of whom to inform and consult. If he recognised a trade union, he could deal with that recognised trade union concerning all workers who may be affected by the proposals in respect of whom the union is recognised. Alternatively, he might invite employees to elect their own employee representatives. However, where the employer did not recognise a trade union or, where he did but the recognition agreement did not cover all categories of employee, he must invite employee representatives not covered by a recognition agreement to elect their own representatives. Singularly lacking in the 1995 Regulations was any detail about the mode of election of employee representatives, the number of employee representatives, how 'representative' they must be, and other matters of some practical importance for employers.

Perhaps not altogether surprisingly, this state of affairs was made the subject of litigation in *R v Secretary of State for Trade and Industry, ex p Unison, GMB and NASUWT.*[37] The arguments raised by the consortium of unions making the complaint were that the arrangements for the selection of representatives were inadequate; protection of organisers of an election was not apparent; there was inadequate provision for facilities such as manpower, information, or financial resources for representatives; no time off was allowed for organisers of the election, nor were facilities for the election of representatives guaranteed; and there was inadequate provision for complaint. None of these arguments found favour with the Divisional Court, which rejected the challenge to the validity of the Regulations in this regard.

---

[34] Article 1(1)(b).
[35] [1994] IRLR 412.
[36] SI 1995/2587.
[37] [1996] IRLR 438. See M Hall, 'Beyond recognition? Employee representation and EU law' (1996) *ILJ* 15.

If that were not enough, the Government introduced, via the 1995 Regulations, a sting in the tail for employees. The Collective Redundancies Directive 75/129 (now consolidated into Directive 98/59) only requires employers to inform and consult where at least a minimum threshold of employee numbers is involved. The EPA 1975 did not take up this opportunity and, although thresholds had to be achieved for certain minimum periods of consultation to apply (at least ten employees for the purposes of 30 days' consultation and at least 100 employees for the purposes of 90 days' consultation), consultation had to begin at the earliest opportunity in respect of even a single proposed redundancy. This had the potential, in an extreme case, to lead to the requirement of information and consultation with a recognised trade union over, say, the non-renewal of an expired fixed-term contract affecting just one employee. To deal with this point, the Government in fact took the opportunity in the 1995 Regulations to claw back some of the more advantageous rights it had enacted over and above what was required by Community law. Thus, in respect of dismissals on or after 1 March 1996, the obligations only bit where 20 or more employees at one establishment were being proposed as redundant. A legal challenge to the *vires* of the Regulations in diminishing employment rights already in existence at the time of the passage of the Regulations was also defeated in the *ex p Unison* case.[38]

The 1995 Regulations certainly fundamentally altered UK industrial relations. Notwithstanding the increase in the threshold for information and consultation obligations to apply, one forecast was that this removed six million workers from the protection of the provisions of TULR(C)A 1992. Whatever their defects, the Regulations now provided that every employer, unionised or not, had to inform and consult with employee representatives where 20 or more redundancies from an establishment were being proposed.

To come full circle, the defects in the 1995 Regulations were amended by the important Collective Redundancies and Transfer of Undertakings (Protection of Employment) (Amendment) Regulations 1999,[39] which dealt with some, if not all, of the problems inherent in the minimalist approach of the 1995 Regulations. The impact of the 1999 Regulations will be discussed in detail in Chapter 11. The divisive approach of allowing an employer who recognises a trade union nonetheless to deal with elected employee representatives has gone. First, if an employee recognises a trade union for a particular category of employees, he must consult with that recognised trade union in respect of that category and may not elect to deal otherwise with elected employee representatives. Second, the arrangements for election of employee representatives where appropriate are hugely strengthened, placing new obligations on employers to ensure the integrity of the election and to protect candidates and representatives from victimisation and discrimination. Third, remedies for breach of the information and consultation have been improved. Never before has the information and consultation regime been so important in the field of redundancies and we make no apology for devoting a significant chapter of this book to this subject.

But to commence our coverage of the law and practice of redundancy we return to the individual dimension and a regime first enacted in 1965, well before our accession to the then European Economic Community (EEC). In Part 1 of this work we expound the law on statutory redundancy payments.

---

[38] Ibid. In retrospect, the analysis of modern 'non-regression clauses' in more recent EU Directives by S Peers, 'Non-regression clauses: The fig leaf has fallen' (2010) 39 *ILJ* (4) 436–443, is instructive.
[39] SI 1999/1925.

1

QUALIFYING FACTORS

A. Eligibility for a Statutory Redundancy Payment	1.01	E. Illegality of Contract	1.138
B. Employment Relationship: Introduction	1.03	F. Continuous Employment Under a Contract of Employment	1.145
C. Employment Relationship: Historical Context	1.14	G. Employees Excluded From Claiming a Statutory Redundancy Payment	1.159
D. Employment Status: Multi-factor Approach	1.21		

A. Eligibility for a Statutory Redundancy Payment

The application of the provisions of the Employment Rights Act 1996 (ERA 1996) relating to **1.01** redundancy payments is confined to a certain category of individuals. In order to qualify for a statutory redundancy payment, an individual must satisfy four essential conditions. These are that:

(a) he is an employee;[1]
(b) he has been continuously employed for a period of not less than two years;[2]
(c) he is not among the excluded categories of employee under the ERA 1996; and
(d) either:[3]
    (i) he is dismissed[4] and the dismissal is by reason of redundancy;[5] or
    (ii) he is eligible for a redundancy payment by reason of being laid off or kept on short time.[6]

In this chapter we examine the first three of these qualifying factors and, in particular, the **1.02** crucial test of employment status; that is, how one determines whether an individual constitutes an 'employee' for these purposes.

---

[1] Subject to the implementation of s 23 of the Employment Relations Act 1999, discussed below.
[2] ERA 1996, s 155.
[3] Ibid., s 135(1).
[4] See Chapter 2.
[5] See Chapter 3.
[6] See Chapter 6.

B. Employment Relationship: Introduction

1.03 The law recognises several classes of employment relationship. Of these, only that relationship where an individual is employed as an employee currently confers on the individual the potential to claim for a statutory redundancy payment.

1.04 Categorisation of the employment relationship is under deep scrutiny. As Professor Mark Freedland remarks in *The Personal Employment Contract*,[7] it was Professor Bob Hepple who was one of the foremost critics of what was previously the 'cornerstone' of the common law contract of service as a model for employment rights. He argued for a new kind of structure for employment relation; rather an 'employment relationship' as opposed to a contract of employment *stricto sensu*.[8]

1.05 Freedland has further critically examined the notion of the contract of employment to which 'a false unity' was attributed.[9] He points out the difficulty of categorising intermittent and triangular employment relationships.[10] He observes the growth of multiple categories of employment in employment legislation, which leads him to argue towards a new definition of a personal employment contract. He has embarked upon an integrated analysis of the law of the personal employment contract as a whole, focusing on the difficulties in the way a purely contractual analysis can 'accommodate the complexity of employment relationships which is encountered in practice'.[11]

1.06 This analysis has, in turn, led Freedland to undertake a research project on personal work contracts in European comparative law.[12] This study of the employment relationship in terms of the development of the concept of the personal work contract has provoked much admiration and comment.[13] Freedland's work may, in the long run, be highly influential in the future categorisation of employment relationships.[14] In the meantime, however, we return to the condition in the Employment Rights Act 1996 that an employment contract must be found for entitlement to a redundancy payment and how this is presently treated by the courts.

1.07 Section 230(1) of the ERA 1996 defines an employee as 'an individual who has entered into or works under (or, where the employment has ceased, worked under) a contract of employment'. The contract of employment is therefore the gateway through which an individual gains access to protection under the redundancy payments legislation. 'Contract of employment' is defined to mean 'a contract of service or apprenticeship, whether express or implied, and (if it is express) whether oral or in writing'.[15] Therefore, a worker does not need to be employed under a written contract of employment in order to qualify as an employee;

---

[7] M Freedland, *The Personal Employment Contract* (OUP, 2003) 5.

[8] BA Hepple, 'Restructuring Employment Rights' (1986) 15 ILJ 225. As Freedland (n 7 above) points out (at 4) other distinguished scholars had, over time, similar misgivings.

[9] Freedland (n 7 above) 15.

[10] Ibid., 33.

[11] Ibid., 34.

[12] M Freedland, 'From the Contract of Employment to the Personal Work Nexus' (2006) ILJ 1–29.

[13] S Deakin, 'Does the "personal employment contract" provide a basis for the re-unification of employment law?' (2007) ILJ 68–83; ACL Davies, 'the contract for intermittent employment' (2007) ILJ 102 to 118.

[14] Leading to a major forthcoming work by Nicola Kountouris: *The Legal Construction of Personal Work Relations* (OUP, 2011, forthcoming). For other works on this subject see M Freedland, *Application of Labour and Employment Law Beyond the Contract of Employment* (2006) Oxford U Comparative L Forum at <http://oucif.iuscomp.org>; M Freedland, 'United Kingdom National Study for the International Labour Organisation' *Workers Protection*, 9 August 1999.

[15] ERA 1996, s 230(2).

contracts of employment can be oral, or implied from a consistent course of dealings. Furthermore, what the parties decide to call the relationship is not conclusive in law.

Despite the manifest importance of being able to distinguish between a contract of service on the one hand, and a contract for services on the other, there remains a high degree of uncertainty as to the criteria by which workers are classified in law.[16] Employment status is a question of mixed law and fact on which employment tribunals faced with the same facts may legitimately disagree.[17] The uncertainty has been exacerbated by the need to accommodate within the existing rigid classifications the growth of flexible labour and the increased number of 'atypical' workers. As we have observed above, a number of commentators have argued that this has resulted in the exclusion from the scope of employment protection legislation of those workers who are most in need of protection.[18]   **1.08**

Moreover, two further factors render the situation even more complicated. First, the tests of employment status are not applied consistently in different statutory contexts, such as tax, social security, and employment law.[19] There are even differences between the statutory tests used within employment protection legislation to determine what constitutes a contract of employment.[20] Thus, principles established in a case decided in one context may not necessarily apply to the determination of employment status for the purposes of qualification for the statutory redundancy scheme.   **1.09**

Secondly, due primarily to the increase in social legislation originating from the European Union (EU), there has been a tendency for recent legislation to confer rights beyond the traditional restricted category of employees. Thus, for example, the National Minimum Wage   **1.10**

---

[16] Research conducted for the Employment Research and Market Analysis Group at the DTI found that 30% of respondents had an employment status which 'had an element of uncertainty and was not completely clear' (Burchell, Deakin, and Honey, 'The Employment Status of Individuals in Non-Standard Employment', DTI, Employment Relations Research Series No. 6, 1999).

[17] See, e.g. the judgment of Lord Hoffmann in *Carmichael v National Power Plc* [2000] IRLR 43 and Mummery LJ in *Brook Street Bureau (UK) Limited v Dacas* [2004] EWCA Civ 217.

[18] See Hepple, (1986) ILJ 15(2) 69; Collins (1990) OJLS 10, 353; Smith (2000) NLJ 150(6920) 84; Collins (2000) ILJ 29(1) 73.

[19] This may be criticised as disturbing the risk allocation inherent in the determination of employment status. One view is that the exclusion of the self-employed from the scope of employment protection legislation is justified on the grounds that they should bear these risks in return for the more beneficial tax treatment they receive. However, the absence of precise congruence between the boundary of employment and self-employment in all contexts means that whilst an individual may not qualify for employment protection, he/she will not necessarily have the concomitant tax advantages available to the self-employed. For example, the Intermediaries Legislation introduced on 6 April 2000 (commonly referred to as IR35) established that individuals who provide services through the intermediary of a personal service company in circumstances in which they would be regarded as an employee of the client for tax purposes if the services were provided under a contract made directly between the individual and the client are deemed to be employees for the purposes of assessing income tax and national insurance contributions. Further, Chapter 9 of the Income Tax (Earnings and Pensions) Act 2003, introduced on 6 April 2007, applies to individuals providing services through a managed service company with the effect that payments received by such individuals are treated as income subject to PAYE and NI contributions where the intermediary meets the definition of a managed service company. However, there is no corresponding provision for those individuals to be deemed to be employees of the client company for employment protection purposes, although they may be employees of the personal or managed service company.

[20] For the purposes of the Sex Discrimination Act 1975, employment is defined to mean 'employment under a contract of service or of apprenticeship or a contract personally to execute any work or labour' (s 82). (See also the Race Relations Act 1976, s 78, and the Disability Discrimination Act 1995, s 68.) See *Mirror Group Newspapers v Gunning* [1985] ICR 145, in which the Court of Appeal held that there was no 'contract personally to execute any work or labour . . .' and *Sheehan v Post Office Counters Limited* [1999] ICR 734.

Act 1998 (NMWA), the Working Time Regulations 1998,[21] the Part-time Workers (Prevention of Less Favourable Treatment) Regulations 2000,[22] and the Public Interest Disclosure Act 1998 apply to 'workers'. The first three of these use the same definition of 'worker':

> an individual who has entered into or works under (or, where the employment has ceased, worked under):

(a) a contract of employment; or

(b) any other contract, whether express or implied and (if it is express) whether oral or in writing, whereby the individual undertakes to do or perform personally any work or services for another party to the contract whose status is not by virtue of the contract that of a client or customer of any profession or business undertaking carried on by the individual.[23]

1.11 The definition contained in the Public Interest Disclosure Act (PIDA) 1998 is in some circumstances wider than that quoted above.[24] Even the other three pieces of legislation differ in the specific provision they make for certain categories of individuals who may or may not be 'workers' as defined.[25] However, in all cases it is clear that the concept of who is a 'worker' is broader than that of who is in law an 'employee'; whereas all employees will be workers, not all workers will be employees.

1.12 The expansion of the scope of employment protection legislation is facilitated by the enactment of s 23 of the Employment Relations Act 1999. This gives the Secretary of State power by order to extend any right conferred on an individual against an employer under the Trade Union and Labour Relations (Consolidation) Act 1992 (TULR(C)A), the ERA 1996, the Employment Relations Act 1999 itself, or a United Kingdom (UK) instrument which implements an EU measure to 'individuals who are of a specified description', including individuals who are at present expressly excluded from exercising such a right. Thus the Secretary of State could extend the right to a statutory redundancy payment to individuals other than employees by statutory instrument, whereas previously this could only have been achieved via the lengthy process of enacting primary legislation. It is possible that this right could be conferred upon all 'workers' as defined in s 230(3) of the ERA 1996.[26] This would include, within the ambit of the statutory redundancy scheme, certain individuals who do not at present qualify for a statutory redundancy payment under the case law as it stands. As yet, however, the Secretary of State has not invoked this power.

1.13 The development of the statutory concept of a 'worker' has been gradual. In effect, the extension of employment rights to workers simply shifts the band of uncertainty further along the spectrum of employment relationships, from the boundary of those who are 'employees' and

---

[21] SI 1998/1833.

[22] SI 2000/1551. These regulations were originally confined to employees, but their scope was extended following representations that this restriction would fail properly to implement the terms of the Part-time Workers Directive (Council Directive 97/81).

[23] NMWA 1998, s 54, Working Time Regulations 1998, reg 2(1), Part-time Workers (Prevention of Less Favourable Treatment) Regulations 2000, reg 1(2) and ERA 1996, s 230(3).

[24] PIDA 1998, sub-ss 1, 15(1) and 18(2) inserting ERA 1996, sub-ss 43K and 230(6).

[25] For example, the NMWA 1998 makes specific provision in respect of homeworkers who are not otherwise 'workers'.

[26] Burchell, Deakin and Honey, 'The Employment Status of Individuals in Non-Standard Employment' (DTI, Employment Relations Research Series No. 6, 1999) concluded that the use of the 'worker' definition might confer employment rights on a further 5% of all those in employment (or about 16% of those whose employment status is unclear because they are employed in non-standard work of some kind).

those who are not, to the boundary between those who are 'workers' and those who are genuinely self-employed.[27] However, this chapter, in the context of qualification for a redundancy payment, is concerned with where the former boundary should be drawn.

C. Employment Relationship: Historical Context

The current test of eligibility is that an individual must be an employee in order to qualify for a redundancy payment. Over the years, the courts have developed various tests to determine whether an individual is an employee. The courts have now evolved a test, known as the 'multiple test', that looks at all the features of the relationship between the employer and the worker in order to determine the nature of the relationship. Before examining this test, it is useful to look at its historical evolution. **1.14**

The control test[28]

The early cases concerning employment status highlighted the element of control as essential to the employment relationship. An employer had the right to control what the worker did, as well as the method of doing it. The courts perceived that the degree of control by the employer was higher in the case of employees than it was in the case of self-employed contractors, who usually retain an element of freedom in how they perform their services. However, it was realised that the control test was both inflexible and reliant upon a fiction. Historically, the test worked in ordinary master-and-servant relationships but did not lend itself to the more sophisticated employment relationships which developed in the twentieth century with, in particular, the growth in the number of skilled employees over whom it was not realistic to expect the employer to have practical as opposed to theoretical control, especially as regards the method of performing their work. Indeed, it could be argued that the presence of control is now equally consistent with either employment or self-employment.[29] **1.15**

The organisational test

Faced with the increasingly artificial control test, the courts looked for a new approach based on the question of whether a worker was integrated into the organisation of the employer. In *Stevenson, Jordan and Harrison Ltd v MacDonald and Evans*,[30] Lord Denning expressed the 'integration' or 'organisational' test as follows: **1.16**

> One feature which seems to run through the instances is that, under a contract of service, a man is employed as part of the business, and his work is done as an integral part of the business; whereas, under a contract for services, his work, although done for the business, is not integrated into it, but is only accessory to it.

Under this test, the definition of an employee is arguably wider than under the control test. A skilled or professional employee may not work under the minute-by-minute control of the employer, thereby failing the strict control test, but he or she may still be integrated into the **1.17**

---

[27] See, for example the Court of Appeal's decision in *RSA Consulting Ltd v Evans* [2010] EWCA Civ 866 and the EAT's decision in *Clarkson v Pensher Security Doors Limited* UKEAT/0107/09.
[28] See Deakin 'The Evolution of the Contract of Employment 1900–1950: the Influence of the Welfare State' in N Whiteside and R Salais (eds), *Governance, Industry and Labour Markets in Britain and France. The Modernising State in the Mid-Twentieth Century*, Work, Employment and Society (1999) 13 170–171, for an account of the evolution of the control test.
[29] Brodie (1998) SLPQ 2, 138.
[30] [1952] 1 TLR 101, CA.

organisation of the employer. But in an age when the boundaries of an organisation are often unclear because more ancillary functions of an enterprise are outsourced[31] to external contractor companies whose own workers may well be 'integrated' into the customer's organisation, whilst clearly not being employees of the customer, this test would also fail as a single, universally applicable test. The growth of 'atypical' workers[32] who arguably deserve employment status also militated against the use of this as the exclusive test of status.

The economic reality test

1.18　In a number of subsequent cases, the courts began to look at employment relationships from the perspective of the allocation of economic risk. This test was first expressed in the UK courts by Cooke J in *Market Investigations Ltd v Minister of Social Security*[33] when he said,

> The fundamental test to be applied is this: is the person who has engaged himself to perform the services performing them as a person in business on his own account? In other words, who bears the risk of economic loss and the chance of profit? Is the worker effectively in business for himself, even though he may be under the control of or within the organisation of the employer?[34]

1.19　This test subsequently found favour in *Lee v Chung and Shun Shing Construction and Engineering Company Ltd*,[35] where the Privy Council said that:

> . . . factors which may be of importance are such matters as whether the man performing the services provides his own equipment, whether he hires his own helpers, what degree of financial risk he takes, what degree of responsibility for investment and management he has, and whether and how far he has an opportunity of profiting from sound management in the performance of his task.

1.20　It is submitted that this is a much more practical and workable test than the more conceptual control and organisational tests. It allows the court to look behind the outward trappings of the contract to determine whether the worker has genuine self-employed status or whether it is an attempt by the employer to avoid statutory protections and obligations. Nevertheless, the test is still based on a comparatively narrow criterion, namely economic risk or financial dependence. It ignores potentially significant factors such as the reason why employment status falls to be determined and it is for this reason that the law has moved towards a much broader-based test.

D.　Employment Status: Multi-factor Approach

1.21　The modern approach of the courts is to consider all the relevant factors and features of the relationship. The test was first propounded by MacKenna J in the case of *Ready Mixed Concrete (South East) Ltd v Minister of Pensions and National Insurance*.[36] This case concerned a lorry driver who used his own lorry to deliver ready-mixed concrete for the company.

---

[31] See Chapter 3.
[32] e.g. homeworkers or tele-workers.
[33] [1969] 2 QB 173.
[34] This test was adopted by the US Supreme Court as early as 1946 (*United States v Silk* 331 US 704 (1946)).
[35] [1990] IRLR 236; [1990] ICR 409, PC.
[36] [1968] 2 QB 497.

However, under the terms of his contract he wore the company's uniform and his lorry carried the company livery. He was required to drive exclusively for the company and had agreed to carry out company instructions 'as if he were an employee'. The question arose as to whether the driver was a contractor or an employee for the purposes of the then National Insurance Act 1965. MacKenna J set out three key questions:

1. Did the driver undertake to provide his own work and skill in return for remuneration?
2. Was there a sufficient degree of control to enable the driver fairly to be called an employee?
3. Were there any other factors inconsistent with the existence of a contract of employment?

Clearly, the question of control is a key element in this analysis, but it is not exclusive. The employer's control of the worker needs to be 'sufficient' but it does not need to be absolute. **1.22**

The test also places a premium on the idea that an employee is contracted to provide a personal service to the employer. On the facts in *Ready Mixed Concrete*, however, the driver was not obliged to actually perform the work himself and was therefore free to employ a substitute driver in his place. This was fatal to the argument that the driver was an employee. An employee does not have the freedom to substitute another worker in place of himself (see the discussion headed 'Personal service' below). **1.23**

The multiple test therefore allows the full range of features of the relationship to be considered, including features such as the degree of control and integration which had previously been regarded as determinative, none of which is necessarily conclusive in itself. It may be, as in *Ready Mixed Concrete*, that there is a vital element missing, such as personal service, and this will be conclusive. However, in the majority of borderline cases, the various factors will have to be weighed against each other and a conclusion drawn. It is important to emphasise that a court will look beyond what the parties have called the relationship and will instead look at the reality of the contract.[37] The fact that the parties may express themselves as employer and employee will therefore carry little weight with a court if all the features of the relationship point to a contract for services. **1.24**

It is important not to be prescriptive in enumerating the factors to be considered by the courts. The range of features to which weight may be given in applying the multiple test includes:[38] **1.25**

(a) the right of control retained, and the degree of control actually exercised, by the employer—whether it is absolute or whether the individual has (whether in theory or in practice) a wide discretion as to how, when, and where he performs his duties;
(b) whether there is 'mutuality of obligation' i.e. whether there are mutual obligations for the employer to provide work and the individual to accept any work which is offered;
(c) whether the individual's interest in the contract involves any aspect of profit or risk of loss, which will involve consideration of the method by which the individual is paid, whether the individual has invested in his business, and whether the individual has the opportunity to profit from sound management of the contract;

---

[37] See, for example, the EAT's decision in *Ahsan v Westmead Business Group Limited* UKEAT/0480/10, in which the tribunal was found to have incorrectly considered post-termination correspondence in determining the nature of the relationship.

[38] See the useful guidance provided by HMRC in connection with IR35 (although this is subject to the point made above about the varying weights which may be given to these factors in different contexts).

(d) whether the individual must perform the work personally or may choose to hire someone else to perform the work for him;[39]

(e) whether the individual is properly regarded as part and parcel of the employer's organisation at the relevant times;

(f) who provides the equipment used by the individual to perform his tasks;

(g) the incidence of tax and national insurance;

(h) the length of the individual's engagement with that employer;

(i) what the parties intended;[40]

(j) the traditional structure of the individual's profession and the arrangements within it;[41] and

(k) whether the contractual terms are more consistent with a contract of service rather than a contract for service (e.g. whether the contract contains detailed provisions as to duties, contractual hours, and place of work, whether the parties are free to terminate the contract without notice,[42] whether the individual is bound by the employer's disciplinary and grievance procedures, and whether the individual is contractually entitled to benefits such as holiday pay, sick pay, and pension provisions).

1.26 Looked at in these terms, the multiple test begins to look like a checklist of features, the results of which will conclusively distinguish a contract of employment from a contract for services. However, the multiple test is not intended to be a strict, mechanical test; the very premise of the test is that the substance of the entire contractual relationship is examined. As Mummery J said at first instance in *Hall (Inspector of Taxes) v Lorimer*:[43]

> [The determination of employment status] is not a mechanical exercise of running through a checklist to see whether [those factors] are present in, or absent from, any given situation. The object of the exercise is to paint a picture from the accumulation of details . . . it is a matter of evaluation of the overall effect, which is not necessarily the same as the sum total of the individual details. Not all details are of equal weight or importance in any given situation.

1.27 A holistic approach is therefore required, illustrations of which are given below. However, it should be noted that it is arguably now settled law that mutuality of obligation, in the sense of obligations for the employer to provide work and the individual to accept any work which is offered, is a *sine qua non* of the existence of a contract of employment. Only if mutuality is established, therefore, will the other factors be of relevance.

Mutuality of obligation

1.28 The case law relating to mutuality can best be considered in the context of various non-standard forms of employment relationship, where employment status often 'founders on the rock of mutuality'.[44]

---

[39] See the discussion in *Express and Echo Publications Ltd v Tanton* [1999] IRLR 367. Arguably this is part of the requirement of mutuality of obligation.

[40] Although in practice this will carry little weight, if other factors are neutral the intention of the parties will be the decisive factor in determining employment status (*Massey v Crown Life Insurance Co* [1978] ICR 580). In relation to so-called 'voluntary' workers, see Morris (1999) ILJ 28(3) 249.

[41] i.e. custom and practice in the industry concerned. This factor was afforded particular importance in *O'Kelly v Trusthouse Forte plc* [1983] IRLR 369.

[42] This was one of the factors which the Court of Appeal in *O'Kelly v Trusthouse Forte Plc* [1983] IRLR 369 said was inconsistent with the existence a contract of employment. However, although it may provide evidence as to the intentions of the parties, this argument is rather circular, since if a contract is a contract of employment the statutory notice provisions of the ERA 1996 will apply.

[43] [1992] STC 599. This passage was subsequently approved on appeal by Nolan LJ [1994] 1 WLR 209.

[44] This was the phrase used by the employment tribunal in *Carmichael v National Power Plc* [2000] IRLR 43.

Casual workers

Over the years there has been a huge increase in the number of workers engaged on a casual **1.29** basis, including a large number on 'zero-hours contracts' where there are no set hours of work. Casual workers provide enormous flexibility for employers, particularly since, historically, employment protection rights were confined to employees and such individuals were not generally regarded as working under a contract of employment although, as discussed above, this flexibility has to some extent been restricted by the extension of certain employment legislation to such workers.[45] However, it should be noted at the outset that the law does not explicitly recognise a specific class of 'casual workers'. Rather, the term is used loosely to define certain individuals whose work is 'not regular or permanent, which is temporary or occasional'.[46] Historically, the courts have had some difficulty in determining the employment status of casual labour, and the issue continues to require a detailed consideration of the facts.

In *O'Kelly v Trusthouse Forte Plc*,[47] the Court of Appeal had to decide whether a number **1.30** of casual waiters and waitresses were employees for the purpose of unfair dismissal proceedings. The workers were described as 'regular' casual staff. They were 'regular' in the sense that they would be offered engagements on a frequent and regular basis and were given preference in the allocation of any available work over and above 'ordinary' casual employees. A number of features indicated that the workers were employed under a contract of employment. They were paid in return for services and did not invest any of their own capital in the enterprise. They worked under the direction and control of the hotel and were clearly part of the hotel organisation. Clothing and equipment were provided by the hotel and the workers were paid weekly in arrears after deduction of income tax and national insurance. The workers were subject to a disciplinary and grievance procedure and there was holiday pay and an incentive bonus calculated by reference to past service. On the other hand, the workers did not receive a regular wage and did not receive sick pay. They were not included in the staff pension scheme. There were no regular or assured working hours and the workers were not given written particulars of employment. The engagement was terminable without notice on either side. The hotel was under no obligation to provide any work and the workers were not obliged to accept work.

The employment tribunal at first instance held that the workers were in business on their **1.31** own account and were independent contractors supplying services; they did not work under a contract of employment. The tribunal paid particular attention to the established custom and practice of the hotel and catering industry in which casual workers were generally regarded as independent contractors. The tribunal applied the multiple test, considering all the aspects of the relationship, with no single factor being in itself decisive. In the tribunal's view, the single most important ingredient missing from the characteristics necessary to find a contract of employment was mutuality of obligations. The fact that the regular casuals were given preference over and above the other casuals

---

[45] e.g. time spent by a worker on a zero-hours contract at the employer's premises waiting to be called to work would be working time for the purpose of the Working Time Regulations 1998 and the worker would be entitled to be paid in respect of that time under the national minimum wage legislation.
[46] *Carmichael v National Power Plc* [1998] IRLR 301, *per* Ward LJ.
[47] [1983] IRLR 369.

was not attributable to any legal obligation on the part of the company to offer work to the regulars and for them to perform that work when offered. On appeal to the Employment Appeal Tribunal (EAT), the EAT disagreed with the decision of the employment tribunal, finding that each individual contract covering a particular catering function was a contract of employment. On appeal to the Court of Appeal, however, the employment tribunal's reasoning was approved. This should be contrasted with the decision of the Court of Appeal in *Nethermere (St Neots) Ltd v Gardiner and Taverna*,[48] in which the court found that there was a mutual obligation to provide and perform work.

Casual workers and the 'mutuality of obligation' test

1.32 Several further cases have emphasised the importance of the 'mutuality of obligation' test in relation to casual workers. The first is *Clark v Oxfordshire Health Authority*.[49] Mrs Clark was a staff nurse who worked on the Oxfordshire Health Authority 'nurse bank'. She had no fixed hours of work, and worked simply when an appropriate vacancy arose at any hospital run by the Authority. She was paid an hourly rate for the work she performed, but was not entitled to any pay when she did not work. Any pay she received was subject to deduction of PAYE, national insurance, and her contributions under the NHS Superannuation Scheme. She had no entitlement to holiday pay or sick leave. Her terms and conditions included provisions relating to discipline and dismissal, a grievance procedure, and a duty of confidentiality. Mrs Clark alleged that she was unfairly dismissed following three years' service between 21 January 1991 and 27 January 1994 during which she had worked in every week but six, save for a break from 23 August 1992 to 25 October 1992, during which she provided no services and had four weeks' leave. The employment tribunal held, however, that Mrs Clark was not an employee and that she could not pursue her claim for unfair dismissal. They concluded that the mutuality of obligation which was an essential feature of a contract of employment was missing; there was no obligation on the Authority to offer Mrs Clark work and no obligation on her to accept work when it was offered, even though in practice she had never refused any work. On appeal, the EAT disagreed with the employment tribunal and held that the contract between Mrs Clark and the Authority was actually a 'global' contract of employment governing successive appointments. The EAT stated that the lack of mutuality of obligation was 'a significant factor but must be seen in the context of the other terms and conditions of the contract'. In other words, it was not conclusive in determining employment status.[50]

1.33 The Court of Appeal, however, reinstated the tribunal's findings as to Mrs Clark's employment status. In the only reasoned judgment, Sir Christopher Slade stated that the court was bound by the Court of Appeal decisions in *Nethermere (St Neots) Ltd v Gardiner and Taverna*[51] and *McLeod v Hellyer Brothers Ltd*,[52] which were authorities for the proposition that no contract of employment can exist 'in the absence of mutual obligations subsisting over the

[48] [1984] IRLR 240. See below.
[49] [1998] IRLR 125.
[50] See also the comments of the EAT in *City and East London FHS Authority v Duncan* (unreported) to this effect.
[51] [1984] IRLR 240.
[52] [1987] IRLR 232.

entire duration of the relevant period'. However, in determining whether this 'irreducible minimum' of mutual obligation was present in this case, Sir Christopher Slade added:

> I would, for my part, accept that the mutual obligations required to found a global contract of employment need not necessarily and in every case consist of obligations to provide and perform work. To take one obvious example, an obligation by the one party to accept and do work if offered and an obligation on the other party to pay a retainer during such periods as work was not offered would, in my opinion, be likely to suffice. In my judgment, however, . . . the authorities require us to hold that some mutuality of obligation is required to found a global contract of employment.

He found that in this case no such mutuality subsisted during the periods during which Mrs Clark was not occupied in a single engagement, any duty of confidentiality binding her during such periods stemming merely from previous single engagements. However, he did not decide whether, at the effective date of termination, there existed a specific engagement which amounted to a contract of service[53] and could provide the basis for a claim for unfair dismissal, as neither the employment tribunal nor the EAT had directed their attention to this question. **1.34**

The second case, which eventually went all the way to the (then) House of Lords, is *Carmichael and Another v National Power Plc*.[54] Mrs Carmichael and Mrs Leese brought claims against National Power Plc under s 1(1) of the Employment Protection (Consolidation) Act 1978[55] for written particulars of the terms of their employment. Their entitlement turned on whether they were employees within the meaning of what is now the ERA 1996. **1.35**

The applicants were engaged to conduct tours around power stations. The tours were normally two hours long and could be at any time during the day. When the jobs were advertised they were done so on a 'casual as required' basis at a rate of £3.77 per hour. Mrs Carmichael and Mrs Leese applied and, after an interview, they were sent a letter in March 1989 noting that they were 'agreeable to be employed by the CEGB [National Power's predecessor] at the Blyth A and Blyth B power stations on a casual as required basis as a station guide' and enclosing a confirmation letter stating 'I am pleased to accept your offer of employment as a station guide on a casual as required basis' to be returned by the offeree. Both applicants signed and returned this letter. **1.36**

Mrs Carmichael and Mrs Leese both received training and worked as guides on most occasions on which they were asked to. The work was not full time and they were paid only for the hours worked. At the time they made the application, they were commonly working for up to 25 hours a week. Income tax and national insurance contributions were deducted at an employed person's rate. However, they were not entitled to sick pay or holiday pay and were not covered by National Power's pension arrangements, although they were allowed to apply for shares on the same basis as employees. When they did work they had to follow the employer's requirements relating to first aid, uniforms, and quality of the tours. In 1995, Mrs Carmichael and Mrs Leese complained to an employment tribunal that National Power had failed to provide them with a written statement of employment particulars. **1.37**

---

[53] As was the case in *McMeechan v Secretary of State for Employment* [1997] IRLR 353.
[54] [1998] IRLR 301, CA; [2000] IRLR 43, HL.
[55] Now s 1 of the ERA 1996.

National Power contended that the tribunal did not have jurisdiction to hear the claim as the applicants were not employed under a contract of employment.

1.38 The employment tribunal found that, as there was no mutuality of obligation to provide and perform work, when not working as guides the applicants were in no contractual relationship of any kind with National Power or its predecessor. *A fortiori*, they were not employed under a contract of employment when not at work. The EAT upheld this ruling. On appeal, the Court of Appeal overturned the tribunal's findings on a split decision. Ward LJ concluded that the March 1989 documentation constituted an offer and acceptance, and therefore a written contract, and that in order to give business efficacy to the contract, a term should be implied that National Power would provide a reasonable share of such guiding work as became available from time to time and a corresponding term that, subject to the qualification of reasonableness, the applicants would accept the work offered. Although National Power could not compel the applicants to accept work, this was due to the absence of an adequate remedy rather than to the absence of a breach of contract. On this basis, Ward LJ considered that when each applicant acted as a guide they did so 'under the umbrella' of the contract between the parties, not in consequence of some ad hoc arrangement effected by the telephone call from National Power requesting them to work and their acceptance of this individual assignment. In the circumstances, and as the contract did not 'founder on the rock of mutuality', he considered that the global contract under which the applicants worked was a contract of employment. In addition, he held that in any event the applicants worked under a contract of service during each single engagement. Chadwick LJ also found that there was a global contract of employment, but on the more restrictive basis that National Power was only under an obligation to ensure that any work which became available would be offered to those recruited and trained as station guides before those who had not been so trained.

1.39 However, this decision was in turn overturned by the House of Lords, which upheld the original decision made by the tribunal that there was no global contract between the parties, let alone a global contract of employment. Rather, the documents did no more than provide a framework for a series of successive ad hoc contracts of service or for services which the parties might subsequently make. The then appointed Lord Chancellor, Lord Irvine, stated that:

> The parties incurred no obligations to provide or accept work, but at best assumed moral obligations in a context where both recognised that the best interests of each lay in being accommodating to the other.

1.40 However, Lord Irvine did not base this decision on the March 1989 documentation alone, as he took the tribunal to have decided that this constituted only one, albeit important, relevant source of material from which they were entitled to infer the parties' true intention, along with the 'other objective inferences which could reasonably be drawn from what the parties said and did in March 1989, and subsequently'. As the documentation contained no provisions relating to how or when work was to be provided, the frequency with which it would be offered, or notice of termination, Lord Irvine considered that they cannot have intended it to constitute 'an exclusive memorial of their relationship'. Thus, what the parties understood to be their respective obligations, and their subsequent behaviour, was relevant evidence of what they in fact were, particularly as they were both of the same understanding. He inferred, from the fact that on several occasions the applicants were unavailable for work but had not been disciplined, that when work was available they were free to undertake it or not as they chose. Rather than the formal subordination required for an employment relationship, the arrangement 'turned on mutual convenience and goodwill'. Even if the March 1989 documentation was capable of bearing the construction favoured by the majority of the Court of Appeal, Lord Irvine said that no terms might be implied on the ground of business efficacy as there was no contract into which they could be implied. However, he expressly left open the question of the applicants' status when they were actually working. In his judgment, Lord Hoffmann indicated that he considered that during each tour the applicants were employed under a contract of service.

The statements of Lord Irvine regarding the sources from which an employment tribunal **1.41** may draw inferences as to the intention of the parties are not purely of relevance to the determination of whether there is a contract and, if so, what the terms of that contract are. As detailed by Lord Hoffmann in his judgment, it is also relevant to the question of whether the appellate bodies are entitled to interfere with the tribunal's decision at first instance. If the issue of employment status turns purely on the construction of a written document, then it is a question of law which the EAT would have jurisdiction to hear on appeal.[56] However, where the intention of the parties, objectively ascertained, has to be gathered partly from documents but also from oral exchanges and conduct, the terms of the contract are a question of fact. Indeed, the question of whether the parties intended a document or documents to be the exclusive record of the terms of their agreement is itself a question of fact. As a tribunal's findings of fact may only be disturbed if they are perverse, this naturally restricts the scope for appealing against decisions on employment status in such cases.

The approach in these cases must be considered in the light of the Court of Appeal's deci- **1.42** sion in *Cornwall County Council v Prater*.[57] Mrs Prater had been engaged as a home tutor by the Council between 1988 and 1998. In respect of this engagement, there was no obligation on the Council to offer pupils to Mrs Prater and no obligation on her to accept those offered. However, once a pupil was offered to and accepted by Mrs Prater, she was obliged to fulfil this commitment and the Council was obliged to give that work to Mrs Prater for as long as was necessary.

Unlike in the previous authorities, Mrs Prater was not arguing that there existed a global or **1.43** umbrella contract. Instead, Mrs Prater's case was based upon there being a succession of teaching contracts which had the necessary mutuality of obligation. In between these contracts, Mrs Prater sought to rely on the provisions of the ERA 1996 relating to continuity of employment on account of a temporary cessation of work (under s 212(3)(b) of the ERA 1996, discussed further below).

The employment tribunal held that Mrs Prater was an employee. In so finding, the tribunal **1.44** referred to the open-ended nature of the engagements, the inability for Mrs Prater to substitute another teacher for herself where necessary and that the lack of control was consistent with a teacher of Mrs Prater's experience. The EAT dismissed the subsequent appeal and upheld the tribunal's decision, finding that the tribunal had been entitled to find as it did on the facts.

---

[56] *Davies v Presbyterian Church of Wales* [1986] IRLR 194.
[57] [2006] EWCA Civ 102.

1.45 The case was thereafter appealed to the Court of Appeal. The Council argued on appeal that the requisite mutuality of obligation was absent in this case. The Council contended that mutuality within each separate contract was not enough to establish a contract of service if there were no continuing obligations on either party after the end of each contract.

1.46 The Court of Appeal dismissed the appeal, holding that there was sufficient mutuality in each contract and that s 212 of the ERA 1996 'took care of the gaps between the individual contracts' (*per* Mummery LJ). Section 212, therefore, operated to establish continuity of employment throughout 1988 to 1998.

1.47 The approach in *Prater* was subsequently followed by the EAT in the case of *North Wales Probation Area v Edwards*.[58] The approach adopted in these cases indicates that the focus is to be shifted towards consideration of the nature of each individual contract, rather than simply attempting to identify an umbrella contract. Indeed, the EAT in the case of *Augustin v Total Quality Staff Limited and another*[59] held that, given the current state of the authorities, the issue to be considered by the tribunal is not just a question of whether there was an overarching contract of employment, but also whether there was a series of short contracts of service.

'Outworkers'

1.48 The concept of mutuality of obligation was originally developed to extend employment status to 'outworkers',[60] but, in the light of *Carmichael*, may be used to deprive them of such status. 'Outworkers' are workers who provide a product or service to an employer, although there may be no specific agreement as to where the work is done. Outworkers typically work from home. In such cases, there may simply be an arrangement whereby the employer provides the materials and the outworker delivers a finished product to the employer. In such arrangements, courts and tribunals have historically been more willing to imply the 'irreducible minimum' of obligation necessary to found a contract of employment.

1.49 For example in *Airfix Footwear Ltd v Cope*,[61] Mrs Cope worked from home making heels for a shoe manufacturer. There was no written contract but the company provided the training, tools, and materials to enable Mrs Cope to make a daily delivery of finished heels. She was paid 'wages' on a piece-work basis, and tax and national insurance were not deducted. Most importantly, the EAT inferred from the conduct of the parties that there was a mutual obligation to provide and perform her work. The EAT, therefore, decided that Mrs Cope was an employee for the purposes of an unfair dismissal claim; although there was no written contract of employment, there was a continuing relationship which had all the characteristics of a contract of employment, even if the arrangement had never been confirmed in writing.

1.50 Similarly, in *Nethermere (St Neots) Ltd v Gardiner and Taverna*,[62] the Court of Appeal confirmed that a long-standing relationship between a company and an outworker could result in an 'umbrella' or 'global' contract from which it could be implied that the company

---

[58] UKEAT/0468/07.
[59] UKEAT/0343/07.
[60] See *Smith*, 15 March 2007.
[61] [1978] IRLR 396.
[62] [1984] IRLR 240.

is obliged to provide work and the worker is obliged to accept and perform that work. As Stephenson LJ in *Nethermere* said:

> I cannot see why well-founded expectations of continuing homework should not be hardened or refined into enforceable contracts by regular giving and taking of work over periods of a year or more, and why outworkers should not thereby become employees under contracts of service like those doing similar work at the same rate in the factory.

This principle should be treated with some caution, however. There is a fine distinction **1.51** between the expectations of the individuals in *Nethermere*, from which the tribunal inferred that there was an obligation to provide work, and those of the regular casuals in *O'Kelly v Trusthouse Forte Plc*,[63] which led to no such inference. In other words it is difficult to distinguish between a contractual right to receive work and a bare expectation that work will continue to be received. It is clear from the House of Lords' decision in *Carmichael* that mutuality will not be implied where in reality it is a fiction.

Employment agency workers

The question of whether a worker is an employee or an independent contractor frequently **1.52** arises if the worker in question has been supplied by an employment agency. The difficulty is that an agency worker performs work pursuant to a tripartite contractual structure. The agency contracts with the worker to provide that worker for a client company. The worker performs the work for the client but is paid by the agency, which is in turn paid a fee by the client company. The worker frequently works under a contract which states that there is no entitlement to holiday or sick pay and that there is no obligation on the agency to provide any work or on the worker to perform any work. The worker would not be paid during any period in which there was no work provided.

In addition, the courts have traditionally held that agency contracts do not constitute a **1.53** contract of service between the agency and the worker. Agency employment contracts usually lack the mutual obligation to provide or do work, which is one of the key features of a contract of service. Similarly, the agency rarely exercises any control over the worker.

This view was confirmed by the EAT in *Wickens v Champion Employment*,[64] in which the **1.54** EAT had to consider whether the 'temporaries' on the agency's books were employees of the agency. The agency was not bound to find work for the temps, nor conversely was the temp bound to accept a booking made by the agency on his behalf. If work was not offered or accepted, there would be no pay. However, there was no evidence that the temps were carrying on business on their own account. Despite this, the EAT concluded that the contracts between the agency and the temps did not create a relationship that had the elements of continuity associated with a contract of employment. The vital elements missing were the obligation of an agency to provide work and the obligation upon the temps to accept a booking. The EAT pointed out that, in order to find that there was no contract of employment, it did not need to be shown that the temp was in business on his or her own account. The test did not include as a necessary element the question of whether the individual carries on a separate business.

---

[63] [1983] IRLR 369.
[64] [1984] ICR 365.

1.55 *Wickens* was followed in *Ironmonger v Movefield Ltd*,[65] in which the EAT again confirmed that there was no contract of employment between the employment agency and the agency worker. The contract in question bore no resemblance to a contract of employment. There was no written contract and the agency exercised no control over the agency worker. Notice of termination could be given by the hiring party, there was no pension provision or holiday pay and, again, there was no obligation on the agency to find work. However, the EAT, whilst accepting that there was no contract of employment, thought that this did not necessarily mean that the agency worker was self-employed. The EAT agreed with the observation of Cooke J in the earlier case of *Construction Industry Training Board v Labour Force Ltd*,[66] when he said that the contracts of agency workers were neither contracts of service nor contracts for services but fell within an entirely different category of *sui generis* contracts which had a unique identity.

1.56 In *McMeechan v Secretary of State for Employment*,[67] however, the Court of Appeal was prepared to find that an agency worker was an employee of an agency. Mr McMeechan was an agency worker who had worked for the agency under a series of temporary contracts. The contracts stated that Mr McMeechan was self-employed. Indeed, he was under no obligation to accept any assignment and the agency had reserved the right to choose whom to assign to a particular client. Mr McMeechan had no contractual entitlement to holiday, pension, or sick pay. However, his contracts contained a number of duties similar to those found in contracts of employment, namely duties of fidelity, confidentiality, and obedience to instructions.

1.57 Furthermore, Mr McMeechan was paid weekly wages calculated on an hourly rate, subject to statutory deductions for national insurance and PAYE. The agency also had power to dismiss Mr McMeechan summarily, whilst there was a grievance procedure which Mr McMeechan could invoke. The question of whether the global agreement under which the applicant provided his services was a contract of employment did not arise before the Court of Appeal, as it concluded that Mr McMeechan was an employee of the agency in respect of the specific engagement in question. Waite LJ, with whom Potter and McCowan LLJ agreed, stated that a temporary worker may have the status of employee of the employment agency in respect of each assignment actually worked, notwithstanding that the same worker may not be entitled to employee status under his general terms of engagement. Although Mr McMeechan was described as a self-employed worker, applying the multiple test, the totality of the conditions in fact created an employment relationship. The factors tipping the balance in favour of employee status included the reservation of the power of dismissal for misconduct, the importation into the contracts of the common law duty to obey reasonable orders and the duty of fidelity, the establishment of a grievance procedure, and the stipulation of an hourly rate of pay subject to deductions for unsatisfactory timekeeping. In considering the question of mutuality of obligation during the individual engagement, Waite LJ said that the fact that the parties would not in future be under an obligation to offer or to accept work was irrelevant.

---

[65] [1988] IRLR 461.
[66] [1970] 3 All ER 220.
[67] [1997] IRLR 353.

Similarly, in *Montgomery v Johnson Underwood Ltd and O & K Orenstein & Kopple Ltd*,[68] the **1.58** EAT found that there was a contract of employment between the agency and the worker for the duration of a specific engagement. The applicant was assigned to work for O & K by her agency. She was paid by the agency but received day-to-day directions as to the details of her hours of work and details of her job from O & K. After two years in the job, at O & K's request, the agency terminated her assignment. Applying the multiple test, at first instance the employment tribunal set out the factors which were inconsistent with the existence of a contract of employment with the agency, such as the express exclusion to that effect, the lack of control the agency had over the applicant's duties, and the fact that she was paid only for work done, together with those factors which were consistent with employee status, such as the power to dismiss the applicant summarily on grounds relating to capacity and/or performance, the fact that the agency determined the applicant's rate of pay, and the treatment of the applicant for tax purposes. Balancing these factors, the tribunal found that the applicant was an employee of the agency for the duration of her engagement with O & K.

The majority of the EAT affirmed this decision on appeal. All members were agreed that **1.59** there was no contract of employment, or indeed contract, between the applicant and O & K. It is instructive, however, to note the terms of Charles J's dissenting judgment. His preferred approach to the question of whether there was a contract of employment was that adopted by MacKenna J in *Ready Mixed Concrete (South East) Ltd v Minister of Pensions and National Insurance*.[69] On this basis, he considered that the irreducible minimum of obligations which must exist in order for a contract to be one of employment extended beyond the mutual obligations to perform and provide work; there must also be a sufficient degree of control and the remaining terms of the contract must not be inconsistent with it being a contract of employment.[70] In effect, therefore, in discharging the onus to show that they are employed, an individual must surmount both the hurdles of mutuality of obligation and of control before the balancing exercise of the remaining relevant factors may be conducted. In practice, the issue of control had become neglected because outside the scope of agency work it was rarely an issue. Charles J considered that the Court of Appeal in *McMeechan* had erred in not considering whether the obligation of the applicant to the agency to carry out the end-user's requirements was sufficient to render the agency the applicant's master. In the instant case, he considered that it did not.

Moreover, although he accepted that, in looking at the status of a self-contained engagement, **1.60** the lack of mutuality as to future engagements was irrelevant, he criticised the failure in *McMeechan* to explain the basis of the mutual obligation to provide and to do work in the context of the individual engagement. On the facts before him, he did not consider that the obligation for the applicant to do the work provided by the agency under the terms of its agreement with O & K was such that the applicant had entered into an obligation to provide her work and skill in the performance of some service for the agency or work provided by it. It is submitted that Charles J's restrictive view of both the mutuality and control issues is the wrong approach.

---

[68] EAT/509/98 and EAT/716/98 (unreported).

[69] [1968] 2 QB 497.

[70] It is worth noting that the element of control was particularly important in the *Ready Mixed Concrete* case because this case concerned vicarious liability for an employee's tort, and it may therefore be inappropriate to give this element similar emphasis in the context of employment legislation.

The quest for a contract between the individual and the client end user

1.61 It has traditionally been even more difficult to demonstrate that there is a contract of employment between an individual and the agency's client. In *Costain Building and Civil Engineering Limited v (1) Mr DR Smith and (2) Chanton Group Plc*,[71] the preliminary issue was whether an agency worker, in this case in the construction industry, was an employee of the building contractor, Costain, to whom he was assigned. Mr Smith, who described himself as being 'nominally self employed' for the whole of his career in the construction industry, was registered on the books of a number of agencies in the business of supplying labour to building contractors. One of those agencies was Chanton. It notified him that Costain required a site engineer, and Mr Smith took the position. He was paid by Chanton, who were in turn paid by Costain under the terms of an agreement between them.

1.62 Mr Smith became unhappy with a number of health and safety issues and he contacted his trade union representative. After some discussion with his trade union, Mr Smith was appointed as the union safety representative on site. The union informed Costain of this on 10 July 1998. Mr Smith then completed a number of safety reports critical of Costain's management of the site.

1.63 On 24 July, Mr Smith was told by Chanton that Costain had informed the agency that it did not want him to work on site again. Consequently Mr Smith claimed that he had been dismissed and moreover that the dismissal was automatically unfair under s 100(1)(b) of the ERA 1996.

1.64 The Employment Tribunal came to this conclusion:

> Weighing up all the facts that we have found and having considered the submissions made to us we find the applicant was not a self employed person but was an employee of Costain at the material times.

1.65 Applying the multiple test, the tribunal identified six factors which were inconsistent with a contract of service between Mr Smith and Costain. These were as follows:

- the method of payment;
- the applicant's tax treatment by the Inland Revenue (self-employed);
- the fact that his relationship with Costain was not permanent;
- the applicant was not issued with a Disciplinary Code, received no holiday pay, had no pension and there was no provision for notice;
- the applicant delivered invoices for payment to him by Chanton;
- the applicant's dismissal was brought about by Costain informing Chanton that they would not require the applicant's services.

1.66 However, the tribunal did not give much weight to these factors. For example, in relation to the fact that the applicant was paid free of tax by Chanton and that the dismissal was brought about by Chanton, the tribunal said that these were artificial devices 'designed to foster the image that the applicant was not an employee of Costain'. The method of payment was dismissed as 'mere mechanics' set up by Costain to escape statutory liabilities arising from employment status.

---

[71] [2000] ICR 215.

Costain, before the EAT, argued that the tribunal had made a fundamental error of law in dismissing these points as it had. On the other hand, Mr Smith argued that the ERA 1996 should be applied 'purposively' in order to grant protection to agency workers.   **1.67**

The EAT pointed out that there were two relevant contracts in this case; the contract between the agency, Chanton, and the building company, Costain, and the contract between Chanton and Mr Smith. There was no contract between Costain and the applicant, let alone a contract of employment. Individuals could not be afforded employee status by being appointed by their union as safety representatives under the Safety Representatives and Safety Committees Regulations 1977.[72]   **1.68**

Importantly, the EAT said that what was clear from the case was that Mr Smith chose to operate as a self-employed agent because he was paid free of tax. The EAT criticised the tribunal for focusing on the potential evasion by Costain of its statutory duties rather than the reality of the situation and the weighty factors negating the presence of a contract of employment. Costain was specifically seeking a site engineer for a temporary period and it went to an agency to supply it with such a person. So far as Costain was concerned, the identity of the site engineer was immaterial. The EAT found no need to apply the law purposively. However, it did not go on to specify what employment status Mr Smith did in fact have.   **1.69**

A turning point in this area came in the Court of Appeal's decision in *Brook Street Bureau (UK) Limited v Dacas*.[73]   **1.70**

Mrs Dacas worked as a cleaner. She was supplied by her agency, Brook Street Bureau, to Wandsworth Borough Council. Mrs Dacas had entered into a written agreement with Brook Street Bureau which provided that the provisions 'shall not give rise to a contract of employment between Brook Street and the Temporary Worker, or the Temporary Worker and the Client'. Brook Street Bureau was responsible for discipline, payments to Mrs Dacas, PAYE and national insurance contributions, and statutory obligations in relation to holiday and sick pay. The Council, on the other hand, exercised day-to-day control and supplied Mrs Dacas with equipment and materials. Mrs Dacas was withdrawn from working at the Council by Brook Street Bureau at the Council's request and she subsequently brought a claim of unfair dismissal against both the Council and Brook Street Bureau.   **1.71**

The tribunal at first instance found Mrs Dacas not to be an employee of Brook Street Bureau at the relevant time. The tribunal considered the intentions of the parties as expressed in the written agreement and determined that the other features of the relationship, such as Brook Street Bureau's entitlement to terminate Mrs Dacas's assignment, were of no assistance in determining her employment status. The tribunal also found there to have been no contract between Mrs Dacas and the Council, absence of which, the tribunal found, precluded any mutuality of obligation.   **1.72**

Mrs Dacas appealed but only against the finding in respect of Brook Street Bureau. On appeal, the EAT held that the tribunal had erred in not finding Mrs Dacas to be an employee of Brook Street Bureau. The EAT's decision in this respect was subsequently overturned by the Court of Appeal. The Court of Appeal found that the relationship between Mrs Dacas   **1.73**

---

[72] SI 1977/500.
[73] [2004] EWCA Civ 217.

and Brook Street Bureau lacked the necessary mutuality of obligation; Mrs Dacas had no obligation to accept work, and Brook Street Bureau had no obligation to provide her with such work.

1.74   In considering Mrs Dacas's relationship with the Council, Mummery LJ, in the majority opinion, concluded that the tribunal had failed to address the possibility of an implied contract of service between them. However, as Mrs Dacas had not appealed against the aspect of the employment tribunal's decision in which her claim against the Council had been dismissed, the Court of Appeal was not entitled to overturn that decision. If that had not been the case, Mummery LJ highlighted that the case would have been remitted to the tribunal to determine whether there had in fact been an implied contract between Mrs Dacas and the Council.

1.75   The subsequent case of *Cable & Wireless Plc v Muscat*[74] followed the view of the majority in *Dacas*. Although the Court of Appeal in *Muscat* recognised that the approach of the Court of Appeal in *Dacas* was not strictly 'binding', it considered it to be 'plainly right' for employment tribunals to heed the guidance provided and consider the possibility that an implied contract might exist.

1.76   This approach has, however, been subject to subsequent criticism for its policy-driven approach. Such was the case in *James v London Borough of Greenwich*.[75] The claimant in this case, Ms James, had a 'Temporary Worker Agreement' with an employment agency which supplied her as a housing support worker to the London Borough of Greenwich (the Council). The Council arranged her instructions, orders, and working conditions. They provided necessary materials and she wore a staff badge which bore the Council's logo and her name. She did not, however, benefit from the Council's sick pay or holiday pay provisions, nor did the Council's disciplinary or grievance procedures apply to her. Ms James subsequently changed agency to an agency which paid her a better hourly wage and she entered a further Temporary Workers Agreement with the new agency. The agency entered a contract with the Council and received reimbursement for pay, expenses, and commission. After Ms James had been replaced following a period of sickness absence, she brought a claim of unfair dismissal. The Council, however, contended that the tribunal did not have jurisdiction to consider the claim on the basis that there was insufficient mutuality of obligation for Ms James to be an employee of the Council.

1.77   Ms James' claim of unfair dismissal was dismissed by the tribunal and her subsequent appeal was also dismissed. The EAT made clear its disagreement with the view of Sedley LJ in *Dacas* that the passage of time could justify an implied contract, stating that 'something more is required to establish that the tripartite agency analysis no longer holds good'.

1.78   The EAT also set out certain observations to assist future tribunals in the task of deciding how to approach the question of implying a contract with the end user:

> In the casual worker cases, where the issue is whether there is an umbrella or global contract in the non-work periods, the relevant question for the tribunal to pose is whether the irreducible minimum of mutual obligations exists. It is not particularly helpful to focus on the same question when the issue is whether a contract can be implied between the worker and end user.

---

[74] [2006] EWCA Civ 220.
[75] [2008] EWCA Civ 35.

The issue then is whether the way in which the contract is in fact performed is consistent with the agency arrangements or whether it is only consistent with an implied contract between the worker and the end user and would be inconsistent with there being no such contract. Of course, if there is no contract then there will be no mutuality of obligation. But whereas in the casual worker cases the quest for mutual obligations determines whether or not there is a contract, in the agency cases the quest for a contract determines whether there are mutual obligations.

If there were no agency relationship regulating the position of these parties then the implication of a contract between the worker and the end user would be inevitable. Work is being carried out for payment received, but the agency relationship alters matters in a fundamental way. There is no longer a simple wage–work bargain between worker and end user.

In *Dacas*, Munby J was surely right when he observed that in a tripartite relationship of this kind the end user is not paying directly for the work done by the worker, but rather for the services supplied by the agency in accordance with its specification and the other contractual documents. Similarly, the money paid by the end user to the agency is not merely the payment of wages, but also includes the other elements, such as expenses and profit. Indeed, the end user frequently has no idea what sums the worker is receiving.

The key feature is not just the fact that the end user is not paying the wages, but that he cannot insist on the agency providing the particular worker at all. Provided the arrangements are genuine and the actual relationship is consistent with them, it is not then necessary to explain the provision of the worker's services or the fact of payment to the worker by some contract between the end user and the worker, even if such a contract would also not be inconsistent with the relationship. The express contracts themselves both explain and are consistent with the nature of the relationship and no further implied contract is justified.

When the arrangements are genuine and when implemented accurately represented the actual relationship between the parties—as is likely to be the case where there was no pre-existing contract between worker and end user—then we suspect that it will be a rare case where there will be evidence entitling the tribunal to imply a contract between the worker and the end user. If any such a contract is to be inferred, there must subsequent to the relationship commencing be some words or conduct which entitle the tribunal to conclude that the agency arrangements no longer dictate or adequately reflect how the work is actually being performed, and that the reality of the relationship is only consistent with the implication of the contract. It will be necessary to show that the worker is working not pursuant to the agency arrangements but because of mutual obligations binding worker and end user which are incompatible with those arrangements.

Typically the mere passage of time does not justify any such implication to be made as a matter of necessity, and we respectfully disagree with Sedley LJ's analysis in *Dacas* on this point. It will no doubt frequently be convenient for the agency to send the same worker to the end user, who in turn would prefer someone who has proved to be able and understands and has experience of the systems in operation. Many workers would also find it advantageous to work in the same environment regularly, at least if they have found it convivial. So the mere fact that the arrangements carry on for a long time may be wholly explicable by considerations of convenience for all parties; it is not necessary to imply a contract to explain the fact that the relationship has continued perhaps for a very extensive period of time. Effluxion of time does not of itself establish any mutual undertaking of legal obligations between the worker and end user. This is so even where the arrangement was initially expected to be temporary only but has in fact continued longer than expected. Something more is required to establish that the tripartite agency analysis no longer holds good.

It will, we suspect, be more readily open to a tribunal to infer a contract in a case like *Muscat*, where the agency arrangements were super-imposed on an existing contractual relationship. It may be appropriate, depending on the circumstances, to conclude that arrangements were a sham and that the worker and end user have simply remained in the same contractual relationship with one another, or that even if the intention was to alter the relationship that has not in fact been achieved. That may be legitimate, for example, where the only perceptible change is in who pays the wages. In such a case the only effect of the agency arrangements may be to make the agency an agent of the employer for the purpose of paying wages. However, in these cases the tribunal is not strictly implying a contract as such but is rather concluding that the agency arrangements have never brought the original contract to an end.

1.79 The Court of Appeal expressly approved the guidance of the EAT and added that:

> . . . it would be very unusual for an appeal to the EAT or this court to have a real prospect of success if the ET's conclusion that a contract of employment with the end user should, or should not, be implied have been reached by applying the correct test of necessity, as explained by *Elias J* in the judgment of the EAT.

1.80 The Court of Appeal in *Muschett v HM Prison Service*[76] confirmed that a contract will only be implied when it is necessary to do so, with Rimer LJ stating that 'nothing less than necessity will do'.

1.81 The courts' unwillingness to imply contracts of employment was demonstrated by the Court of Appeal in the more recent case of *Tilson v Alstom Transport*.[77]

1.82 The agency relationship that existed in this case was complex in its nature. Mr Tilson's services were provided to Alstom Transport by an agency, Morson Human Resources Limited, who paid Mr Tilson via a service company, Silversun Solutions Limited.

1.83 There was no express contractual relationship between Mr Tilson and Alstom Transport. It was accepted, however, that Mr Tilson was very fully integrated into Alstom Transport's business. The tribunal at first instance had identified the fact that Mr Tilson needed to apply to his line manager to take annual leave, he worked Monday to Friday each week, he ordered materials, he had network access, and he was not at liberty not to turn up to work or to send a substitute to replace him. It was asserted on behalf of Alstom Transport, however, that whilst it might appear that Mr Tilson was an employee, in fact he was not. Indeed, he had been offered a position as an employee which he had refused, seemingly on account of the higher rate of pay he received under the agency relationship and the tax advantages of this arrangement. The tribunal, however, determined that it was necessary to imply a contract of employment to explain the basis of his relationship.

1.84 The EAT overturned this decision. The EAT took into account Mr Tilson's refusals to accept an offer of employment and his intention to work as an independent contractor and deemed that, although Mr Tilson had been integrated into the business, the conduct of the parties pointed firmly against an employment relationship.

1.85 On appeal to the Court of Appeal, it was argued on behalf of Mr Tilson, having regard to his integration into the business, the degree of control exercised over him by Alstom, and the need for him to notify his line manager before taking holidays, that taken together these factors justified the conclusion that there was an employment contract in force. On behalf of Alstom, it was contended that it was contrary to contractual principles to imply a contract against the parties' intentions.

---

[76] [2010] EWCA Civ 25.
[77] [2010] EWCA Civ 1308; [2011] IRLR 169.

The Court of Appeal dismissed Mr Tilson's appeal and highlighted that: **1.86**

> ... the mere fact that there is a significant degree of integration of the worker into the organisa-
> tion is not at all inconsistent with the existence of an agency relationship in which there is no
> contract between worker and end user. Indeed, in most cases it is quite unrealistic for the
> worker to provide any satisfactory service to the employer without being integrated into
> the mainstream business.

Further, the fact that Mr Tilson needed to apply to his line manager for annual leave was not
sufficient to justify the implication of a contract. The Court of Appeal found that the parties
would have acted in exactly the same way if there had been no contract, which was fatal to
the implication of a contract.

The Court of Appeal highlighted that the practice of implying a contract of employment **1.87**
involves an objective analysis of the circumstances, but the parties' understanding of their
relationship and their inability to reach an agreement on the terms will be strong indicators
against the necessity to imply a contract of employment.

The position of agency workers is set to improve in line with the EU's Temporary Agency **1.88**
Worker's Directive 2008,[78] which was required to be implemented by Member States by
5 December 2011. As a result, the Agency Workers Regulations 2010[79] are intended to come
into force in the UK in October 2011. The Directive requires that 'basic working and
employment conditions of Temporary Agency Workers shall be, for the duration of their
assignment at a user undertaking, at least those that would apply if they had been recruited
directly to occupy the same job'. However, given that alternative arrangements can be
established by Member States, the UK Government has provided that this right will only
apply after completion of a 12-week qualifying period.

The basic rights which will apply to those agency workers who have completed the relevant **1.89**
qualifying period will include rights in relation to duration of working time, overtime,
breaks, rest periods, night work, holidays, public holidays, and pay as if they had been
recruited directly by the end user. Agency workers from their first day of assignment will also
acquire the right to information regarding vacancies and in respect of access to facilities.

The provisions of the Employment Act 2008 which came into force on 6 April 2009 further **1.90**
strengthen the regulation of agencies by providing the Employment Agency Standards
Inspectorate with additional powers and increasing the penalties that can be imposed for
offences under the Employment Agencies Act 1973.

Personal service

In *Express and Echo Publications Ltd v Tanton*,[80] the Court of Appeal was faced with a situ- **1.91**
ation where the preponderance of factors supported the conclusion that the applicant was an
employee. However, it was a term of the agreement between the applicant and his employer
that:

> In the event that the worker is unwell or unable to perform the services personally, he shall
> arrange at his own expense entirely for another suitable person to perform the services.

---

[78] Council Directive (EC) 2008/104.
[79] SI 2010/93. See now the BIS Guidance on the Agency Workers Regulations (http://www.bis.gov.uk/
assests/biscore/employment-matters/docs/a/11-905-agency-workers-regulations-guidance.pdf).
[80] [1999] IRLR 367.

1.92 In practice, the applicant occasionally utilised the right to provide a substitute and, exceptionally, throughout a six-month period during which he was ill. During that time the applicant paid the substitute, and received remuneration from his employer. The employment tribunal therefore concluded that this clause was not a sham. The Court of Appeal stated:

> Where a person who works for another is not required to perform his services personally, as a matter of law, the relationship between the worker and the person for whom he works is not that of employer and employee . . . without such an irreducible minimum of obligation, it cannot be said that the contract is one of service.

1.93 Although in his judgment Peter Gibson LJ did not explicitly refer to the fact, this is in reality merely an application of the principle of mutuality of obligation. If the individual is not under an obligation to perform work provided by his employer personally, there cannot be a contract of service. A similar clause proved conclusive in the *Ready Mixed Concrete* case.[81]

1.94 However, *Tanton* was distinguished by the EAT in *Glasgow City Council v MacFarlane and Skivington*.[82] Whilst not casting doubt on the decision in *Tanton*, the EAT considered on the facts before it that although there was scope for the individuals in question to arrange for a substitute to perform their work, they may only do so if they themselves were unable to attend work. They also had to choose a substitute from an approved list (the employer sometimes organised the substitute itself) and the substitutes were paid directly by the employer. In effect, this arrangement came within the limited exception identified by MacKenna J in the *Ready Mixed Concrete* case that a 'limited or occasional power of delegation may not be . . . inconsistent with a contract of service'. The EAT drew a distinction between cases where theoretically the individual need not perform any services personally, such as in *Tanton*, where there could be no mutuality, and cases where in limited circumstances it would not be a breach of contract for an individual to arrange for a replacement to perform the individual's work, where there was mutuality.

1.95 The position was considered further by the EAT in *Staffordshire Sentinel Newspapers Ltd v Potter*.[83] Mr Potter signed an agreement for services which contained the right to substitute suitable people to ensure the obligations were fully complied with. There was no finding that such a clause was a sham, nor that it had been varied, and the fact that the company had from time-to-time not approved substitutes proffered by Mr Potter was consistent with the wording of the clause. The clause was, therefore, found to be inconsistent with a contract of service in accordance with *Tanton* (which was said to be entirely consistent with *MacFarlane*).

1.96 This issue was further considered in the case of *James v Redcats (Brands) Limited*.[84] The contract in that case provided that, 'you need to ensure that a suitable alternative courier is available to carry out the terms of this agreement when you are unable. This might happen during holidays or if you are ill.' This wording relieved Mrs James from the duty to perform the work only when she was unable, and this was narrower than the obligation found in *Tanton*. Therefore, the EAT held that when Mrs James was able, she was required to perform the work personally.

---

[81] [1968] 2 QB 497.
[82] EAT/1277/99 (unreported).
[83] [2004] IRLR 752.
[84] [2007] IRLR 296.

To be contrasted are the instructive facts of *Kuncharalingam v Word by Word Translations Ltd*[85] where an interpreter had an 'unfettered', as opposed to limited, right of substitution. In 2007 he carried out 37 assignments personally, declined 4 and sent substitutes on 20 assignments. In 2008 he carried out 35 assignments, declined 6 and sent substitutes on 3 assignments. He had the unfettered power to delegate and was mostly able to do so without even telling the Company. Against this factual matrix it was held that there was no requirement for personal service and the claimant was neither an employee or a worker.

1.97

A right of substitution on its own will therefore not necessarily lead to the conclusion that an individual is not an employee. The factors to be considered in determining this issue include the limitations on the right to delegate, when that right arises, the nature and extent of the delegable duties under the contract, and who benefits from the power to delegate. As HH Judge Peter Clark stated in *Kuncharalingam* the situation must be judged by 'the whole of the factual matrix'.[86]

1.98

The parties' choice

As can be seen from the points made above, the contractual documentation between the parties will be scrutinised when determining the nature of the parties' relationship and their intentions. Whether the documentation amounts to a 'sham' will often fall to be considered in such cases.

1.99

It had previously been the case that, to establish a 'sham', it was necessary for the parties to have a 'common intention that the acts or documents are not to create the legal rights and obligations which they give the appearance of creating' (*Snook v London & West Riding Investments Ltd*[87]).

1.100

However, this approach was reconsidered by the Court of Appeal in the case of *Protectacoat Firthglow Ltd v Szilagyi*.[88]

1.101

Mr Szilagyi had approached Protectacoat for work and had been asked by Protectacoat to enter into a partnership agreement with a colleague and thereafter the partnership entered into a contract with Protectacoat for the provision of services. Mr Szilagyi claimed, however, to have been an employee of Protectacoat and that, following a dispute, he had been unfairly dismissed.

1.102

The employment tribunal at first instance held that the written documents were a sham and that the true relationship was that of employer and employee. In this respect, the tribunal highlighted that there existed a document referring to the tools and van being hired to the partnership by Protectacoat when in fact no charge was made. The tribunal also considered the fact that payment for work was made directly to the individuals (rather than the partnership) with tax deducted, and that Mr Szilagyi was required to attend Protectacoat's yard every morning before going to his next site and could not work for anyone else, despite that the contract stated to the contrary. The EAT, on appeal, upheld the decision of the tribunal in finding that Mr Szilagyi was an employee.

1.103

---

[85] EAT/0269/10.
[86] Ibid., at para 10.
[87] [1967] 23 QB 786.
[88] [2009] EWCA Civ 98.

1.104   The Court of Appeal highlighted that, when assessing whether to disregard express contractual provision,

> The question is always what the true legal relationship is between the parties. If there is a contractual document that is ordinarily where the answer is to be found. But, if it is asserted by either party, or in some cases by a third party, that the document does not represent or describe the true relationship, the court or tribunal has to decide what the true relationship is.

1.105   In applying the principles established in the previous cases, the Court of Appeal in *Protectacoat* held that the tribunal had been entitled to conclude that the contractual documentation was a sham and did not 'describe or represent the true intentions or expectations of the parties' and that it was not necessary to establish an intention to deceive a third party.

1.106   The Court of Appeal in the case of *Autoclenz Limited v Belcher & Ors*[89] further considered the issue of sham contracts.

1.107   The case concerned the legal status of 20 car valets at the Autoclenz Limited site in Measham. The valets claimed entitlement to certain statutory rights, including holiday pay and thus sought a declaration that they were either workers or employees. Autoclenz Limited challenged this entitlement, arguing that the valets were self-employed contractors.

1.108   The valets' contracts referred to them as sub-contractors and included a substitution clause and a right to refuse work. The assessment of the Inland Revenue (as it was then) in 2004 had found that the arrangements were consistent with self-employment for tax purposes. However, the control of the processes of cleaning and the materials and methods used by the valets was said to be strictly exercised by Autoclenz Limited.

1.109   The employment tribunal at first instance found that the valets were employees. The judgment highlighted the lack of control of the valets over the way the work was carried out and their integration into Autoclenz's business. Notwithstanding the substitution clause, the tribunal found that the valets were required to provide a personal service. The contract was held not to reflect what had actually been agreed between the parties. The employment judge further commented that, if he was wrong and the valets were not employees, he would have found them to be workers.

1.110   The EAT, however, in reliance upon guidance from case law since overruled, set aside the finding that the valets were employees based on the assumption that it was necessary for there to be an intention on behalf of both parties to mislead someone in order for an express term to be regarded as a sham. In considering whether the valets were in fact workers, the EAT held on the facts that the valets' services were not being provided to a client or customer and they were, accordingly, workers. Autoclenz appealed against this finding, and the valets cross-appealed against the finding that they were not employees.

1.111   In regards to the issue of disregarding an express clause in a contract, the Court of Appeal held that it was not necessary for there to be a common intention to mislead someone; it was enough that the written term did not represent the intentions or expectations of the parties.

---

[89]   [2009] EWCA Civ 1046.

The Court of Appeal found that, after considering the terms of the contract and the conduct **1.112** of the parties, the tribunal had been entitled to hold that the contract did not genuinely reflect the rights and obligations of the valets. The Court of Appeal concluded that the valets were in fact workers within s 230(3) of the ERA. In going on to consider whether the valets were also employees, the Court of Appeal held that the tribunal had been entitled to hold that they were employees even though the valets had accepted their self-employed status for a number of years. The Court of Appeal held that the irreducible minimum of mutual obligation had been established and the appeal was therefore dismissed and the cross-appeal allowed.[90]

Non-standard workers: a clear way forward?

There remains a degree of confusion over the process through which a tribunal should set **1.113** about analysing arrangements relating to non-standard workers. If a contract is found to exist,[91] then the tribunal should proceed to stage two and classify the contract. The case law indicates that the presence of the mutual obligation to provide and personally perform work is essential if the contract is to be classified as a contract of employment. It is also possible that the individual must show that the employer had a sufficient degree of control as to how, where, and when he performed his duties.[92] Even if both of these are present, the tribunal must go on to consider the other relevant factors to determine whether they are on balance consistent with the existence of a contract of employment.

It is possible that on a proper analysis the individuals might be held to work under a series of **1.114** separate contracts of employment.[93] In classifying such a contract, the fact that the parties will not in future be under an obligation to offer or to accept work is irrelevant,[94] and the concept of mutuality of obligation will not provide such a hurdle to gaining employment status. However, as such contracts will inevitably be of a short duration, the individuals may have problems demonstrating that they have the necessary continuity of service to qualify for the various employment protection rights.[95]

In practice, therefore, notwithstanding the use of the multiple test, the requirement that **1.115** there be mutuality of obligation has often proved determinative in excluding casual workers from protection. Since such mutuality must be expressed in a contract, this will often turn on the evidence presented to the tribunal of the way in which the parties in fact conducted their relationship, as given the casual nature of the relationship there will often not be any express written or oral agreement to this effect.[96] Therefore, as discussed above, the important question of employment status is subject to the vagaries of findings of fact and the weight

---

[90] Permission was granted to appeal to the Supreme Court on 21 December 2009. Judgement was reserved on 11 May 2011.

[91] This will be a question of law.

[92] *Ready Mixed Concrete (South East) Ltd v Minister of Pensions and National Insurance* [1968] 2 QB 467; *Montgomery v Johnson Underwood Ltd and O & K Orenstein & Kopple Ltd* EAT/509/98 and 716/98 (unreported).

[93] See, e.g. *Cornwall CC v Prater* [2006] EWCA Civ 101.

[94] *McMeechan v Secretary of State for Employment* [1997] IRLR 353; cf. the dissenting judgment of Charles J in *Montgomery v Johnson Underwood Ltd and O & K Orenstein & Kopple Ltd* EAT/509/98 and 716/98 (unreported).

[95] See below for a brief discussion of the provisions of the ERA 1996 relating to continuity.

[96] An employer will only be under an obligation to supply a written statement of particulars of employment under s 1 of the ERA 1996 if the individual is an employee; where the individual's employment status is in dispute, therefore, the individual is unlikely to have been provided with such a statement. See the *Carmichael* case.

accorded to those findings by employment tribunals which has led to inconsistent and patchy coverage. It is questionable whether qualification for employment protection rights, such as the right to a redundancy payment, should in fact be determined in this manner.[97]

Freelance workers

1.116   In *Hall (Inspector of Taxes) v Lorimer*[98] the Court of Appeal had to determine whether a freelance television vision mixer was an employee for tax purposes.[99] Mr Lorimer operated from home on projects for various clients' studios, which usually lasted one or two days each. He had worked 800 days over the period from 1985 to 1989. He worked at his clients' studios using equipment provided by the clients. He had no employees of his own but did occasionally employ an agent. Mr Lorimer never entered formal written conditions of engagement with any of his clients and was paid on an agreed lump sum basis. The question therefore arose as to whether Mr Lorimer was taxable under Schedule D, on the basis that he was self-employed, or under Schedule E, on the basis that he was an employee. The Inland Revenue argued that Mr Lorimer was an employee who simply worked under a series of contracts of service and that he could not be described as being in business for himself. He did not provide his own equipment and had no financial risk apart from the risk of bad debts and being unable to find work. The time, place, and nature of his work were controlled by the client.

1.117   At first instance, Mummery J disagreed with the Inland Revenue. Applying the multiple test, he thought it significant that Mr Lorimer exploited his abilities in the market place and therefore bore his own financial risk in the sense that he risked bad debts and insufficient work. Conversely, he also had a chance to increase his profits by providing an efficient service, thereby enhancing his reputation and, therefore, the demand for his services, for which he would be able to charge accordingly. Mr Lorimer was therefore self-employed and his remuneration was properly taxable under Schedule D rather than Schedule E. The Inland Revenue appealed, but the Court of Appeal agreed with Mummery J. The court emphasised the importance of the traditional contrast between a servant and an independent contractor. The extent to which Mr Lorimer was dependent on, or independent of, a particular paymaster was therefore significant. The outstanding feature on the facts was that Mr Lorimer usually worked for 20 or more production companies and the vast majority of his assignments lasted only for one day.

Other categories

1.118   Certain other specific categories of worker are not usually treated as employees without some evidence of employment status.

Apprenticeships

1.119   The definition of a contract of employment contained in s 230(2) of ERA 1996 specifically includes a contract of apprenticeship. Under the more traditional model the apprentice is bound to the employer in order to learn a trade, and the apprenticeship will usually be for a

---

[97]   Hepple, (1986) ILJ 15(2) 69 asserted that 'The coverage of labour legislation has degenerated into a mass of isolated decisions of industrial tribunals'.

[98]   [1994] 1 All ER 250.

[99]   Some caution may therefore be needed in applying these principles in the context of employment legislation.

fixed term and entered into under a written contract or deed. The apprenticeship is therefore governed by normal contractual rules entitling the apprentice to damages for wrongful dismissal.[100] However, the apprentice does not qualify for a redundancy payment if he or she is not kept on by the employer at the end of the apprenticeship.[101]

1.120 The emergence of the concept of a 'modern apprenticeship' has, however, created certain difficulties in establishing the status of the apprentice. Unlike the traditional model, the training is done by a third party and the qualification provided by a central body. The employer is, however, required to give the apprentice time off and fund the cost of attendance at classes.

1.121 The position of apprentices under a modern apprenticeship scheme was considered in the case of *Flett v Matheson*.[102] The Court of Appeal in this case held that a modern apprenticeship arrangement could in fact constitute a common law contract of apprenticeship, although this was dependent upon the nature and duration of the employer's obligations under the agreement. The Court of Appeal found that the essential features of an apprenticeship were present in a modern apprentice scheme and the fact that a third party provided certain aspects of the training, did not 'deprive the relationship between the employer and apprentice of a long term character which persists until the end of the training period contemplated'.

1.122 This area has, however, been the subject of extensive reform by the Apprenticeship, Skills, Children and Learning Act 2009, which received Royal Assent on 12 November 2009. The apprenticeship-specific provisions of the Act are due to come into force in 2013. Section 35 of the Act specifically provides that the relationship will no longer be a contract of apprenticeship but a contract of service.

Office holders[103]

1.123 Office holders are not within the scope of the ERA 1996 *per se*.[104] There are three categories of office holders:[105]

- office holders whose rights and duties are defined by the office they hold, such as police officers;
- office holders who are both office holders and have a contract of service, as is commonly the case with company directors; and
- 'office holders' so called who in reality are employees under a contract of service.

1.124 It is only the first of these categories of office holder who are excluded from the right to claim a statutory redundancy payment. In relation to the last of the categories, the EAT in *102 Social Club and Institute Ltd v Bickerton*[106] laid down the following points to be considered in determining whether there was in fact a contract of service:

(1) Is payment for the position by way of honorarium or a payment made contractually for services rendered, i.e. salary?

---

[100] e.g. *Wallace v CA Roofing Services Ltd* [1996] IRLR 435.
[101] *North East Coast Ship Repairers Ltd v Secretary of State for Employment* [1978] IRLR 149.
[102] [2006] IRLR 277.
[103] See Burbridge, *Solicitors Journal*, 23 June 2000 at 582.
[104] Contrast the position in the Sex Discrimination Act 1975 following the decision in *Perceval-Price v Department of Economic Development*, *The Times*, 28 April 2000.
[105] *Johnson v Ryan* [2000] ICR 236, 242.
[106] [1977] ICR 911.

(2) Is the payment fixed in advance or paid on a periodic basis, or is the amount varied in token of the officer's work?

(3) Is there a right to payment, or is payment made *ex gratia*?

(4) What is the size of the payment?

(5) Does the officer exercise the functions of an independent office or is he subject to the control and orders of his employer?

(6) What is the extent of the officer's duties? The greater the obligations, the more likely the officer is to be an employee.

(7) How is the payment described and how is it treated for tax and national insurance purposes?

1.125　In *Johnson v Ryan*,[107] Morison J held that the ERA 1996 should be construed in a wide, inclusive way. On this basis, he held that a rent officer could bring a claim for unfair dismissal as an employee, despite also being an office holder, as she had been promoted from a position as a clerk, in which she had clearly been an employee, and it would be inequitable to deprive her of protection. However, the legitimacy of this approach has been queried in other cases.[108]

1.126　Lord Nicholls of Birkenhead in the case of *Percy v Church of Scotland Board of National Mission*[109] in the House of Lords called for caution to be exercised lest the use of the term 'office' leads to a 'false dichotomy: a person either holds an office or is an employee. He cannot be both at the same time. This is not so. If "office" is given a broad meaning, holding an office and being an employee are not inconsistent.'

1.127　Some office holders who do not have a contract of employment are included in the statutory redundancy scheme by virtue of regulations made under ss 171 and 172 of the ERA 1996.[110]

Shareholders

1.128　Section 166 of the ERA 1996 allows employees to claim statutory redundancy payments owed to them by an insolvent employer from the Secretary of State for Trade and Industry.[111] Section 182 makes similar provision in respect of certain other debts. In recent years, there has been a spate of cases regarding whether a director of the insolvent company, who was also a shareholder in it, qualifies as an employee for these purposes.

1.129　In *Buchan and Ivey v Secretary of State for Employment*,[112] the EAT concluded that since both of the individuals in question controlled their companies to the extent that they could block any attempt to terminate their employment or vary the terms of service, they could not for policy reasons be regarded as employees. This flew in the face of a body of case law which suggested that the real issue was whether the alleged contract of service was a bona fide arrangement between the company and the director, the issue of control being only one factor to take into account. However, in *Fleming v Secretary of State for Trade and Industry*,[113]

---

[107] [2000] ICR 236.

[108] e.g. *Costain Building and Civil Engineering Limited v (1) Mr D R Smith and (2) Chanton Group Plc* [2000] ICR 215, discussed above.

[109] [2006] ICR 282. In *Moore v President of the Methodist Conference* (EAT/021 9/10), the EAT held that a methodist minister was an employee for the purposes of an unfair dismissal claim. See also *New Testament Church of God v Stewart* [2008] ICR 282. *Moore* is due to be heard by the Court of Appeal during 2011.

[110] See below.

[111] See Chapter 8.

[112] [1997] IRLR 80.

[113] [1997] IRLR 62.

the Court of Session made it clear that whether a person is an employee is a matter of fact to be decided by a tribunal.

The traditional approach was reasserted by the Court of Appeal in *Secretary of State for Trade & Industry v Bottrill*.[114] Mr Bottrill and others bought an off-the-shelf company called Magnatech UK Limited which had one share, which Mr Bottrill owned. The intention was that another company, Magnatech Inc, would invest in Magnatech UK Limited and acquire 80 per cent of the equity. A draft agreement was prepared to this effect but was never executed. The company got into some financial difficulty and ultimately went into liquidation. Mr Bottrill remained the sole shareholder. He claimed certain payments from the Secretary of State. The Court of Appeal held that ownership of a majority shareholding does not necessarily mean that the individual concerned is not an employee:

> ... whether or not an employer/employee relationship exists can only be decided by having regard to all the relevant facts. If an individual has a controlling shareholding that is likely to be significant in all situations and in some cases it might prove to be decisive, but it is only one of the factors which is relevant and is not to be taken as determinative.[115]

1.130

Other factors which may be taken into account include:

1.131

(i) whether there existed a 'genuine contract' between the company and the shareholder;
(ii) if there was, how and when the contract came into existence and whether, for example, it was made at the time insolvency loomed; and
(iii) whether the contract is genuinely a contract of employment (considering the degree of control exercised by the company over the shareholder and the other factors usually taken into account in the multiple test).

This question was revisited by the Court of Appeal in the case of *Secretary For Business, Enterprise and Regulatory Reform v Neufeld and Howe*[116] following the uncertainty created by various EAT decisions subsequent to *Bottrill*.

1.132

Both appeals, those of *Mr Neufeld* and *Mr Howe*, arose out of insolvency situations with the issue to be determined being whether Mr Neufeld and Mr Howe were employees of the insolvent companies. Mr Neufeld held 90 per cent of the company's issued shares and acted as one of three directors. He was also recognised by the employment tribunal at first instance as having an oral contract of employment for the purposes of s 182 ERA of the 1996. Mr Howe held 100 per cent of the insolvent company's shares and was the sole director. Both Mr Neufeld and Mr Howe were paid subject to tax and national insurance contributions.

1.133

The Court of Appeal concluded that the principle that someone who is a shareholder (even a controlling shareholder) and a director can also be an employee of the company under a contract of employment remained intact and fell to be determined in each case from the facts. The Court of Appeal highlighted that the first issue that will need to be determined will be whether the putative contract is genuine or a sham. The second issue will be whether, if the contract is genuine, it amounts to a contract of employment.[117]

1.134

---

[114] Ibid., 326.
[115] See also, e.g. *Secretary of State for Trade & Industry v Smith* [2000] IRLR 6.
[116] [2009] EWCA Civ 280.
[117] See, too, *Nesbitt and Nesbitt v Secretary of State for Trade & Industry* (EAT/0091/07). See also the case of *Ashby v Monterry Designs Limited* UKEAT/0226/08, in which the decision in *Neufeld* was applied. In Case C-232/09 *Dita Danosa v LKB Lizings SIA* [2010] All ER (D) 178 (Nov), the European Court held that a

Partners

1.135　A relationship between partners (such as equity partners) is not an employment relationship, although the position in respect of salaried partners is less clear.[118] A 'partner' will not qualify as an employee and has no right to receive a redundancy payment on dissolution or termination of the partnership agreement.[119]

1.136　The issue of whether a person was a 'partner' within the meaning of section 1(1) of the Partnership Act 1890 or an 'employee' within the meaning of section 230(1) of the ERA was recently considered by the EAT in the case of *Tiffin v Lester Aldridge LLP*.[120] The Claimant was found by the Tribunal to have contributed capital and shared profits with his fellow partners, and that the success of the business depended upon meeting client demands and accepting a particular management structure.[121] The documents governing the relation were also found not to be shams. Accordingly, the Claimant was initially a salaried partner in a partnership, which then became a Limited Liability Partnership (LLP) in which the claimant then became a fixed share partner. He was found not to be an employee for the purpose of section 230 of the ERA. This decision was upheld on appeal.

Agents

1.137　Agents, such as sales agents who sell products on behalf of a company, are not necessarily employees, although calling an employee an 'agent' (as often happens in practice) does not prevent there being a contract of employment if the facts indicate that a contract of service exists. In *J C King Ltd v Valencia*,[122] an employment tribunal determined that an agent was nevertheless an employee of the company, since the agent was paid a weekly remuneration plus commission and was subject to precise and definite terms governing what he could and could not do in the course of his work.

E. Illegality of Contract

1.138　The distinction between an employment contract and legitimate self-employment raises the issue of legality if the parties have both got it wrong and are regarded by the law as culpable in so doing. One risk that the parties (particularly the employee) run in a reckless (or of course, wilful) misclassification is that the contract will be illegal and therefore void *ab initio* if it is *ex facie* illegal, or else unenforceable by any party who is not innocent of the illegality. An employee who works under a contract of employment that is tainted by illegality may therefore not qualify for a redundancy payment or employment protection rights, as there will be no contract on which to found the rights. Although it is now established that in most

---

member of a capital company's board of directors who provides services to that company and is an integral part of it must be regarded as having the status of worker for the purposes of the Pregnant Workers Directive (92/85/EEC).

　[118] *Steikel v Ellice* [1973] 1 WLR 191 and *Briggs v Oates* [1990] IRC 473 demonstrate that a salaried partner can be either a true partner or an employee.

　[119] *Cowell v Quilter Goodison Company Ltd and QC Management Services Ltd* [1989] IRLR 392, CA.

　[120] UKEAT/0255/10. On appeal to the Court of Appeal, to be heard on 8 November 2011.

　[121] Section 4(4) of the Limited Liability Partnerships Act 2000 states that: 'A member of a limited liability partnership shall not be regarded for any purpose as employed by the limited liability partnership unless, if he and the other members were partners in a partnership, he would be regarded for that purpose as employed by the partnership'.

　[122] [1966] 1 ITR 67.

cases an individual working under a contract tainted by illegality may bring a claim under the Equality Act 2010 even if he/she is aware of the illegality,[123] it is submitted that if the contract is void or unenforceable by the employee then the employee will not be able to claim a statutory redundancy payment as the claim itself is based on a termination of the contract of employment in specific circumstances.

A contract that seeks to defraud HM Revenue and Customs is illegal and therefore void. **1.139** Similarly, a contract of employment to procure an illegal or immoral act, such as a contract of employment the sole purpose of which is to procure stolen goods, would clearly be illegal and void. The fact that the parties are innocent of any intent to be party to illegality is no defence. If the contract is incapable of performance without illegality on the part of one or both of the contracting parties, the contract will be void and cannot be relied upon by either party to establish contractual or statutory rights.

In *Corby v Morrison*,[124] the EAT held that the employee could not present a claim for unfair **1.140** dismissal because her pay packet was regularly made up by the amount of tax and national insurance which had been deducted, and the additional payment was never declared. The contract was illegal and void, even though the employee claimed she was unaware of the illegal nature of the arrangement. The EAT decided that the employee must have known the true purpose and effect of the agreement.

Similarly, in *Salvesen v Simons*,[125] the EAT confirmed that ignorance of the illegality of a tax- **1.141** evading arrangement did not prevent the contract being void. In this case, an employee was paid partly by way of salary and partly by way of a 'management fee' that was paid to a partnership that the employee operated with his wife. Even though the parties did not know, believe, or suspect this was illegal, the EAT found that the contract was illegal because it patently defrauded the Revenue and could therefore not be used as a basis for an action by the employee against the employer.

In contrast, other cases show a more pragmatic approach by the courts to finding illegality. **1.142** In *Lightfoot v D & J Sporting Ltd*,[126] the EAT stressed that there was a fine line between lawful tax avoidance and unlawful tax evasion. In this case, a gamekeeper arranged to have part of his salary paid to his wife who had assisted her husband on an unpaid basis. No income tax or national insurance were paid on the proportion of income paid to the wife. The EAT found that this was a commonplace and lawful mechanism of tax avoidance.

Where, however, the contract is, on its face, lawful and one party alone has some illegal pur- **1.143** pose, the innocent party is usually able to enforce the contract if they can show that they honestly did not know of the illegality. The test is not whether the innocent party ought to have known of the illegality. Needless to say, whilst the purely innocent party may be able to rely on the contract, the guilty party cannot. This was confirmed in *Newland v Simons and Willer (Hairdressers) Ltd*,[127] in which an employee was paid cash-in-hand but believed that the employer still paid the proper tax thereon to the Inland Revenue. Even though this was

---

[123] *Leighton v Michael* [1995] ICR 1091; *Hall v Woolston Hall Leisure Limited* [2000] IRLR 578. See also the reference to the European Court of Justice made by the Court of Appeal in *Crehan v Courage Ltd* (unreported) (a competition law case).
[124] [1980] IRLR 218.
[125] [1994] IRLR 52.
[126] [1996] IRLR 64.
[127] [1981] IRLR 359.

not the case and the contract was therefore illegal, the employee was entitled to an unfair dismissal remedy because she was innocent of any illegality.

1.144 In terms of the entitlement to a redundancy payment, therefore, a *prima facie* illegal contract will confer no right to a redundancy payment on the employee unless, on a pragmatic view of the facts, it can be shown that the employee was wholly innocent of any illegal intent or knowledge.

F. Continuous Employment Under a Contract of Employment

1.145 Continuity of service is of dual importance in the context of redundancy payments. First, in order to qualify for a statutory redundancy payment, an employee must have been continuously employed for two years.[128] Second, the amount of statutory redundancy pay to which an employee is entitled is dependent on the employee's period of continuous service.[129] Continuity is a statutory concept and the parties cannot validly agree to disapply the statutory rules.[130]

Calculating continuity

1.146 The rules for calculating a period of continuous employment are contained in the ERA 1996, Pt XIV. There is a presumption[131] that continuity is unbroken between the actual commencement of employment with that employer and the 'relevant date',[132] and therefore that the period between them yields the total number of calendar months for calculating qualifying service or the total calendar years for calculating a redundancy payment.

1.147 Section 212(1) of the ERA 1996 prescribes that a week counts towards continuity if, during the whole or part of that week, the employee's relations with the employer are governed by a contract of employment.[133] For these purposes a week is defined as meaning a week ending with a Saturday.[134] However, in *Roach v CSB (Moulds) Limited*[135] the EAT held that, notwithstanding the fact that an employee had worked for the same employer in consecutive weeks, continuity was broken where the employee sought and obtained work from another employer in the intervening period. Doubts over the correctness of this decision were expressed by the EAT in *Carrington v Harwich Dock*

---

[128] ERA 1996, s 155. The (then) two-year service qualification for unfair dismissal was challenged as being indirectly discriminatory in *R v Secretary of State of Employees, ex parte Seymour Smith Percy* [2000] IRLR 263, but the challenge was unsuccessful.

[129] See Chapter 8.

[130] *Collison v BBC* [1998] IRLR 238.

[131] ERA 1996, s 210(5).

[132] Ibid., s 211(1). 'Relevant date' is defined and discussed in full in Chapter 8.

[133] It used to be a condition that the said 'contract of employment' had to be one that normally involved at least eight hours of work per week. However, *R v Secretary of State for Employment, ex p EOC* [1994] 1 All ER 910 established that the former 16- and 8-hour minima were contrary to ex-Art 119 of the Treaty of Rome (now Art 157 of the TFEU) and the Equal Treatment Directive (76/207). The provisions of the legislation pre-dating the ERA 1996 were amended by the Employment Protection (Part-time Employees) Regulations 1995 so that the number of hours worked is now irrelevant in calculating continuous employment for redundancy purposes.

[134] ERA 1996, s 235(1).

[135] [1991] IRLR 200.

Co Limited,[136] and in *Sweeney v J&S Henderson (Concessions) Limited*[137] the Scottish EAT went a step further and held that *Roach* was wrongly decided. Mr Sweeney began working for the company in 1995. On Saturday 15 February 1997 Mr Sweeney resigned. He immediately took up another job with a new employer. However, within a few days he regretted this decision, resigned from his new employment and returned to his old employer on Friday 21 February 1997.

Thus in Mr Sweeney's case there was no week in which his relations with the company were not governed by a contract of employment. Looking at Mr Sweeney's position the EAT said that s 212(1) clearly takes account of the fact that the concept of continuous employment includes the possibility of gaps in employment. The EAT said that continuity of service cannot be determined on the basis of whether or not the termination of employment which created the gap is caused by the employee rather than the employer. **1.148**

Breaks in continuity

Subject to the provisions of the ERA 1996 which allow for continuity to be preserved in certain specific circumstances, any week which does not count towards continuity in accordance with the rules of s 212(1) must break continuity.[138] Any period of time prior to a break in continuity must be excluded from a calculation for the purposes of a qualifying period and a redundancy payment. **1.149**

Briefly, the basic principle set out in s 212(1) does not apply in the following circumstances: **1.150**

    (1) Any week during the whole or part of which an employee is:
        (a) incapable of work in consequence of sickness or injury;
        (b) absent from work on account of a temporary cessation of work;[139]
        (c) absent from work in circumstances such that, by arrangement or custom, he is regarded as continuing in the employment of his employer for any purpose,[140] or
    (2) If an employee has escaped dismissal in the past by accepting alternative employment, any gap in employment which is created by his trial of such alternative employment will count towards continuity.[141]
    (3) Similar provisions apply to a gap of up to eight weeks between the death of an employer, which causes the employee to be deemed to have been dismissed, and re-engagement by the employer's personal representatives.[142]
    (4) There is no break in continuity if an employee switches from one employer to an associated employer.[143]
    (5) If circumstances exist in which the 'relevant date' is postponed,[144] the gap between termination of employment and the relevant date can be counted as continuous

---

[136] [1998] IRLR 567.
[137] [1999] IRLR 306.
[138] ERA 1996, s 210(4).
[139] See also Chapter 6.
[140] See below.
[141] ERA 1996, s 213(2).
[142] Ibid., sub-s 174(2), (3) and 213(2).
[143] Ibid., s 218(6).
[144] Ibid., s 145(5). See Chapter 8.

employment for the purposes of determining qualification for, and calculating of, a redundancy payment.[145]

(6) Payment of a previous statutory redundancy payment is deemed to break continuity for the purposes of the redundancy scheme,[146] but only if the payment is made in respect of a true liability[147] or the employee has been paid a sum in respect of the payment by the Secretary of State.[148] Continuity is deemed to have been broken on the date which is the relevant date for the purposes of the payment made.[149]

(7) A week of employment does not count in computing the period of employment for the purposes of ss 155 and 162 of the ERA 1996 if the employee was employed outside Great Britain during the whole or part of that week and no secondary class one national insurance contributions were payable in respect of him during that week.[150] Continuity is nevertheless preserved during a period of employment overseas, even though it may not be counted.[151]

(8) A week does not count if during any part of it the employee takes part in a strike, although this does not break continuity.[152] In such cases, the date from which continuous service is deemed to commence is postponed by the number of days between the last working day before the strike and the day on which work was resumed.[153]

(9) If an employee is re-engaged or reinstated following a complaint of unfair dismissal or discrimination, continuity of the employee's period of employment is preserved and also the period between dismissal and re-engagement or reinstatement will count towards continuity.[154]

(10) Employees in local government service (as defined) can rely upon continuous employment in local government as a whole, and not just continuous employment with the employer from whom the payment is claimed.[155] Similar provisions apply to employees in the National Health Service.[156]

1.151 Perhaps the most problematic issue is determining where an employee is absent from work in circumstances such that he has no contract of employment but, by arrangement or custom,

---

[145] Ibid., s 213(3).

[146] Ibid., s 214. This rule has, however, been amended by the Employment Protection (Continuity of Employment) Regulations 1996 (SI 1996/3147), reg 4, which states that continuity will not be broken where an employee is re-instated or re-engaged and he repays the redundancy payment.

[147] *Rowan v Machinery Installations (South Wales) Ltd* [1981] ICR 386, EAT, confirmed in *Gardner v (1) Haydn Davies Catering Equipment (1988) Ltd (In Liquidation) (2) ABE Catering Equipment Ltd* (EAT, 9 January 1992). See also *Senior Heat Treatment v Bell* [1997] IRLR 614.

[148] *Lassman and Others v (1) Secretary of State for Trade and Industry (2) Pan Graphics Industries Limited (In Receivership)*, CA (unreported). See also ERA 1996, s 167 and Chapter 8.

[149] Ibid., s 214(4).

[150] Ibid., s 215(2).

[151] Ibid., s 215(3). For each week which does not count under this subsection, the date on which the employee commenced employment will be deemed to be postponed by seven days.

[152] Ibid., s 216.

[153] Ibid., ss 211(3) and 216(2).

[154] Employment Protection (Continuity of Employment) Regulations 1996 (SI 1996/3147).

[155] The Redundancy Payments (Continuity of Employment in Local Government etc) (Modification) Order 1999 (SI 1999/2277), reg 1.

[156] SI 1993 No 3167. Finally, continuity is preserved where there is more than one employer where there has been a transfer of a trade, business, or undertaking (see ERA, s 218). See also the other examples quoted in s 218.

he is regarded as continuing in employment. Absence in this context simply refers to the interval between two successive contracts of employment.[157]

This provision has, however, been interpreted restrictively by the courts. For example, in **1.152** *Booth and Others v United States of America*,[158] the three applicants were employed by the United States Army as maintenance workers under a series of fixed-term contracts. The total period of employment was more than two years but in between each contract there was a break of about two weeks.

At the end of each fixed term the employees were informed in writing that the contract had **1.153** terminated and they received all outstanding holiday pay and other benefits. After a break, the individuals completed new application forms and other relevant documentation for employment. They were then employed under new contracts. When the employees returned to work they were given the same employee number, used the same tools and clothing provided by the employer, and were given the same lockers.

On termination of the last fixed-term contract the applicants claimed redundancy payments **1.154** and/or unfair dismissal compensation. Those claims were dismissed by the employment tribunal on the basis that they did not have two years' continuous service. For their part the employees argued that continuity was preserved, notwithstanding the gaps between fixed-term contracts, 'by arrangement or custom' under s 212(3) (c).

At the EAT the employees argued that the underlying purpose of these contracts and the **1.155** breaks was to prevent them building up sufficient continuity of service to gain employment rights and that when the contracts were terminated the parties well understood that the employees would be re-employed after a short break. They argued that it was clear that there was some arrangement by which the employees and employer knew that the particular individuals would be returning to the same work in the same place following each break. For its part, the USA argued that, as it never intended the employment to continue during a break, there could be no 'arrangement'.

The EAT stated that the concept of 'by arrangement' means that something must be said or **1.156** done by the employer to justify the conclusion that the parties regarded the employment relationship as continuing despite the termination of the contract of employment. The arrangement must be in place before the employee returns from his absence.[159] The EAT also said that a custom does not have to be a custom of the trade but rather a custom in the sense of 'custom and practice' as commonly understood in industrial relations. This does not require that anything is said or done but does require there to be an established custom and practice that such breaks in employment are treated as though the employment continued. On the facts the EAT said that at best it could be said that there was a 'settled expectation' that the employees would return to their old job after a short break, but that that fell short of the statutory requirement that the arrangement should be one pursuant to which the employee is regarded as still being in the employment of the employer. For example, there was no evidence that any of the applicants had a right to enter the premises

---

[157] *Ford v Warwickshire County Council* [1983] IRLR 126. Continuity may therefore be preserved notwithstanding the fact that the employee has been dismissed (as his contract has expired), and the employee may claim that that dismissal was unfair whilst still being in continuous service by virtue of s 212(3) (*Pfaffinger v City of Liverpool Community College* [1996] IRLR 508).

[158] [1999] IRLR 16.

[159] *Morris v Walsh Western UK Limited* [1997] IRLR 562.

during the break and the documentation suggested that employment had ended and new employment commenced. The EAT considered that, although the whole purpose of the breaks was to defeat continuity, the statute does not prevent an employer from structuring his employment relations in order to do so.

1.157   The decision in the case of *Booth* was subsequently applied by the EAT in the case of *Mark Insulations Limited v Bunker*.[160] However, the EAT warned of the need for caution in relation to *Booth*, stating that:

> . . . the dictum in *Booth v USA*, that there must have been some discussion or agreement to the effect of the parties regarded the employment relationship as continuing despite the termination of the contract of employment must be read with a little caution. The discussion does not have to establish that the employment relationship was to be regarded as continuing for all purposes—only for some purpose.

The position of non-standard workers

1.158   If one considers the position of non-standard workers, it can be seen that the absence of a global contract of employment will not necessarily mean that the worker cannot establish the two years' continuous service needed to qualify for a statutory redundancy payment. If the worker works for the employer at least once in each week, and is deemed to work under a separate contract of employment during each specific engagement, continuity will be established under s 212(1). However, as soon as the individual misses a week, continuity will be broken unless one of the rules outlined above deem otherwise. Perhaps the most relevant of these would be s 213(3)(c), as the individual may be able to argue that there was an 'arrangement or custom' that continuity would be preserved. Given the restrictive application of this section, however, and the refusal of the EAT in *Booth* to construe it purposively in order to prevent employers structuring their relationships in such a way as to prevent individuals attaining employment rights, it would appear that it will be relatively rare that an individual could demonstrate that there was such an arrangement or custom.[161]

G. Employees Excluded From Claiming a Statutory Redundancy Payment

1.159   Even if a person is an employee with the requisite period of continuous service, he may still lose the right to a statutory redundancy payment if he falls within certain classes of employees who are excluded from the right to a statutory redundancy payment or, alternatively, if his personal circumstances effectively disqualify him from the right to a redundancy payment.

1.160   The ERA 1996 expressly excludes from the right to claim a statutory redundancy payment the following categories of employee:

(a)   Crown employees (including members of the armed forces)[162] and parliamentary staff;[163]

---

[160]   UKEAT/0331/05.
[161]   cf. Collins [2000] ILJ 29(1) 73.
[162]   ERA 1996, s 191.
[163]   Ibid., ss 194 and 195.

(b) public office holders and civil servants;[164]
(c) employees of overseas governments;[165]
(d) domestic servants in a private household where the employer is a relative of the employee;[166]
(e) share fishermen;[167]
(f) employees excluded by order of the Secretary of State where there is in force a collective agreement entitling employees to payments on termination of their contract of employment;[168] and
(g) employees who have contracted out of the right to receive a statutory redundancy payment.[169]

Formerly there was an additional exclusion in respect of overseas employees who 'ordinarily worked outside Great Britain'.[170] This was repealed by the Employment Relations Act 1999, which means that whether or not an employee can claim a statutory redundancy payment when he works outside Great Britain will be determined by the principles governing conflicts of laws,[171] although given the rules for calculating continuity of service where an employee works overseas, this question may not arise often.[172] **1.161**

Age limits

The statutory redundancy payment lower age limit of 18 and the upper age limit of 65 which previously applied were removed by the Employment Equality (Age) Regulations 2006, which came into force on 1 October 2006. **1.162**

Extensions of the right to claim a redundancy payment

Section 171 of the ERA 1996 permits the Secretary of State for Trade and Industry to extend the right to a redundancy payment to certain individuals who are not employees as defined. Thus the right has been granted to:[173] **1.163**

(a) clerks of the peace;
(b) justices' clerks;
(c) airports' policemen;
(d) registrars of births, marriages and deaths;
(e) rent officers; and
(f) immigration medical inspectors.

In addition, regulations made under s 172 have extended the right to a redundancy payment to chief constables of police.[174] **1.164**

---

[164] Ibid., ss 159 and 191(6).
[165] Ibid., s 160.
[166] Ibid., s 161.
[167] Ibid., s 199(2).
[168] Ibid., s 157(2) and (3)—see also Chapter 2.
[169] Ibid., s 197—see also Chapter 2.
[170] Ibid., s 196(6).
[171] See Dicey & Morris, *Conflict of Laws* (13th edn, Sweet & Maxwell, 2000).
[172] ERA 1996, s 215; see above.
[173] Redundancy Payments Office Holders Regulations 1965 (SI 1965/2007).
[174] Redundancy Payments Termination of Employment Regulations 1965 (SI 1965/2022).

2

THE REQUIREMENT OF DISMISSAL

A. Termination of Employment Law by Operation of Law   2.08

B. Other Cases   2.10

2.01 The right to a redundancy payment cannot be exercised unless the employee has been dismissed. A dismissal is defined in ERA 1996, s 136 as occurring when the contract is terminated by the employer with or without notice (i.e. an employer-initiated termination);[1] where a limited-term contract terminates by virtue of the limiting event without its being renewed;[2] and where the employee terminates his contract of employment with or without notice in circumstances such that he is entitled to terminate it without notice by reason of the employer's conduct (i.e. an employee-initiated termination in response to a serious breach of contract, or, as it is commonly known, a 'constructive' dismissal).[3] Detailed text books on employment law should be consulted for further detail of the case law and analysis on the three types of dismissal listed above.[4] But we discuss briefly here their implications for redundancy law before dealing with a number of problem cases, again commonly arising in the law of redundancy.

2.02 Express dismissal by the employer under s 136(1)(a) of the ERA 1996 (often referred to as an employer-initiated termination) is usually straightforward, although in this chapter we highlight some situations where whether a dismissal has occurred may be ambiguous.

2.03 Ambiguity may also occur in the words actually used by an employer, although this is unlikely to occur frequently in practice in the context of redundancy. According to the learned editors of *Harvey on Industrial Relations and Employment Law* the preponderance of authority is 'in favour of the objective view, i.e. that the question to be answered is how a reasonable listener would have construed the words used in all the circumstances of the case, and that this is the test whether the words used are ambiguous or not'.[5]

2.04 Dismissals may be made with notice or without notice. If without notice, in the context of redundancy a claim for damages for wrongful dismissal will apply in addition to the claim

---

[1] ERA 1996, s 136(1)(a).

[2] Ibid., (1)(b).

[3] Ibid., (1)(c).

[4] See I Smith and A Baker, *Smith & Wood's Employment Law* (10th edn, OUP); S Deakin and GS Morris, *Labour Law* (5th edn, Hart Publishing).

[5] *Harvey on Industrial Relations and Employment Law* D1 [248]. See the (often conflicting) cases discussed at D1 [225]–[249].

for a statutory redundancy payment together with the ability, subject to a qualifying period to pursue a claim for unfair dismissal (see Chapter 10).

The House of Lords has recently held, for the purposes of the effective date of termination in unfair dismissal law, that where a dismissal occurs without notice the effective date of termination is when the employee is informed of the dismissal or has had a reasonable opportunity of discovering that the employee has been dismissed.[6] **2.05**

It is often not appreciated by employers that the non-renewal of a limited-term contract is a dismissal which may, subject to the definition of redundancy, be by reason of redundancy. Many employees, mainly researchers in universities, are employed on externally funded fixed-term contracts. When these are not renewed through lack of funding, a redundancy payment liability (and obligations to inform and consult appropriate employee representatives under s 188 of the Trade Union and Labour Relations (Consolidation) Act 1992—subject to the number of terminations involved) will arise. **2.06**

A constructive dismissal may occur where the employer commits or threatens to commit a repudiatory breach of the employee's contract. In practice, in redundancy cases, constructive dismissal occurs upon a unilateral decision by the employer to move work location in the absence of an enabling mobility clause in the employment contract. This aspect is covered in Chapter 3. **2.07**

A. Termination of Employment Law by Operation of Law

A termination by operation of law, e.g. through frustration, is not a dismissal, save only where s 136(5) (see Chapter 5) applies and the event affects the employer (e.g. the employer's death[7]). It is clear that the doctrine of frustration applies to the employment contract.[8] The authorities, such as *Marshall v Harland and Wolff Limited (No 2)*,[9] *Egg Stores (Stamford Hill) Ltd v Leibovivi*,[10] *FC Shepherd & Co Ltd v Jerrom*,[11] *Notcutt v Universal Equipment Co (London) Ltd*,[12] and *Collins v Secretary of State for Trade and Industry*[13] support the doctrine. However, it can often be difficult for an employer to rely on the doctrine save in the case of imprisonment or long-term sickness.[14] Thus, in *Gryf-Lowczowski v Hinchingbrooke Healthcare NHS Trust*,[15] the High Court refused to allow an employer to rely upon the doctrine of frustration where, following a referral to the National Clinical Assessment Authority after a disciplinary complaint, an employee, a consultant surgeon, had been on special leave for almost two years and could not resume his duties for his employer until he had undergone a period of re-skilling at another trust. The employment contract had not yet become incapable of performance. Notwithstanding the length of time of the incapacity from performing duties, in this case, because the employment was of a highly skilled nature and its termination by frustration would have had the catastrophic effect of making it highly unlikely **2.08**

---

[6] *Gisda Cyf v Barratt* [2010] UK SC 41.
[7] [1972] ICR 101.
[8] [1977] ICR 260.
[9] [1972] ICR 101.
[10] [1977] ICR 260.
[11] [1986] ICR 802
[12] Ibid., 414.
[13] [2001] All ER (D) 286.
[14] See *Shepherd* and *Notcutt*, respectively.
[15] [2005] EWHC 2407 (QB); [2006] ICR 425; [2006] IRLR 100.

that the employee would find similar work elsewhere, it was reasonable to expect the employers to wait longer than might be the case in other circumstances. On the facts there remained a realistic possibility that a placement could be found to enable the surgeon to be re-skilled and, afterwards, to resume his former duties. Accordingly, the contract was not frustrated.

2.09   In *Hatton Logistics Ltd v Waller*,[16] the EAT upheld the tribunal's decision that a lorry driver's contract of employment had not been frustrated, when, having been off sick from work for six months with heart palpitations he raised the possibility with his employer of a pacemaker having to be fitted. Finally, although the authority of *Shepherd* (see above) holds that an employment contract may be frustrated through imprisonment, it has been held that being charged and bailed will not, *per se*, frustrate the employment contract (even if bail conditions impede further work). This is especially so if the employer has chosen to use its powers to suspend the employee during this period.[17]

B.   Other Cases

Advance warning of dismissal contrasted with notice of dismissal

2.10   It is important to note that an employer's warning of impending redundancy may not be a dismissal. The reason why such a warning may sometimes not amount to a dismissal or even a notice of dismissal is because a notice of dismissal must give the employee precise information as to when the employment will end; many warnings do not do this. Thus, in *Morton Sundour Fabrics Ltd v Shaw*,[18] an employee was warned by his employer that the department in which he was employed would close down at some date in the future. As a result, the employee decided to seek alternative employment and anticipate the termination of his employment. He was successful in his efforts and gave notice to his employer of resignation and left. But as stated, in order to terminate the contract of employment the notice given to an employee must specify the date or contain material from which the date of termination is ascertainable. Here there was none and so it was held that there was no dismissal and that the employee had resigned. As the employee had resigned, he lost his rights. This principle has been upheld in a number of other cases[19] and it is equally applicable to unfair dismissal law as well as to redundancy. In all of these cases an employer's warning of a future dismissal was held not to be an express dismissal. Nor, it seems, will such an advance warning of dismissal amount to a constructive dismissal, at least if the length of the employer's warning of impending dismissal is long enough to allow the employer, within that period to serve a valid notice of dismissal of the appropriate length.[20]

2.11   A contrasting case in this area where, on the facts, an employer's threat to dismiss on notice was held to give rise to a constructive dismissal is *Greenaway Harrison Ltd v Wiles*.[21] However, there were particular features to the case perhaps not applicable to the

---

[16]   EAT/0298/06.

[17]   See *Four Seasons Healthcare Ltd v Maughan* [2005] IRLR 324, EAT.

[18]   (1967) 2 ITR 84.

[19]   *Burton Group Ltd v Smith* [1977] IRLR 351, EAT; *International Computers v Kennedy* [1981] IRLR 28, EAT; *Pritchard-Rhodes Ltd v Boon and Milton* [1979] IRLR 19, EAT; *Haseltine Lake & Co Ltd v Dowler* [1981] ICF 222, [1981] IRLR 25, EAT; *Secretary of State for Employment v Greenfield*, EAT 147/89. See also *Ingersoll-Dresser Pumps (UK) Ltd v Taylor*, EAT 391/94.

[20]   *Devon County Council v Cook* [1977] IRLR 188; *Haseltine Lake & Co Ltd v Dowler* [1981] ICR 222, EAT.

[21]   [1994] IRLR 380, EAT.

discussion here.[22] It seems unlikely that the proposition that the giving of lawful notice by the employer could give rise to a constructive dismissal would be followed in future cases. In *Kerry Foods Ltd v Lynch*,[23] an employer gave an employee notice that if he did not agree to new employment terms his current contract would terminate at the end of the notice period (which was the required notice period under his employment contract) and he was offered immediate re-engagement on its expiry under the new terms. However, before the employer's notice expired, the employee resigned and claimed constructive dismissal. The EAT emphasised that for a constructive dismissal the employee must leave in response to a breach of contract. The employer here had given a lawful notice of termination which could not amount to a repudiatory breach of contract. As Judge Peter Clark stated: 'There is no . . . breach of the existing terms nor an anticipatory breach in indicating lawful termination of the contract on proper notice.'

Anticipating the expiry of the employer's notice

If the employer has given a valid notice of dismissal it is possible for an employee to anticipate the expiry of that notice and leave early, although this too is not without its pitfalls. First, it is possible for an employee and an employer to agree, during the period of notice served upon the employee, to foreshorten that period of notice in order to allow an employee to leave early. In such circumstances, the courts may be prepared to say that all that has happened is that the employer and employee had agreed consensually to change the date of expiry of the notice without taking away the essential character of the dismissal by reason of redundancy.[24] Another interpretation is that the employer and employee have superimposed upon the original dismissal a termination of employment by mutual agreement; and a termination by agreement is not a dismissal within the meaning of the statute. Such an arrangement would therefore be disastrous for an employee. However, it is submitted that the courts would, on the whole, be reluctant to find a termination by mutual agreement in a case where a redundancy dismissal notice has already been served. It is probably more likely that they would construe the agreement as one simply altering the date on which the employee leaves as a result of his earlier notice of dismissal.[25] **2.12**

Alternatively, there is no reason why the termination date cannot, by agreement, be postponed as in Mowlem *Northern Ltd v Watson*.[26] An example of a case where it was held that the terms of an original notice of dismissal can be varied by agreement between the parties is *Palfrey v Transco Plc*.[27] In this case, Mr Palfrey was given notice of dismissal on the ground of redundancy in a letter from the employers dated 24 February 2003. The letter stated that his notice period would commence on 25 February 2003 and his last day of employment would be 19 May 2003. Mr Palfrey informed his employers that he would like to leave on 31 March. He therefore received a further letter dated 17 March confirming that his notice period would be adjusted so that his last day of employment would be 31 March and as a result of him not working his full period of 12 weeks' notice he would be given seven weeks in lieu of notice. He duly ceased working on 31 March. Over three months following the date of 31 March he brought a claim for unfair dismissal which, of course, was time-barred. The employment tribunal then had to consider his argument that his effective date of **2.13**

---

[22] And see criticism by McMullen, *In House Lawyer*, September 1994, 39.
[23] [2005] IRLR 680 (EAT).
[24] *McAlwane v Boughton Estates Ltd* [1973] ICR 470.
[25] But cf. the case of *Scott v Coalite Fuels and Chemicals Ltd* [1988] ICR 355; [1988] IRLR 131, EAT.
[26] [1990] IRLR 500, EAT.
[27] [2004] IRLR 916.

termination was 19 May, as specified in the original termination letter (in which case his application would be in time) or, instead, the earlier date of 31 March, which would mean that his application was time-barred. The tribunal found that the employer's letter of 17 March had the effect of causing the termination of employment to be brought forward to 31 March and therefore his application was out of time. The EAT upheld the employment tribunal. The employment tribunal had viewed the termination date as being varied by agreement. The EAT considered that the effect of the letter of 17 March was to withdraw the original notice of termination and substitute another one incorporating Mr Palfrey's new leaving date.

2.14 However, the EAT did not concur with the theory that there can never be a variation of an original notice of termination unless it has been positively withdrawn. Had it been necessary to do so the EAT would have concluded that the majority decision of the Court of Appeal in *TBA Industrial Products Ltd v Morland*[28] was *per incuriam* and should not be followed. That particular decision had been reached without reference to a number of significant decisions of the NIRC, the High Court, and the EAT, all of which allowed for variation of original notices of dismissal without the procedural superfluity of an express, or possibly implied, withdrawal of the original notice. Account must be taken of what has happened between the parties over time. Where there is a variation of notice, the notice expires on the new date, as does the contract of employment.

2.15 Apart from cases of altering the date of leaving by agreement, it may be possible for an employee unilaterally to anticipate the expiry of the employer's notice and still preserve his rights. By virtue of ERA 1996, s 142 it is provided that where the employer has given notice to an employee to terminate the contract of employment, and, at a time within the 'obligatory period' of that notice, the employee gives notice in writing to the employer to terminate the contract of employment on a date earlier than the date on which the employer's notice is due to expire, the employee shall, notwithstanding his counter notice, still be taken to be dismissed by his employer.[29] However, the main pitfall for employees here is that the employee's notice must be given during the 'obligatory period' of the employer's notice. The obligatory period is a period equal to the minimum period which is required to be given by an employer to terminate the contract of employment either by virtue of ERA 1996, s 86 or under the contract of employment, whichever is the greater, worked back from the date of expiry of the period of notice that the employer has actually given.[30] Now, in most cases, this will cause few problems because the period of notice that the employer has given will be equal to the obligatory period, i.e. will be equal to the period of notice he is required by law to give. But suppose an employer gives notice more generous than the minimum which he is required to give and suppose too that the employee gives his counter notice to the employer outside (i.e. before the commencement of) the obligatory period. In this case, the employee's rights are lost entirely and he will be deemed to have resigned and will have lost his redundancy payment.[31] Of course, if the employee's action was with the agreement of the employer, a mutual agreement to vary the date of termination might have been struck along the lines discussed above.[32] But if the employee unilaterally attempts to anticipate the expiry of the employer's notice outside the obligatory period he will lose his rights.

---

[28] [1982] ICR 686; [1982] IRLR 331 (CA).
[29] ERA 1996, s 142(1)(a).
[30] Ibid., s 136(4).
[31] *Pritchard-Rhodes Ltd v Boon and Milton* [1979] IRLR 19, EAT.
[32] See *CPS Recruitment Ltd v Bowen* [1982] IRLR 54, distinguishing *Pritchard-Rhodes*, on this ground, on the facts.

If the employee's notice is given at the appropriate time, i.e. within the obligatory period of **2.16** the employer's notice, it is not clear what amount of notice has to be given to the employer. ERA 1996, s 86 says that the minimum period of notice to be given by an employee to an employer under statute (in the contract it may be greater) is one week. However, it has been held in *Ready Case Ltd v Jackson*[33] that notice given by the employee for present purposes may be less than that which is required by law and still be effective. Nonetheless, it has also been held that there must be at least some notice which is sufficient to indicate to an employer that there is an intention to anticipate the expiry of the employer's notice[34] and ERA 1996, s 142 does, of course, require an employee to give notice in writing of his intention to anticipate the expiry of the employer's notice.

Assuming the employee has given a valid counter notice the employer may, before the **2.17** employee's counter notice is due to expire, give him a counter counter notice (again in writing) requiring him to withdraw his counter notice and to continue in employment until the date on which the employer's original notice was due to expire.[35] The employer's counter counter notice must also state that unless he does so, the employer will contest any liability to make a redundancy payment to the employee in respect of the termination of the contract of employment.[36] If the employer does serve this notice and if the employee does not comply with it, the employee will be disentitled to the redundancy payment that would otherwise be due except to the extent that it appears to the employment tribunal, having regard both to the reason for which the employee seeks to leave the employment and those for which the employer requires him to continue in it, to be 'just and equitable'.[37] This, therefore, gives the employment tribunal a discretion to order payment of the entire redundancy payment or such part of it as the tribunal thinks fit, notwithstanding the employer's counter counter notice and the employee's failure to comply with it.[38]

Voluntary redundancy and termination by mutual agreement

As has been mentioned above, a termination by mutual agreement will not be a dismissal for **2.18** the purposes of ERA 1996, s 136. In the context of redundancy, however, it is common for volunteers to be solicited and voluntary redundancies have some similarities with consensual termination. Does an employee run the risk of disentitlement merely because he has volunteered for redundancy? The answer is 'not necessarily'.

There are two common situations. One is where there is a genuine mutual agreement between the **2.19** employer and employee, where no pressure is applied by the employer for termination of employment to take place. The other is a termination which results from the initiative of the employer notwithstanding that it is accepted or even invited by the employee. In the former case, there will be no redundancy dismissal; in the latter case, there will. Thus, in *Burton Allton and Johnson Ltd v Peck*[39] it was held that when an individual volunteered for redundancy—the employer having already declared that redundancies would have to be implemented—there was a dismissal within the meaning of ERA 1996, s 136 and therefore a right to a redundancy payment.

---

[33] [1981] IRLR 312, EAT.
[34] *Walker v Cotswold Chine Holme School* (1977) 12 ITR 342, EAT.
[35] ERA 1996, s 142(l).
[36] Ibid., (2).
[37] Ibid., (3) and (4).
[38] Ibid.
[39] [1975] ICR 193; [1973] IRLR 87. See also *Morley v CT Morley Ltd* [1985] ICR 499, EAT.

Also to be noted is the case of *Optare Group Ltd v Transport and General Workers Union.*[40] Here the EAT considered whether the termination of employment of three employees who volunteered for redundancy and whose applications were accepted was a dismissal by the employer or was a termination by mutual agreement. The EAT upheld the tribunal's decision that the three volunteers had been dismissed. On the facts they had not volunteered prior to the redundancy selection exercise occurring but had done so when volunteers were invited by Optare to mitigate the impact of the redundancies. In this case, this meant that these three volunteers were to be added to the number of employees proposed to be dismissed in the establishment within a period of less than 90 days, bringing the total to more than 20 and thus triggering the information and consultation provisions of TULR(C)A 1992, s 188. As the employer had not complied with s 188 and informed and consulted with the recognised trade union, the Transport & General Workers Union, a protective award was made.

2.20 However, in *Birch v University of Liverpool*[41] the employees applied for retirement under the Universities Retirement Compensation Scheme. Their applications to retire happened after the university had announced to its staff that there had been a reduction in funds and that there would have to be a reduction in the number of staff employed. It was held in this case that there was a genuine consensual termination and therefore no dismissal. In some cases, the dividing line is very fine indeed.

2.21 Also to be noted is *Scott v Coalite Fuels and Chemicals Ltd*,[42] where an employee already under notice of dismissal for redundancy was given the option of early retirement so as to trigger pension benefits. It was held in this case that he had come to an agreement to end his employment and had not been dismissed.[43]

2.22 Perhaps some guidance can be taken from the Court of Appeal decision in *Jones v Mid Glamorgan County Council.*[44] In that case, Mr Jones was employed by the council as an assistant area surveyor. He applied for promotion and when it was unsuccessful his relationship with his employers soured. He was instructed to transfer to a different post but refused. Having first attempted to resist it on health grounds he then applied for early retirement. His application was successful but the terms offered were less favourable than those to which Mr Jones believed he was entitled. When he failed to either respond to the offer or to transfer as instructed he was sent a letter terminating his employment. Subsequently he agreed to take voluntary early retirement on the terms offered instead of being dismissed. Mr Jones commenced two claims, one in the county court in respect of a pension dispute, and one in the employment tribunal in respect of unfair dismissal. In both cases Mr Jones essentially argued that he had been under such pressure to retire that he had in law been dismissed and moreover, that his agreement to retire was subject to duress. Much of the debate on appeal turned on the words of the tribunal in quoting extensively from the findings of the county court in making its decision. In the Court of Appeal, however, it was also submitted for the council that the tribunal would have been justified in any event in holding that Mr Jones' complaint

---

[40] [2007] All ER (D) 135 (Jul).
[41] [1985] ICR 470; [1985] IRLR 165, CA.
[42] [1988] ICR 355; [1988] IRLR 131, EAT.
[43] See also (in a different context) *Sheffield v Oxford Controls Ltd* [1979] ICR 396, EAT and *Logan Salton v Durham County Council* [1989] IRLR 99, EAT. For two later cases with contrasting outcomes see *Gateshead Metropolitan Borough Council v Mills* (EAT 610/92) and *Renfrew District Council v Lornie* (Court of Session, 23 June 1995).
[44] [1997] IRLR 685.

was unarguable on the fundamental ground that because Mr Jones had three alternatives to choose from: retirement, dismissal, or transfer, the threat of dismissal was not the sole factor in his decision to retire.

This submission was not accepted by the Court of Appeal. The Court concluded that the **2.23** concept of dismissal by forced resignation was too valuable and too flexible to be constrained by a precondition that the threat of dismissal must be the sole factor inducing the resignation. The fact that there were three options did not nonetheless mean that it was impossible for the employee to claim that his resignation was induced by threat of dismissal. Indeed, Waite LJ pointed out that:

> At one end of the scale is the blatant instance of resignation preceded by the employer's ultimatum: retire on my terms or be fired—where it would not be surprising to find the tribunal drawing the inference that what had occurred was a dismissal. At the other extreme is the instance of the long serving employee who is attracted to early retirement by benevolent terms of severance offered by a grateful employer as a reward for loyalty, where one would expect the tribunal to draw the contrary inference of termination by mutual agreement. Between those two extremes there are bound to lie much more debatable cases to which, according to their particular circumstances, the tribunal are required to apply their expertise in determining whether the borderline has been crossed between a resignation that is truly voluntary and a retirement unwillingly made in response to a threat. I doubt myself whether, given the variety of circumstances, there can be much scope for assistance from authority . . . . in cases where precedent is nevertheless thought to be of value, the authority that will no doubt continue to be cited is *Sheffield v Oxford Controls Co Ltd*.

In *Sheffield v Oxford Controls Co Ltd*,[45] (which was not concerned with redundancy) the EAT **2.24** held that where terms of resignation emerge which are satisfactory to the employee (i.e. the terms of finance) the threat of dismissal is no longer the operative factor in the employee's decision to resign. Accordingly, the causation of the resignation is no longer the threat of dismissal but it is the negotiated terms. Given, however, the view expressed in *Jones*, it would appear that a factual analysis will need to take place in each case.

A similar approach was taken by the EAT in the case of *Matthews v Pearl Assurance Plc*,[46] **2.25** where the EAT concluded that Mr Matthews had three options:

(a) remaining in his original employment for a period up to likely redundancy;
(b) accepting alternative employment; and
(c) accepting the early retirement terms;

and, accordingly, Mr Matthews had not been dismissed.[47]

In *Sandhu v Jan de Rijk Transport Ltd*,[48] Mr Sandhu was employed as an operations manager. **2.26** He was asked to attend a meeting at the head office of the company in the Netherlands on 6 December 2002. He was not told in advance what the meeting was about. There was conflicting evidence about what actually occurred but, on any view, the meeting opened with Mr Sandhu being told that he was being dismissed. There was a proposal that he should finish at the end of December 2002. Mr Sandhu negotiated an agreement that he would

---

[45] [1979] IRLR 133.
[46] EAT/0552/97/AM, 2 March 1998, unreported.
[47] See also *Catherall v Michelin Tyre Plc* [2005] ICR 28, EAT; *Cole v London Borough of Hackney* EAT, 17 October 2000.
[48] [2007] IRLR 519 (CA).

remain employed until 3l March 2003 retaining the use of his company car until the end of January 2003 and that he would retain the use of his mobile phone, albeit paying for the calls himself from 9 December 2002. He subsequently brought a claim in the employment tribunal for unfair dismissal. The employer conceded that had Mr Sandhu left the meeting immediately after hearing the opening remark to the effect that he was being dismissed, he would have been dismissed and this would have been procedurally unfair. But the employer argued that it did not dismiss Mr Sandhu. What had happened was that having negotiated satisfactory severance terms during the course of the meeting, Mr Sandhu resigned. The EAT accepted this argument and the tribunal decision was upheld.

2.27 The Court of Appeal, however, allowed Mr Sandhu's appeal and remitted the case for hearing before a different tribunal as to the merits of the unfair dismissal claim. The EAT had been wrong to uphold the employment tribunal's decision that Mr Sandhu had resigned. It had misdirected itself as to the law. Had it directed itself properly, the only conclusion that it could probably have reached was that Mr Sandhu had been dismissed. Resignation implies some form of negotiation and discussion; it predicates a result that is a genuine choice on the part of the employee. If the employee had had the opportunity to take independent advice and then offered to resign, that would be powerful evidence pointing towards resignation rather than dismissal. But the Court of Appeal pointed out that in none of the cases where an employee has been held to have resigned did the resignation occur during the same interview/discussion in which the question of dismissal had been raised. And there was no case in which termination of the employee's employment had occurred in a single interview where a resignation had been found to take place. Wall LJ analysed the meeting as:

> [Mr Sandhu] was being dismissed. In my judgment it simply cannot be argued that he was negotiating freely. He had no warning that the purpose of the 6 December meeting was to dismiss him; he had had no advice, and no time to reflect. In my judgment, he was doing his best on his own to salvage what he could from the inevitable fact that he was going to be dismissed. This, in my judgment, is the very antithesis of free, unpressured negotiation.

3

THE DEFINITION OF REDUNDANCY

A. General	3.01	E. Bumped Redundancies	3.94
B. The Presumption of Redundancy	3.05	F. Bumping—A Different View	3.99
C. The Definition Analysed	3.08	G. Summary	3.107
D. The Contract Test Versus the Job Function Test	3.77		

A. General

3.01 The definition of redundancy for redundancy payment purposes is contained in s 139(1) of the ERA 1996. This states that an employee is entitled to a redundancy payment either on dismissal by reason of redundancy or when he is laid off or kept on short-time working.[1] Verbatim, the definition from s 139 is as follows:

(1) For the purposes of this Act an employee who is dismissed shall be taken to be dismissed by reason of redundancy if the dismissal is wholly or mainly attributable to:

    (a) the fact that his employer has ceased, or intends to cease—

        (i) to carry on the business for the purposes of which the employee was employed by him, or

        (ii) to carry on that business in the place where the employee was so employed, or

    (b) the fact that the requirements of that business—

        (i) or employees to carry out work of a particular kind, or

        (ii) for employees to carry out work of a particular kind in the place where the employee was employed by the employer, have ceased or diminished or are expected[2] to cease or diminish.

3.02 However, for the purposes of information to and consultation with worker representatives in the context of collective redundancies,[3] the definition is somewhat wider. Section 195(1) of the TULR(C)A 1992 states that 'references to dismissal as redundant are references to dismissal for a reason not related to the individual concerned or for a number of reasons all of which are not so related'.

---

[1] Within the meaning of s 147 of the 1996 Act (see Chapter 6).

[2] For a rare case on the concept of a redundancy dismissal where the requirements of the employer were expected to cease or diminish, see *Strathclyde Buses Limited v Leonard* (EAT 507/97), where the EAT held that four depot workers dismissed on a merger were redundant on the ground of expected reductions in labour due to new technology even though the technology was some way from being in place.

[3] See Chapter 10.

3.03 In this chapter we are principally concerned with the traditional definition of redundancy in the ERA 1996 for individual employment law purposes, whereas Chapter 11 deals with collective redundancies. But it is important to highlight the difference between the two definitions. The provisions in the TULR(C)A 1992 dealing with collective redundancies emanate from the EC Collective Redundancies Directive 75/129 (now Directive 98/59), which defines redundancy in terms now expressed in s 195(1) of the TULR(C)A 1992. This section, as presently drawn, was introduced by TURERA 1993, s 34(1) and (5) with effect from 30 August 1993.[4] Prior thereto, s195 (as it was) of TULR(C)A 1992 (which was carried forward from s 99 of the EPA 1975) adopted the traditional definition of redundancy in s 139(1) of the ERA 1996 for collective purposes also. But Directive 75/129 contained a wider definition for the purposes of consultation on mass redundancies, and the EC Commission pointed out this discrepancy to the UK Government. In response to this warning, s 195(1) of the TULR(C)A 1992 (as it had by then become) was amended by the TURERA 1993.[5] There was no obligation on the UK to widen the definition of redundancy for individual redundancy payment purposes because redundancy payments law is not based on Directive 75/129 (now Directive 98/59), nor any similar European obligation. As such, it can stand independently and, indeed, it was left alone.

3.04 In summary then, the narrower definition of redundancy, comprising two aspects, applies for the purposes of individual entitlement to redundancy payments; the wider definition under s 195(1) of the TULR(C)A 1992 applies for the purposes of collective redundancies consultation under that Act. Clearly, s 195(1) of the TULR(C)A 1992 includes instances of redundancy falling under s 139(1) and (2) of the ERA 1996, but it arguably goes wider, as explained in Chapter 11, including reorganisational dismissals not strictly falling under the traditional definition of redundancy.

B. The Presumption of Redundancy

3.05 Another point to bear in mind is that s 163(2) of the ERA 1996 provides that there is a presumption of redundancy. That is to say, an employee is presumed to have been dismissed by reason of redundancy unless the employer is able to prove the contrary.[6] In fact, notwithstanding the difference between the two redundancy definitions discussed above, this presumption also applies in the case of s 188 of the TULR(C)A 1992.[7]

3.06 For the purposes of individual employment law, the presumption applies to Pt XI of the ERA 1996, i.e. redundancy payments. So, if an employer alleges that a redundancy dismissal is fair for the purposes of unfair dismissal, in particular that he has a fair reason (redundancy) for dismissal, the presumption of redundancy does not apply; the employer has to prove the redundancy reason for dismissal and, if he cannot do so, the dismissal will be unfair (see s 98(1) of the ERA 1996, where the onus is firmly placed on the employer to prove the reason for dismissal for unfair dismissal purposes). This would be so even if the

---

[4] SI 1993/1908.
[5] In the end, the Commission proceeded to sue the UK for infraction of Directive 75/129, notwithstanding the fact that this complaint and a number of others had been addressed in the TURERA 1993. The outcome, in the EC's favour, is recorded in *Commission of the EC v the UK* [1994] IRLR 412.
[6] *Willcox v Hastings* [1987] IRLR 298.
[7] See also s 195(2) of that Act and Chapter 11 herein.

employee had benefited from the presumption of redundancy for the purposes of redundancy payments. This was confirmed by the EAT in *Shawkat v Nottingham City Hospital NHS Trust*.[8] Thus:

> We agree with the submission made on behalf of the Respondent that the section only applies to a question arising under Part XI of the Act [redundancy payments]; it follows that the presumption does not arise in respect of the claim for unfair dismissal under Part X of the Act [unfair dismissal] if that is treated as a discrete issue.[9]

Thus in *Midland Foot Comfort Centre Ltd v Moppett*,[10] Moppett claimed a redundancy **3.07** payment and unfair dismissal compensation. It was held that she was entitled to the benefit of the presumption of redundancy for her redundancy payments claim. However, that having been established (and a redundancy payment having been held due) the employer sought to use the finding in the context of proving a fair reason for dismissal for unfair dismissal purposes. It was nevertheless held that the presumption of redundancy did not apply for this purpose and the employer had to prove the reason for dismissal, in this case redundancy. On the facts he was unable to do so and Mrs Moppett therefore succeeded twice.

C. The Definition Analysed

(1) Closure of the business or movement of work location

It is critical here to determine for the purposes of whether a redundancy case arises on **3.08** movement of work location to ascertain where the employee was employed.[11]

There were for many years two conflicting interpretations. The first was that the employee **3.09** is employed at the place where he actually works, whether or not this coincides with the contractual place of work (which often, of course, it will). The second was that the employee is employed at the location where he works or could be required to work under his employment contract. These two views gave rise to the contest between the 'geographical' and 'contract' tests of employment. Often (and probably mostly) the contract test and the geographical test would produce the same result—in other words, where an employee is employed to work is where he both actually works and where he is employed to work under his employment contract. But this would not always be the case. An employee may, for example, actually work at location A but in theory may be contractually mobile to work at places B, C, D, and E,

---

[8] [1999] IRLR 340 (affd by the Court of Appeal in *Shawkat v Nottingham City Hospital NHS Trust (No. 2)* [2001] IRLR 555).

[9] [1999] IRLR 340 at para 8. It is to be noted that in *Church v West Lancashire NHS Trust* [1998] IRLR 4, the EAT (Morison J presiding) stated at para 21 that 'if a question of redundancy is referred to an employment tribunal then any dismissal is presumed to be by reason of redundancy unless and until the contrary is shown', suggesting that the presumption applies to all questions of dismissal referred to in an employment tribunal, whether in the context of redundancy payments or unfair dismissal. But with respect, this is not the case and the presumption clearly only applies to redundancy payment issues as confirmed by the EAT in *Shawkat*.

[10] [1973] IRLR 141.

[11] Of course, there may also be a fundamental issue as to whether there is a closure of the business, a subject relatively neglected in case law. See, however, *Whitbread Plc t/a Whitbread Berni Inns v Flattery* (EAT 287/94), where when a Berni Inn closed for refurbishment and opened one month later as a brasserie, it was held that the employers had not demonstrated that there was a permanent cessation of the business and therefore employees were not redundant (see *IDS Brief* 630, February 1999, p 13).

and so forth. In this latter set of circumstances, closure of the business at location A would not trigger a redundancy payment under the contract test. So the geographical test for redundancy payments law was more favourable to employees. The decision of the Court of Appeal in *High Table Ltd v Horst*[12] put an end to this interesting, if diverting, debate by proposing a more common sense and holistic test of where the employee is employed. But first, we track the history of the area and the development of the law as it is now in *High Table v Horst*.

3.10 Initially, the majority of case law tended to favour the contract test as opposed to the geographical test. In short, for the purposes of our present discussion, this meant that if there were a mobility clause in the employee's contract and the employer asked the employee to move within the scope of that term to do other work, there would not be a redundancy for the purposes of the ERA 1996. This was because the employer had not ceased work at the place where the employee was employed to work. Thus, in *United Kingdom Atomic Energy Authority v Claydon*,[13] Claydon was employed under a contract which required him to work at any of his employer's establishments in the UK. The employer closed the unit where he worked in Suffolk and asked him to transfer to Berkshire. He refused and was dismissed. It was held that the place where the employee was employed meant any place where he could be required to work under his contract, that is to say, any of the employer's establishments. And so no redundancy payment was due.

3.11 Similarly, in *Sutcliffe v Hawker Siddeley Aviation Ltd*,[14] Sutcliffe was employed under an employment contract which required him to be mobile anywhere in the UK. He was employed at RAF Marham but this unit was closed by his employer and he was asked to move to RAF Kinloss. He refused and was dismissed. He lost his claim for a redundancy payment because his place of work was, again, anywhere he could lawfully be required to work under his employment contract.

Mobility obligations: must they always be express or can they be implied?

3.12 In order to rely upon employee mobility to defeat a redundancy payment, the employer must show that the mobility obligation was part of the contract. If it is express, the position is relatively straightforward, subject perhaps only to construction of the clause or any question as to whether the clause was incorporated into the contract.

3.13 Thus, in *Anglia Regional Co-operative Society v O'Donnell*,[15] an employee was held to be unfairly dismissed by reason of redundancy for refusing to transfer to a new location on the ground that the mobility clause on which the employers tried to rely was not part of her contract of employment. Her employer had recently issued new terms and conditions which contained an extended mobility clause.

3.14 However, the employee did nothing to indicate acceptance of the new terms and conditions. When the employer attempted to rely upon the new mobility clause in order to require the employee to relocate from Beccles to Lowestoft, the employee refused and was dismissed. The EAT upheld the employment tribunal's decision that the dismissal was unfair. The employee's

---

[12] [1997] IRLR 513.
[13] [1974] ICR 128.
[14] [1973] ICR 560.
[15] EAT 655/91.

original contract contained a mobility clause which covered the Beccles area only and the employer was not entitled to rely upon this to move the employee as far as Lowestoft. However, the EAT did find that the offer of a transfer to Lowestoft had been an offer of suitable alternative employment which the employee had unreasonably refused.[16] (Hence the employer was under no obligation to make a statutory redundancy payment and the basic award for unfair dismissal was reduced to nil.)

The latest case in this area is *Aparau v Iceland Frozen Foods plc*,[17] where, on the facts, a mobility **3.15** clause imposed by the employer was not expressly part of the contract, even though an employee had worked on for 12 months after its unilateral imposition.[18]

Whether a term can be implied, in the absence of an express term, is a more difficult issue. **3.16** Largely this question depends upon the particular type of employment. If it is customary to be mobile across sites in a particular location, a term may be implied. But otherwise the courts will treat the possibility with caution.

In *Stevenson v Teeside Bridge and Engineering Ltd*[19] the employee was a steel erector working **3.17** at one particular site. Work finished at that site and the employee was asked to move to another site. He refused and was dismissed. It was held that it was customary for steel erectors to move from site to site without objection and therefore it was implied by custom and practice in the industry that he could be required to work at any site at the employer's request.

In *Courtaulds Northern Spinning Ltd v Sibson*[20] the employee was employed as a lorry driver **3.18** working out of one transport depot in Greengate, Lancashire. His contract contained no express mobility clause. At his depot all employees belonged to one trade union but the employee resigned from that union. In order to head off industrial action in protest by other employees, the employer stipulated that the employee must either re-join the union or transfer to another depot at Chadderton one mile away. The employee refused to either re-join or transfer and resigned, claiming constructive dismissal. Although the claim he submitted was for unfair dismissal, the issue in this case was whether there was a contractual right to transfer him to Chadderton which, of course, is relevant to our discussion. It was held that there was an implied term in the contract entitling the employer to transfer the employee to work at any place within reasonable daily reach of his home.

In *Jones v Associated Tunnelling Co Ltd*[21] Browne-Wilkinson J attempted to summarise the **3.19** position thus:

> The term to be implied must depend on the circumstances of each case. The authorities show that it may be relevant to consider the nature of the employer's business, whether or not the employee has in fact been moved during the employment, what the employee was told when he was employed and whether there is any provision made to cover the employee's expenses when working from daily reach of his home.

---

[16] See Chapter 4.
[17] [1996] IRLR 119.
[18] For other cases on express mobility see *Parry v Holst & Co Ltd* (1968) 3 ITR 317 and *Rank Xerox Ltd v Churchill* [1988] IRLR 280. Another dimension is the case of *Meade-Hill and National Union of Civil and Public Servants v British Council* [1995] IRLR 478, in which the Court of Appeal struck out a mobility clause on the ground that it indirectly discriminated against female employees.
[19] [1971] 1 All ER 296.
[20] [1988] ICR 451.
[21] [1981] IRLR 477.

3.20   In *O'Brien v Associated Fire Alarms Ltd*,[22] O'Brien was employed by a company which supplied and installed fire and burglar alarms in the UK. The country was divided into two areas each controlled from an area office. O'Brien worked in the North-Western area and lived in Liverpool, from which the North-Western area was controlled. He had always worked in and around Liverpool and parts of the North-West that were within commuting distance of Liverpool. He was then directed to work in Barrow-in-Furness, which is 120 miles from Liverpool. It was held that, while there was an implied term that employees would be mobile to places within daily travelling distance from their homes, Barrow-in-Furness was too far. Therefore, when dismissed, O'Brien was entitled to a redundancy payment. In *Aparau* (see above) it was held that there was no implied term to the effect that an employee could be transferred from branch to branch of a retail group. (Each case, of course, depends on its own facts.)

3.21   Conversely, in *Managers (Holborn) Ltd v Hohne*,[23] an office manageress working in High Holborn could legally be asked to move to Regent Street. It was held, therefore, that the employee, a commuter, could be required by implication to work anywhere in Central London.

3.22   In *Little v Charterhouse Magna Assurance Co Ltd*[24] a general manager employed under a contract based in Uxbridge was asked to move to Bletchley. It was held that it was possible to imply a UK-wide mobility obligation, having regard to the status of the individual in all the circumstances.[25]

The limits to the contract test

3.23   On the other hand, as a caveat to the operation of the contract test it was held that if an employer wants to rely upon a mobility clause he must do so at the time. An employer who does not invoke a mobility clause cannot say that its mere existence entitles him to claim, after he has closed down the workplace where employees were employed, that he might have required them to work elsewhere (even though he did not), so dis-entitling the employees from redundancy payments. In the EAT in *Curling v Securicor Ltd*, Knox J said:[26]

> The employer can invoke the mobility clause in the contract and require the employee to go to a new location or job, if the clause entitles him to do so whereupon no question of redundancy will arise. Alternatively, the employer can decide not to invoke the mobility clause and rely instead on alternative suitable offers of employment as a defence to claims for redundancy payment. In the former example the original employment continues, in the latter it ceases but is replaced in circumstances which unless the employee reasonably refuses the offer of suitable alternative employment, provide the employee with continuity of employment but relieve the employer of liability to make a redundancy payment. What the

---

[22]   (1968) 3 ITR 182.
[23]   [1977] IRLR 230.
[24]   [1980] IRLR 19.
[25]   Even if there is a mobility term in the contract, it may cause hardship if it is unreasonably applied by the employer. The EAT adapted the implied term to this possibility in *McAndrew v Prestwick Circuits Ltd* [1988] IRLR 514 by holding that, in that particular case, it was an implied term that the employee would not be transferred to another location except on reasonable notice. This was arguably taken a step further in *United Bank Ltd v Akhtar* [1989] IRLR 507, where the EAT also held that an express mobility clause could be overridden by the employer's implied obligation to maintain trust and respect. Another division of the EAT in *White v Reflecting Roadstuds Ltd* [1991] ICR 733 refused to accept a proposition that this meant that it was now implied that all express terms had to be exercised reasonably. But even so these cases support the view that an arbitrary or capricious exercise of a power such as in the case of a mobility clause may breach the implied term of trust and respect contained in every contract of employment. For unfair dismissal law generally, see Chapter 10.
[26]   [1992] IRLR 549.

employers cannot do is dodge between the two attitudes and hope to be able to adopt the most profitable at the end of the day.

However, for the avoidance of doubt, *Curling v Securicor Ltd* does not prevent an employer **3.24** from lawfully invoking a mobility clause to avoid a redundancy payment when a redundancy situation has arisen and where there is work to direct the employee to pursuant to the mobility clause. The Court of Appeal in *Home Office v Evans*[27] so held, reversing the EAT which had over-literally applied the prior decision of the EAT in *Curling*. In this case, the claimants were immigration officers employed at Waterloo International Terminal. Their employment contracts contained mobility clauses. In the Spring of 2004 the Home Office decided to close static immigration control at Waterloo and sought to rely upon the mobility obligations, common in civil service contracts. Consultations took place but the claimants refused to engage in these. In August 2004 the Home Office informed the claimants that they would, pursuant to the mobility clause, be transferred to Heathrow. They resigned, claiming unfair dismissal. The employment tribunal held that they had been constructively unfairly dismissed and purportedly relied upon the authority of *Curling v Securicor Ltd* to the effect that the Home Office was *not* entitled to invoke the mobility provisions to transfer the claimants from Waterloo to Heathrow. This was primarily because the employment tribunal considered that the Home Office had failed to apply its own stated procedures established by a Home Office notice (HON) incorporated in the staff handbook. This, in effect, was a redundancy procedure. The employees alleged that the employer had been in fundamental breach of the implied term of trust and confidence in refusing to follow the redundancy procedure.

The employment tribunal and the EAT accepted that there was no principle of law that if an **3.25** employer was closing down a business it was not entitled to invoke a mobility clause. However, in accordance with the *Curling* decision, there could be no 'dodging' between the two, mobility and redundancy. The employer with the mobility clause could not invoke it and in effect 'trump' a contract incorporating a redundancy procedure. The employer's position had been that the redundancy HON would apply until, following legal advice, it changed its position, deciding then that the mobility clause would apply instead. According to HH Judge McMullen QC in the EAT:

> That, in our judgment, represents the kind of dodging to be found unacceptable in *Curling* [the employer] invoked the mobility clause after changing its position and thus *Curling* applies.

The EAT held that the tribunal had been correct in holding that there was a breach of the **3.26** implied term of trust and confidence by the simple fact that the employer would not adhere to the redundancy HON and its motive was irrelevant in considering whether this was a fundamental breach of the implied term of trust and confidence.

However, the Court of Appeal overruled the EAT. *Curling* was clearly a case where the employer **3.27** was not entitled to rely upon the mobility obligations in the contract as it had already implemented the redundancy procedure, in which the employees had participated and the employer had not sought to rely upon the mobility obligations until the hearing, by which time the tribunal considered that it was too late to raise a new point.

---

[27] [2008] IRLR 59.

3.28 In the present case there was no question of the Home Office 'dodging' from one contractual procedure to another, having left it too late to invoke the mobility obligations or having waived its rights to invoke them. If the Home Office preferred to invoke a mobility clause in order to avoid redundancy dismissals it was entitled to make that choice. If it did it was unnecessary, on the facts, to follow its redundancy procedure and to apply the redundancy HON to the claimants.

3.29 In other words, an employer cannot rely upon the mere existence of a mobility clause to defeat a redundancy payment claim. But if it has a mobility clause in the contract and it has other work to direct the employee to under that mobility clause, it may rely upon the mobility clause to defeat the claim for a redundancy payment.

The movement away from the rigidity of the contract test

3.30 In *Bass Leisure Ltd v Thomas*[28] Mrs Thomas was employed by Bass as a collector, collecting takings from pub fruit machines. She had worked for Bass for more than 10 years in its Coventry depot, which was about 10 minutes' drive from her home and was especially convenient for her. Bass decided to close its Coventry depot and offered Mrs Thomas relocation in Erdington, some 20 miles west of Coventry. Mrs Thomas agreed to give the change a try but subsequently terminated her employment and sought a redundancy payment. Bass sought to defend Mrs Thomas's claim on the basis of a mobility clause which purported to give the company the right to transfer employees to an alternative place of work subject to certain conditions. Her dismissal arose because Bass had breached the mobility clause by not complying with the conditions contained within it and this entitled Mrs Thomas to claim constructive dismissal. Nevertheless, it was still necessary to consider the employer's power under the mobility clause to deploy her to another geographical location. The EAT, however, held that an employee's place of work for redundancy purposes is a question of fact taking into account an employee's fixed or variable place of work and any contractual terms that provide (simply) evidence of that place of work.

3.31 Therefore, the compromise solution suggested in *Bass Leisure* seemed to be, first, that the contract could be relevant as to where the place of work was, but only as part and parcel of the overall picture. Second, the issue of where the employee works was essentially a question of fact.

The death of the contract versus geographical test debate

3.32 The circle was squared in *High Table Ltd v Horst,*[29] where the facts were as follows. Three employees were employed as silver service waitresses by High Table Ltd, which was a company providing catering services for companies and firms in the City. They worked for one particular client, Hill Samuel, from 10.00am to 4.00pm on weekdays. However, the staff handbook, which was part of the employment terms, said

> . . . your place of work is as stated in your letter of appointment which acts as part of your terms and conditions. However, given the nature of our business, it is sometimes necessary to transfer staff on a temporary or permanent basis to another location. Whenever possible this will be within reasonable daily travelling distance of your existing place of work.

---

[28] [1994] IRLR 104.
[29] [1997] IRLR 513.

In 1993 Hill Samuel cut its catering budget and re-negotiated the services provided by High Table, which resulted in a need for fewer waitresses working longer hours. So the three employees were dismissed as redundant. Certain alternative work was offered to the employees but they rejected that work as unsuitable. They claimed unfair dismissal initially on the basis of unfair selection and insufficient attempt to redeploy them, but they then brought in at a later stage a further point that the dismissal was unfair because there was no valid reason for dismissal and they were not, technically, redundant. The EAT decided that it was relevant that there was a contractual mobility clause in the contract and remitted the case to the employment tribunal to consider this. Before the Court of Appeal, the main issue was whether there was a contractual or functional test to determine the place where the employee was employed.

The Court of Appeal held that these tests were not appropriate. The place where an **3.33** employee was employed for the purposes of the employer's business is to be determined by a consideration of the factual circumstances which obtained until the dismissal. More particularly, the idea that there is a contractual test so that if the contract contains a mobility clause 'the place where the employee was so employed' extends to every place where the employee might be required to work, could not be accepted. Even if an employee has worked in any one location under his contract of employment for the purposes of the employer's business:

> . . . it defies commonsense to widen the extent of the place where he was so employed merely because of the existence of a mobility clause. If the work of an employee for his employer has involved a change of location, as would be the case where the nature of the work required the employee to go from place to place, then the contract of employment may be helpful to determine the extent of the place where the employee was employed. It cannot be right however to let the contract be the sole determinant, regardless of where the employee actually worked. It would be unfortunate if the law were to encourage the inclusion of mobility clauses in contracts of employment to defeat genuine redundancy claims. The refusal by the employee to obey a lawful requirement under the contract to move may constitute a valid reason for dismissal but the issues of dismissal, redundancy and reasonableness in the actions of the employer should be kept distinct.

So in the present case, the place where the employees were employed was at the particular **3.34** client for whom they worked and there was a redundancy situation which caused their dismissals. They were therefore not unfairly dismissed.[30]

(2) Cessation or diminution in requirement for employees in the business

The second limb of s 139(1) of the ERA 1996 covers the case where there is a need to shed **3.35** labour because there is less work or because the work is rationalised and made more efficient so that there is a need for fewer employees to do the work or, finally, where the requirement for work of a particular kind itself disappears, i.e. where a job disappears entirely or where work done previously by one particular job-holder is required to be done in the future by an entirely different type of job-holder.

---

[30] This case was applied in *Morgan v Davies Bros (Pecander) Ltd* (EAT, 23 March 1999), when the EAT concluded that a mobility clause in the employees' contract of employment did not operate in the employer's favour because the employees had for many years worked in Trimsaran, Wales and not Carmarthen, to which the employer wished to transfer them.

3.36   Employees often dispute an employer's reliance on the reason of redundancy where the need by the employer for work to be done is undiminished but fewer employees are needed. How can an employee be redundant, the employee asks, if my work is still there? That is not the point. The question is whether requirement of the employer for employees to do work of a particular kind has ceased or diminished, as Burton J (P) stated in *Kingwell v Elizabeth Bradley Designs Ltd*:[31]

> . . . it appears to us that there is a fundamental misunderstanding about the question of redundancy. Redundancy does not only arise where there is a poor financial situation at the employers, although, as it happens, there was as such in this case. It does not only arise where there is a diminution of work in the hands of an employer, although, as happens, here again, there was in this case. It can occur where there is a successful employer with plenty of work, but, who perfectly sensibly as far as commerce and economics is concerned, decides to re-organise his business because he concludes he is over-staffed. Thus, even with the same amount of work and the same amount of income, the decision is taken that a lesser number of employees are required to perform the same functions. That too is a redundancy situation.

Downsizing and absorption of duties

3.37   One of the simpler forms of redundancy under this part of the definition is where fewer employees are needed to do the work in the business as a result of a reduced order book, technological change, or increased efficiency. Thus, in *Sutton v Revlon Overseas Corporation Ltd*,[32] the employer dismissed a chief accountant and re-allocated the work previously done by him amongst three of his colleagues. The work was still required to be done but fewer employees (three instead of four) were needed to do it. The dismissed employee was entitled to a redundancy payment.

3.38   In *Carry All Motors Ltd v Pennington*[33] both a transport clerk and a depot manager were employed at a transport depot. The company considered that the two posts could be merged and the work carried out by one employee alone. Accordingly, the transport clerk was dismissed. It was held that the transport clerk was entitled to a redundancy payment.

3.39   In *McCrea v Cullen and Davison Ltd*,[34] a company in which Mr McCrea was the general manager, was taken over. The new owner appointed himself managing director and the general manager was required to work alongside the managing director. After a while, the managing director found he could perform both the functions of the managing director and the general manager and accordingly dismissed the general manager. It was held that the general manager had been dismissed by reason of redundancy and was entitled to a redundancy payment.[35]

3.40   In the somewhat controversial EAT decision in *Frame It v Brown*,[36] it was held that a reduction of workers from four to three with re-allocation of the dismissed employee's work among the remaining three was not a redundancy. However, this must plainly be wrong.

---

[31] EAT/0661/02.
[32] [1973] IRLR 173.
[33] [1980] ICR 806.
[34] [1988] IRLR 130.
[35] See also *Millat Housing Association v Nijhar* (EAT, 11 February 1999) and *Governing Body of Thomas Mills High School v Rice* (EAT, 17 February 1998).
[36] EAT 177/193.

In *Polyflor Ltd v Old*[37] the claimant claimed unfair dismissal. He was senior project controller **3.41** above and independent of four regional sales managers. He was informed that he was redundant, his duties to be absorbed by those four regional managers. The employment tribunal decided that the dismissal was unfair, for the reason, *inter alia*, that the employer had not demonstrated the need for the reorganisation and had not provided an economic justification for the redundancy. Although the employment tribunal also found that the employer was liable for unfair dismissal on ground of procedural fairness, it also found that the employer had not made out redundancy as a potentially fair reason for dismissal. It was held by the EAT that the post of senior project controller had disappeared and that there was therefore no longer a requirement for an employee to do that particular kind of work: 'it is a classic redundancy dismissal. No economic justification was required of the respondent.'

Replacing direct labour with outside contractors: 'outsourcing'

It used to be the case that replacement of direct labour with self-employed workers or an **3.42** outside contractor firm would also mean that the direct labour, dismissed to make way for the indirect labour, would be dismissed by reason of redundancy. This is because there would be a cessation of the requirement for employees to do work of a particular kind.[38]

However, this is now subject to the provisions of the Transfer of Undertakings (Protection of **3.43** Employment) Regulations 2006 (TUPE). The question of whether there is a cessation or diminution in requirement of work of a particular kind to be done by employees whose jobs are outsourced now depends on TUPE. If TUPE applies to the outsourcing there will be no redundancy. This is because, if TUPE applies, the employment contracts transfer and there is no cessation in requirement for work to be done. The possibility of TUPE applying when work is outsourced is greatly enhanced by reg 3(1)(b) of the TUPE Regulations 2006, which provides that, as long as service activities cease to be provided by one employer and are taken up by another, there will be a transfer of an undertaking, provided that prior to the service provision change there was an organised grouping of employees, the purpose of which was to provide the services on behalf of the client. This is a broader definition of a TUPE transfer than applied under the TUPE Regulations 1981,[39] and most cases of outsourcing to an external

---

[37] EAT/0482/02.

[38] See *Lang v Briton Ferry Working Mens Club and Institute* [1967] 2 ITR 35.

[39] The law governing TUPE 1981 was, principally, *Ayse Süzen v Zehnacker Gebäudereinigung GmbH Krankenhausservice* [1997] IRLR 255, in which the European Court of Justice held that a mere replacement by a client of a contractor with a new contractor was not of itself a transfer of an undertaking for the purposes of the Directive. What was required was a transfer of significant tangible or intangible assets or, in lieu, a taking over by the new employer of a major part of the workforce in terms of numbers and skills. Regulation 3(1)(b) of TUPE 2006, triggering the provisions of TUPE on the change of service provider itself (subject to certain conditions) effectively reverses *Ayse Süzen* in the UK. *Ayse Süzen* is, of course, still good authority in terms of the Acquired Rights Directive itself and indeed binds most EU Member States' post-domestic legislation, which does not contain the wider definition of a TUPE transfer on a service provision change as is contained in reg 3(1)(b) of the TUPE Regulations 2006. For more detail on the provisions of the TUPE Regulations 2006, see J McMullen, *Business Transfers and Employee Rights* (looseleaf, LexisNexis Butterworths). See also, J McMullen, 'An Analysis of the Transfer of Undertakings (Protection of Employment) Regulations 2006' (2006) ILJ 113–139. Over the last few years case law has begun to emerge on reg 3(1)(b) of TUPE 2006 (see J McMullen, *Business Transfers and Employee Rights,* Chapter 5). This includes *Hunt v (1) Storm Communications Limited (2) Wild Card Public Relations Limted (3) Brown Brothers Wine (Europe) Limited* (EAT/2702456/06); *Kimberley Group Housing Limited v Hamberley and Others* [2008] IRLR 682; *Clearsprings Management Limited v Ankers* (EAT/0054/08); *Metropolitan Resources Limited v Churchill Dulwich (In Liquidation)* [2009] IRLR 700; *OCS Group UK Limited v Jones* (EAT/0038/09); and *Ward Hadaway Solicitors v Love* (EAT/0471/09).

contractor will now attract TUPE protection for employees, thus negating the redundancy that would otherwise apply.

Reduced hours

3.44 Sometimes an employer reacts to a reduced order book not by dismissing employees but by reducing hours. That might result in a constructive dismissal, which would lead to a redundancy payment as there has been a diminution in the requirement of work of a particular kind to be done by employees. Thus, in *Hanson v Wood (Abington Processing Gravers)*,[40] the employing company suffered a temporary recession but instead of laying off or expressly dismissing individual workers, the employer decided to reduce the hours of all of the workers. It was held that this might amount to a constructive dismissal, which would be by reason of a redundancy for the reasons stated above. In *Temple Grove School v Gorst*[41] it was seemingly accepted by the EAT that where work in a department had diminished but there was still half a post left, a redundancy situation still applied as there was, overall, a diminution in the requirement of the employer for work of a particular kind to be performed by the employee.

3.45 A case which bucks this trend is *Aylward v Glamorgan Holiday Home Ltd t/a Glamorgan Holiday Hotel*.[42] In this case, in order to save costs, the employer, which provided respite and holidays for the elderly, disabled, and disadvantaged in a hotel in South Wales decided to close the hotel during January and February on an accountant's advice, the business showing profit in the 10 months from March to December but losses in January and February. The net effect of the proposals to employees was to change the existing terms and conditions from 52 to 42 weeks paid work per annum, reducing paid sick leave entitlement and other changes. Twenty of the twenty-nine members of staff accepted the new contract but nine objected and issued employment tribunal proceedings. On the question of whether the employees objecting to the change were entitled to a redundancy payment following the termination of their old contracts, the EAT upheld the employment tribunal's decision to the effect that the requirement for employees at the hotel had not altered. The number working there was to be the same before and after the reorganisation. What had occurred was a business reorganisation which involved a change in the terms and conditions of employment of the employees and in particular the number of days that were to be worked by the same number of employees. With respect it is questionable whether this decision is correct. It is inconsistent with *Hanson* (see above). The better view, we submit, is that termination of employment on ground of reduced demand *should* satisfy the statutory definition.[43]

3.46 See also the relationship with short-time working and the particular statutory regime in that regard discussed in Chapter 6.

Reduction in requirements of the business for work of a particular kind

3.47 It has been argued that if an employer has dismissed employees because he can no longer afford to keep them, but really the business would, but for financial constraints, have accommodated them, the redundancy definition is not satisfied.

---

[40] [1986] 3 ITR 46.
[41] EAT, 15 October 1998.
[42] EAT/167/02.
[43] See the criticism by *Harvey on Industrial Relations and Employment Law,* Division E, paras 803–816.

Thus in *Delanair Ltd v Mead*,[44] Delanair, a manufacturer of heaters for the car industry, depended heavily on a contract with Ford. Ford reduced its order book with Delanair considerably, and as a result Mr Mead was made redundant. His work was absorbed by other existing members of staff, but they needed to do overtime to cover the additional duties allocated to them which had previously been performed by Mr Mead. The employer argued that there was no redundancy because there was no diminution in the output of the department. The employment tribunal agreed. However, the EAT disagreed and stated that the wrong test had been applied: the statute required attention to be paid to the requirements of the business for employees to do the work rather than to whether there is an overall diminution in work. The dismissal was, therefore, by reason of redundancy. **3.48**

In *Association of University Teachers v University of Newcastle upon Tyne*,[45] because of a failure of outside funding the university was obliged to discontinue a course for which there was still student demand. The lecturer was consequently dismissed and his union claimed the employer had not consulted with it as required by what is now s 188 of the TULR(C)A 1992. The case, therefore, turned on the definition of redundancy in s 188, at that time the same as the ERA 1996 definition.[46] It was argued that there was no redundancy dismissal because the overall need for the course had not ceased or diminished. The university simply could no longer afford to run the course. It was held that, although, in an ideal world, the services of the lecturer would be required, in practical terms the university had made a decision to shed labour and to discontinue the course. Fewer employees were therefore required by the employer. The correct approach was to focus on the cause of the dismissal and not the cause of the redundancy which gave rise to it. Therefore, as the services of the lecturer were not required, his dismissal was by reason of redundancy. **3.49**

In *Halfords v Roache*[47] the employer dismissed a telephonist as part of a cost-efficiency exercise. Her work was absorbed by and distributed among other employees. Despite the fact that the dismissal arose out of economic grounds, it was by reason of redundancy. There had been an appraisal of staffing requirements and the decision made was that that particular employee was surplus and that the work could be re-distributed. There was a diminution in the requirement for employees to do work of a particular kind, and thus a redundancy. **3.50**

Of course, not all economic dismissals will be by reason of redundancy. There has to be a cessation or diminution in the requirement for employees to do the work. The case of *Chapman v Goonvean and Rostowrack China Clay Company Ltd*,[48] discussed below in the context of reorganisation, is an example where the definition of redundancy was not satisfied. **3.51**

Entire change in job function

A redundancy can also occur where the employee's job changes so much through a reorganisation or re-definition of the job that it emerges as an entirely new job. The old job, being work of a particular kind, has disappeared and the employer's requirement for employees to do it has ceased. Whether the reorganisation or re-definition is significant enough for this to happen is a question of fact and degree in each case. **3.52**

---

44 [1976] ICR 522.
45 [1987] ICR 317.
46 But now see TULRCA 1992, s 195.
47 *IDS Brief* 396, 1 May 1989, p 2.
48 [1973] 2 All ER 1063.

3.53 In *Robinson v British Island Airways Ltd*[49] the posts of flight operations manager and a general manager (operations and traffic) were both discontinued at the insistence of the employer and a post of operations manager was created. Robinson, who failed to get the job of operations manager, was redundant, as the new job was very different from his old job.

3.54 In *Murphy v Epsom College*,[50] a plumber was dismissed and replaced by a heating technician. It was held that the plumber had been dismissed by reason of redundancy because the new job was substantially different from the old job.

3.55 In *Hall v Farrington Data Processing Ltd*,[51] the job of a salesman with managerial functions was sufficiently different from that of a salesman without managerial functions so as to cause a redundancy when the requirement for a mere salesman ceased.

3.56 In *Denton v Neepsend Ltd*,[52] an employee worked on a cold saw. His employers wanted to introduce an abrasive cutting machine. It was held that the job of using the new machine required different skills and techniques and was more demanding. A redundancy therefore arose when the job was changed.

3.57 A general test has been coined in *Amos v Max-Arc Ltd*,[53] where the National Industrial Relations Court said 'Work of a particular kind means work which is distinguished from other work of the same general kind by requiring special aptitudes, skills or knowledge.'

3.58 In *Loy v Abbey National Financial and Investment Services Plc*[54] the Court of Session, Outer House, confirmed that the definition of redundancy is not satisfied simply because there are changes imposed by the employer in the way the work is to be done. After a takeover the claimant suffered changes in the way that his job, as manager, was to be performed. In particular, he lost exclusive control of allocating particular sales managers to the individual national accounts which he controlled and he no longer had control over the training and education budget allocated to those accounts. It was accepted that these changes were significant and were uncongenial to him. However, the changes, according to the Court, had no real bearing on the nature of the job itself. The work which he was expected to do had not ceased or diminished; it was simply required to be done in different ways. Whilst a serious change in working conditions or how the work is to be done may or may not be a repudiatory breach of contract entitling an individual to resign and claim constructive dismissal, it did not follow, as a result, that a redundancy payment was due or the definition of redundancy under s 139(1) of the Employment Rights Act 1996 was satisfied. Thus:

> . . . redundancy in these circumstances does not automatically follow simply because of changes in a way a job is done. The statutory definition of redundancy . . . envisages that redundancy can only arise when the requirements of the employer's business for employees to carry out work of a particular kind have diminished or ceased. In the present case, there was no suggestion that the work which the pursuer was expected to do in the merged company had in any way ceased or diminished; all that was proposed, at best, for the pursuer, was that the work would be done in a different way.[55]

---

[49] [1978] ICR 304.
[50] [1985] ICR 80.
[51] [1969] 4 ITR 230.
[52] [1976] IRLR 164.
[53] [1973] ICR 46.
[54] [2005] CSOH 47.
[55] The Court relied on a dictum by Lord Clyde in *Murray v Foyle Meats Ltd* at p 59 H 260 A.

Change of attributes or qualifications for a job function

3.59 If the reason for the dismissal, generally, was that the employer required different personal attributes or qualifications from an employee but the work required from employees was basically the same, no redundancy payment will be due and no redundancy reason will apply in an unfair dismissal case.

3.60 In *Vaux & Associated Breweries Ltd v Ward (No. 2)* [56] Mrs Ward, who was aged 57, was dismissed from her post as a barmaid when her employers wished to turn the pub in which she worked into a modern road-house with a younger and 'more glamorous' barmaid. It was held that there was still work of a particular kind required to be done (i.e. that of a barmaid) and, therefore, Mrs Ward was not entitled to a redundancy payment. (This may seem harsh in modern times; but she would now claim unfair dismissal and, of course, the employer would have failed in his defence of an unfair dismissal claim, not being able to establish a redundancy reason for dismissal.)

3.61 In *Pillinger v Manchester Area Health Authority*,[57] the employee, Pillinger, was a research officer paid on grade II. He was then promoted to grade IIS. The employer decided that the work only justified it being done by a grade II officer. It was held that, as the work required was just the same after as before the dismissal, there was no redundancy upon the decision to dismiss the grade IIS employee and replace him with a grade II employee.

3.62 The point seems to have been stretched in *British Broadcasting Corporation v Farnworth*,[58] where Farnworth was a radio producer on a fixed-term contract which was not renewed. Her contract expired on 21 October 1996. Meanwhile, in July 1996, the British Broadcasting Corporation (BBC) advertised for a more experienced radio producer to work on a programme on which Farnworth had been working. It was held by the EAT that the definition of redundancy was satisfied in that the business needed fewer of a particular kind of employee and therefore the dismissal that arose by virtue of the non-renewal of the applicant's contract was by reason of redundancy. This sits uneasily with *Pillinger*. However, the EAT was heavily influenced by the employment tribunal's finding of fact with which it was unwilling to interfere in that:

> We decide that there are different levels of producer depending on experience and ability, in the same way that there are different levels of teachers, and that the BBC needed a varied range. When [the new producer] was appointed, clearly the BBC's needs for as many producers at the applicant's level had diminished or was likely to diminish.

Reorganisation not necessarily giving rise to a redundancy

3.63 The mere fact that there is a business reorganisation does not mean the statutory definition of redundancy is satisfied. As Burton J (P) stated in *Kingwell v Elizabeth Bradley Designs Ltd*,[59]

> . . . it is not an automatic consequence of there being a business re-organisation that there is a redundancy; nor is there a need for a business reorganisation where there should be a redundancy situation. The two are entirely self-standing concepts. If a business reorganisation leads to a diminution in the requirement for employees carrying out the relevant work, then that business reorganisation leads to a redundancy situation and if not, not.

---

[56] [1970] 5 ITR 62.
[57] [1979] IRLR 430.
[58] [1998] ICR 116.
[59] EAT/0661/02.

3.64   In *Chapman v Goonvean and Rostowrack China Clay Company Limited*[60] the arrangements made by the employer included the provision of transport to and from work. Ten workers were involved and eventually three were made redundant. The employer then decided that it was no longer economic to provide transport for the seven remaining employees and so the employer ceased the provision of free transport. This was a serious breach of contract and, therefore, a constructive dismissal but it was held that this was not by reason of redundancy. The requirements of the business for employees had not diminished beyond the need to reduce the workforce by three and, notwithstanding the withdrawal of free transport, the seven remaining members were still employed to do the work they were previously employed to do.

3.65   In *Johnson v Nottinghamshire Combined Police Authority*[61] the employer decided to alter the time of day at which the work was to be performed. The two employees concerned worked five days a week, 9.30am to 5.00pm or 5.30pm. The employer decided to change the hours of work to two shifts of 8.00am to 3.00pm and 1.00pm to 8.00pm, six days a week on alternate weeks, but the work that the employees were doing remained exactly the same after the change as it was before. It was held that there was no redundancy entitlement, and that work of a particular kind refers to the work that is being done, so that a mere alteration of the time and day at which it is done does not necessarily result in a redundancy payment.

3.66   Similarly, in *Lesney Products & Co Ltd v Nolan*[62] the employer decided to reorganise the day shift by splitting up one single day shift into two. The existing hours were Monday to Thursday 8.00am to 5.00pm and Friday 8.00am to 2.30pm. After the change, the employees were required to work 7.30am to 3.30pm or 2.00pm to 10.00pm Monday to Friday. Those who refused to go along with the change were dismissed, but it was held that they were not entitled to redundancy payments. There was no diminution in the requirement of work of a particular kind to be done, but simply an alteration of the times of day at which the work was to be done.

3.67   The *Johnson* line of authority was applied in *Barnes v Gilmartin Associates*,[63] in which it was held that a secretary, who worked part-time and who was dismissed to make way for a new, full-time secretary, was not redundant on the basis that there was no diminution of a requirement for employees to carry out work of a particular kind.

3.68   Conversely, however, where an employer decided to employ four full-time workers instead of 10 part-time workers in order to achieve the same output with fewer employees, there was a reduction in the number of employees required by the business in accordance with the statutory definition.[64] Thus:

> The simple approach is synthesised by the [employment tribunal's] own statement that four employees now carried out the same work instead of ten . . . It is quite apparent that, for good economic and commercial reasons, the employer reorganised the work so that the same (in fact, diminishing, but that does not matter) work was now to be carried out by four employees instead of ten, and consequently the six employees were dismissed, because the requirements

---

[60] [1973] All ER 1063. Noted by PP Craig (1974) ILJ 108–109.
[61] [1974] 1 All ER 1082; noted by P Elias (1974) ILJ 163–164. Applied in *Barnes v Gilmartin Associates* (EAT, 29 July 1998).
[62] [1974] 1 All ER 1082.
[63] EAT 825/97.
[64] *Kingwell v Elizabeth Bradley Designs Ltd* (EAT/661/02).

of the business for employees to carry out work of a particular kind, namely knitting work, in the place where the employee was employed by the employer, had diminished. As Lord Denning [in *Johnson v Nottinghamshire Combined Policy Authority* [1974] ICR 170] pointed out, that could have diminished simply by virtue of a laudable desire to reorganise in an overstaffing situation. It could have resulted, as it did here, in circumstances of financial stringency. But however, it resulted in the diminution of the employer's requirement for employees, to the tune of six employees. Those six employees are, in our judgment, plainly entitled to redundancy payments.

In *Shawkat v Nottingham City Hospital NHS Trust (No. 2)*[65] Dr Shawkat was employed by the hospital in a staff grade thoracic surgery post. The Trust sought to merge the thoracic and cardiac departments in the hospital. This involved reorganisation of the work of thoracic surgeons by cutting down their thoracic work and requiring them also to carry out cardiac work. Dr Shawkat did not wish to do cardiac work as he felt he would be unable to do this as well as he did thoracic work. He was dismissed following his rejection of proposed changes to his employment contract under which his theatre and clinical sessions in thoracic surgery would be reduced and he would thereafter be obliged to do cardiac as well as thoracic work. He claimed that he had been dismissed by reason of redundancy. The employment tribunal held that redundancy did not apply as there was no diminution in the requirement of the employer for employees to carry out work of a particular kind.[66] The EAT allowed his appeal against the decision that he was not redundant and remitted the case to the employment tribunal to make further findings. On remission the employment tribunal reiterated its finding that there was no diminution in the requirement of the employer for employees to do work of a particular kind, namely thoracic surgery. There was no reduction in the amount of thoracic surgery that needed to be performed. The reason that his thoracic surgeries were reduced was because they wanted him to do cardiac work part of the time. The EAT dismissed Dr Shawkat's second appeal. He appealed to the Court of Appeal. The Court of Appeal concluded that the employment tribunal and the EAT were correct and there was no diminution of the employer's requirements for employees to carry out work of a particular kind. Thus: **3.69**

> . . . the mere fact of reorganisation is not conclusive of redundancy . . . . In the present case the employment tribunal did, in its first decision, decide that the reorganisation of the cardiac and thoracic departments changed the work that its employees in the thoracic department were required to carry out. It was for that reason that the tribunal decided that Dr Shawkat had been *unfairly dismissed* in the course of the Trust seeking to implement that change. But it cannot follow of itself that Dr Shawkat was dismissed by reason of redundancy, because the tribunal had to go on to decide . . . whether that 'change has had any, and if so what, effect on the employer's requirement for employees to carry out a particular kind of work'. The tribunal has found that, despite the change that did occur, the employer's requirement for employees to carry out thoracic surgery had not ceased or diminished and that is a conclusion which was open to them on the facts and must be the end of the matter.

It is important to note that it was found, as a fact, that the Trust had reorganised its staff to do more cardiac surgery than before. However, the requirements for thoracic surgery still existed, undiminished.[67] **3.70**

---

[65] [2001] IRLR 555.

[66] His complaint of unfair dismissal succeeded on other grounds.

[67] The outcome of the decision (no redundancy) may be contrasted with the outcome in *Murphy v Epsom College* [1985] ICR 80 (discussed above) (redundancy). This is because the facts in the cases were different, as explained by Cox J in *Corus & Regal Hotels Plc v Wilkinson* (EAT/0102/03) (see below). See also *Shrewsbury v*

3.71 In *Handford v Nationwide Building Society*[68] Handford was employed by Nationwide as a human resources (HR) manager. He was employed under a generic job description he shared with three colleagues. Handford himself was responsible for Nationwide's HR strategy and planning. In June 1996 it was decided that the HR department should be restructured and only three HR managers retained. The roles were allocated to Handford's colleagues and Handford was offered the job as a manager responsible for manpower and planning. This was at the same pay and grade as his previous job. He alleged that the job was significantly different from his former role but agreed to take the job on a three-month trial. He then found alternative employment with a new employer and brought proceedings against Nationwide for a redundancy payment. He claimed he had been made redundant by Nationwide as the result of the reorganisation had been to undermine his position, causing him to lose status and that his new post involved merely mechanistic tasks. Nationwide said that he had been given an important strategic role falling within his generic job description and denied redundancy. It was held that no redundancy arose. Handford was given a job within his current job description at an equivalent grade and at the same level of remuneration. It was an important strategic role. There was no redundancy on the facts.

3.72 In *Martland v Co-operative Insurance Society Limited*,[69] the duties of financial advisers employed by the Co-operative Group, which included changes in the method of performance and the reduction of regular links with clients, did not justify a conclusion that there was a different kind of job being performed which was still, notwithstanding the change, essentially selling insurance products to members of the general public.

3.73 The EAT coined a general test in *Camps Mount Farm Estate v Kozyra*,[70] that 'In truth a reorganisation may or may not end in redundancy; it all depends on the nature and the effect of the reorganisation.'

3.74 In *Corus & Regal Hotels Plc v Wilkinson*[71] the EAT confirmed that 'the question whether, following a business restructuring or re-organisation, a redundancy situation exists is a matter of fact for the employment tribunal to decide applying the test set out in s 139 (1) (b) of the 1996 Act . . .'.

3.75 According to Elias J (as he then was) in *Martland v Co-operative Insurance Society Ltd*,[72] 'this is classically an area for the tribunal to determine'.

The employee recruited in anticipation of a diminishing need

3.76 If the diminution in requirement for an employee to do work of a particular kind was always anticipated, even at the outset, will the employee, when eventually dismissed, be able to claim a redundancy payment? A curious theory based on this question was adopted by the EAT in *Lee v Nottinghamshire County Council*.[73] In this case, an employee was invited to become a lecturer at

---

Telford Hospitals NHS Trust v Lairik Yengbam (EAT/0499/08), where the EAT held that an employment tribunal had erred in characterising the non-renewal of a locum consultant appointment on appointment of a permanent consultant as redundancy since it was willing to regard the locum post as distinct and different from the substantive posts.

[68] [2000] All ER(D) 2018.
[69] EAT/0200/07.
[70] EAT 499/85. See also *Robinson v British Island Airways Ltd* [1977] IRLR 477, para 13, *per* Phillips J.
[71] EAT/0102/03.
[72] EAT/0220/07.
[73] [1980] IRLR 284.

a teacher training college and it was understood that it was a temporary job for one or two years at the most. The reason why it was temporary was because the fall in birth rate meant a reduced demand for teachers and hence those who were employed to teach them. Upon the termination of the employee's contract, the employment tribunal awarded a redundancy payment. The EAT reversed the employment tribunal's decision holding that, as the cessation or diminution had already been anticipated prior to the commencement of the employment, the Act did not apply. However, the Court of Appeal reversed the EAT's decision, holding that the legislation must be given its plain meaning; as a matter of fact, during the course of the employee's employment there had been a cessation or diminution of a requirement of work of a particular kind to be performed and, therefore, a redundancy payment was due.[74]

D. The Contract Test Versus the Job Function Test

Much the same as in the case of the discussion about mobility clauses, a tension arose in the test of whether there is any longer a requirement for work of a particular kind. The question was, is the work that is required defined by what is required under the contract (the contract test) or by what the employee is actually doing (the job function test)? **3.77**

As with the discussion on mobility clauses there were two schools of thought. The job function test said that you were not to look at the contract but instead you should look at what job the employee was actually performing, see whether that function had disappeared and if so, he would be entitled to a redundancy payment. The other (contract) test school said that if under the terms of the contract of employment the employee might be required to perform jobs other than the one which has disappeared then he would not genuinely be redundant and therefore should not be entitled to a redundancy payment. Of course, in many situations the job function test did not produce a different result from the contract test because the employee might be both employed to do one specific thing and might actually be performing that job and nothing else. If so, when the job function disappeared so did the job as defined by the employee's contract, and a redundancy payment was due whichever test applied. However, a different result might be possible where the employee's employment contract contained a very wide job description listing other tasks to be performed if required and if it went beyond the specific job that was being undertaken at present. Here, if the job function test were applied, the redundancy payment would be due. But if the contract test were applied it would not. **3.78**

The point arose first not in a redundancy claim proper but from some unfair dismissal cases in which the employee sought to dispute that there had been a valid reason for dismissal under the heading of redundancy under s 98(2) of the ERA 1996. **3.79**

In *Nelson v BBC (No. 1)*[75] Nelson was employed as a producer in the BBC Caribbean Service. Under his contract he was required to be mobile and move to any department at the request of the BBC. Ultimately the Caribbean Service was closed down and the BBC offered Nelson alternative work. He refused to accept this and was dismissed, claiming unfair dismissal. **3.80**

---

[74] See also *Pfaffinger v City of Liverpool Community College* [1996] IRLR 508.
[75] [1977] ICR 649.

The BBC sought to resist the claim for unfair dismissal on the basis that there was a redundancy because he was employed only in the Caribbean Service and therefore when this closed down it was a genuine redundancy and therefore a fair dismissal for that reason. The Court of Appeal held that, as under the contract Nelson was obliged to work elsewhere outside the Caribbean Service at the request of the employer, the dismissal was not by reason of redundancy. So, it was unfair as the employer had no alternative permitted reason apart from redundancy. (In hindsight, of course, the employer should have pleaded some other substantial reason under s 98(1)(b) of the ERA 1996.)

3.81   The case came before the Court of Appeal a second time in *Nelson v BBC (No. 2)*[76] on the issue of compensation for unfair dismissal. As such, the basic point here was not discussed in detail but the Court did not disapprove of the analysis in *Nelson (No. 1)*.

3.82   In *Haden v Cowen Ltd*,[77] Mr Cowen was employed as a regional surveyor. After a heart attack he was made a divisional contracts surveyor with a view to making his life easier. Under his contract he also had to undertake other duties if required which reasonably fell within his capabilities. Later the company found that it could do without a divisional contracts surveyor and he was therefore dismissed. The company defended the claim on the basis that there was a genuine redundancy and therefore the dismissal was fair. The EAT felt obliged to follow what it saw as the contract test applied in the *Nelson* case and held that Mr Cowen was not redundant because there was other work available under the terms of his contract as divisional contracts surveyor. In the Court of Appeal it was held that, on the facts of the case, the position of divisional contracts surveyor was a special one and could be differentiated from the post of any other surveyor and therefore when the need for a divisional contracts surveyor ceased, Mr Cowen was redundant. In this particular case, the clause in his contract requiring him to do other work falling within his capabilities had to be construed in a way which meant that he was required to do other work within his capabilities as a divisional contracts surveyor. The work of any other surveyor was outside the clause. There was on this finding no other work he could be required to do under his contract when the post of divisional contracts surveyor was dispensed with.

3.83   *Obiter*, the Court of Appeal stated that, nonetheless, the ratio of *Nelson v BBC (No. 1)* was that the test of redundancy was whether there had been a cessation of diminution of the requirement under the contract for employees to perform the kind of work that Nelson was employed to do. In other words, the contract test was supported.

3.84   But the debate between the contract test on the one hand, and the job function test, on the other continued to rage.[78]

3.85   As has been stated, the difference between the job function test and the contract test was immaterial when the job function performed by the employee was the same as the job description in the employment contract. Where, however, the contract of employment contained an extremely wide job description, theoretically embracing duties other than those actually performed by the employee, the result of the contract test was to deny an employee a redundancy payment. That was notwithstanding that the contract test was to the

---

[76] [1980] ICR 110.
[77] [1983] ICR 1. Noted by H Collins (1982) ILJ 225–257.
[78] See also *Pink v White and White and Co (Earls Bartion) Ltd* [1985] IRLR 489 and *Horton v Farnell Electronic Services Ltd* (EAT 755/95).

advantage of the employee in unfair dismissal cases like *Nelson* because, if there were no redundancy and the employer provided no other reason for dismissal, the dismissal was unfair.

The turning of the tide

In *Johnson v Peabody Trust*[79] the EAT urged, instead, an holistic approach to be taken whilst at the same time acknowledging that the contract test was the orthodox one to be applied. Johnson began employment with a housing association as a labourer. In 1985 he was promoted to the skilled position of roofer. In 1988, because of a reduction in the amount of day-to-day repair work needed by the association, a flexibility clause was introduced into the employee's contract. So, although under his contract, Johnson was still employed and paid as a roofer, he was in theory required as a tradesperson to carry out multi-trade operations where possible. If there was no roofing work for him to do he carried out other work, predominantly plastering. In 1993 nine redundancies were proposed, including a roofer, and Johnson was selected as the one roofer to be dismissed. At that time, a downturn in roofing work had meant that he had recently been carrying out multi-trade operations for more of his time than he was actually doing roofing work. He claimed unfair dismissal but the employment tribunal found that he had been fairly dismissed by reason of redundancy. He was employed as a roofer and the employer's occasional requirements to carry out roofing work had diminished. **3.86**

On appeal, Mr Johnson relied upon the contract test to say that he was not actually redundant and therefore there was no fair reason for his dismissal. This would be another example, as in the case of *Haden v Cowen* of the contract test being to the employee's advantage in an unfair dismissal case (although if he had been arguing for a redundancy payment it would clearly have been to his disadvantage). The EAT upheld the employment tribunal and found that Johnson had been employed as a roofer notwithstanding the flexibility clause in his contract which required him to carry out multi-trade operations when necessary. Therefore he had been dismissed by reason of redundancy. The EAT said that where an employee is employed to perform a particular, well-recognised and well-defined category of skilled trade it is that basic contractual obligation that has to be looked at when deciding whether the employer's requirements for employees to carry out work of a particular kind have ceased or diminished. This is rather than looking at any work which the employee could be required to carry out in accordance with a contractual flexibility clause. Clearly, the contract test is the right one to apply, it said, but it should not be applied in an over-technical or legalistic way; rather, it should be looked at in a commonsense way in order to ascertain the basic task which the employee was contracted to perform. Mindful of the arguments affecting employers in this area, the EAT said: **3.87**

> Were it otherwise an employer could in practice never establish that any skilled tradesman employed as such who had accepted a flexibility clause of the kind in this case had become redundant without establishing that a redundancy situation existed in every other trade encompassed within the ambit of such a flexibility clause. In our judgment so to construe [s 139(1)(b) of the 1996 Act] would be to subject the wording to an artificial and overly legalistic construction that would impose an unreasonable burden on employers.

Disappearing job—the end of the contract and job function tests

The law on the definition of redundancy on a disappearing job was revised, root and branch, by the EAT (Judge Peter Clark presiding) in *Safeway Stores Plc v Burrell*.[80] Here, Burrell was **3.88**

---

[79] [1996] IRLR 387.
[80] [1997] IRLR 200.

employed as a petrol station manager at a filling station located at one of the Safeway super-markets. It was decided that the management structure at store level needed de-layering and a reorganisation took place. Under the new structure, the post of petrol station manager disappeared and a new post of petrol filling station controller was created. The job description for the new post differed to some extent from Mr Burrell's job description as petrol station manager. Each former manager had to be assessed for suitability for the new role and the process was competitive as overall there were going to be fewer management positions than before and, hence, possible redundancies. Burrell decided not to apply for the new job because it paid him £2,000 per annum less. He received a redundancy payment and a payment in lieu of notice but he subsequently claimed unfair dismissal, claiming that the new position was exactly the same as his old job and therefore he was not technically redundant. The employers resisted the claim on the basis that there was a genuine redundancy.

3.89 The majority of the employment tribunal said that the employer had not established redundancy and therefore the dismissal was unfair. Although his job description as manager contained some responsibilities not contained in the controller's job, in practice he was not called upon to exercise them and so in effect he was doing the job of a petrol station controller before the reorganisation. They therefore applied the job function test and decided that the job had not in effect disappeared. The Chairman, however, in the minority, decided in favour of the employer, using the contract test. He concluded that the additional responsibilities in the manager's post were responsibilities that the employer could have called upon the applicant to have exercised quite lawfully; he was not fully doing the work he was employed to do or could be called on to do and therefore the job that he was employed to do as manager on this basis no longer existed.

3.90 On appeal the EAT held that the majority had erred in holding that the function test applied. But it also said that the Chairman had erred in applying the contract test. The correct approach for determining what is a dismissal by reason of redundancy involves a three-stage process:

(1) Was the employee dismissed? If so,
(2) Had the requirements of the employer's business for employees to carry out work of a particular kind ceased or diminished or were they expected to cease or diminish? If so,
(3) Was the dismissal of the employee caused wholly or mainly by that state of affairs?

3.91 In determining at stage two whether there was a genuine redundancy situation, the only question to be asked is, was there a diminution/cessation in the employer's requirements for employees (not necessarily the claimant) to carry out work of a particular kind? The terms of the claimant's contract of employment are irrelevant to that question.

> It is impermissible for the employment tribunal to re-write the words of the statute to import a further stage, that there must be a diminishing need for employees to do the kind of work for which the applicant was employed.

3.92 At stage three, in determining whether the dismissal was attributable wholly or mainly to the redundancy, the tribunal is concerned with causation; thus, even if a redundancy situation arises, if that does not cause the dismissal, the employee has not been dismissed by reason of redundancy.

3.93 The contract versus the job function test debate was based on a misreading of the statute and the decisions in *Nelson* and *Cowen*. According to the EAT, *Nelson* is authority for no more than the proposition that where a redundancy situation arises and a potentially redundant employee is directed to transfer to other work within the scope of his contract of employment, if he refuses that transfer and is then dismissed the reason for dismissal is not redundancy. Save for the limited circumstances arising from *Nelson*, an employee's terms and conditions of employment are irrelevant to the questions raised by the statute.

E. Bumped Redundancies

The analysis of Judge Peter Clark also allowed survival of the principle of bumped redundancies. **3.94**

Bumping occurs as follows. An employee may be redundant but perhaps because of his long **3.95** service it may be thought desirable to retain his services and give him another employee's job. The employee whose job is given to the redundant employee may have to be dismissed to make way.

Whether it is appropriate from an industrial relations point of view and for unfair dismissal **3.96** purposes for an employer to consider bumping another employee out of his or her job (which that employee may have been performing perfectly satisfactorily to date) is a question of fact in each case. In considering the position as far as the employer's duty under unfair dismissal law to act reasonably, the EAT in *Burne v Arvin Meritor LVS (UK) Ltd*[81] stated that the obligation on an employer to act reasonably is not one which imposes absolute obligations, and certainly imposes no absolute obligation to 'bump', or even consider 'bumping'. The issue is, what a reasonable employer would do in the circumstances, in particular, by way of consideration by the tribunal, whether what the employer did was within the of band of reasonable responses of a reasonable employer.[82] And in *Alvis Vickers Limited v Lloyd*[83] the EAT confirmed the decision that to place the individual within a pool for selection for redundancy was a matter concerning whether the employer acted within the reasonable range of decisions available to it, and it is not open for an employment tribunal to substitute its own judgment for that of the employer so acting within the band of reasonable responses.

The question we are concerned with in this chapter is that, if an employer does 'bump' **3.97** another employee to make way for an employee who is redundant, is the 'bumped' employee entitled to a redundancy payment?

Thus in *Gimber and Sons Ltd v Spurrett*[84] a warehouse manager was dismissed because his job **3.98** was given to a sales representative who had lost his own job through redundancy. It was held that when there is a reduction in the requirements for employees in one area of an employer's business and a consequently redundant employee is transferred to another area, an employee who is displaced by the transfer and dismissed by reason of the transfer is dismissed by reason of redundancy. In *Safeway Stores Plc v Burrell* Judge Peter Clark considered the following example:

> If a forklift truck driver delivering materials to six production machines on the shop floor, each with its operator, is selected for dismissal on the basis of last in first out within the department following the employer's decision that only five machines are needed and one machine operator

---

[81] EAT/239/02, Burton J (P).
[82] See also *Green v A & I Fraser (Wholesale Fish Merchants) Limited* [1985] IRLR 55; see also further discussion in *Barrett Construction Limited v Dalrymple* [1984] IRLR 385 and *Leventhal Limited v North* (EAT/0265/04).
[83] EAT/0785/04. And for a discussion about whether bumping is necessary in disability discrimination law to discharge the employer's obligation to make reasonable adjustments for a disabled employee, see *Dixon v Automobile Association Ltd* (EAT/0874/03).
[84] [1967] 2 ITR 308.

with longer service is transferred to driving the forklift truck, the truck driver is dismissed by reason of redundancy. Although under both the contract and the function test he is employed as a forklift truck driver and there is no diminution in the requirements for forklift drivers, nevertheless there is a diminution in the requirement for employees to carry out the machine operators' work and that has caused the driver's dismissal.

F. Bumping—A Different View

3.99   In *Church v West Lancashire NHS Trust*,[85] Church was employed by the Trust as a helpdesk operator in its computer services group. The post of co-ordinator in the department became surplus to requirements. The employers decided that the remaining positions would be filled by competitive selection process. Employees had to apply for each remaining position. A person judged to be the least well qualified in the department would become redundant. On this basis Mr Church was bumped and selected for redundancy, even though his job remained the same and was filled by another employee who would have been dismissed. The employment tribunal, relying upon *Gimber v Spurrett*, and, of course, *Safeway Stores Plc v Burrell*, found that he had been dismissed by reason of redundancy. Church, who was claiming unfair dismissal, disputed the redundancy and relied upon the contract test coined by the Court of Appeal in *Nelson* and argued that he could not be redundant if his own job remained in existence.

3.100   The EAT applied *High Table Ltd v Horst* in holding that the contract test was not relevant. The proper test was neither contractual nor functional but the sensible blend of the two applied to the question of the place where the employee was employed. This is essentially, of course, the test in *Safeway Stores Plc v Burrell*. But Morison J parted company from Judge Peter Clark in *Safeway Stores Plc v Burrell* by disagreeing that bumping gave rise to a redundancy.

> A bumped employee cannot be regarded as having been dismissed by reason of redundancy within the meaning of s 139(1)(b) of the Employment Rights Act, which provides that an employee shall be taken to be dismissed by reason of redundancy if the dismissal was wholly or mainly attributable to a diminution of the requirements of the business 'for employees to carry out work of a particular kind'. Even though the statute does not say anything to link the particular kind of work to the relevant employee whose dismissal is being considered, the proper meaning of the words 'work of a particular kind' is that it is work of a particular kind which the dismissed employee was employed to do. Section 139 is dealing with the reason for dismissal which is an issue of causation. The dismissal of a bumped employee is not wholly or mainly attributable to the diminution in the requirements of the business for employees to do work of a particular kind but rather to the method by which the employers sought to manage that diminution in requirements.

3.101   A 'bumped' employee, according to Morison J, was therefore not redundant (*sed quaere*).

3.102   If this were correct, in such cases the only avenue for an employer to justify a bumped redundancy would be to plead some other substantial reason. This had not been done in the *Church* case. The case took a cruel twist in *Church v West Lancashire NHS Trust (No. 2)*,[86] where Morison J ruled that as a litigant must raise all relevant points at the trial of his complaint, this

---

[85] [1998] IRLR 4. Applied in *Russell v London Borough of Haringey* (EAT, 8 February 1999).
[86] [1998] IRLR 492.

means that when a case is remitted after an appeal has been allowed an employer cannot revive a different ground (in this case, some other substantial reason) to justify the case.

Shawkat v Nottingham City Council NHS Trust

Returning to the central definition point in a case with quite complicated facts that need not **3.103** be set out here, Charles J in *Shawkat v Nottingham City Council NHS Trust (No. 2)*[87] in the EAT considered that the phrase 'work of a particular kind' in s 139(1)(b)(i) of the Employment Rights Act 1996 should not be qualified by adding the words 'which the dismissed employee was to do' but had to be applied by reference to the requirements of the employer's business. In Charles J's view this involved elements of both contract and function tests, although neither would be decisive. The case was remitted to the employment tribunal to be reconsidered.[88] But clearly this is another example of a broader approach to the wording in s 139(1)(b)(i).

Disappearing work—the House of Lords settles the issue

The House of Lords decision in *Murray v Foyle Meats Ltd*,[89] in which the principal opinion **3.104** was given by Lord Irvine of Lairg LC now settles the issue.[90] In a case on art 2(7) of the Industrial Relations (Northern Ireland) Order 1976,[91] *Murray* was concerned with the issue of the disappearing job. In an admirably short opinion, Lord Irvine of Lairg LC supported the decision of Judge Peter Clarke in *Safeway Stores Plc v Burrell*[92] discussed above and settled the debate tracked in this chapter.

Murray and Doherty were 'meat plant operatives' normally working in the company's slaugh- **3.105** ter hall but under their employment contracts could be required to work elsewhere and occasionally did so. In 1995 there was a decline in business and the company decided to reduce the number of 'killing lines' in the slaughter hall from two to one so that fewer employees were required in the hall. Murray and Doherty were, amongst others, selected for redundancy. Their claim, however, was not for a redundancy payment but for unfair dismissal. Because their contract said they could do other things than work in the slaughter hall, they disputed whether the employer had a valid reason for dismissal under art 22(1) of the 1976 Order. Clearly, they relied on the contract test to say that they were not redundant and, therefore, as the employer relied on redundancy as the reason, they had been unfairly dismissed.

Lord Irvine swept away 20 years of case law by saying that the statute asked two questions of **3.106** fact, namely, had the requirements of the business for employees to carry out work of a particular kind ceased or diminished? Second, was the dismissal attributable wholly or mainly to that state of affairs? It was simply a question of causation.[93] As fewer workers were needed

---

[87] [1999] ICR 780.
[88] On the eventual outcome, see *Shawkat v Nottingham City Hospital NHS Trust (No. 2)* [2001] IRLR 555, discussed above.
[89] [1999] ICR 827.
[90] It was stated in *Stamkovic v Westminster City Council* (EAT, 17 October 2001) that any authority on the proper interpretation of the phrase 'work of a particular kind' in s 139(1)(b) of the ERA 1996 prior to the House of Lords decision in *Murray v Foyle Meats Ltd* had to be treated with considerable reserve, save in one instance, that of reliance on the decision of the EAT in *Safeway Stores Ltd v Burrell*. The authorities of *Safeway Stores Plc v Burrell* and *Murray v Foyle Meats Ltd* were followed in *Wilkinson v Corus and Regal Hotels Plc* [2004] All ER(D) 370 (Mar).
[91] SI 1976/1043.
[92] [1997] IRLR 200.
[93] Applied in *Hachette Filipacchi UK Ltd v Johnson* (EAT/0452/05).

in this case, the workers were dismissed by reason of redundancy. As well as simplifying the test to be applied in typical downsizing exercises the decision clearly also allows bumping redundancies (cf. *Church*) to be redundancies under the statutory definition because a cessation or diminution in requirement for employees to do work of a particular kind does not mean that there must be cessation, necessarily, of the work of a particular kind that the employee himself was actually contracted to perform.

G. Summary

3.107 (1) The erstwhile predominance of the contract test for both disappearing job and disappearing workplace versus the job function and geographical tests respectively, meant that few employees would be redundant and therefore fewer employees would receive redundancy payments.

(2) The death of the contract test (and also the job function test) allowing the tribunal to take a broader approach means that more employees will be entitled, as a matter of course, to redundancy payments.

(3) Conversely, however, it will be easier for employers to establish a fair dismissal as it will be easier to establish the fair reason of redundancy.

(4) The recent decisions, therefore, which appear to be, on the face of it, employee-orientated in their nature are really cases advantaging the employer. It must be remembered that in *Safeway Stores v Burrell*, *High Table v Horst*, and *Murray v Foyle Meats* the courts were defeating the employees' claim for unfair dismissal.

(5) The validity of bumping as a redundancy dismissal has now been robustly confirmed.

(6) Whither mobility clauses? Does this mean that an employer may no longer be able to use a mobility clause lawfully to direct an employee to another job or another place of work without the fear of a redundancy being triggered? The case law is now clear that the mere existence of a mobility or flexibility clause cannot defeat the operation of redundancy if the job the employee is actually doing disappears (or moves) (see *Curling v Securicor* and *High Table v Horst*). On the other hand, if there is a specific mobility clause under which the employer is entitled lawfully to direct the employer to a different job or a different work location, it is argued that this would be a case of legitimate reliance upon contractual terms by an employer, refusal to go along with which would be correctly attended with dismissal for refusal to follow a reasonable and lawful instruction. Arguably in that case, there would be no redundancy (see *Home Office v Evans*). What an employer cannot do, however, is rely upon the mobility/flexibility clause to defeat the redundancy claim where no such alternative work is available or offered.

4

RE-EMPLOYMENT

A. General	4.01	E. Acceptance of an Offer of	
B. Scope of Sections 138 and 141	4.06	Re-employment	4.32
C. The Distinction Between Renewal		F. Unreasonable Refusal	
and Re-engagement	4.07	of Re-employment	4.58
D. The Offer of Re-employment	4.16		

A. General

Although the right to a redundancy payment provides some compensation for the loss of **4.01** a job, many employees would choose to forgo such a payment if this meant they could be redeployed within their employer's organisation. Equally, it is no doubt more efficient for the labour market as a whole if employees who would otherwise be made redundant could be retained by their employers, albeit in a different capacity. The ERA 1996 recognises this by encouraging the employer to offer, and the employee to accept, new or renewed employment as an alternative to redundancy. This is achieved by ss 138 and 141. Accordingly, s 138(1) provides that an employee shall not be regarded as dismissed by reason of redundancy if:

(a) [his] contract of employment is renewed, or he is re-engaged under a new contract of employment in pursuance of an offer made before the end of his employment under the previous contract; and

(b) the renewal or re-engagement takes effect either immediately on, or after an interval of not more than four weeks after the end of that employment.

This has been described by some commentators[1] as the 'vanishing' or 'disappearing' dismissal **4.02** and means that, where re-employment is accepted under the terms of s 138(1), there is no redundancy dismissal and therefore no right to a redundancy payment.

However, it is clearly necessary to ensure that the employee is not pressurised into accepting **4.03** inappropriate work. Section 138(2) therefore goes on to provide that where the new job is to be on different terms to the old, the employee is allowed a statutory trial period during which time he can try out the new job without prejudicing his redundancy rights. On the other

---

[1] See *Harvey on Industrial Relations and Employment Law*, para E [1557].

hand, the employee should not be allowed to benefit from capricious behaviour and s 141 makes it clear that if the employee:

(a) unreasonably refuses an offer of suitable alternative work or renewed employment made before the old contract finishes; or

(b) unreasonably terminates (or gives notice to terminate) a suitable new job during the statutory trial period

then, although the redundancy dismissal continues in existence, there is no right to a redundancy payment in these circumstances. Conversely, if the employee acts reasonably in rejecting the employer's offer or in terminating the new job during the trial period, the entitlement to a redundancy payment will remain.

4.04 Although the principles underlying ss 138 and 141 are simple enough to state, the sections are in fact fairly technical and need to be considered carefully before any action is taken. However, if the appropriate steps are followed, their combined effect is to allow an employer to avoid liability to make a redundancy payment to an employee if he makes a suitable offer of alternative employment in accordance with s 141 and this is unreasonably refused either at the outset or during the statutory trial period.

4.05 In this chapter we look in some detail at the provision of ss 138 and 141 and examine their implications for both employers and employees.

B. Scope of Sections 138 and 141

4.06 It is important to emphasise at the outset that neither s 138 nor s 141 has any application outside the context of redundancy. (There used to be some ambiguity on this point in the original legislation, but s 138 is now clearly drafted to confine its effect to the sphere of redundancy.[2]) As a result, in *Jones v Governing Body of Burdett Coutts School*[3] the EAT held that an employee who had accepted his employer's offer of alternative employment was nonetheless entitled to bring a claim for unfair dismissal, notwithstanding the fact that under s 138(1) there was no dismissal for the purposes of statutory redundancy rights. The same principle was demonstrated in *Trafalgar House Services Limited v Carder*,[4] where it was held that an employee who accepted alternative employment but terminated his new contract within the statutory trial period was not necessarily dismissed for the purposes of an unfair dismissal claim—even though he was clearly dismissed for redundancy purposes under the provisions of s 138(4).

---

[2] Section 138 was originally enacted as s 3 of the Redundancy Payments Act 1963. This made it clear that the dismissal was only to be ignored for redundancy purposes. However, when this provision was subsequently consolidated in s 84 of the Employment Protection (Consolidation) Act 1978 the wording was ambiguous, although the better view was that such a limitation was implicit in any event (see *Hempell v WH Smith & Sons Limited* [1986] IRLR 95, [1986] ICR 365, EAT; cf. *EBAC Limited v Wymer* [1995] ICR 466, EAT). Fortunately, when s 84 was re-enacted by the current s 138 any ambiguity disappeared, as the section only applies 'for the purposes of this Part' i.e. Pt XI of the Employment Rights Act 1996, which deals with redundancy payments.

[3] [1997] ICR 390 EAT. The EAT's reasoning on this point was subsequently upheld by the Court of Appeal, although the employer's appeal was allowed on other grounds; see [1998] IRLR 521.

[4] EAT 306/96. This case and *Jones v Governing Body of Burdett Coutts School*, above, are discussed in IRLB 571 (June 1997) at p 7.

C. The Distinction Between Renewal and Re-engagement

Both s 138 and s 141 envisage two types of re-employment, namely 'renewal' of the old **4.07** employment and 're-engagement' under a new contract. However, the sections do not define these concepts and the difference between them is not entirely clear. It has been suggested that renewal of employment means employment on precisely the same terms, whereas re-engagement implies different terms.[5] However, this cannot be the case, as s 138(2) (which deals with the statutory trial period) is clearly drafted on the basis that renewal can be on terms that vary from the previous contract.

Alternatively, it is argued that re-engagement requires a gap between the two periods of **4.08** employment whereas renewal takes place where the contractual relationship is continuous. Although some support for this view can be found in s 235(1) of the ERA 1996, which defines 'renewal' to include the extension of a contract, this is clearly not meant to be an exhaustive definition. Moreover, as s 138(1)(b) specifically refers to the possibility of a renewal occurring after an interval of 'not more than four weeks' from the end of the previous employment, it is apparent that continuity is not essential to a renewal in this context.

A third means of distinguishing renewal from re-engagement is put forward by the authors **4.09** of *Harvey on Industrial Relations and Employment Law*. They suggest, by analogy with the concept of reinstatement in the law of unfair dismissal, that renewal covers a situation where the employer agrees 'to treat the employee in all respects as if he had not been dismissed'.[6] However, although this provides a useful test in many cases even this approach is hard to reconcile with the fact that, as we have seen, s 138 clearly envisages situations in which the terms of a renewal can be different from those of the previous contract.

In truth, the distinction between the two terms has never been properly explained and **4.10** although re-employment on the same or substantially the same terms as before is likely to amount to a renewal whereas redeployment in a completely different job will not, there is a grey area between these two extremes where uncertainty remains.

Does the distinction matter?

The reason this question is important is that s 138 treats renewals and re-engagements rather **4.11** differently. If the employer wishes to re-engage the employee under a new contract, s 138(1) makes it clear that the dismissal will only vanish for redundancy purposes if the re-engagement is offered before the end of the old employment.

By contrast, if the employer wants to renew the old contract, s 138(1) does not require any **4.12** offer to be made before the end of the old employment. All that is required is that the old contract is actually renewed within four weeks of the former employment ending. If this occurs, then s 138(1) applies automatically and there is no dismissal.[7]

---

[5] See *Camelo v Sheerlyn Productions Limited* [1976] ICR 531, EAT.
[6] *Harvey* (n 1 above) para E [1523].
[7] See *SI (Systems and Instruments) Ltd v Grist and Riley* [1983] IRLR 391, EAT.

4.13   However, despite the wording of s 138, the employer should wherever possible ensure that any offer to renew the old contract is made before the old employment terminates. This is because s 141 (which denies the right to a redundancy payment if an offer of renewal or re-engagement is unreasonably rejected) only applies if such an offer is made before the old employment ends. As a result, if the employer's offer to renew the old contract is made after this date the employee is free to refuse it on any grounds whatsoever without forfeiting his right to a redundancy payment.

4.14   The importance of the timing of an offer is seen where the redundancy takes effect (i.e. the old contract ends) before any kind of offer has been made. Suppose, however, that almost immediately business picks up (e.g. because an unexpected order is placed). In this situation any offer of re-engagement under a new contract will be too late to take advantage of s 138(1) and if such an offer is made and accepted a redundancy payment may still have to be made. However, if the employer offers to renew the old contract within the four weeks following dismissal s 138(1) can still apply. This means that if the employee accepts the offer the dismissal will vanish and the right to a redundancy payment will be lost. If, on the other hand, the employee rejects the offer, then no matter how unreasonable that rejection might be, the dismissal stands and, because the timing of the offer precludes the operation of s 141, the employee retains his entitlement to a redundancy payment.

4.15   In practice, therefore, it will always be better for the employer to make a specific offer of re-engagement or renewal well before the end of the old employment, if possible. This means that even if there is no obvious vacancy at the start of the redundancy process the employer should continue to monitor the situation. If a job subsequently arises, the aim should be to make the offer as quickly as possible and in any event before the redundancy takes effect. This puts the onus on the employee to decide whether to accept—knowing that, under s 141, an unreasonable refusal could destroy his right to a redundancy payment. The employer who is able to plan ahead and make his offer in good time is therefore always going to be in a stronger position, although clearly this will not always be achievable.[8]

D. The Offer of Re-employment

4.16   It follows from the above that if the employer decides to re-employ the employee (whether by renewal or by re-engagement) rather than make him redundant, then to take full advantage of ss 138 and 141 he should make him an offer as soon as he can and at the latest before the old employment ends. However, a number of points need to be made in respect of any such offer.

---

[8] Note that certain employees have to be given priority consideration for redeployment. Top of the list are women on maternity leave who, unlike other employees, are entitled to be offered a suitable vacancy and will be treated as automatically unfairly dismissed if they are not (see Maternity and Parental Leave Regulations 1999, reg 10). This is the case even if an employee with much longer service than the woman on maternity leave is consequently dismissed. In addition, an employer risks a disability discrimination claim under the Equality Act 2010, s 6 if he offers alternative employment to someone who would otherwise be made redundant, in preference to a disabled person who is no longer fit to do his old job. This was the case in *Kent County Council v Mingo*, EAT (reported in EOR No. 89 January/February 2000, p 55), where the County Council was held to have discriminated against a disabled worker because their redeployment policy gave preference to those at risk of redundancy rather than to disabled employees. Although a justification defence is available under the Equality Act 2010, s 19(3) the case suggests that giving priority to redundant employees is not of itself sufficient and that a specific justification, relevant to the disabled individual in question, must be shown.

Oral or written offer

Sections 138(1) and 141(1) make it clear that the employer's offer can be made orally, **4.17**
although a prudent employer will always put it in writing. Not only does this prove deci-
sively that an offer has been made, it also reduces the risk of disputes—particularly if the new
job is to be on different terms and conditions.

It follows from the fact that the offer can be made verbally that there is no prescribed form **4.18**
for such an offer, although in the majority of cases the offer is made in a letter from the
employer to the employee.

Offer from an 'associated employer'

An offer of alternative employment can be made by the same or an 'associated employer'.[9] **4.19**

'Associated employer' is defined, by virtue of s 231 of the ERA 1996, as follows: **4.20**

> 'For the purposes of this Act any two employers shall be treated as associated if—
>
> (a) one is a company of which the other (directly or indirectly) has control, or
> (b) both are companies of which a third person (directly or indirectly) has control and 'associ-
> ated employer' shall be construed accordingly.

This provision clearly allows the offer to be made not just by the old employer but also by **4.21**
another company within the same group. However, the exact parameters of s 231 have
caused some difficulty and the provision has been subject to a great deal of litigation, which
can be summarised as follows:

(a) The balance of the case law suggests that in general 'control' is determined by looking at
who has the majority of votes in the general meeting of the company. The crucial issue is
therefore numerical control in terms of voting shares rather than how decision-making
power has been exercised in practice.[10] In this connection it appears that when looking
at the question of control, shares held by the nominee of a beneficial owner cannot be
aggregated with shares held by the nominee in his own right; instead, any nominee
shares should be counted as belonging to the beneficial owner for these purposes.[11]

(b) There is a view that two companies can be controlled by a third person even if there is no
single person who owns more than 50 per cent of the shares in either company. This
would occur where a group of third parties together hold the majority of shares in both
companies and in practice act in concert as one.[12] However, this approach has been
questioned by *South West Laundrettes Limited v Laidler*[13] and *Strudwick v Iszatt Bros
Limited*,[14] which suggests that even if the third person can be more than one individual,

---

[9] ERA 1996, s 146(1).
[10] See *Secretary of State for Employment v Newbold* [1981] IRLR 305, EAT; *Washington Arts Association v
Forster* [1983] ICR 346; *Hair Colour Consultants Limited v Mena* [1984] ICR 671, [1984] IRLR 386, EAT;
Umar v Pliastar Ltd [1981] ICR 727; *South West Laundrettes Limited v Laidler* [1986] ICR 455, [1986] IRLR
305, CA.
[11] See *Cann v Fairfield Rowan Limited* (1966) 1 KIR 510 and *Secretary of State for Employment v Chapman*
[1989] ICR 771.
[12] See *Zarb and Samuels v British and Brazilian Produce Company (Sales) Ltd* [1978] IRLR 78, EAT and
Harford v Swiftrim Limited [1987] ICR 429, [1987] IRLR 360, EAT.
[13] [1986] ICR 455, [1986] IRLR 305, CA.
[14] [1988] ICR 796, [1988] IRLR 457, EAT.

it must be the same people (and not a varying combination of individuals) who have voting control over each relevant company. In practice this will seldom be the case.

(c) It has been held that a partnership and a company were associated employers where the partnership exercised de facto control over the company.[15]

(d) A number of cases have held that the definition in s 231 is exhaustive and that company means 'limited company'.[16] This means that some bodies corporate (such as local authorities) are not covered by the section and it has therefore been necessary to legislate to fill this gap. Delegated legislation now allows an employee in local government or related employment to be offered alternative employment by either the original employer or any other local government employer (as defined).[17] Similarly, an employee of the health service may receive an offer from the employer who dismisses him or from any other NHS employer.[18] The EAT has also been prepared to hold that the term 'company' includes a partnership of companies[19] and also that an overseas (American) company falls within the definition.[20]

(e) A person can be an associated employer even though at the time the offer is made it has never employed anyone. This could cover a group company which has been newly incorporated or which has previously been dormant.[21]

Timing of the offer

4.22 As discussed above, s 138(1) draws a distinction between renewal of the old contract and re-engagement under a new contract, providing that an offer of re-engagement must be made before the old contract ends if the dismissal is to disappear when the employee accepts the offer. However, this is not the case with renewal—the dismissal will disappear regardless of the timing or existence of any offer if renewal actually takes place within four weeks of the old contract ending.

On the other hand, if the employee wishes to rely on s 141 then, whether his offer is of renewal or re-engagement, it must be made before the old contract ends. If this is done the employer is freed from liability to make a redundancy payment if a suitable offer is unreasonably refused.

4.23 Note that an offer made on the last day of the old employment will qualify as an offer made before the end of the original employment. However, in practice such a late offer should be avoided if possible. This is because refusal by the employee at this stage may well be reasonable (e.g. because he has found employment elsewhere) and the employee's right to a redundancy payment may therefore be preserved.

Communication of the offer

4.24 The offer is made when it has been effectively communicated to the employee. So, for instance, an offer of re-employment sent by post is not communicated until the letter is received.

---

[15] See *Tice v Cartwright* [1999] ICR 769.

[16] See, for example, *Gardiner v London Borough of Merton* [1980] IRLR 472, CA.

[17] See Redundancy Payments (Continuity of Employment in local Government, etc) (modification) Order 1999 (SI 1999/2277).

[18] See Redundancy Payments (National Health Service) (Modification) Order (SI 1993/3167).

[19] See *Pinkney v Sandpiper Drilling Limited* [1989] IRLR 425.

[20] See *Hancill v Marcon Engineering Limited* [1990] ICR 103, [1990] IRLR 51.

[21] See *Lucas v Henry Johnson (Packers and Shippers) Limited* [1986] ICR 384, EAT. For more detail, see McMullen, 'The concept of continuity of employment', in *Butterworths Employment Law Guide*, paras 7.59–7.61, which discusses these cases (in a different context).

In *Smith v Brown Bayley Steels Ltd*,[22] an offer of re-employment was posted to the employee's house on 29 March, the day before his notice of dismissal for redundancy expired. However, the letter did not arrive until 31 March. The offer was to be disregarded because it was not effectively communicated to the employee in time.

The onus is on the employer to ensure that the offer is effectively communicated to each **4.25** employee and the employee is therefore under no duty to ascertain whether a new job is available. However, the offer does not have to be put to each employee individually; it can be made collectively. A valid offer was therefore made by posting a notice on a company notice board (see *McCreadie v Thomson and MacIntyre (Patternmakers) Ltd*[23]). The offer on the notice board was valid because it was 'in writing, brought to the notice of the employee, capable of being understood by him and in fact read by him'. Nonetheless, despite the *McCreadie* case it is much better practice to send an individual offer to each employee. This is because it is too easy for things to go wrong with a collective offer. For example, such an offer will be invalid if the employee does not see or hear of it because he is away sick or on holiday (*Maxwell v Walter Howard Designs Ltd*[24]). An employer should also take special care to ensure that any employees with aural or visual impairment know about such an offer (see, in a different context, *Tomczynski v JK Millar Ltd*[25]).

An employee may, of course, make it clear from the outset that he does not want any alternative **4.26** work with his old employer and may ignore or reject that employer's attempts to make an offer. However unreasonable, this type of employee behaviour will not of itself relieve the employer of his duty: the employer must make the offer if he is to rely on the employee's unreasonable refusal of suitable alternative employment in order to avoid liability for a redundancy payment. As an example, in *Simpson v Dickinson*[26] a shop changed hands and the assistant was made redundant. She told the new managers that she was no longer interested in shop work and intended to take a holiday and then seek work in a hospital. Accordingly, no offer of alternative employment was made, with the result that the employee was entitled to a redundancy payment.

Contents of the offer and new start date

Under general contractual principles, an offer must be sufficiently precise to be capable of **4.27** acceptance. In other words, it should be clear enough for the employee to understand what is being offered. It is therefore not enough for an employer to state that he will 'try to fit [an employee] in' (*Anderson v David Winter & Sons Ltd*[27]). Whilst the EAT has held it unnecessary for the offer to contain all of the items required to be included in the written statement of particulars of employment required by s 1 of the ERA 1996, it made it clear that a tangible offer would '. . . embody important matters such as remuneration, status and job description'. In addition, it would be prudent to specify in what ways (if any) the new employment is to differ from the old.

---

[22] [1973] 8 ITR 606.
[23] [1971] 2 All ER 1135.
[24] [1975] IRLR 77.
[25] [1976] ICR 127, EAT.
[26] [1972] ICR 474.
[27] [1966] 1 ITR 326.

4.28 It is not necessary to state precisely when the re-employment will commence; 'in the new year' or 'in the near future' will do.[28] However, both ss 138 and 141 make it clear that the re–employment must start 'either immediately on, or after an interval of not more than four weeks after' the end of the old contract. However, this requirement is relaxed slightly where the old employment ends on a Friday, Saturday, or Sunday. In this situation, s 146(2) provides that the new job must start no later than the Monday four weeks later. Note that any uncertainty about the start date may be taken into account when deciding whether any refusal to accept alternative work is reasonable (see below).

4.29 In summary, the prudent employer will ensure that the offer clearly states the job description, nature of duties, location, hours of work, pay (including any overtime entitlement and bonuses), details of any other benefits (e.g. pension, private health, car) and, where possible, the commencement date.

Multiple job offers

4.30 The employee may be offered several jobs by the employer. However, quality rather than quantity is important, the onus being on the employer to ensure that at least one of the multiple offers is sufficiently detailed to qualify under the rules.

Requirement that the offer is genuine

4.31 The offer of re-employment must be genuine in that the employer must reasonably expect to be able to fulfil the offer. In one case, it was held unsurprisingly that an offer that was a sham would not constitute a genuine offer (see *Kaine v Raine*[29]).

E. Acceptance of an Offer of Re-employment

4.32 There is no obligation on an employee to accept an offer of re-employment in any particular way; simply reporting for work in a new job will be enough. However, most employers will require a rather more definite, and earlier, indication of acceptance.

4.33 If the new job differs from the old in more than trivialities, the employee has a right to a statutory trial period which, depending on the circumstances, will be at least four weeks in length. This is an important right and is discussed in greater detail below. Subject to that right, an employee who accepts an offer of re-employment made in accordance with the terms of s 138(1) is deemed not to have been dismissed and therefore loses any entitlement to a redundancy payment.

4.34 As we have seen, if the new job takes the form of a renewal of the old contract, then it is not strictly necessary for the offer to have been made before the old contract ends. As long as the renewal actually takes effect within four weeks of the old contract ending there is no dismissal and therefore no right to a redundancy payment. However, if the re-employment amounts to

---

[28] See *Lonmet Engineering Limited v Green* [1972] 7 ITR 286; *Kaye v Cooke's (Finsbury) Limited* [1973] 3 All ER 434.

[29] [1974] ICR 300 (NIRC). In this case the fact that the offer was not genuine meant that there was no valid offer and s 141 was therefore irrelevant. However, in other cases evidence that the offer is a sham, whilst not negating the offer, may well mean that the employee's rejection of the offer is reasonable. So, for example, in *Hart v CE Payne & Sons Limited*, South London tribunal, 7 March 1985 (COIT 1633/21) an employee who was offered re-employment as a sales representative was held to be reasonable in rejecting the offer because he had every reason to be sceptical about whether the offer was genuine.

're-engagement under a new contract' then unless the employer offers such re-engagement before the old contract ends, s 138(1) will not apply, the dismissal will remain valid, and even if the employee accepts a later offer, his entitlement to a redundancy payment will remain.

Under s 138(1), re-engagement under a new contract must be 'in pursuance of an offer'. This **4.35** means that if the terms and conditions of the job turn out to be different from those contained in the offer, re-engagement 'in pursuance of an offer' has not taken place and the employee is still entitled to a redundancy payment. For example, in one case, the employer underestimated average earnings for piece-rate workers. This meant that the actual terms under which operatives were employed were inferior to those offered by some £13 per week. Accordingly, the operatives were never genuinely re-employed under that offer.[30]

As seen above, ss 138 and 141 only apply if the job being offered starts no later than four **4.36** weeks after the old contract ends. There may therefore be an interval between the old contract and the new. In this situation, continuity is expressly preserved by virtue of s 213(2) of the ERA 1996 so that the employee's seniority for the purposes of any future redundancy dismissal is maintained.

Of course, even if the employer has complied with the terms of ss 138 and 141 an employee **4.37** is not compelled to accept an offer of re-employment by the employer and he has two other options available to him, both of which preserve his right to a redundancy payment. First, he will, in certain circumstances, be entitled to a statutory trial period during which time he can try out the new job without prejudice to his redundancy rights. Second, he could refuse any such offer and still claim a redundancy payment as long as his refusal is reasonable. Each of these options will be discussed in turn.

Acceptance subject to a statutory trial period

General

In order to protect the employee and give him time to consider his options, it is provided in **4.38** s 138(2) of the ERA 1996 that, where the capacity, place, or other terms or conditions on which the employee is to be re-employed differ wholly or in part from the corresponding provisions of the previous contract, a trial period is allowed in relation to the contract as renewed. In other words, if the terms differ in any respect from the old employment the employee is entitled to the statutory trial period without prejudice to his redundancy rights. This apparently applies even if the terms are more favourable to the employee (see *Rose v Henry Trickett & Sons Limited (No. 2)*[31] and *Baker v Gill*[32]). In the *Rose* case it was held that the new terms differed if they were not identical in all respects, i.e. it was not sufficient to take an overall view of the contract and look at whether the employee lost out in some ways but gained in others. This means that, trivial differences aside, unless the individual terms are the same, the right to the statutory trial period arises.

Length of the statutory trial period

The trial period begins with the termination of the employee's employment under the previous **4.39** contract and ends with the expiration of a period of four weeks beginning with the date on

---

[30] See *Clarke and Others v Wolsey Limited* [1975] IRLR 154.
[31] [1971] 6 ITR 211, DC.
[32] [1970] 6 ITR 61, DC.

which the employee starts work under the new contract (ERA 1996, s 138(3)). In other words, the statutory trial period may well be longer than four weeks if there is an interval between the two jobs.

4.40 It has been held by the Court of Appeal that the length of the statutory trial period will be strictly construed. 'Four weeks' means four calendar weeks, not four full working weeks during which the employee has had the opportunity of working. This seems harsh, but the Court said that it would not read into the legislation words that were not there. Thus, in *Benton v Sanderson Kayser Ltd*,[33] an employee whose employment terminated on 21 December 1986 and whose trial period started forthwith did not have the right to have a seven-day Christmas closure excluded from the trial period. His trial period ended on 18 January 1987, even though this meant that he had, in reality, only three weeks in which to try out the new job. He therefore lost his right to a redundancy payment when he resigned on 19 January 1987, one day late.

4.41 Exceptionally, under s 138(3)(b)(ii) of the ERA 1996, the statutory trial period may be extended by agreement between the employer and the employee for the purposes of re-training the employee for employment under the new contract. However, under s 138(6) such an agreement has to be made in writing between the employer and the employee (or the employee's representative) before the employee starts work under the new contract. It must also specify the date when the period of re-training will end. (It is to be noted that the statute imposes no time limit on the extended trial period). In addition, the agreement must set out the terms and conditions of employment that will apply in the employee's case after the end of the re-training period. However, although these detailed conditions have to be followed in full for an extension to apply, the courts have been prepared to interpret them rather generously. So, for example, although the written agreement should refer to the most important terms that will apply after the extended trial period is over, it does not have to cover all the particulars that have to be inserted in a written statement of terms under s 1 of the ERA 1996.[34] Note that if the conditions of s 138(6) are not satisfied, the employee may lose his right to a redundancy payment. For example, if he decides to terminate the new employment more than four weeks after the new job starts, wrongly believing there to be an extended trial period, then as long as the conditions of s 138(1) are satisfied there will be no redundancy dismissal on the ending of his old contract and therefore no entitlement to a redundancy payment.[35]

Termination of employment during the trial period

4.42 Section 138 provides that if, during the trial period (which, as we have seen, includes any interval between the old job and the new), the employee (for whatever reason) terminates the contract or gives notice to terminate it, then he is treated as having been dismissed on the date on which his employment under the old contract ended: s 138(2)(b)(i). Similarly, if the employer 'for a reason connected with or arising out of' any difference between the old contract and the new terminates the new contract or gives notice to terminate during the trial period the employee's dismissal takes effect at the end of the old contract. In both cases

---

[33] [1989] ICR 136.
[34] See *McKindley v William Hill (Scotland) Limited* [1985] IRLR 492, EAT.
[35] The strictness of the trial period and the limited basis on which it can be extended was emphasised in *Reality (White Arrow Express) Ltd v O'Hara* (EAT/0447/03) and *Optical Express Ltd v Williams* [2007] IRLR 936.

the dismissal is treated as being for the reason for which he was originally dismissed (i.e. redundancy). However, if the employee is unreasonable in taking such action and the new employment was suitable for him, the right to a redundancy payment will be lost (see s 141(4), discussed below).

Note that if the employer or employee chooses to give notice to terminate during the trial period it is irrelevant that the notice expires after the trial period. **4.43**

As seen above, the employer's right to terminate is conditional upon there being a reason 'connected with or arising out of' the change in terms. This phrase was discussed in *Bailey v Whitehead Bros (Wolverhampton) Limited*,[36] where a redundant works manager agreed to an extended trial period as a storekeeper/librarian. The employee was dismissed at the end of the trial period—he was often ill and proved physically incapable of performing his new role. It was held that this dismissal was '. . . for a reason connected with or arising out of the change . . .' and that the employee was thus to be treated as dismissed for redundancy on the day his old contract ended and so entitled to a redundancy payment. The same reasoning will apply if an employee simply cannot perform the tasks his new job requires. **4.44**

However, if the employer dismisses the employee for a reason unconnected with or not arising from the change in terms (e.g. for misconduct) the employee is not entitled to a redundancy payment but will, as is the case with any dismissal, benefit from all of the other protections afforded by statute and common law (for example, unfair dismissal). **4.45**

The right to reinstate the dismissal by reason of redundancy pursuant to s 138(2)(b)(i) is strictly construed. In *Optical Express Ltd v Williams*[37] Williams was employed by Boots (the chemists) as a manager from April 1978. She was responsible for two dental practices in Southport and Bolton, a chiropody practice in Chester, and some 33 employees. In January 2005 Optical Express Ltd bought all Boots dental practices by way of a TUPE transfer. This excluded the chiropody practice. Williams remained a multi-site manager, but now excluding the chiropody practice and with few staff. In January 2005 she was told by Optical Express that the Southport practice would cease to exist. She was offered a position as a dual services manager in Bolton managing a dental and optical service. However, in August 2005 Optical Express decided to close the dental clinic in Bolton and as a result, she was informed that her position would become redundant. During consultation meetings it was suggested that she could become manager of the Bolton optical store, thus relieving her of all dental responsibilities and also her previous multi-site responsibility (although her salary would be protected). Mrs Williams responded, expressing the view that the offer of the Bolton optical store with a protected salary was not a suitable alternative. It was suggested that she try the position as store manager in Bolton for a four-week trial period. She agreed to do this. The expiry of that period was 13 January 2006. During that period her solicitors sent Optical Express a number of letters expressing the view that the employment was not suitable but *not* terminating her employment (pursuant to s 38(2)(b)(i)). Two weeks *after* the end of the trial period Williams gave notice terminating her employment contract. She then claimed a redundancy payment from the employment tribunal. It was held that the terms of s 38 are clear. The right to claim dismissal, express or constructive, is barred after the expiry of the trial period unless the employee exercises rights given by s 138(2) **4.46**

---

[36] COIT 1265/232.
[37] [2007] IRLR 936.

and (3). The EAT expressed the view that both parties went into the arrangement 'with their eyes open'. The EAT noted that although Mrs Williams had reservations, she had legal advice and she could have exercised her right of termination in time, before the expiry of the trial period.

4.47   In *Reality (White Arrow Express) Ltd v O'Hara* [38] the EAT emphasised that the trial period of four weeks can only be extended under very limited circumstances i.e. where an extension of the trial period is agreed for the purposes of re-training and *only* if the provisions of s 138(6) (see above) are complied with. In this case, the employee was informed of redundancy but given a new position to try under a trial period. The claimant, having tried out the trial period, only gave notice to terminate the employment two weeks outside the trial period and there was no agreement to extend the trial period by virtue of an agreement for re-training. It was not sufficient, for example, as the EAT pointed out to write a letter during the trial period indicating an intention to terminate the contract 'at some stage in the future'. [39]

Successive trial periods

4.48   It is possible to have a succession of trial periods. So, for example, if it becomes clear during the first trial period that the new job is not suitable for the particular individual the employer can offer a further alternative and if the employee decides to accept this further offer a new statutory trial period will apply. This subsequent contract may be terminated either by the employee (on any grounds) or by the employer (on the limited grounds set out above). In either case, the employee will then be treated as dismissed for redundancy on the day his original contract ended. The time limit for applying to a tribunal for a redundancy payment in such a case will run from the date on which the final contract of employment ended (s 145(4)(a)).

Working beyond the statutory trial period

4.49   The statutory trial period is strict and the employee will be deemed to have accepted the new employment if he carries on working beyond the end of this period. If he subsequently leaves, he will therefore be regarded as having resigned and will have no right to a redundancy payment. This is demonstrated by *Meek v (1) J Allen Rubber Co Ltd and (2) Secretary of State for Employment*. [40] In that case, the employee, a lorry driver shuttling between two of the employer's depots, was dismissed when one depot closed. He was offered a redundancy payment or work on a different route on at least a six-month trial. His new job involved driving irregular hours, mostly at night. The employee tried the work and after about seven months rejected it. He was moved elsewhere but eventually left, claiming a redundancy payment. The employee argued that a 'common law trial period' applied (see below) and that he had left within a reasonable time of the trial period agreed with his employers. However, the EAT held that the employee was only entitled to the statutory four-week trial period because he had been expressly dismissed from his original job and had accepted an offer of alternative employment. As the employee had neither left nor given notice during the statutory trial

---

[38] EAT/0447/03.

[39] As is noted in Chapter 2 the cases of, *inter alia*, *Morton Sundour Fabrics v Shaw* [1967] ITR 84 and *The Burton Group v Smith* [1977] IRLR 351 are authority for the rule that a notice to terminate by an employer must contain, and cannot be effective without, a termination date. The EAT in *Reality (White Arrow Express) Ltd v O'Hara* (EAT/0447/03) considered that the rule applies equally to any purported notice of termination by an employee.

[40] [1980] ICR 24, EAT.

period, he was not to be treated as having been dismissed for redundancy when his old contract ended. Although it was accepted that an extended trial period had been agreed with the employers, it was not extended for the purpose of re-training and was therefore outside the statutory scheme.

This seems rather hard on the employee and it is possible that if the employer has made a **4.50** promise to extend the trial period which does not meet the statutory conditions, the promise will nevertheless be binding on the employer as a matter of contract law. A contractual claim would therefore have to be made for a payment equivalent to the statutory redundancy payment, and not for the statutory payment itself. There is no reported instance of this happening but it seems a sound proposition on first principles. Success would, however, depend on the terms of the promise made by the employer, i.e. whether they are precise enough to amount to an unequivocal promise to make a payment in any event.

The so-called 'common law trial period'

As we have seen there is a strict time limit on the statutory trial period which begins at the **4.51** end of the old employment and ends no later than four weeks after work under the new contract begins. There are only two exceptions to this rule. First, as discussed above, the statutory trial period can be extended by agreement for the purposes of re-training. Second, in certain situations a common law trial period may apply and it is to this concept that we now turn. If an employee is dismissed for redundancy and his dismissal takes effect on notice or by a payment in lieu of notice his contract will end at the expiry of the notice or on payment of the sum in lieu. Should he be offered a new contract and become entitled to the statutory trial period it is then clear that this period starts at the end of the old employment and (subject to any extension for re-training) finishes, without fail, four weeks after he starts work under the new contract.

But what if, in a redundancy situation, the employer does not dismiss but instead simply **4.52** imposes new terms and conditions in breach of contract? This might arise, for example, where an employer unilaterally requires the employee to change location or job duties in circumstances where the contract does not oblige the employee to work at the changed location or to perform the new job duties. If the employee, faced with such unilateral change, simply accepts it, arguably that is an agreed variation of contract and there is no right to a trial period of any kind. Equally, there will be no dismissal and so no right to claim a redundancy payment. However, if he does not agree to the change, then it may be that there is a repudiatory breach of contract.

Such a repudiatory breach of contract, however drastic, does not of itself terminate the **4.53** contract of employment (see *Gunton v London Borough of Richmond upon Thames*[41]). It needs an acceptance by the injured party to bring it to an end, particularly if the employee indicates his reservations or otherwise says that he is 'testing the water' or working under protest under the new conditions (see, for example, *Marriott v Oxford & District Co-operative Society (No. 2)*[42]). In this situation, the employee will not be deemed to have accepted the new employment (and thereby to have treated the old employment as at an end) merely by working under the new conditions. He will be allowed a reasonable trial period at common law in

---

[41] [1981] 1 Ch 448.
[42] [1970] 1 QB 186.

which to make up his mind and in which to make his election to treat the employment as at an end. This period is not set and its length depends on the circumstances of each case. It is clear that it can be longer than the statutory trial period, although if the employee delays too long he will be taken to have accepted the new terms, with the result there is no dismissal and no right to a redundancy payment.

4.54 There are two leading cases on the subject. In *Air Canada v Lee*[43] the employee was employed as a switchboard operator. The employer moved its business to new premises, where the switchboard was located in the basement of the building. The employee found this very unsatisfactory and uncongenial but tried out the new conditions for about two months. After this period the employee resigned and claimed constructive dismissal and a redundancy payment. Although the period was longer than the length of the statutory trial period it was held that she was nonetheless entitled to a redundancy payment. Following the employer's repudiation of the original contract, the employee had a reasonable time at common law in which to decide whether or not to accept the breach as terminating the contract or to affirm the contract. In these circumstances, two months was not an unreasonable time. Although this case suggested that the statutory trial period only came into play once the old contract had been terminated, the one view is that the statutory trial period is irrelevant in these circumstances. Either the employee accepts the breach and resigns (in which case no further trial period is appropriate) or he elects to continue working, in which case there is no dismissal.[44]

4.55 The second case is *Turvey v CW Cheyney & Sons Ltd*.[45] Here the employee was employed as a polisher, but work diminished and he was persuaded to take a job in a different department of the employer's business. This was a breach of the employment contract, but the employee agreed to try out the new employment and he stayed on for a period of a little over four weeks. Only then did he resign. It was held that he could nonetheless be entitled to a redundancy payment in these circumstances. This was not an express dismissal but a case of employer repudiation which was not effective until the employee treated the employment as at an end. In this situation the employee was therefore entitled to a reasonable period during which he was able to make up his mind as to whether he wanted to accept the breach as terminating the contract or affirm the new contract without losing his rights. Again, the statutory trial period was held to be irrelevant until the old employment terminated, when it could be 'tacked on' to the common law trial period.[46] *Turvey v C W Cheyney & Sons Ltd* was followed by the EAT in *Kentish Bus & Coach Company Ltd v Quarry*.[47]

4.56 The legal problems generated by the juxtaposition of common law and statutory trial periods can be avoided altogether if the employer expressly terminates the old contract and offers the new job under a new contract. It is then clear that the employee is only entitled to a statutory

---

[43] [1978] ICR 1202.

[44] See *East Suffolk Local Health Services NHS Trust v Palmer* [1997] ICR 425.

[45] [1979] ICR 341. The case is discussed in *IDS Brief* 151, February 1979, at p 13 and was followed by the EAT in *Kentish Bus & Coach Co Ltd v Quarry* (EAT 287/92).

[46] For the reasons outlined above this reference to the statutory trial period is arguably misguided. Certainly, there is very little evidence that the legislation was intended to create two consecutive trial periods in this situation.

[47] EAT/287/92 (employee entitled to a reasonable period to consider whether or not he should accept the new terms offered by his employers as a repudiation of his existing contract, before the statutory trial period was engaged).

trial period (*Sheet Metal Components Ltd v Plumridge*[48]). On the other hand, many employers like to persuade employees to accept redeployment in a redundancy situation without expressly dismissing and offering to re-hire. However, if they choose this less confrontational approach they should be aware that it could give rise to a common law trial period which, with or without the statutory period, may be of more than four weeks' duration. On the other hand, there is a risk to the employee in this situation. The distinction between a repudiatory breach of contract, which the employee grudgingly accepts, and a variation of the contract to which he agrees is far from clear, yet the consequences are far reaching. This is because if the employee is taken to have agreed to a variation there will be no dismissal and no prospect of a redundancy payment. The employee who is reallocated to a new job without an express dismissal and where there is no contractual authority for the change should therefore indicate wherever possible that he is reluctant to accept the new terms so that he can subsequently resign and argue that he was constructively dismissed and entitled to a redundancy payment.

4.57 Finally, it is to be noted that if the dismissal is by way of non-renewal of an expired fixed-term contract followed by re-employment under a new contract, then an employee will be allowed the statutory trial period but not the common law trial period. This is because the old contract clearly terminates on the expiry of the fixed term (see s 136(1)(b)).

F. Unreasonable Refusal of Re-employment

4.58 As stated above, the right to a redundancy payment will be lost if the new employment is the same as the old employment or, if it is not, it is suitable in relation to the employee and, in either case, the employee's refusal of the offer of new employment or (if applicable) his resignation during the trial period, is unreasonable.[49] However, as we have seen, for s 141 to apply any offer of new or renewed employment must be made before the end of the old employment. This means that whether the old contract is to be renewed or whether there is to be re-engagement under a new contract, the employer can only take the benefit of s 141 if the offer of re-employment has been made by this date. In addition, the job offered must start no later than four weeks after the old job ends.

4.59 Assuming s 141 does apply, then if the terms of the new job are the same there is no statutory trial period and the only issue is whether the employee acted reasonably in turning the offer down. If he did, then he will be entitled to a redundancy payment.[50] If, on the other hand, the terms of the new job are different then there will be a right to a statutory trial period and two questions come into play. First, was the new employment suitable in relation to the employee and, second, did the employee refuse the offer or opt out of any trial period unreasonably? If the answer to both these questions is yes then the right to a redundancy payment will be lost. It is therefore necessary to examine the meaning of 'suitable' and 'unreasonable' in this context.

---

[48] [1974] IRLR 86.

[49] See s 141.

[50] Obviously, it will be comparatively rare for the employee not to want his old job back again but this could occur where, for example, he has been offered employment elsewhere, in which case any refusal is likely to be reasonable.

Suitability of the job and unreasonableness of refusal

4.60   Whether a job is 'suitable' and whether refusal is 'unreasonable' are questions of fact in each case [51] and although the two concepts of suitability and reasonableness are separate in theory they are often hard to distinguish in practice [52] The onus is on the employer to show that the job offered was suitable and that the employee's refusal was unreasonable (*Kitching v Ward* [53] and *Jones v Aston Cabinet Co Limited* [54]).

4.61   It seems that whether the job is 'suitable' in relation to an employee involves an objectively based approach including job comparison (for example, comparing the new and the old conditions, such as pay, status, location of work, and so on and then taking an overview of the job as a whole). As the EAT in *Inchcape Retail Limited v Large* [55] remarked, the tribunal has to consider objectively whether the employment offered was suitable (though it has to do so in relation to the particular employee concerned i.e. objectively viewed, is it suitable for him?) 'Reasonableness', on the other hand, may allow more subjectively based factors to be taken into account, including all an employee's personal circumstances. So, in *Cambridge & District Co-operative Society Ltd v Ruse* [56] the EAT stated that, 'we consider that, as a matter of law, it is possible for the employee reasonably to refuse an objectively suitable offer on the ground of his personal perception of the employment offered'. In *Carron Company v Robertson* [57] the Lord President of the Court of Session stated:

> In deciding as to the suitability of employment in relation to an employee, one must consider not only the nature of the work, hours and pay, the employee's strength, training, experience and ability but such matters as status in the premises of the employer and the benefits flowing from that status. A decision as to the reasonableness or unreasonableness of his refusal depends on a consideration of the whole circumstances in which he would have been placed if he had accepted the offer.

4.62   The EAT has rejected any notion that the unreasonable refusal provision in s 141(2) requires the adoption, by analogy, of the 'range of reasonable responses' test applicable to fairness of a dismissal under s 98(4) of the ERA 1996 (test of unfair dismissal). In *Hudson v George Harrison Ltd*,[58] and *Commission for Healthcare Audit & Inspection v Ward*,[59] Judge Peter Clark (sitting in both cases) relied on and endorsed the analysis of Phillips J in *Executors of Everest v Cox* [60] where he stated:

> . . . the employee's behaviour and conduct must be judged looking at it from her point of view, on the basis of the facts that they appeared, or ought reasonably to have appeared, to her at the time the decision had to be made.

---

[51]   See *Rice v Mr & Mrs T Walker t/a Kitchen Shop* (EAT/0498/05).

[52]   On occasion it is difficult for tribunals to separate the two. It has been recognised by the EAT that there can be occasions of overlap. Thus, in *Commission for Healthcare Audit & Inspection v Ward* (EAT/2549/07) Judge Peter Clark considered, for example, 'it seems to us that in an appropriate case where the new job offer is overwhelmingly suitable it may be a little easier for the employer to show that a refusal by the employee is unreasonable. It is part of the balancing exercise which the tribunal is charged to carry out.'

[53]   [1967] 2 ITR 464, and Divisional Court.

[54]   [1973] ICR 292 (NIRC); endorsed by Judge Peter Clark in *Commission for Healthcare Audit & Inspection v Ward* (EAT/0579/07)).

[55]   EAT/0500/03.

[56]   [1993] IRLR 156; *Commission for Healthcare Audit & Inspection v Ward* (EAT/0579/09).

[57]   [1967] 2 ITR 484.

[58]   EAT/0571/02 (at paras 7–12).

[59]   EAT/0579/07.

[60]   [1980] 1CR 415, 418 C–D.

To illustrate the above, suppose an employee is employed as an engineering foreman at **4.63** location A. Suppose also that a redundancy arises because the employer wishes to change the place of work to location B (we assume for the sake of argument in this example that there is no implied or express mobility clause (see Chapter 3)). It is to be assumed that the employer is happy to offer the employee a job as an engineering foreman at the different location, and the offer made to the employee is likely to be suitable. However, whether the employee's refusal of that job is reasonable or unreasonable may involve personal considerations. For example, it might be reasonable for an employee to refuse the suitable alternative employment on the ground that the travelling time to work is much greater than in the old employment and that factor might affect different employees differently. Some employees may have difficulty with public transport, some may have problems with getting children to school, and some may, for example, have health or domestic considerations which make the new arrangements unsatisfactory and their rejection, in the circumstances, reasonable.[61]

There is a plethora of reported cases concerning findings of fact by employment tribunals as **4.64** to suitability and as to the reasonableness of refusals on the part of employees. These are mainly to be found in the Industrial Tribunal Reports (ITR), originally published by HMSO (subsequently reprinted by Professional Books Limited) but discontinued in 1977. However, we have resisted the temptation to provide an endless list of examples, as it must be stressed that each case depends upon its facts. What is clear is that there are a number of factors that can be taken into account in relation to suitability and reasonableness (and some of them, from time to time, are employed by tribunals in either category[62]). We have given several examples below in relation to each factor, some of which resulted in the finding in favour of the employee and some which did not. Nevertheless, it is to be stressed that the issue is always a question of fact for the employment tribunal. In practice this uncertainty can lead employers to make a redundancy payment even though an offer of suitable alternative employment has been unreasonably refused. This then avoids a challenge in the employment tribunal (which for tactical reasons may also include an unfair dismissal claim) the outcome of which cannot be predicted with any certainty.

'Suitability' factors

Status

In *Taylor v Kent County Council*,[63] a very experienced headmaster was offered a job working **4.65** in a mobile pool of teachers. Although there was no drop in pay the job was considered by the Divisional Court to be 'quite unsuitable'.[64]

In *Eltringham v Sunderland Co-operative Society Ltd*[65] the employee had held the position of **4.66** branch manager for the Sunderland Co-op for 18 years. The employer decided to close the employee's department and offered him a job as an assistant branch manager elsewhere. He refused and so his employment was terminated. The majority of the tribunal decided that an offer of suitable employment had been made. On appeal to the High Court it was held that the tribunal was entitled, on the evidence before it, to come to the conclusion that the

---

[61] The way in which an employee considers a suitable offer and whether he responds or does not respond to it is relevant to the issue of reasonableness; see *Lincoln & Louth NHS Trust v Cowan* (EAT/395/99).
[62] See, e.g. *Souter v Henry Balfour & Company Ltd* [1966] 1 ITR 383 referred to below.
[63] [1969] 2 QB 560.
[64] See also *Harris v E Turner & Sons (Joinery) Ltd* [1973] ICR 31.
[65] [1971] 6 ITR 121.

employment was suitable. Lord Parker CJ said, 'the question of status, whether a man has been demoted, is of course a very relevant consideration when one is determining whether an offer is an offer of suitable employment'. But here it was counterbalanced by the fact that he was going to a much larger branch where, notwithstanding he was an assistant manager under a manager, he had five people under him, namely two section heads and three assistants, and the chances of getting more wages and commission were also relevant factors.

Location

4.67 In *Bass Leisure Ltd v Thomas* [66] the closure of one depot resulted in a woman with domestic responsibilities being offered alternative employment 20 miles away, adding a number of hours to her day. It was not suitable.

4.68 In contrast, in *Gotch & Partners v Guest* [67] an architect was employed at the respondent's Bournemouth office which was then closed. The employee was offered other employment at an increased salary in Bristol and a contribution to his removal expenses. An offer of suitable employment had been made which was unreasonably refused.

Hours of work

4.69 In *Kykot v Smith Hartley Ltd* [68] a weaver was transferred from a night shift to a day shift following a reorganisation of working patterns. It was held that a change in shift is a relevant concern in assessing whether an offer is suitable.

Pay and skills

4.70 In *Souter v Henry Balfour & Company Ltd* [69] the employee had worked all his life as a pattern maker and was offered work as a progress clerk at a lower rate of pay. The employee declined the offer of employment partly because of the immediate drop in earnings but mainly because he had been employed as a craftsman for the whole of his working life and he wanted to continue in the job that he understood and for which he was trained. The tribunal considered that the employer had made an offer of suitable employment but in the circumstances he was not acting unreasonably in refusing the offer and deciding to find a job with another firm as a pattern maker. [70]

4.71 Similarly, in *Michaelson v Arthur Henriques Plc* [71] 15 jacket machinists were offered work as dress machinists. They tried the new work but resigned shortly afterwards. The tribunal held that the offer was unsuitable because dress machining demanded completely different skills, which the machinists might not be able to acquire. In addition, the new work attracted considerably lower piece rates. In *Granger v White* [72] an offer to re-employ a qualified hairdresser who had been manager of a salon as an assistant in a sports and equipment shop was held to be unsuitable. The employee was a highly qualified and skilled hairdresser and the work offered did not reflect this.

---

[66] [1994] IRLR 104.
[67] [1966] 1 ITR 65.
[68] [1975] IRLR 372.
[69] [1966] 1 ITR 383.
[70] The case could equally, we suggest, have been decided on the basis that the offer of alternative employment was not suitable.
[71] Manchester tribunal, 27 August 1985 (COIT 1680/214).
[72] Brighton tribunal, 1 March 1985 (COIT 1631/134).

'Reasonableness' factors

As noted above the concern here is not with what a reasonable employee would have done **4.72** but rather whether the particular individual was, in light of his personal circumstances, acting reasonably in rejecting the offer.[73]

Fringe benefits

In *Carron Company v Robertson*[74] the employee had been employed for 20 years as a pattern **4.73** maker at the employer's Bathgate foundry. He was then offered alternative work at another foundry but refused it. He did so because he had staff status at the Bathgate foundry and the benefits attached to it and the work offered to him did not have that status. The Lord President of the Court of Session held that, when the matter was remitted to an employment tribunal, it was open to it to decide that the refusal was reasonable on grounds of loss of status and benefits including, in particular, significant sick pay.

Lateness or vagueness of the offer

In *McNulty v T Bridges & Company Ltd*[75] Mr McNulty was dismissed as redundant but was **4.74** subsequently offered alternative work at another site on similar terms. By the time this occurred, however, he had found other employment and refused the offer and left. The offer had been received only two days before the period of notice terminated. The employment tribunal accepted that the lateness of an offer (and the acceptance of an offer from another employer) was certainly a factor to be taken into account when considering reasonableness. But on the facts of that case, lateness did not justify the refusal by the employee of the company's offer of alternative employment. Therefore, he had acted unreasonably.

On the other hand, in *Bryan v George Wimpey & Co*,[76] Mr Bryan was given notice terminating **4.75** his employment but just before the notice expired the employers sought to withdraw it as they wanted him to continue in their employment. He left, however, as he had already got a job else-where. It was held by the employment tribunal that the employers were not able to withdraw the notice without the consent of the employee and therefore their attempt to do so was to be treated as an offer to renew the contract. The offer was suitable but the refusal of it was not unreasonable. One of the factors taken into consideration was that the offer was made on the evening of the day before the employment came to an end at a time when he had only nine-and-a-half hours left to work. The applicant was entitled to honour his contractual obligation to his new employer.[77]

It has also been held that making a number of insufficiently specific offers is no adequate **4.76** substitute for a single offer of suitable alternative employment.[78]

---

[73] See *Executors of Everest v Cox* [1980] ICR 415; *Hudson v George Harrison Ltd* (EAT/057/02); *Commission for Healthcare Audit & Inspection v Ward* (EAT/0579/07).

[74] [1967] 2 ITR 484.

[75] [1966] 1 ITR 367.

[76] [1968] 3 ITR 28. It has also been held, in a different context (whether the employer had acted reasonably for unfair dismissal purposes in formulating an offer of alternative employment in lieu of redundancy) that, normally, the employer should inform the employee of the financial prospects of a particular position (*per* HH Judge Birtles in *Fisher v Hooper Finance Ltd* (EAT/0043/05), explaining the earlier EAT decision in *Modern Injection Moulds Ltd v Price* [1976] IRLR 72.

[77] cf. *McNulty v T Bridges & Company Limited* [1966] 1 ITR 367, referred to above.

[78] *Curling v Securicor Limited* [1992] IRLR 549.

Housing and schooling considerations

4.77   In *Bainbridge v Westinghouse Brake and Signal Company Ltd* [79] the employee had been employed for five years at the respondent's Newcastle site. He was married, lived locally, and had two children at local schools. In 1963 it was proposed to close the Newcastle site and he was offered work by his employer in Glasgow (which was expected to last for three years) and thereafter Leeds. He refused to move and he was dismissed. The offer of alternative employment was suitable but the majority of the employment tribunal held that he had not acted unreasonably in refusing it as he would have been required to move his family and principally his children at a particularly crucial stage of their education—one was about to sit a GCE examination and the other the 11-plus. In addition, the refusal had been reasonable because it was unlikely he would have been able to obtain council housing in the new location and he could not afford to buy a house.

Domestic problems

4.78   In *MacGregor v William Tawse Ltd* [80] the employee was employed in the civil engineering and contracting industry and was dismissed at the end of a contract. He was offered alternative employment on the Island of Mull but refused it. Among the considerations were that this involved working away from home and if he accepted the offer he would get one weekend at home every six weeks. However, he suffered no loss of wages and the working rules for the industry accepted that employees would have to work away from home on occasions owing to the nature of the industry. He had therefore acted unreasonably and was not entitled to a redundancy payment.

4.79   In *Rose v Shelley & Partners Ltd* [81] the employee worked for the employer for several years. During 1965 the employer moved premises from North London to Huntingdon. The new premises were 60 miles away from the old. The employee was asked to move but because his wife refused to move he rejected the offer. She was adamant and said that if her husband did go to Huntingdon she would remain in Tottenham and even went so far as to get a job in order to support herself and the children. It was held that the employee had not acted unreasonably, although another ground for the decision was that the offer had not been made before the ending of the old employment and therefore it did not comply with the re-employment provisions.

Medical reasons

4.80   In *Williamson v National Coal Board* [82] Williamson was a coal miner made redundant when the colliery closed down. He was offered work at another colliery but did not accept it and left when his notice expired. He then claimed a redundancy payment and only at a hearing before the employment tribunal did he produce a medical certificate to the effect that he was unable to work underground. The tribunal by majority decided that the offer made to the employee had been unreasonably refused because he had acted unreasonably in failing to inform his employers of his condition. The Court of Session upheld the decision, pointing out that if he had got in touch with the employer and explained that by reason of his age and physical condition he was no longer able to work at the face, he might have been offered work

---

[79] [1966] 1 ITR 89.
[80] [1967] 2 ITR 198.
[81] [1966] 1 ITR 169.
[82] [1970] 5 ITR 43.

of another kind or have been given treatment or become eligible for an incapacity pension. He did none of these things and therefore was unreasonable.

In contrast, in *Denton v Neepsend Ltd*[83] an employee was offered alternative work operating **4.81** a machine that emitted dust and vapour. Although the work was held to be suitable, the employee had an obsession about the health risks as his father and father-in-law had died from chest trouble and pneumoconiosis, respectively. The tribunal considered that the employee's fears about his own health might be 'utterly groundless' but nevertheless they were genuine fears and the refusal was reasonable.

Financial uncertainty of the employer

In *GD Systems Ltd v Woods*,[84] during a period of severe financial difficulty, an employee working **4.82** with a very small company was given notice of termination. He was subsequently asked to carry out some work for the company. The EAT held that, bearing in mind the dire financial circumstances of the employer, the fact that the cheque for his last month's salary had not been honoured, and the fact that he had been barred from entering on one occasion, the employee's refusal of the offer was reasonable.

Alternative job prospects

In *Michaelson v Arthur Henriques Plc*[85] a tribunal held that the refusal by jacket machinists **4.83** to accept alternative work as dress machinists was reasonable because there was no shortage of jacket machining jobs in the locality and the employees clearly preferred that work. Conversely, in *Granger v White*,[86] the fact that a 53 year-old hairdresser would find it difficult to find another job did not make her refusal to work in a sports and equipment shop unreasonable.

Collective offers

Where a collective offer is made to a number of employees (see above) any question of **4.84** suitability must be determined in relation to each individual employee. In addition, where the offer is conditional upon it being accepted by all the employees involved then the new jobs must be suitable for each individual. If this is not the case then even if only one of the jobs is unsuitable there will have been no suitable job offer in relation to any of them.[87] Similarly, the reasonableness of any refusal must also be determined on an individual basis.[88]

---

[83] [1976] IRLR 164.
[84] EAT 470/09.
[85] COIT 1680/214, Manchester Industrial Tribunal, 1985.
[86] COIT 1631/134, Brighton Industrial Tribunal, 1985.
[87] See *E & J Davies Transport Limited v Chattaway* [1972] ICR 267.
[88] See *John Fowler (Don Foundry) Limited v Parkin* [1975] IRLR 89.

5

DEATH OF AN EMPLOYER OR EMPLOYEE

A. General	5.01
B. Death of an Employer	5.02
C. Death of an Employee	5.04

A. General

5.01 The death of a party to a contract of personal service might be regarded as a frustrating event at common law.[1] A frustrating event affecting an employee or employer will cause the contract to end by operation of law with no dismissal at all. But the following discussion deals with situations under statutory redundancy payments law where the rigours of this rule are modified.

B. Death of an Employer

5.02 The basic rule is that a redundancy payment only arises following a dismissal. Notwithstanding the above, s 136(5) of the ERA 1996 deems the death of an employer to be a dismissal of an employee by reason of redundancy, and a redundancy payment is then due. Section 136(5) also applies to any other termination of the employee's contract by operation of law where this is as a result of an act on the part of the employer or any event affecting the employer, but in practice the most common circumstance under this section would be the death of an individual employer and, by extension, the dissolution or winding-up of an employer (if not otherwise a dismissal).

5.03 If the employee is taken on by the deceased employer's personal representatives, the legal position is covered by s 174 of the ERA 1996, which mirrors the operation of the re-employment provisions on change of employer but with some differences. Principally, it is permissible for the new employment to commence as late as eight weeks after the ending of the old employment;[2] further, it is not specifically provided (as a matter of common sense!) that the offer from the personal representatives of the new employment has to be made before the ending of the old contract.[3] Subject to these points, rules similar to the standard re-employment

---

[1] For a case of frustration by employer's death see *Farrow v Wilson* [1869] LR 4 CP 744. For cases of frustration involving an employee, see *Marshall v Harland and Wolff Ltd (No. 2)* [1972] ICR 97; *Egg Stores (Stamford Hill) Ltd v Leibovici* [1977] ICR 260; FC *Shepherd & Co Ltd v Jerrom* [1986] ICR 802; and *Notcutt v Universal Equipment Co (London) Ltd* [1986] 3 All ER 582. For a further discussion see Chapter 2.

[2] Compared to four weeks in the case of the standard re-employment provisions discussed in Chapter 4.

[3] Again, cf. the standard re-employment provisions discussed in Chapter 4.

provisions apply. That is to say, the employee may reject with impunity the new employment on the point of offer if it is different from the old and not suitable, or during the trial period of four weeks if it is not suitable or, in either case, if suitable, it is reasonable so to do. A redundancy payment is then due in the above circumstances, but it will be lost if the employment was held to be suitable or the rejection or termination unreasonable.

C. Death of an Employee

Certain statutory provisions cover the case of death of an employee. Unlike the circumstance **5.04** of death of an employer, the death of an employee is not deemed to give rise to a redundancy dismissal (or, indeed, any dismissal). But there are special rules once a redundancy notice has been given to an employee and the employee should then die. These provisions involve a considerable amount of speculation as to what would have happened had the employee survived.

First, if the employer has given notice to an employee to terminate the contract of employ- **5.05** ment for redundancy and before that notice expires the employee dies, then, for the purposes of the statutory redundancy scheme provisions, the contract is deemed to have been duly terminated by the employer by notice expiring on the date of the employee's death.[4] Second, when an employer has given notice to an employee to terminate the contract of employment and has offered to renew the contract of employment or re-engage under a new contract, then, if the employee dies without either having accepted or refused the offer and the offer has not been withdrawn before his death, the entitlement of the deceased employee's estate to the redundancy payment depends on whether it would have been unreasonable on the part of the employee (had he lived) to have refused the offer.[5] Third, when an employee's contract of employment has been renewed or he has been re-engaged under a new contract of employment and during the trial period the employee dies without having terminated or having given notice to terminate the contract, then the entitlement of the employee's estate to a redundancy payment will depend on whether it would have been reasonable for the employee (had he lived) to have terminated the employment during the trial period.[6] Fourth, if an employee gives notice to terminate his employment during the trial period but dies before the expiry of that notice, then his notice is deemed to have expired upon his death and the entitlement of the estate to a redundancy payment depends on whether it would have been reasonable for the employee (had he lived) during the trial period to have terminated the contract.[7]

There are also rules about lay-off, short-time working and other matters where they are **5.06** affected by the death of an employer or employee. For these more arcane situations, the rules are set out in the ERA 1996, ss 174–176.[8]

---

[4] ERA 1996, s 176(1).
[5] ERA 1996, s 176(3).
[6] Ibid., (4).
[7] Ibid.
[8] Finally, death of an employer arose in a different context, concerning information and consultation obligations arising from the Collective Redundancies Directive 98/59/EC (see Chapter 11) in a referral to the ECJ by the *Tribunal Superior de Justica de Madrid (Spain)* in the case of Case C-323/08 *Ovidio Rodriguez Mayor and Others v Herencia Yacentre de Rafael de las heras Dávila and others*. In a judgment of 10 December 2009 the Court ruled that the Spanish law according to which the termination of employment contracts of workers as a result of death of their employer (being a natural person) is not classified as collective redundancy, did not infringe on the Directive. (And so it also followed that the Directive does not preclude natural legislation, which provides for different compensation depending on whether the workers lost their jobs as a result of the death of the employer or as a result of a collective redundancy).

6

LAY-OFF AND SHORT-TIME WORKING

A. General   6.01   D. Implied Contractual Terms   6.07
B. Common Law Rules   6.03   E. The Statutory Scheme   6.15
C. Express Contractual Terms   6.04

A. General

6.01 Sometimes, when work is scarce and an employer needs to reduce costs, he may be tempted to consider laying-off employees by asking them not to come to work for a period of time.[1] Alternatively, he may consider putting them on short-time work by asking them to work fewer hours per day or fewer days per week. These options may be considered as an alternative to redundancy, perhaps in the hope that work will pick up again in the near future. For an employer, the two options may provide a positive alternative, as not only is the employer able to retain a skilled workforce, but he also avoids the need to remunerate his workforce to the extent of his full contractual obligation to do so and further may avoid making redundancy payments. But whilst these options may be seen by employers as alternatives to redundancy, these solutions are not always welcome to employees who may, in circumstances where they are not receiving full pay,[2] prefer to be released from their employment, to make a claim for a statutory redundancy payment and perhaps commence alternative employment elsewhere.

6.02 The immediate implications of lay-off or short-time working will depend, in part, on the contracts of employment of the employees concerned. If these contain provision (whether express or implied) for the employer to lay-off employees or put them on short-time work, the employer will at least not be acting in breach of contract. However, detailed statutory provisions may come into play, providing a complicated method by which an employee may claim a redundancy payment notwithstanding the employer's contractual rights. If the employer does breach the employee's contract in laying-off employees or putting them on short-time work when there is no enabling term in the contract, such a breach is likely to

---

[1] See 'Lay-offs and Short-time working', IRLB 589 (March 1998), which refers to lay-off as 'the suspension of a contract of employment when work is unavailable'.

[2] Although such employees may be entitled to statutory guarantee payments (See Chapter 9) and/or job seekers' allowance.

permit an employee to resign and claim constructive dismissal. If successful, the employee will[3] be awarded a redundancy payment as the reason for the dismissal will be a diminishing work requirement (see Chapter 3). In such a case an employee would not therefore need to rely on the statutory rules.[4]

B. Common Law Rules

Is there a contractual right for the employer to impose a lay-off or short-time work?

There is a clear principle of law that where an employee is laid off by an employer in the **6.03** absence of contractual authority to do so, the employer will repudiate the contract and the employee will be entitled to treat himself as dismissed.[5] There is clearly a fundamental breach of contract in circumstances where an employer seeks, as occurs when an employee is laid off, not to pay his workers, albeit that they are not expected to work.[6] If eligible,[7] the employee can then claim a redundancy payment.[8] So, in the absence of either an express or implied right to lay-off or to put an employee on short-time work, an employer will be in breach of contract and could find himself faced with a constructive dismissal claim where he is potentially liable for a redundancy payment.[9] If an employment tribunal were to find that the employer had acted unfairly, then the employer may also have to pay compensation for the unfair dismissal.[10]

C. Express Contractual Terms

Clearly, the first exercise for an employer when considering these measures is to examine **6.04** whether there is an express power in the employment contract[11] to lay-off employees or to impose short-time work on them. But even if there is an express provision, the employer must then check that it covers the situation in which he finds himself. So, for example, in *Jewell v Neptune Concrete Limited*,[12] a reference to the employer being permitted to lay-off as a result of inclement weather or similar did not 'constitute authority for lay-offs due to lack of orders'.

In *A Dakri & Co Limited v Tiffen*[13] Mrs Tiffen was laid off without pay in accordance with an **6.05** express term in her contract which said, 'if there is a shortage of work or the firm is unable to operate because of circumstances beyond its control it has the right to lay you off temporarily and without remuneration'. After four weeks of being laid off, Mrs Tiffen wrote to her employers, who explained that the closure was only 'temporary'. One week later, Mrs Tiffen

---

[3] Subject to eligibility.
[4] Unless perhaps he had waived the employer's breach of contract by implied or express consent.
[5] *Jewell v Neptune Concrete Limited* [1975] IRLR 147.
[6] In the absence, of course, of the appropriate contractual authority.
[7] See eligibility requirements in Chapter 1.
[8] And possibly unfair dismissal (see Chapter 10).
[9] The employer may be able to argue in its defence that the employee has impliedly or expressly waived the breach by conduct, for example.
[10] But this would depend on the facts (see Chapter 10).
[11] The employment contract may, of course, include terms of a collective agreement which are incorporated into it. Commonly of relevance in these circumstances would be a 'Guaranteed Week Agreement' provided, of course, it was incorporated into the employee's contract.
[12] [1975] IRLR 147.
[13] [1981] IRLR 57.

applied to the employment tribunal for a redundancy payment. The tribunal held that because of the period of time over which the lay-off extended, it was not 'temporary' and therefore Mrs Tiffen was entitled to regard herself as being constructively dismissed. The EAT upheld the employment tribunal's decision, and stated that unless a period is specified in an express contractual term, any period of lay-off must be reasonable. What is reasonable, will, of course, be a question of fact for the employment tribunal. In this case, a four-week limit was suggested.[14]

6.06   The scope of *Dakri* was considered by the EAT in *Kenneth McRae & Co Limited v Dawson*.[15] Mr Dawson was laid off for four weeks and the employment tribunal, following the EAT in *Dakri* held that, notwithstanding that the company was contractually expressly entitled to lay Mr Dawson off without pay 'indefinitely', it could only do so for a reasonable period of time without being in material breach of an implied term that the express power in the contract would be exercised reasonably. The EAT, however, overturned the employment tribunal's decision and held that where an express right to lay-off existed without the words of temporal limitation operative in the *Dakri* case, an employer cannot be regarded as being in breach of its obligation simply because of the passage of time. So, an express contractual right to lay-off indefinitely is not subject to a reasonableness test in terms of its length but, of course, that may be largely irrelevant given that if any employee thinks that too long a time has elapsed, he can follow the statutory procedure (see below) in order to terminate his employment and obtain his redundancy payment.

D. Implied Contractual Terms

Lay-off

6.07   If there is no express contractual provision permitting an employer to lay-off or put an employee on short-time work, the question is whether such a term can be implied into an employee's contract of employment. Generally, the courts will be reluctant to do this. A good starting point is the Court of Appeal's decision in *Devonald v Rosser & Sons*.[16] Following a shut down of the business, the employee sought to recover damages for breach of an implied agreement by the employer to provide the employees with work.

In its defence the employer sought to establish that an implied term existed which enabled it to lay- off its employees without notice and to cease to provide work and pay. This applied, argued the employer, when it, 'was unable to obtain remunerative orders or specifications', in addition to situations such as 'lack of water or coal ... breakage of machinery, repairs'.

6.08   The Court of Appeal held:

> Now in order to succeed the defendants must prove a custom or general usage so well known, as to be properly read into the contract. It must be a custom so universal that no workman could be supposed to have entered into his service without looking to it as part of the contract.

The Court of Appeal went on to say, 'a claim to be good must be reasonable, certain and notorious'.

---

[14]   But this entirely depends on the facts, of course.
[15]   [1984] IRLR 5.
[16]   [1906] 2 KB 728.

Whilst it may therefore be possible to imply a right to lay-off in circumstances wholly beyond **6.09** the employer's control (such as a failure of supplies or power or machinery breakdown), slackness of trade will not generally be sufficient, nor will an absence of remunerative orders.

There are, of course, certain other circumstances in which the right to lay-off will be implied **6.10** into a contract of employment. In *Puttick v John Wright & Sons Limited*,[17] Mr Puttick had been employed as a regular casual worker for over 23 years but on a job-by-job basis. Consequently, he frequently had short periods in between jobs in which he was laid off. It was held that the employer had an implied contractual right to lay Mr Puttick off. The National Industrial Relations Court found that it was clearly part of the ongoing arrangement between the parties that Mr Puttick could be laid off for periods in which no work was available and so a term to that effect could be implied into his contract of employment.

Another example of the implication of a term into a contract may be found in *Waine v R* **6.11** *Oliver (Plant Hire) Limited*.[18] The EAT held that where there is no express provision in a contract of employment or a collective agreement, whether there is an implied right to lay-off 'depends upon what the expectation would be, according to customs in the particular trade, as to the terms upon which an employee in the position of the employee in this present case was to be employed at the time his employment commenced'. So, on this authority, an employer must be able to persuade an employment tribunal that the implied term was in existence at the time the employee began work. The EAT made specific reference in that case to 'customs of a particular trade'. Consequently, it is far more likely that an employer will be able to argue an implied contractual right to lay-off in these circumstances in industry sectors such as the building trade, where it is a common occurrence to lay people off when there is a shortage of work, than generally. On a practical note, employers must not, once an employee has agreed on one occasion to be laid off, assume that they have a contractual right to lay-off on future occasions, as such an acceptance on one occasion will not mean that the employee has accepted the existence of an implied term. It is at least equally likely that a court would say that the employee simply waived the employer's breach on that one occasion.[19]

Short-time

In *Miller v Hanworthy Engineering Ltd*[20] the contract of employment of a section foreman **6.12** stated: 'Your salary is at the annual rate shown above, payable in arrears at the end of each calendar month. Adjustments for overtime, lost time or other alterations are made at the end of the month following such overtime or short-time.' There was also in place a collective agreement which applied in respect of Mr Miller and which made provision for work sharing. It said: 'Where work sharing is accepted as an alternative to immediate redundancies, the terms and conditions of employment as regards periods of notice, remuneration etc shall be temporarily waived …'. Although there had been other occasions when Mr Miller had worked short-time without complaint, in October 1982 a further period of short-time work began which had not been agreed to by Mr Miller's union. Mr Miller claimed his lost wages

---

[17] [1972] ICR 457.
[18] [1977] IRLR 434.
[19] See *Waine*; although repeated acceptance may give rise to an estoppel or to a variation of the contract or may be taken into account as evidence of what the parties agreed at the time.
[20] [1986] IRLR 461.

from the periods during this non-agreed short-time working. The case was eventually heard by the Court of Appeal, which upheld Mr Miller's claim. The Court of Appeal stated:

> Where there is an admitted contract of employment under which a salary is payable, if the provision as to payment of salary in that contract is to be displaced, the employers must show some agreed variation of the actual term.

6.13   The Court of Appeal held, first, that the reference to an 'adjustment' or 'alteration' in the context of short-time work 'did not give the [employer] authority to refuse to pay an employee who was willing and able to return his contractual duties simply because of the [employer's] inability to provide him with work'. Second, it held that the relevant term in the collective agreement 'was applicable only where work sharing was accepted by the union'. So, a clause must clearly and unambiguously provide an employer with the right to put employees on short-time work, as there can be no implied contractual right for an employer to impose short-time working on a salaried employee who is ready, able, and willing to perform the duties required of him under his contract of employment.

An employee's choices

6.14   Where there is no express or implied term allowing an employer to lay-off or impose short-time work, an employee may, of course, decide not to act upon the employer's breach by resigning, and seeking to claim a statutory redundancy payment by claiming constructive unfair dismissal, but may continue to be employed. However, even if an employee who is laid off does not resign, he may[21] bring a contractual claim for his lost wages.[22] Alternatively, the employee may bring a claim under Pt II of the ERA, as a failure to pay the employee what he is due under his contract may constitute an unlawful deduction from wages. Finally, the employee may[23] seek to rely on the statutory scheme.

E. The Statutory Scheme

Statutory right to a redundancy payment

6.15   The statutory scheme enables an employee to claim a redundancy payment where either the employer has a contractual right (express or implied) to lay him off or put him on short-time work, or where an employer has acted in breach of contract but the employee has chosen not to resign in response to that breach.

6.16   Sections 147 and 148 of the ERA 1996 contain details of the scheme by virtue of which an employee can claim a redundancy payment without actually being dismissed by his employer. This scheme operates when an employee has been laid off or kept on short-time work for the time periods set out in the ERA 1996, subject to the satisfaction of certain statutory conditions.[24] The scheme can be relevant in the absence of a contractual entitlement enabling

---

[21] Providing he does not 'accept' the employer's breach.
[22] Or, rather, damages in lieu if he has wrongfully been prevented from supplying the consideration (i.e. work) for the wages due (see *Miller v Hamworthy Engineering Ltd* (above)).
[23] In addition to a breach of contract/unlawful deduction from wages claim if he so chooses.
[24] As stated above, it may not be necessary for an employee to rely on the statutory scheme if there is no contractual power to lay-off or impose short-time working on the particular occasion in question: common law principles may classify this as a repudiation, leading to (if accepted) a constructive dismissal which will probably be by reason of redundancy, allowing the employee to resign and claim a redundancy payment by virtue of the constructive dismissal.

an employer to lay-off or impose short-time work as an alternative to the employee resigning and claiming constructive dismissal in order to claim a redundancy payment. It will, however, be most useful to employees who are subject to a contractual power on the part of the employer to alter working patterns in this way.

Lay-off and short-time: the definitions under the statutory scheme

There are specific statutory definitions of lay-off and short-time working. Section 147(1) of the ERA 1996 states that an employee shall only be taken to be laid off 'where [he] is employed under a contract on terms and conditions such that his remuneration under the contract depends on his being provided by the employer with work of the kind which he is employed to do'. Such an employee is treated as laid off during any week in respect of which he is not provided with work as a result of which he is not contractually entitled to remuneration.[25]   **6.17**

Short-time working under statute occurs where there is a diminution in the work provided for an employee under the contract and as a result the employee's remuneration for any week is less than half a week's pay.[26] Consequently, it may be possible to place an employee on short-time work, but so that he still receives more than half a week's pay and avoid the statutory scheme.   **6.18**

Spinpress Limited v Turner,[27] provides some assistance on the interpretation of the statutory definition of short-time work. Mr Turner was a polisher on 'piece work'. When there was a downturn in business, Mr Turner was offered some work which he refused, on the ground that the rate of pay was too low for that work. Consequently, there was not enough work to keep him employed on a full-time basis and he was put on short-time work. He applied for a redundancy payment. The employment tribunal found that he was entitled to a redundancy payment as the work was merely 'offered' and not 'provided'. The employer appealed. The EAT held that, had he accepted the work, he would have received more than half a week's pay. He was therefore not on short-time and was not entitled to a redundancy payment. So, work is 'provided' if it is offered.   **6.19**

What an employee must do to claim a redundancy payment

Section 148 of the ERA 1996 states that an employee shall not be entitled to a redundancy payment by reason of being laid off or kept on short-time unless he gives notice in writing to his employer 'indicating (in whatsoever terms) his intention to claim a redundancy payment in respect of lay off or short-time'.[28] Such a notice is referred to as 'a notice of intention to claim', and it must be in writing.   **6.20**

Before service of that notice, the employee in question must have been laid off or kept on short-time for four or more consecutive weeks.[29] The last of those weeks must have ended   **6.21**

---

[25] Employees who are entitled to a minimum wage, for example, under a guaranteed week agreement will not therefore qualify (although guarantee payments (see Chapter 9) are irrelevant for those purposes).

[26] ERA 1996, s 147(2). Note that this is the statutory definition and that short-time work does not necessarily need to satisfy the statutory definition in order to enable an employee to resign and claim constructive dismissal. Also, the amount of a week's pay is calculated in accordance with statutory guidance.

[27] [1986] ICR 433.

[28] ERA 1996, s 148(1).

[29] A notice served before this period has expired is invalid (see, e.g., *Allinson v Drew Simmons Engineering Ltd* [1985] ICR 488).

not more than four weeks before the date on which the notice was served.[30] Alternatively, the employee must have been laid off or kept on short-time for a series of six or more weeks, of which no more than three were consecutive, within a period of 13 weeks.[31] In the latter case, the last week of the series before the service of the notice must have ended on the date of service of the notice or not more than four weeks before the date of service.

Employer's counter notice

6.22   An employee is not entitled to a redundancy payment in pursuance of a notice of intention to claim if the employer gives a counter notice under s 149 of the ERA 1996. This notice must be in writing and given within seven days of the service on the employer of the employee's notice of intention to claim. The notice must state that the employer will resist any liability to make a redundancy payment in pursuance of the employee's notice of intention to claim.[32] In addition, it must be established that, on the date of service of the employee's notice of intention to claim, it was reasonably to be expected that had he continued to be employed by the same employer the employee would, not later than four weeks after that date, enter upon a period of employment with the employer of not less than 13 weeks, during which he would not be laid off or kept on short-time for any week.[33] If, however, during the four weeks following the date of service of the employee's notice of intention to claim, the employee is laid off or kept on short-time for each of those weeks, it is conclusively presumed that it cannot reasonably be expected that the employee will not be laid off or kept on short-time for the 13-week period mentioned above.[34]

6.23   Where the employer gives a counter notice within seven days of the service of the employee's notice of intention to claim and does not withdraw the counter notice by a subsequent notice in writing to the employee, the employee is not entitled to a redundancy payment except in accordance with a decision of an employment tribunal.[35]

Requirement for employee to terminate employment

6.24   The final additional hurdle that the employee must surmount to be entitled to a redundancy payment in pursuance of his notice of intention to claim is that he must terminate his contract of employment. This must be by at least one week's notice (whether given before, after, or at the same time as the notice of intention to claim), or more if the period of minimum notice that he would normally have to give to terminate his contract is longer.[36] In *Walmsley v C & R Ferguson Limited*[37] it was held that no particular mode of articulation is required to indicate the necessary notice of termination of employment. So, when Mr Walmsley, having referred to the fact that he had been laid off for the requisite number of weeks, said in writing to his employer '... I am left with no option but to resign and instigate industrial tribunal proceedings against you. I look forward to hearing from you within seven days', the Court of Session held that the letter was capable

---

[30] ERA 1996, s 148(2)(a).
[31] Ibid., (b).
[32] See, e.g. *Fabar Construction Ltd v Race* [1979] ICR 529.
[33] ERA 1996, s 152(1).
[34] Ibid., (2).
[35] Ibid., s 149.
[36] Ibid., s 150(2).
[37] [1989] IRLR 112.

of bearing the meaning that the employee had duly served the one week's notice required of him.

Notice of termination of employment must be given within certain periods in differing circumstances. First, if the employer fails to give a counter notice within seven days of the service of the employee's notice of intention to claim, the period is the three weeks after the end of those seven days.[38] Second, if the employer has given a counter notice within those seven days but withdraws it by a subsequent notice in writing, the period is the three weeks after the service of the notice of withdrawal.[39] Third, if the employer gives a counter notice within seven days and does not withdraw it and the question of the employee's right to a redundancy payment in pursuance of the notice of intention to claim is referred to an employment tribunal, the period is the three weeks after the industrial tribunal has notified the employee of its decision.[40] **6.25**

Strikes and lock-outs

In all these calculations, no account should be taken of any week during which an employee is laid off or kept on short-time working where the lay-off or short-time is wholly or mainly attributable to a strike or a lock-out, whether the strike or lock-out is in the trade or industry in which the employee is employed or not, and whether it is in Great Britain or elsewhere.[41] **6.26**

'Strike' and 'lock-out' are defined in s 235(5) and (4) of the ERA 1996.[42] **6.27**

It is important to note that other forms of industrial action short of a strike, for example a go-slow or a work-to-rule, are not covered and their existence need not be taken into account if the employee is laid off or put on short-time work as a result. **6.28**

---

[38] ERA 1996, s 150(3)(a).
[39] Ibid., (b).
[40] Ibid., (c).
[41] Ibid., s 154.
[42] Under s 235 of the ERA:

    (4) 'lock-out' means:
        (a) the closing of a place of employment;
        (b) the suspension of work; or
        (c) the refusal by an employer to continue to employ any number of persons employed by him in consequence of a dispute done with a view to compelling persons employed by the employer, or to aid another employer in compelling persons employed by him, to accept terms or conditions of or affecting employment.
    (5) 'strike' means:
        (a) the cessation of work by a body of employed persons acting in combination; or
        (b) a concerted refusal, or a refusal under a common understanding, of any number of employed persons to continue to work for an employer in consequence of a dispute, done as a means of compelling their employer or any employed person or body of employed persons or to aid other employees in compelling their employer or any employed person or body of employed persons, to accept or not to accept terms or conditions of or affecting employment.

7

MISCONDUCT AND STRIKES

A. The Overall View	7.01	D. Strike Action: Treatment of	
B. Misconduct: The General Scheme	7.03	Entitlement to a Redundancy Payment	7.13
C. Misconduct and Strike Action	7.06	E. Appendix to *Simmons v Hoover Ltd*	7.16

A. The Overall View

7.01 The statutory provisions dealing with the effect of misconduct or strike action on redundancy payment entitlement are of labyrinthine complexity. Phillips J remarked in the EAT case of *Simmons v Hoover Ltd*[1] that ' . . . it is plain that no Chairman of an [employment] tribunal has embarked with any enthusiasm on the task of construing these [provisions]. We share this reluctance . . .'.

7.02 To be fair to the learned judge, it should be noted that, despite his remarks, the EAT then went on helpfully to publish, with the assistance of counsel, a tabular guide to the legislative scheme as an appendix to its decision. This guide is reproduced at the end of this chapter.

B. Misconduct: The General Scheme

7.03 Subject to the ERA 1996, s 140,[2] under s 140(1) of the ERA 1996, an employee may be disentitled to a redundancy payment where the employer is entitled to terminate the contract of employment by reason of the employee's conduct and the employer does actually do so:

(a) without notice; or
(b) by giving shorter notice than that which, in the absence of conduct entitling the employer to terminate the contract without notice, the employer would be required to give to terminate the contract, or
(c) by giving notice which includes, or that is accompanied by, a statement in writing that the employer would, by reason of the employee's conduct, be entitled to terminate the contract without notice.

---

[1] [1977] 1 QB 284.
[2] See below.

Purpose of the provision: through a glass darkly

At first glance it is hard to see why this provision is included in the legislation at all. Effectively, **7.04**
it says that if the employer is entitled to dismiss by reason of misconduct (in effect because of
a repudiatory breach of contract on the part of the employee), there is no right to a redundancy
payment. It could be supposed that such a dismissal was not by reason of redundancy in
any event but a dismissal for misconduct, thus raising no question about entitlement to a redundancy payment in the first place. However, it is thought that the section is meant to catch
cases where, for example, the employee is dismissed by reason of redundancy but there are
also independent grounds which would have entitled the employer to dismiss summarily for
misconduct, and where, but for s 140(1), the employee would still be entitled to the redundancy
payment because of the presumption of redundancy.[3]

The provision might also apply where the dismissal is by reason of redundancy and the **7.05**
employer is unaware at the time of dismissal that there is misconduct, which would have
entitled the employer to dismiss without due notice on that ground. This will not usually
be where the dismissal is with full notice as the employer, being unaware of the misconduct,
will not have included the obligatory written statement to the effect that the employer
would have been entitled to dismiss with no notice (see above). But it might include a case
of a summary dismissal ostensibly on the ground of redundancy which occurs prior to an
employer's knowledge of actual misconduct. Thus, in *X v Y Limited*[4] an employee dismissed
summarily by reason of apparent redundancy was disentitled to a redundancy payment
because of his employer's subsequent discovery of misconduct, which then entitled the
employer to rely upon s 140(1) of the ERA 1996. The Parliamentary debates on the provisions are contained in Hansard;[5] they do not, however, unequivocally explain the issues
outlined above.

C. Misconduct and Strike Action

It was held in *Simmons v Hoover Ltd*[6] that conduct entitling the employer summarily to **7.06**
dismiss for the purposes of s 140(1) of the ERA 1996 includes strike action which (contrary
to some previous case law discussion) is repudiatory of the contract of employment and
therefore misconduct within the terms of that section of the 1996 Act. There has always been
controversy on whether a strike with notice amounts to a breach of contract.[7] But in *Simmons*
it was suggested that the effect of a strike notice would simply be notice of an intended breach
of contract. It seems that the better view is that it depends on the wording of a strike notice:
if appropriately worded it could be construed as a lawful notice of termination by an
employee,[8] in which case there would be no breach of contract (but a resignation would not
entitle an employee to statutory rights). The effect of *Simmons* is nevertheless that in most
cases a strike will be a repudiatory breach of contract. In practice, the last thing strikers
intend to do is to terminate their employment contracts by lawful notice.

---

[3] ERA 1996, s 163(2).
[4] [1969] 4 ITR 204.
[5] HC vol 716 col 1708 (21 July 1995); and HL vol 269 cols 206–246 (3 August 1965).
[6] [1977] 1 QB 284.
[7] See, e.g., *Morgan v Fry* [1968] 2 QB 710, in which Lord Denning MR suggested it might have the effect
of suspending the contract.
[8] *Boxfoldia Ltd v National Graphical Association* (1982) [1988] ICR 752.

7.07   Lord Denning MR in *Secretary of State for Employment v Aslef (No. 2)*[9] also regarded 'working to rule' as a breach of contract in this context. In this case, involving industrial action by rail unions in 1972, members were instructed to strictly observe all of the British Railway Board's (BRB) rules i.e., to work strictly 'to rule' to ban Sunday and rest day working and to impose a general ban on overtime working. It was accepted that the object of these instructions was to make it impossible for the BRB to carry on its commercial activity of running the railways. Rules were to be observed to the very letter in order to disrupt the railway service. Lord Denning MR stated:

> Now I quite agree that a man is not bound positively to do more for his employer than his contract requires. He can withdraw his goodwill if he pleases but what he must not do is wilfully to obstruct the employer as he goes about his business. This is plainly the case where a man is employed singly by a single employer . . . It is equally the case when he is employed as 'one of the many' to work in an undertaking which needs the service [of all]. If he, with the others, takes steps wilfully to disrupt the undertaking, to produce chaos so that it will not run as it should, then each one who is a party to those steps is guilty of a breach of contract. It is no answer for any one of them to say 'I am only obeying the "rule book"' or, 'I am not bound to do more than a 40 hour week'. That would be all very well if done in good faith without any wilful disruption of services; but what makes it wrong is the object with which it is done. There are many branches of our law when an act which would otherwise be lawful is rendered unlawful by the motive or object with which it is done. So here it is the wilful disruption which is the breach.

7.08   However, in *Burgess v Stevedoring Services*[10] the Privy Council did not find that an overtime ban by port workers called by the Bermuda Industrial Union fell within the definition of industrial action or was an anticipatory repudiation on behalf of all of its members of their contractual obligation to work overtime. In this case, it was held the overtime ban was not in breach of the contracts of employment or terms and conditions of the service of the participants. The way in which the overtime ban was implemented was that the union, in breach of an obligation under the collective agreement, refused to make up overtime gangs. This was not in itself a breach of any individual contract of employment. The employee's obligation was to report for duty if, but only if, he had been assigned to an overtime gang and the effect of the overtime ban was to prevent this from happening. In fact, a number of employees were willing to report for duty whenever they were called upon to do so. The employees had simply stayed at home because they had not been assigned overtime work. If they had been assigned work and as part of concerted action declared themselves not available, the *Aslef* case might have been relevant but it was not, where it could be distinguished, in the present case.

7.09   There are exceptions to disentitlement to a redundancy payment in the case of misconduct or strike action. These are when the misconduct or strike action occurs during the notice period that follows an earlier dismissal by reason of redundancy. First, under s 140 of the ERA 1996, if an employee has been given notice of dismissal by reason of redundancy but subsequently takes part in a strike and is for that reason dismissed with short notice, and if the second dismissal takes place during the 'obligatory period'[11] of the employer's notice, the

---

[9] [1972] 2 QB 455.
[10] [2002] IRLR 810.
[11] See Chapter 2.

strike will not affect entitlement to the redundancy payment.[12] Second, if, during notice of dismissal for redundancy, an employee commits an act of misconduct (other than going on strike) and the dismissal occurs during the obligatory period of the employer's notice, the employee is *prima facie* disentitled to the redundancy payment, but an employment tribunal may at its discretion award all or part of the redundancy payment notwithstanding the misconduct.[13]

'Strike', by virtue of s 235(5) of the ERA 1996 means: **7.10**

(a) the cessation of work by a body of employed persons acting in combination, or

(b) a concerted refusal or a refusal under a common understanding, of any number of employed persons to continue to work for an employer in consequence of a dispute, done as a means of compelling their employer or any employed person or body of employed persons, or to aid other employees in compelling their employer or any employed person or body of employed persons, to accept or not to accept terms or conditions of or affecting employment.[14]

It is important to note that there must be two dismissals for s 140 of the ERA 1996 to apply;   **7.11**
the first for redundancy and the second during the notice period on account of a strike or misconduct. In *Simmons v Hoover Ltd*[15] the employees went on strike. During this strike the employer sent notices of dismissal giving the employees one week's notice of termination on the ground that it was necessary to reduce the labour force. The employee in question had an entitlement to six weeks' notice of termination of employment and was therefore dismissed with short notice for the purposes of s 140(1) of the ERA 1996. He claimed a redundancy payment. It was held that the employee was disentitled to a redundancy payment and could not rely upon s 140 of the ERA 1996 as that required a second dismissal on account of an ensuing strike. Here, there was only one dismissal, ostensibly on the ground of redundancy, after the strike had started.

Section 140 of the ERA 1996 also applies to cases under s 148 of that Act, i.e. to lay-off and   **7.12**
short-time working, so that if an employee has served notice of intention to claim a redundancy payment through lay-off or short-time and thereafter is dismissed by reason of strike action or misconduct, the above provisions apply *mutatis mutandis*.

D. Strike Action: Treatment of Entitlement to a Redundancy Payment

It can be seen from the above that, in the case of a dismissal subsequent to an original   **7.13**
dismissal for redundancy on account of a strike or misconduct, employees dismissed on account of a strike are more favourably treated (i.e. they have an absolute right to a redundancy payment) than employees dismissed by reason of misconduct (where the payment is discretionary[16]). However, by virtue of s 143 of the ERA 1996 an employer may have some additional redress in practical terms in the case of strikes. Where, during the notice of dismissal by reason of redundancy, the employee begins to take part in the strike, the

---

[12] ERA 1996, s 140(2)
[13] Ibid., (3) and (4).
[14] Ibid., s 235.
[15] [1977] ICR 61.
[16] *Lignacite Products Ltd v Krollman* [1979] IRLR 22.

employer may serve on the employee a notice in writing requesting him to agree to extend the contract of employment beyond the expiry of the notice. This extension may be by an additional period comprising the number of days lost by striking.

7.14 The notice from the employer has to indicate the reasons for making the request and has to state also that, subject to certain conditions, the employer will contest any liability to pay the redundancy payment in respect of the original dismissal.[17] The conditions attaching to the notice are threefold: the employee complies with the request; or the employer is satisfied that, in consequence of sickness, injury, or otherwise, the employee is unable to comply with it; or in other circumstances the employer is satisfied that it is not reasonable for the employee to comply with it.

7.15 An employee is taken to comply with the request in the notice of extension if, on each available date within the proposed period of extension, he attends work and is ready and willing to work.[18] It is then provided that the notice period is deemed to be extended to the last day on which the employee attends ready and willing to work within the period of the extension.[19] If the employee does not comply with the request and does not attend for work during all of the available days during the proposed extension, he is disentitled to a redundancy payment unless the employer agrees to make such a payment notwithstanding the failure to comply. However, an employment tribunal may award part or all of the redundancy payment as seems appropriate if it is considered reasonable for the employee not to have complied with the request.[20]

E. Appendix to *Simmons v Hoover Ltd*[21]

7.16 Table from the judgment in *Simmons v Hoover Ltd* (reproduced with the kind permission of The Incorporated Council of Law Reporting for England and Wales).

X is a redundant employee of Y Company and is entitled, under his contract of employment, to three months' notice.

---

[17] ERA 1996, s 143(1) and (2).
[18] Ibid., s 144(1).
[19] Ibid.
[20] Ibid., s 143(5) and (6).
[21] [1977] ICR 61.

No	Situation	[Counsel for employers]			[Counsel for employees]		
		[s 140(1)]	[s 140(2)–(4)]	Redundancy payment	[s 140(1)]	[s 140(2)–(4)]	Redundancy payment
1	X is dismissed on 1 January with two months' notice:						
	(a) Y knew on 1 January that X had been stealing.	✓	X	No	✓	✓ [140(3), (4)]	Discretionary
	(b) Y subsequently discovered that X had been stealing before his dismissal.	✓	X	No	✓	✓ [140(3), (4)]	Discretionary
2	X is dismissed on 1 January with three months' notice. On 1 February Y discovers that X has been stealing and terminates the contract forthwith.	✓	✓ [140(3), (4)]	Discretionary	✓	✓ [140(3), (4)]	Discretionary
3	X is dismissed on 1 January with six months' notice. Y terminates the contract forthwith or on short notice:						
	(a) X had been found stealing on 1 February and was dismissed on that day;	✓	X	No	✓	X	No
	(b) Y discovered that X had been stealing prior to 1 January and dismissed him on 1 February;	✓	X	No	✓	X	No
	(c) X was found stealing on 1 May and was dismissed on that day.	✓	✓ [140(3), (4)] ✓ [140(2)]	Discretionary	✓	✓ [140(3), (4)]	Discretionary
4	X is dismissed on 1 January with three months' notice. X goes on strike immediately afterwards. X terminates contract forthwith on 1 February by reason of strike.	✓	X	Yes	If circumstances of strike justify summary dismissal ✓	✓ [140(2)]	Yes
5	X is dismissed on 1 January with six months' notice. X goes on strike immediately afterwards. Y terminates the contract forthwith on 1 February.	✓	X	No	If circumstances of strike justify summary dismissal ✓	X	No
6	X is dismissed with six months' notice on 1 January. On 1 February X is caught stealing. Y gives X one months' notice of termination (contract of employment terminates on 1 March).	✓	X	No	✓	X	No

Notes:

(1) The statutory provisions are square-bracketed because the table as originally given in the judgment refers to the Redundancy Payments Act 1965 provisions (e.g. s 140(1) of the ERA 1996 is the equivalent of s 2(2) of the RPA 1965; s 140(2)–(4) of the ERA 1996 is the equivalent of s 10 of the RPA 1965).

(2) The table shows respective views of counsel for the employers and the employees regarding the situations posed in the left-hand column.

8

CLAIMING AND CALCULATING

A. Time Limits	8.01	D. Failure or Inability to Pay: The	
B. The 'Relevant Date'	8.03	National Insurance Fund, the Old	
C. Amount, Seniority Issues, and the		Redundancy Fund, and the (Defunct)	
Equality Act 2010	8.12	Redundancy Rebate	8.32

A. Time Limits

8.01 A redundancy payment is not payable unless, before the end of six months beginning with the 'relevant date' (see below), either the payment has:

been agreed and paid;

or the employee has made a claim for the payment by notice in writing given to the employer;[1]

or a question as to the right of the employee to the payment or as to the amount of the payment has been referred to an employment tribunal;[2]

or an unfair dismissal complaint has been presented by an employee to an employment tribunal;

If the employee fails to ensure any of these steps is taken but, within an additional period of six months, either;

makes a claim by notice in writing given to the employer;

or refers the issue of a redundancy payment to an employment tribunal;

or makes an unfair dismissal complaint;

and it appears to the tribunal to be just and equitable that the employee should receive a redundancy payment having regard to the reasons shown by the employee for his failure to take any of the relevant steps within the first six months and to all the other relevant circumstances, then a redundancy payment may be payable nonetheless.[3]

---

[1] In *Hetherington v Dependable Products Limited* (1971) 6 ITR 1 it was held by the Court of Appeal that such a notice *must* refer to redundancy pay in some way. But as long as this notice is given during the six-month period the claim may be activated at any time thereafter.

[2] The duty on ACAS (Advisory, Conciliation and Arbitration Service) to conciliate extends to redundancy payment claims submitted to an employment tribunal: Employment Tribunals Act 1996, s 18 (1)(d). It is to be noted that if an unfair dismissal claim is lodged, that is sufficient to protect redundancy payment rights even if beyond the three months limit to be observed for unfair dismissal claims (as long as it is submitted within six months of the relevant data: *Duffin v Secretary of State for Employment* [1983] ICR 766).

[3] ERA 1996, s 164.

It has been held, however, that where there is a dispute about a contractual redundancy **8.02** payment in respect of civil servants of the type mentioned in what is now ERA 1996, s 171(3) and where there is a reference to an employment tribunal under s 170 allowed by the contract of employment, no six-month time limit applies. The time limit is the contractual limitation period of six years.[4] Any other claim for a contractual redundancy payment is, presumably, also governed by the contractual limitation period (see chapter 12).[5]

B. The 'Relevant Date'

The 'relevant date' triggers the start of the limitation period for submitting a claim. It fixes **8.03** the end of employment for the purposes of deciding whether an employee was employed for at least two years before termination (i.e. whether the employee qualified to make a claim) and it also fixes the end of employment for the purposes of determining how long the employee's employment lasted when calculating the size of the redundancy payment. Although the question of size of payment is discussed later, the concept of 'relevant date' is discussed here.

When the employee's contract of employment is terminated by notice, whether given by the **8.04** employer or by the employee, the relevant date is the date on which the notice expires.[6] When the contract of employment is terminated without notice, it is the date on which the termination takes effect.[7] When the employee is employed under a contract for a fixed term and that term expires, it is the date on which the term expires.[8]

In a re-employment case under ERA 1996, s 138, (see Chapter 4) where there is a reasonable **8.05** termination by an employee during a trial period and, as a result, the employee is treated as having been dismissed on the termination of his employment under the previous contract, the relevant date is the relevant date as defined above in relation to the renewed or new contract for the purposes of time limits for putting in a claim for a redundancy payment. But for any other purposes (such as, for example, calculating the length of continuous employment for the purposes of calculating the size of the redundancy payment) the date is the relevant date as defined above in relation to the previous contract.[9]

Where an employee is taken to be dismissed by virtue of ERA 1996, s 136(3) (see Chapter 4— **8.06** employee anticipating expiry of employer's notice), the relevant date is the date on which the employee's notice to terminate the contract of employment expires.[10]

In a case where there has been a lay-off or short-time working and an employee puts in a **8.07** notice of intention to claim a redundancy payment, the relevant date in a case falling under ERA 1996, s 148(1)(a) (right to put in a notice of intention to claim following lay-off or short-time working for four or more consecutive weeks) is the date on which the last of the four or more consecutive weeks before the service of the notice came to an end. In a case

---

[4] *Greenwich Health Authority v Skinner and Ward* [1989] ICR 220, EAT.
[5] Unless a claim is being brought before a employment tribunal under its breach of contract jurisdiction—in which case the time limit will be three months.
[6] ERA 1996, s 145(2)(a).
[7] Ibid., (2)(b).
[8] Ibid., (2)(c).
[9] Ibid., (4).
[10] Ibid., (3).

falling within s 148(1) (b) (right to submit a notice of intention to claim as a result of lay-off or short-time working for a series of six or more weeks within a period of 13 weeks) it is the date on which the last series of six or more weeks before the service of the notice came to an end.[11]

8.08 In cases of summary dismissals with or without a payment in lieu of notice, ERA 1996, s 145(5) allows the relevant date to be postponed by the amount of statutory minimum notice to which the employee was entitled under ERA 1996, s 86(1). However, this is only for limited purposes, that is to say for calculating the two-year qualifying period under ERA 1996, s 155; for calculating the length of service to arrive at the amount of the redundancy payment (ERA 1996, s 162(1)); and for calculating a week's pay to arrive at the redundancy payment amount (ERA 1996, s 227(4)), for example to give the employee the benefit of any increase in the amount of a week's pay that can be taken into account that may have occurred between the date of the summary dismissal and the date of the notional expiry of the statutory minimum period of notice.

8.09 There is a difference between the rules for redundancy payments and unfair dismissal here. In unfair dismissal, employment can be extended by a period equivalent to statutory notice on a constructive dismissal without notice as well as an employer-initiated dismissal (ERA 1996, s 97(4)). This is not the case under s 145(5).

8.10 ERA 1996, s 86(3) says that nothing in s 86 is to be taken as preventing a party from waiving his right to notice or from accepting a payment in lieu. If a payment in lieu is accepted, does this mean that s 145(5) does not apply? The EAT in *Secretary of State, for Employment v Stafford County Council*[12] held that acceptance of a payment in lieu of notice did indeed mean that s 145(5) could not extend the employment to a later 'relevant date'. However, this decision was reversed by the Court of Appeal, where it was held that even if a party had waived all or part of his statutory notice or accepted a payment in lieu, s 145(5) still operated to extend the 'relevant date'.[13]

8.11 Where the employee dies during the period of notice of dismissal the contract is deemed duly terminated by the employer by notice expiring on the employee's death.[14] Where the employee dies after the termination of the contract but before the date on which it ought to have terminated if proper notice under ERA 1996, s 86 had been given then, for the purposes of the three cases mentioned in s 145(5) (see above), the relevant date is taken to be the date of death.[15]

C. Amount, Seniority Issues, and the Equality Act 2010

8.12 The amount of a redundancy payment is calculated under the rules in ERA 1996, s 162. This area has been affected by the changes made to the statutory scheme by the then Employment Equality (Age) Regulations 2006 where the relevant date falls after 1 October 2006. First, the minimum age threshold of 18 for a redundancy payment was removed.

---

[11] Ibid, s 153.
[12] [1987] ICR 956, [1988] IRLR 3.
[13] [1989] ICR 664.
[14] ERA 1996, s 176(1).
[15] Ibid., (2).

Second, the upper age limit of 65 was also removed. Finally, the old 'tapering' provision which provided for reduction of a redundancy payment by one-twelfth per month between the age of 64 and 65 if the relevant date fell between the employee's 64th and 65th birthday was also, consequentially, removed.[16] The banding of redundancy payments is still, as will be seen below, dependent on age. The system of differential payments according to age was retained by the government on the basis it considered that this was justifiable, notwithstanding the requirement of non-discrimination on grounds of age under the EU Equal Treatment Directive.

The then Parliamentary-Under Secretary of State for Trade and Industry, Mr Gerry Sutcliffe, **8.13** stated the government's position with regard to amending the statutory redundancy payment scheme in the light of the Equal Treatment Directive and the then forthcoming Employment Equality (Age) Regulations 2006 in a written statement to Parliament on 2 March 2006:[17]

> The Government have been considering what amendments might be needed to the statutory redundancy payments scheme to bring it into line with the EU Employment Directive [*sic*] which requires Member States to outlaw discrimination on the grounds of age, among other things, in the employment field. The current scheme contains three age bands and directs greatest financial support to older workers and those with long service.
>
> We have been discussing the way forward with key stakeholders over the last few months, including the CBI, EEF and TUC. In the course of those discussions the Government became concerned that a system using a single multiplier might not meet our overall policy aims. We have therefore carefully examined the rationale for the current scheme and come to the conclusion that this provides the best fit with our aims.
>
> Evidence the Government have gathered demonstrates that younger, prime age and older workers fall into three distinct economic categories, with older workers facing a particularly difficult position in the employment market. Young workers tend not to be out of work for long, and see only a small fall in pay when switching jobs. Older workers are much more likely to be long-term unemployed, and to experience a substantial fall in pay when finding a new job. Prime age workers fall into the middle. We therefore believe it is sensible for the level of support provided through the scheme to reflect these three categories. A system using a single multiplier would leave a significant group of older workers substantially worse off than at present, and we believe this would be unacceptable. Even if a substantial amount of money were injected into the scheme so as to leave older workers no worse off, the enhanced benefits to younger workers are not justified by their position in the employment market.
>
> The Directive provides for the possibility of Member States providing for different treatment on the grounds of age, where the difference of treatment is objectively and reasonably justified by a legitimate aim, including employment policy. We have looked at this question very closely and are confident that retaining the age bands is permitted by the Directive.
>
> The Government have however decided to remove the lower and upper age limits in the redundancy scheme (at 18 and 65 respectively) and the taper at the age of 64 because we believe, as employees are living and working longer, these cannot be justified under the Directive . . . .

The weighting of redundancy payments according to age under the statutory scheme in the **8.14** ERA 1996 is therefore exempt from challenge under what is now the Equality Act 2010 (EA 2010), Sch 22, para 1(1), which states that a person does not contravene the protection

---

[16] See the former ERA 1996, s 162(4) and (5), repealed with effect from 1 October 2006 by the Employment Equality (Age) Regulations, 2006, Sch 8, para 32.

[17] HC Hansard—written ministerial statements for 2 March 2006.

against discrimination on the grounds of age as a protected characteristic if he is acting in accordance with a requirement in an enactment.[18]

8.15 It is to be noted, however, that the EA 2010 makes discrimination as to contractual and non-contractual benefits on grounds of age unlawful unless it can be justified. Thus, an enhanced redundancy compensation scheme which differentiates payments on grounds of age is potentially unlawful unless objectively justifiable. However, provided that the same structure is used to circulate contractual redundancy terms as for statutory redundancy terms (even though the amounts are higher than the statutory redundancy payments themselves) these enhanced, contractual terms are lawful under the Regulations without the need for objective justification by the employer. This is expressly provided for by para 13 of sch 9 of the EA 2010. In other words, provided that the employee follows the statutory seniority scheme exactly he can, for example, treat a week's pay under the enhanced scheme as not being subject to a maximum amount as is the case under the statutory scheme, remove the two-year qualifying period, and compensate those who volunteer for redundancy but who are not technically dismissed as defined, without falling foul of the EA 2010. Enhanced redundancy schemes and age discrimination issues are more fully discussed in Chapter 12.

The formula

8.16 Under the statutory scheme in the ERA the employee is entitled to one-and-a-half week's pay for every year during which he was 41 years of age or over. He is entitled to one week's pay for every year during which he was aged 22 years or over but less than 41. And he is entitled to half a week's pay for every year during which he was under 22. The maximum amount of a week's pay that can be taken into account is usually altered periodically by statutory instrument and with effect from 1 February 2011 is £400.[19] A maximum of 20 years' service

---

[18] Replacing Equality (Age) Regulations 2006, reg 27.

[19] As stated above, the maximum amount of a week's pay that can be used for the calculation is currently £400 (The Employment Rights (Increase of Limits) Order 2010 (SI 2010/2926). Previously, this limit was reviewed annually by the Secretary of State for Trade and Industry, who could vary it at his discretion. However, s 34 of the ERA 1999 provides for the indexation of various payments and employment tribunal awards which arise under the ERA 1996 and TULR(C)A 1992, including the limit on a week's pay. The first such increase took effect on 1 February 2000 and reflected the change in the Retail Prices Index (RPI) between September 1997 and September 1999 (the maximum week's pay rose from £220 to £230) (SI 1999/3375). The Secretary of State is now under an obligation to increase (or decrease) the limit in line with the change in the RPI over the preceding year, using September's indices as the reference points. The limit will be rounded up to the nearest multiple of £10. Although this change, which means that in real terms redundancy payments should maintain their value, is to be welcomed, it does nothing to remedy the erosion in value of statutory redundancy payments that has occurred since the enactment of the Redundancy Payments Act 1965. As discussed in our Introduction, most employees now earn more than the current statutory maximum amount and the maximum has lost considerable value in real terms since inception. According to the 2009 Annual Survey of Hours and Earnings the median gross weekly pay was £489 in the UK. Meanwhile, the maximum compensatory award for unfair dismissal has been increased from £12,000 to (currently) £68,400. Although the government never explicitly stated that this was its intention, this increase restored the value of the maximum in real terms to the same level as it was when the right to complain of unfair dismissal was introduced. However, it seems that redundancy payments will not benefit from the same treatment. The previous maximum of £380 (raised from £350) was made by the Work and Families (Increase of Maximum Amount) Order 2009 pursuant to the power in s 14 of the Work and Families Act 2006, given the financial crisis and concerns of business and unions. But the government rejected the option of increasing the limit to £450 (the then average weekly earnings) and further froze the increase until 2011, thereby missing out the annual review which would have been due in February 2010. The maximum is now set at £400 with effect from 1 February 2011. Where an employee earns in excess of the maximum amount, the statutory limit is used in the formula for calculation set out above. As stated, the 2009 Annual Survey of Hours and Earnings revealed that in April 2006 the median gross weekly earnings were £489. For men earnings were £531, compared with £426 for women. It can be inferred from

worked back from the relevant date can be taken into account for the purposes of calculating the redundancy payment (thus yielding a maximum payment at the time of writing of £12,000 (30 x £400). This means that this is the present maximum redundancy payment under statute. A redundancy payments ready reckoner is reproduced at Appendix 1.

Calculating a week's pay

As stated, the maximum amount of a week's pay available for a redundancy payment **8.17** calculation is £400. Where the employee's pay is less than the statutory maximum the rules for the calculation of a week's pay are contained in ss 220–229 of the ERA 1996. There is a distinction between the situations where there is employment with normal working hours on the one hand and where there is employment with no normal working hours on the other. The rules are highly complex. A more detailed treatment may be found in *Harvey on Industrial Relations and Employment Law.*[20] A summary of the basic rules follows here.

Employments with normal working hours

It is ss 221 and 223 which determine the amount of a week's pay where there are normal **8.18** working hours for the employee when employed under the employment contract in force on the calculation date.[21]

If the employee's remuneration for the employment in normal working hours does not vary **8.19** with the amount of the work done in the period, the amount of a week's pay is the amount which is payable by the employer under the employment contract in force on the calculation date if the employee works throughout his normal working hours in any week.[22]

If the employee's remuneration for employment in normal working hours does vary with the **8.20** amount of work done in the period, the amount of a week's pay is the amount of remuneration for the number of normal working hours in a week calculated by the average hourly rate of remuneration payable by the employer to the employee in respect of the period of 12 weeks ending:

(a) where the calculation date is the last day of a week, with that week and;
(b) otherwise, with the last complete week before the calculation date.[23]

---

this that the weekly earnings of considerably more men than of women exceed the statutory maximum. It is therefore possible to argue that its imposition infringes Art 157 of the Treaty on the Functioning of the European Union (TFEU) (see *Barry v Midland Bank Plc* [1991] ICR 859). Even if there is a *prima facie* infringement of Art 157 of the TFEU, however, it is highly probable that the limit would be capable of objective justification (see in a different context the comments of Lord Hoffmann in *Mann v Secretary of State for Employment* [1991] IRLR 566, 570)). Where an employee earns less than the statutory maximum, a week's pay must be calculated for him in accordance with the provisions of ERA 1996, ss 220 to 229 (see below). Although there is no express provision in the ERA 1996 as to whether the applicable statutory maximum is that which is in force on the calculation date or that which is in force on the relevant date, it may be inferred from s 227(3) (now repealed) that it is the latter.

[20] *Harvey on Industrial Relations and Employment Law* H [800]–[1100].
[21] ERA 1996, s 221 (1). Voluntary overtime does not come into normal working hours (*Armstrong Whitworth Rolls Ltd v Mustard* [1971] 1 All ER 598). But if the employer becomes obliged to offer overtime and the employee is obliged to work those overtime hours compulsory overtime comes into normal working hours: *Armstrong Whitworth Rolls Ltd v Mustard*; *Tarmac Roadstone Holdings Ltd v Peacock* [1973] 2 All ER 485; *Gascol Conversion Ltd v Mercer* [1974] IRLR 155; *Lotus Cars Ltd v Sucliffe and Stratton* [1982] IRLR 381; *Colne Valley Spinning Ltd v Yates* (EAT/1091/02).
[22] ERA 1996, s 221 (2). Termed by *Harvey* as 'flat rate' workers.
[23] Ibid., (3). Termed by *Harvey* as 'variable rate' workers.

8.21   Section 223 of the ERA 1996 provides, for the purposes of ss 221 and 222, in arriving at the average hourly rate of remuneration only:

(a)   the hours when the employee was working and;

(b)   the remuneration payable for or apportionable to, those hours should be brought in. If for any of the twelve weeks mentioned in sections 221 and 222 no remuneration was payable by the employer to the employee account shall be taken of remuneration in earlier weeks so as to bring up to twelve the number of weeks of which account is taken.

8.22   Finally, where:

(a)   in arriving at the average hourly rate of remuneration, account has to be taken of remuneration payable for, or apportionable to, work done in hours other than normal working hours and;

(b)   the amount of that remuneration was greater than it would have been if the work had been done in normal working hours

account shall be taken of that remuneration as if that work had been done in such hours and the amount of that remuneration had been reduced accordingly.

8.23   In *British Coal Corporation v Cheesbrough*,[24] The House of Lords ruled that where an employee works hours in excess of his normal working hours and receives overtime premium in respect of those hours, s 223 (3) provides that for the purposes of calculating the average hourly rate, the amount of remuneration should not include the overtime premium. The House of Lords noted that the underlying purpose of s 223 (3) was to prevent inflation of redundancy payments to employees who worked longer hours of overtime attracting a large element of overtime premium in the concluding weeks of employment.

Remuneration

8.24   References to remuneration varying with the amount of work done includes remuneration which may include any commission or similar payment which varies in amount.

8.25   Otherwise remuneration is not defined. According to *Secretary of State for Employment v John Woodrow & Sons (Builders) Limited*[25] remuneration means gross pay. The National Industrial Relations Court (NIRC) authority of *S & U Stores Limited v Wilkes*[26] held that remuneration included wages and salaries; expenses are excluded (to the extent that they do not represent a profit in the employee's hands); benefits in kind are excluded; and cash payable by someone other than the employer are excluded. Bonus and commission payments may be included in the calculation if the employee is *entitled* to such payments by way of the employment contract, even if the level of payment may fluctuate according to the employee's performance.[27] Thus, it has been held by the EAT in *Canadian Bank of Commerce v Beck*[28] that for the purposes of calculating a week's pay for reason of assessing the amount of the protective award, a discretionary bonus should not be included.

8.26   Where remuneration varies according to the time of work, the following rules apply.[29] If the employee is required, under the employment contract, to work normal working hours on days of the week or times of the day which differ from week to week or over a longer period

---

[24] [1990] IRLR 148.

[25] [1983] IRLR 11.

[26] [1974] IRLR 283.

[27] *Weevsmay Ltd v Kings* [1977] ICR 244.

[28] EAT/0141/10.

[29] Termed by *Harvey* as 'rota' workers.

so that the remuneration payable for or portionable to any week varies according to the incidences of those days or times,[30] the amount of a week's pay is the amount of remuneration for the average number of weekly normal working hours at the average hourly rate of remuneration.[31] For this purpose the average number of weekly hours is calculated by dividing by 12 the total number of the employee's normal working hours during the relevant period of 12 weeks and the average hourly rate of remuneration is the average hourly rate of remuneration payable by the employer to the employee in respect of the relevant period of 12 weeks.[32] 'Relevant period of 12 weeks' means the period of 12 weeks ending:

(a) where the calculation date is the last day of a week, with that week and;
(b) otherwise with the last complete week before the calculation date.[33]

Employment with no normal working hours

When this is the case, the amount of a week's pay is the amount of the employee's average weekly remuneration in the period of 12 weeks ending   **8.27**

(a) where the calculation date is the last day of a week, with that week, and;
(b) otherwise, with the last complete week before the calculation date.[34]

In arriving at the average weekly remuneration no account is to be taken of a week in which no   **8.28**
remuneration was payable by the employer to the employee and remuneration in earlier weeks is to be brought in so as to bring up to 12 the number of weeks of which account is taken.[35]

Calculation date

The calculation date is   **8.29**

(a) where the relevant date is postponed by virtue of Section 145 (5), the date on which the contract of employment ends or otherwise;
(b) the date x weeks before the relevant date, where x weeks is the notice which is required by Section 86 of the ERA 1986 (statutory minimum notice) to terminate the contract

Written statement

An employee is entitled to a written statement from an employer indicating how a redun-   **8.30**
dancy payment is calculated unless an employment tribunal has already fixed the amount of a redundancy payment by a decision of the tribunal.[36] If the employer fails to comply with this obligation without reasonable excuse he commits a criminal offence.[37] Further, the employee may demand a statement if not already supplied with one, giving the employer at least one week to comply therewith. If the employer fails to comply with this request without reasonable excuse he may commit a further criminal offence.[38] If an employer fails to give a written statement or indeed any sort of voluntary statement indicating how the redundancy

---

[30] ERA 1996, s 222 (1).
[31] Ibid., (2).
[32] Ibid., (3).
[33] Ibid., (4).
[34] Ibid., s 224(2).
[35] Ibid., (3).
[36] Ibid., s 165(1).
[37] Ibid., (2).
[38] Ibid., (3).

payment is calculated he runs the risk, in cases where he makes a general *ex gratia* payment to an employee on termination of employment which exceeds the amount of the statutory payment, of the employee later asserting that it was not intended that the *ex gratia* payment should include the statutory redundancy payment. This might allow the employee a fresh opportunity to claim a redundancy payment in addition to the *ex gratia* payment even if, all along, the employer may have intended the *ex gratia* payment to include the redundancy payment.[39]

Repealed provisions

8.31 Finally, there were formerly complicated provisions that allowed an employer to reduce or extinguish any redundancy payment entitlement due to accrual by an employee of a pension on or soon after the dismissal by redundancy. These were repealed with effect from 1 October 2006 by the Employment Equality (Age) Regulations 2006.[40]

D. Failure or Inability to Pay: The National Insurance Fund, the Old Redundancy Fund, and the (Defunct) Redundancy Rebate

8.32 Until the Employment Act 1989 an employer was, under what was then s 104 of the Employment Protection (Consolidation) Act 1978 (EPCA), entitled to a rebate on redundancy payments paid by him out of what was previously known as the Redundancy Fund. From 1985 the rate of rebate was 35 per cent. But the Wages Act 1986 denied the right to claim rebate to employers who had more than nine employees. The Employment Act 1989 abolished the right to rebate altogether.[41]

8.33 The Redundancy Fund was replaced by the National Insurance Fund with effect from 1 February 1991.[42] Under ERA 1996, s 167, where an employee claims that his employer is liable to pay him a redundancy payment and the employee has either taken all reasonable steps (other than legal proceedings) to recover the payment from the employer and the employer has refused or failed to pay it or has paid part of it and has refused or failed to pay the balance or the employer is insolvent and the whole or part of the payment remains unpaid, then the employee may apply to the Secretary of State for a payment under ERA 1996, s 166.[43] The claim is made using form RP1, which is reproduced at Appendix 9. When a payment is made by the Secretary of State to an employee all rights and remedies of an employee in respect of the payment reimbursed by the Secretary of State are transferred to the Secretary of State, who may then recover from the employer.[44] Any dispute with the Secretary of State about liability of an employer or the amount of the sum payable may be referred to an employment tribunal.[45]

---

[39] *Collin v Flexiform Ltd* (1966) 1 ITR 253; *Galloway v Export Packing Services Ltd* [1975] IRLR 306.

[40] See ERA 1996, s 158 and the Redundancy Payments Pensions Regulations 1965, SI 1965/1932, repealed by the Employment Equality (Age) Regulations 2006, Sch 8, para 31. In the DTI partial regulatory impact assessment in respect of statutory redundancy pay and the proposed changes in the light of the then forthcoming Employment Equality (Age) Regulations 2006 it was proposed that these Regulations be revoked on the ground that they 'no longer serve a useful purpose and . . . have fallen into disuse'.

[41] Employment Act 1989, s 17. See the discussion on the effects of this change at para 20.05.

[42] Employment Act 1990, s 13 (now administered by the Department of Business Innovation and Skills).

[43] ERA 1996, ss 166(1) and 167(1).

[44] Ibid., s 170(3).

[45] Ibid., (2).

Part II

EMPLOYMENT PROTECTION RIGHTS ASSOCIATED WITH REDUNDANCY

9

GUARANTEE PAYMENTS AND TIME OFF TO LOOK FOR WORK OR TRAINING

A. Guarantee Payments	9.01
B. Time Off to Look for Work or Training	9.24

A. Guarantee Payments

Qualifying factors

The statutory right to a guarantee payment is found in Pt III of the ERA 1996. Guarantee **9.01** payments are not part of the statutory redundancy scheme, but are minimum fall-back payments to which certain categories of employees are entitled during periods of lay-off.[1]

The right of an employer to lay-off his employees without pay, due to the unavailability of **9.02** work, will constitute breach of contract if the employer has no express or implied contractual right to do so. Where there is no contractual right to lay-off, employees are entitled to receive normal pay and benefits, even though there is no available work. Failure to make these payments may therefore lead to claims for breach of contract, constructive unfair dismissal, or claims under Pt II of the ERA 1996 for unauthorised deductions from pay (see Chapter 6). Where, however, the employer does have a contractual right to lay-off without pay, the employer may still be obliged to make statutory guarantee payments to qualifying employees in respect of days when no work is provided during normal working hours.

Certain categories of employees are excluded from the right to guarantee payments. The **9.03** excluded categories are:

(a) share fishermen;[2]
(b) police officers;[3]
(c) members of the armed forces.[4]

---

[1] Lay-off is considered fully in Chapter 6.
[2] ERA 1996, s 199(2).
[3] Ibid., s 200(1).
[4] Ibid., s 192(2).

9.04 Neither crown servants nor parliamentary staff are excluded.[5] Formerly, an employee could not qualify for a guarantee payment if he was employed wholly or mainly outside Great Britain;[6] however, this provision has now been repealed.[7]

9.05 In order to claim a guarantee payment, an employee must normally be continuously employed for a qualifying period of one month, ending with the day before that for which the guarantee payment is claimed.[8] It should be noted that days on which an employee is actually laid off will count as days of continuous employment.

9.06 An employee who has no normal working hours on any particular day also has no right to a guarantee payment[9] because the very purpose of the right is to compensate the employee for the loss of earnings which would have been earned in normal circumstances but for the failure of the employer to provide work.

The workless day

9.07 An employee will only be entitled to a guarantee payment if the reason that the employee was not provided with work by his employer is due to either:

(i) 'a diminution in the requirements of the employer's business for work of the kind that the employee is employed to do';[10] or

(ii) 'any other occurrence affecting the normal working of the employer's business in relation to work of the kind that the employee is employed to do'.[11]

9.08 An 'occurrence' in (ii) above has been interpreted as meaning some external 'involuntary' interruption to the employer's business, such as natural disaster, power supply failure, fire, or flood. In *North v Pavleigh Ltd*[12] the employer's voluntary closure of his factory for Jewish holidays fell outside the restricted meaning of an 'occurrence'. The test therefore seems to be whether the closure is involuntary,[13] although in *Newbrooks and Sweet v Saigal*[14] an employment tribunal found that employees had been laid off because the employer wanted fewer employees at work whilst he was hospitalised.[15]

The right to claim

9.09 An employee is entitled to be paid a statutory guarantee payment in respect of a 'workless day'.[16] A 'day' is a period of 24 hours from midnight to midnight,[17] and it is 'workless' if, during those 24 hours, the employee is given no work to do at all[18] and, in normal circumstances, his contract would require him to work at least part of that day. However, where a

---

[5] Ibid., ss 191(2), 194(2), and 195(2).
[6] Ibid., s 196.
[7] Repealed by the ERA 1999.
[8] ERA 1996, s 29(1).
[9] Ibid., s 30(1).
[10] Ibid., s 28(1).
[11] Ibid., s 28(1)(b).
[12] [1977] IRLR 461.
[13] See also *Robinson v Claxton and Garland (Teeside) Ltd* [1997] IRLR 159.
[14] 29695/77.
[15] See also *Miller v Harry Thornton (Lollies) Ltd* [1978] IRLR 430.
[16] ERA 1999, s 28(3)(a).
[17] Ibid., (4).
[18] Even if the work is provided outside normal working hours.

working day straddles two calendar days, as in the case of night workers, only one day may be treated as a qualifying workless day, depending on whether most hours of the shift fall before or after midnight.[19]

In order to claim the guarantee payment, the employee must be able to show that he would **9.10** be 'normally required to work in accordance with his contract of employment' on the relevant day.[20] The employee cannot therefore claim the payment if he would have been absent on the relevant day due to holiday or sickness.

The question of whether there is a normal requirement to work has been considered in a **9.11** number of cases.[21] The situation is that the day must be one on which under normal circumstances the employer can require the employee to attend for work. In *Mailway (Southern) Ltd v Willsher*[22] the applicant was a casual worker who worked such hours as were available, but she was under no obligation to work if she did not want to. She was not, therefore, required to work on any particular day and it was held that she was not entitled to a guarantee payment. In *Miller v Harry Thornton (Lollies) Ltd*,[23] an employment tribunal held that there was a normal requirement to work on the relevant day as employees were expected under their contracts to attend on any weekday on which they were called for work by the employer. However, a more restrictive interpretation was applied in *Christopher Neame Ltd v White and Others*,[24] in which the EAT found that employees employed under loose contractual arrangements allowing them to attend for work on any given day that they liked did not amount to a normal requirement to attend for work, even though there was substantial regularity in the employment.

It should also be noted that a variation in the employee's contract of employment, even if **9.12** made in unilateral breach of contract by the employer, may disentitle the employee to a guarantee payment. In *Clemens v Peter Richards Ltd*,[25] the employer reduced the employee's working week from five days to four days and finally to a two-day week. Even though the employer was in unilateral breach of contract, the employee was not entitled to a guarantee payment in respect of the three days a week on which he did not work, because there was no normal requirement to work on those days. This is a very harsh decision but indicates the generally restrictive interpretation adopted by the employment tribunals. The position is different, however, if the variation is one which is specified to cover a period of short-time working, in which case normal working hours will include those worked under the original contract.[26]

Finally, no guarantee payment is payable on any day where working is voluntary, where **9.13** the employee should be on holiday or sick, or on a non-working day if the employee is part-time.

---

[19] ERA 1996, s 28(5).
[20] Ibid., (1).
[21] See also *North and Others v Pavleigh Ltd* [1977] IRLR 461.
[22] [1978] IRLR 322.
[23] Ibid., 430.
[24] EAT 451/79 (1980, unreported).
[25] [1977] IRLR 332.
[26] ERA 1996, s 50(5).

Exclusions from the right to a guarantee payment

9.14 Section 29 of the ERA 1996 provides that an employee will not be entitled to a statutory guarantee payment in three circumstances:

Where the failure to provide work is due to industrial action[27]

9.15 An employee is not entitled to a guarantee payment in respect of a workless day if the failure to provide him with work occurs in consequence of a strike, lock-out, or other industrial action involving any[28] employee of the employer or an associated employer.[29] It has also been held that the employee is excluded from the right to a guarantee payment if the industrial action is the immediate cause of the lay-off, even if it is not the only cause.[30]

The employee unreasonably refuses alternative work[31]

9.16 An employee is not entitled to a guarantee payment in respect of a workless day if the employer has offered to provide alternative work for that day,[32] and the work is suitable in all the circumstances (whether or not it is work that the employee is employed to perform under his contract), and the employee has unreasonably refused that offer.[33] Whilst this requirement does, at first glance, look similar to the test of suitable alternative employment in a redundancy situation (see Chapter 4), it is generally thought that the test of suitability in s 29(4)(a) of the ERA 1996 is wider than in the context of redundancy. An employment tribunal will have regard to the temporary nature of the alternative work and will usually expect more versatility from an employee in assessing the suitability of the alternative work and the reasonableness of the refusal.[34]

9.17 In *Purdy v Willowbrook International Ltd*[35] a coach-building firm laid off a trimmer but offered him temporary work in the finishing shop. The employee contended that the work was unsuitable because it was not his trade. However, the employment tribunal found that he had unreasonably refused the work because he was capable of doing it and, indeed, had done it in the past. There was no danger of the employee becoming a 'permanent fixture' in the finishing shop. The employee therefore disqualified himself from claiming a statutory guarantee payment.

The employee does not comply with reasonable requirements of the employer with a view to ensuring that his services are available[36]

9.18 An employee is not entitled to a guarantee payment in respect of a workless day if he does not comply with reasonable requirements imposed by the employer with a view to ensuring that the employee's services are available. In *Meadows v Faithful Overalls Ltd*[37] the employer's factory ran out of oil for the central heating system and the employees were asked to wait in

---

[27] Ibid., s 29(3).
[28] And not only the employee in question.
[29] ERA 1996, s 29(3).
[30] *Thompson v Priest Lindley Ltd* [1978] IRLR 99.
[31] ERA 1996, s 29(4)(a).
[32] The offer must be made before the workless day; see *Newbrooks and Sweet v Saigal* Case No. 29694/77.
[33] ERA 1996, s 29 (4)(b).
[34] Ibid., s 29(4) provides that the alternative work may be suitable even though it is outside the contract of employment.
[35] [1977] IRLR 388.
[36] ERA 1996, s 29(5)(b).
[37] [1977] IRLR 330.

the canteen for oil to be delivered by 10.00am or soon thereafter. The workers refused to wait until after 9.45am and went home. It was held that the employees had failed to comply with the employer's reasonable requirements and were not entitled to guarantee payments.

Calculation of a guarantee payment

Guarantee payments are payable in respect of working days on which the employee is provided with no work at all. Payments are calculated by multiplying the number of normal working hours for the day in question by the 'guaranteed hourly rate'.[38] The 'guaranteed hourly rate' varies according to whether or not the employee has fixed normal working hours, as follows: **9.19**

(i)   Where normal working hours do not differ from week to week, the guaranteed hourly rate is a week's pay divided by the fixed normal weekly working hours.[39]

(ii) If normal working hours do differ from week to week[40] or over a longer period, the guaranteed hourly rate is a week's pay divided by the average normal weekly working hours during the preceding 12 weeks.

(iii) Where normal working hours do differ from week to week and the employee has been employed for less than 12 weeks, the guaranteed hourly rate is a week's pay divided by an estimated number which fairly represents the number of normal weekly working hours.[41]

In practice, such elaborate calculations are rarely necessary because guarantee payments are subject to a maximum daily rate (presently) of £22.40.[42]

The number of days for which the payment may be claimed is also limited.[43] An overall maximum of five days may be claimed for in any one period of three months.[44] However, an employee is not entitled to guarantee payments for more than the number of days he works in a week[45] (subject again to a limit of five). Thus, if the employee works less than five days a week, he may claim a guarantee payment only for such lesser number of workless days per quarter. When the number of working days varies week by week, the specified number of days is either the average number of such days (not exceeding five) over the preceding 12 weeks or a fair representation of that number, having regard to the employee's expectations from his contract of employment and the work pattern of comparable employees.[46] The three-month period is a rolling period, so that an employee who has received his maximum guarantee payment entitlement over a three-month period will have to wait for three months before being able to claim again. **9.20**

---

[38] ERA 1996, s 30(1).
[39] See Ibid., (2).
[40] As in the case of a worker whose hours differ from day to day because, for example, he is a piece-worker.
[41] ERA 1996, s 30(3) and (4). A new s 31(7) inserted by the ERA 1999, s 35, as from 25 October 1999 allows the Secretary of State to vary, by order, either the length of the period specified in s 30(2) or the limit specified in sub-s (3) or (4).
[42] Effective where appropriate date falls on or after 1 February 2011.
[43] ERA 1996, s 31(2).
[44] Ibid., (3).
[45] Within the meaning of s 235(1).
[46] ERA 1999, ss 31(4) and (5).

Other points

9.21 It is not uncommon for employees to have, in addition, a contractual right to guaranteed minimum pay in respect of workless days under the contract of employment.[47] The right to a statutory guarantee payment does not affect the contractual payment, although s 32(2) of the ERA 1996 does provide that any contractual remuneration paid to an employee in respect of a workless day shall go towards discharging any liability of the employer to pay a statutory guarantee payment in respect of that day. Also, any statutory guarantee payment paid in respect of a workless day goes towards discharging any contractual liability of the employer. In other words, there is a mutual set-off between statutory and contractual guarantee payments. If the employee is paid contractual remuneration for any workless day, that day will be taken into account when assessing his entitlement to a guarantee payment.[48]

9.22 Payment of a statutory guarantee payment by an employer does not prevent the employee claiming that he was laid off on the day for which the payment is made for the purposes of claiming a redundancy payment. If the lay-off continues for a sufficient period, the employer may be obliged to pay both the guarantee payments and a redundancy payment in respect of the lay-off (see Chapter 6). It is to be noted, however, that an employee who is entitled to a statutory guarantee payment is disqualified from claiming unemployment benefit for the workless day in question.

9.23 Where the employer has failed to pay the whole or part of a guarantee payment that was due to an employee, the employee may present a complaint to an employment tribunal.[49] The complaint must be presented before the end of the period of three months beginning with the day for which the employer has failed to make the payment. However, the tribunal may extend the time limit allowed if it is satisfied that it was not reasonably practicable for the employee to have presented the complaint earlier. If the tribunal upholds the complaint, the employer will be ordered to pay the amount of the guarantee payment that is due.[50]

B. Time Off to Look for Work or Training

Qualifying factors

9.24 Sections 52 and 53 of the ERA 1996 provide that, in certain circumstances where an employee has been given notice of dismissal by reason of redundancy, he will be entitled to reasonable paid time off during working hours to look for new employment or make arrangements for training for future employment. It should be noted that the 1996 Act does not give an employee the right to take time off without his employer's consent, but, instead, a right to request 'reasonable' time off and be compensated if it is not given.

9.25 To qualify, a claimant must be an employee and must not fall within the excluded worker category. The categories of workers who are excluded from redundancy payments are

---

[47] For example, a minimum wage payable under a Guaranteed Work Agreement provided no exemption order has been made under ERA 1996, s 35.
[48] *Cartwright v G Clancey Ltd* [1983] IRLR 355.
[49] ERA 1996, s 34(1).
[50] Ibid., (3). Any jobseeker's allowance received by the employee may be recouped.

considered in more detail in Chapter 1; some of those workers are nevertheless entitled to time off to look for work and are thus protected by ss 52 and 53 of the ERA 1996. The only workers not entitled to time off to look for work or training are:

(i) share fishermen;[51]
(ii) members of the police service;[52] and
(iii) merchant seamen.[53]

The employee must in addition have two years' continuous employment calculated in accordance with s 226 of the ERA 1996.[54] And he must have been given formal notice that his employment will terminate, not merely an indication that the employer's business might be closing down within the next few months.[55] However, in one respect, entitlement to a redundancy payment is not a requirement of eligibility for paid time off to look for work or for training: an employee who refuses to accept suitable alternative employment (and therefore loses his right to a redundancy payment) would still be entitled to reasonable paid time off for present purposes. **9.26**

Taking time off

Section 52(1) of the ERA 1996 states that a qualifying employee is entitled to 'reasonable' time off. How much time off is 'reasonable' will, of course, depend on the individual circumstances of each case. It would seem that the statute envisages a maximum of the equivalent of two working days, since the maximum award for failure to allow time off is two-fifths of a week's pay (ERA 1996, s 53(5)).[56] But this does not mean that all employees are entitled to two days off. What is 'reasonable' depends on factors such as how difficult it may be to find alternative employment, how far the employee may need to travel to do so, the needs of the employer, and so on. **9.27**

The statute states[57] that an employee is to be given time off 'during the employee's working hours'.[58] Section 53(1) of the ERA 1996 states that any period of absence occasioned by the permitted time off should be remunerated at the 'appropriate hourly rate'. The method of calculation of the 'appropriate hourly rate' is dependent on the regularity of the hours worked by the employee. If he works the same hours weekly, the rate should be calculated by dividing a week's pay by the number of hours normally worked.[59] If, however, his normal working hours vary from week to week, then an average of the last 12 weeks is taken, ending with the last complete week before the date on which notice of redundancy was given.[60] It would therefore follow that if notice was given on a Friday, the week up to that Friday would not be included in the computation. **9.28**

---

[51] ERA 1996, s 199(2).
[52] Ibid., s 200(1).
[53] Ibid., s 199(4).
[54] See Chapter 1; ERA 1996, s 52(2).
[55] See Chapter 2.
[56] For a discussion of how a week's pay is calculated see Chapter 8.
[57] ERA 1996, s 52(1).
[58] Section 50(11) of the ERA 1996 defines 'working hours' as 'any time when, in accordance with his contract of employment, the employee is required to be at work'.
[59] ERA 1996, s 53(2).
[60] Ibid., (3).

Unreasonable action by an employer

9.29 There are two circumstances which give cause for complaint under the ERA 1996 through unreasonable action by the employer concerning time off. These are where an employee:

(a) has been unreasonably refused reasonable time off to look for new employment or make arrangements for training for future employment;[61] or

(b) has been allowed time off but has been refused remuneration at the appropriate hourly rate.[62]

9.30 To make a complaint, the employee must make an application to an employment tribunal within three months, beginning with the day on which it is alleged that the time off should have been allowed, or within such further period as the tribunal considers reasonable in a case where it is satisfied that it was not reasonably practicable for the complaint to be presented within the period of three months.[63]

9.31 For an employee's claim under (a) above to be successful, he must show that his request for time off has been unreasonably refused. Whether or not the employer's refusal is reasonable will depend on the facts of each individual case. If, for example, an employer has an urgent contract that needs completing and that could lead to jobs being saved, then an employer is arguably likely to be considered reasonable in refusing an employee time off. Alternatively, an employer is unlikely to be considered reasonable if he refuses an employee the opportunity to attend an interview with a prospective employer when the employer has been given advance warning.

9.32 But will an employer necessarily act reasonably if he refuses time off when there is no actual interview or appointment made? Not according to the case of *Dutton v Hawker Siddeley Aviation Ltd*,[64] where the applicant was given two weeks' notice and within that period demanded time off with pay to seek alternative employment. His employer requested that he produce evidence of an appointment and refused to permit the time off when the applicant failed to produce such evidence. The EAT held that there was no reason why an employee should not be entitled to time off to look for other work without an appointment. After all, an interview is normally a final stage in job-hunting and will generally take place after some preparatory work. A visit to a job centre, for example, during working hours should therefore be permitted. It was held on the facts that the refusal to allow time off was unreasonable.

9.33 An employment tribunal in *Hasler v Tourell Precision Engineers Ltd*[65] followed the foregoing decision, and held that an employer acted unreasonably by making it a pre-requisite that the employee have a 'firm lead' before time off would be allowed. In this case, the tribunal said that the employer might be reasonable in refusing to pay employees who took days off and then subsequently asked for pay because they said they had been looking for work during that time; it was not reasonable, however, to require an employee to have a set interview appointment before permitting him the time off.

9.34 An example of a case where an employer acted reasonably in refusing time off is *Seldon v Kendall Company (UK) Ltd*.[66] Despite being offered re-employment by the employer who

---

61 Ibid., s 54(1).
62 Ibid.
63 Ibid., (2).
64 [1978] IRLR 390.
65 Case No.1426/103.
66 Case No.1669/22.

had, in addition, made enquiries in the area in which the employee wanted to look for work (all of which drew a blank), the employee brought a claim for refusing to permit reasonable time off. The employee had in this case requested two days off to go to Devon and Cornwall to look for jobs as a warden of a camping or caravan site. Definite leads were requested by the employer, but the tribunal held that in this case he was merely testing the employee's sincerity and checking his motives in the light of what had already been done, therefore, the employer did not unreasonably refuse the employee's request.

Remedy for unreasonable employer action

9.35 On finding for an employee in these types of cases, an employment tribunal must make a declaration to the effect that the employer has breached ss 52 or 53 of the ERA 1996 and must order the employer to pay to the employee the amount it finds due to him.[67] This amount may be:

(i) the remuneration to which the employee is entitled because of the time off he was allowed to take by the employer; and/or

(ii) compensation of an amount equal to the remuneration to which the employee would have been entitled had he been allowed the time off.

9.36 It can be seen that where the complaint is of unreasonable refusal to allow time off, an employee could actually be paid twice for the same amount of time, i.e. once by the employer for the time worked and secondly by virtue of the award from the employment tribunal. The tribunal in the *Hasler* case considered this to be correct, and the award was therefore a bonus to the employee and a penalty to the employer.

9.37 If both situations are applicable, then the amounts can be aggregated but in no case shall the amount awarded to the employee be more than two-fifths of a week's pay.[68] This acts as a ceiling, but it should be noted that there is no limit on the amount of a week's pay as there is when calculating a redundancy payment. The issue of whether a week's pay should be calculated as net or gross was also discussed in *Hasler*. The tribunal concluded that it should be gross, since deductions such as national insurance were not due because all such appropriate contributions had already been made. Under s 225(2) of the ERA 1996, the relevant date for establishing the rate of pay is the date on which notice of redundancy was given.

9.38 In *Seldon v Kendall Company* the EAT discussed s 53(7) of the ERA 1996, which precludes the possibility of double recovery where time off has been allowed. The employment tribunal held that this section precluded any financial compensation being made in a case where the employee had received more than his strict contractual entitlement. It is submitted, however, that this is not the case at all: as discussed above, double recovery is permitted in respect of unreasonable refusal of time off. In such a situation, the employee can claim up to two-fifths of a week's pay in addition to any payment received under the contract of employment, but not where time off has been allowed.

9.39 Finally, in this context, s 203 of the ERA 1996 invalidates any provision that purports to exclude or limit the right of compensation, except so far as settlement achieved under the auspices of an ACAS officer precludes the right in relation to a particular complaint. Conciliation is available for this matter under ss 18–19 of the Employment Tribunals

---

[67] ERA 1996, s 54(3).
[68] Ibid., ss 53(5) and 54(4).

Act 1996 in the normal way. The compromise agreement procedure under s 203 of the ERA 1996 is also available.

Exemption Orders

9.40 The Secretary of State may make an order under s 35 excluding certain employees from the operations of right to a guaranteed payment under s 28. This applies where, at any time, there is in force a collective agreement or an Agricultural Wages Order, under which employees to whom the agreement or order relates have a right to guaranteed remuneration and on the application of all parties to the agreement or of the Board making the order, the appropriate minister (having regard to the provisions of the agreement or order) is satsified that s 28 should not apply to those employees.[69]

---

[69] Section 35(1). The following Guarantee Payments Exemption Orders in force at the time of the introduction of this provision have effect as if made under the provision by virtue of s 241 and Sch 2, part 2, paras 1–4 of the ERA 1996 namely: No. 1 (SI 1977/156) Federation of Civil Engineering Contracts; No. 2 (SI 1977/157) National Federation of Demolition Contractors; No. 5 (SI 1977/902) British Footwear Manufacturers' Federation; No. 6 (SI 1977/1096) Steeplejacks and Lightning Conductor Engineers; No. 7 (SI 1977/1158) Paper and Board Industry; No. 8 (SI 1977/1322) Smiths Food Group; No. 9 (SI 1977/1349) British Leather Federation; No. 10 (SI 1977/1522) Fibreboard Packing Case Industry; No. 11 (SI 1977/1523) Henry Wiggin & Co Ltd; No. 12 (SI 1977/1583) Refractory Users Federation; No. 13 (SI 1977/1601) Multiwall Sack Manufacturers; No. 14 (SI 1977/2032) Tudor Food Products; No. 15 (SI 1978/153) British Carton Association; No. 16 (SI 1978/429) Henry Wiggin & Co; No. 17 (SI 1978/737) NJC for Workshops for the Blind; No. 18 (SI 1978/826) Employers' Federation of Card Clothing Manufacturers; No. 19 (SI 1979/1403) NJC for the Motor Vehicle Repair Industry; No. 21 (SI 1981/6) Plant Hire Working Rule Agreement; No. 23 (SI 1987/1757) National Agreement for Wire and Wire Rope Industries (revoking No. 4); No. 24 (SI 1989/1326) Rowntree Mackintosh Confectionery Ltd (revoking No. 22 as amended); No. 25 (SI 1989/1575) Building and Allied Trades Joint Industrial Council (revoking No. 20); No. 26 (SI 1989/2163) Airflow Streamlines; No. 27 (SI 1990/927) G & G Kynock plc; No. 28 (SI 1990/2330) Bridon Ropes Ltd; No. 30 (SI 1996/2132) National Joint Council for the Building Industry.

Part III

UNFAIR DISMISSAL

10

REDUNDANCY AND UNFAIR DISMISSAL

A. General	10.01	D. The Selection Process	10.119
B. The Standard of Reasonableness Expected of Employers	10.37	E. Alternative Employment	10.176
		F. Remedies	10.185
C. The Warning and Consultation Process	10.78	G. Automatically Unfair Dismissal	10.230

A. General

A common misconception is that a redundancy dismissal has no consequence other than **10.01** liability for a statutory (or contractual) redundancy payment and for notice entitlement. This is not so; any employee who has been dismissed, including by reason of redundancy, has, subject to qualifying factors, the right not to be unfairly dismissed for the purposes of Pt X of the ERA 1996. In fact, redundancy dismissals give rise to a significant number of unfair dismissal claims each year. Common complaints concern failure to inform and consult, unfair selection, and failure to consider alternative employment. The level of claims is, of course, exacerbated by the present economic crisis.

In this chapter we shall identify and examine those elements of a redundancy procedure that **10.02** an employment tribunal would expect to see in order that the procedure may be considered as fair and reasonable. To do this we shall look at the standard of reasonableness in relation to the major elements of the redundancy procedure, namely those of warning and consultation, selection, and alternative employment, before going on to examine the elements themselves. We shall consider what remedies are available for the unfairly dismissed individual, and finally we evaluate some of the more recent changes to the law allowing individuals greater scope to claim that their selection for redundancy and dismissal has been automatically unfair.

Qualifying factors

An employee who wishes to claim unfair dismissal must, in general, prove first that (subject **10.03** to certain exceptions) he or she had been employed for one year continuously up to the effective date of termination of employment and, second, that he or she has been dismissed. The ERA 1996 also imposes other conditions of entitlement to bring a claim, although these are not discussed in detail here.

It will be noted that the one-year qualifying period for unfair dismissal claims no longer **10.04** equates to the two-year qualifying period for redundancy payment entitlement (see Chapter 1).

The original two-year qualifying period for unfair dismissal claims was under continual threat (see, for example, *R v Secretary of State for Employment, ex parte Seymour-Smith*,[1] in which the Court of Appeal held that, for the period between 1985 and 1991, the two-year qualifying threshold for an unfair dismissal complaint indirectly discriminated against women and was incompatible with the EC's Equal Treatment Directive).[2] The change from a two-year to a one-year qualifying period was effected by the Unfair Dismissal and Statement of Reasons for Dismissal (Variation of Qualifying Period) Order 1999.[3] At the time of writing the Coalition Government has announced its intention to increase, once again, the qualifying period for unfair dismissal claims from one year to two. This section therefore needs to be read in the light of that proposal.[4]

10.05 The Government made the change from a two-year qualifying period to a one-year qualifying period prior to the determination of the issues in the *Seymour-Smith* litigation. After the Court of Appeal had heard the case, the House of Lords got its chance to consider the matter.[5] The House of Lords criticised the Court of Appeal, which had made a declaration that the two-year qualifying period necessary to complain of unfair dismissal was indirectly discriminatory contrary to the Equal Treatment Directive. The House of Lords said that a declaration of incompatibility would not enable the employees to pursue their claims in the tribunal. A directive has no effect upon the private rights of employees and their employers where the employer is not the State or one of its emanations.[6] The House of Lords determined that in order to give judgment it would be necessary to request the European Court of Justice (ECJ) to give preliminary rulings on certain questions on the construction of what was then Art 119 of the European Treaty (now Art 157 of the TFEU).

10.06 The House of Lords therefore posed five questions to the ECJ. These were as follows:

(i) Does an award of compensation for breach of the right not to be unfairly dismissed under national legislation constitute 'pay' within the meaning of Article 119?

(ii) If the answer to question 1 is 'yes' do the conditions determining whether a worker has the right or not to be unfairly dismissed fall within the scope of Article 119 or that of Directive 76/207?

(iii) What is the legal test for establishing whether a measure adopted by a Member State has such a degree of disparate effect as between men and women as to amount to indirect discrimination for the purposes of Article 119 of the E.C. Treaty unless shown to be based upon objectively justified factors other than sex?

(iv) When must this legal test be applied to a measure adopted by a Member State? In particular, at which of the following points in time, or at what other point in time, must it be applied to the measure:

(a) When the measure is adopted?

---

[1] [1995] IRLR 464.

[2] Directive 76/207 of 9 February 1976 on the implementation of the principle of equal treatment for men and women as regards access to employment, vocational training and promotion, and working conditions. See BIS consultation paper: Resolving workplace disputes, January 2011. (<http://www.bis.gov.uk/consultations/resolving-workforce-disputes?cat-open>).

[3] SI 1999/436.

[4] See BIS consultation paper: Resolving workplace disputes, January 2011, (n 2 above).

[5] [1997] IRLR 315, HL; [1997] ICR 371; [1997] All ER 273.

[6] See the decisions of the European Court of Justice in *Marshall v Southampton and South West Hampshire Area Health Authority* [1986] IRR 140, ECJ and C-91/92 *Faccini Dori v Recreb Srl* [1994] ECR I-3325, ECJ.

   (b) When the measure is brought into force?

   (c) When the employee is dismissed?

 (v) What are the legal conditions for establishing the objective justification, for the purposes of indirect discrimination under Article 119, of a measure adopted by a Member State in pursuance of its social policy? In particular, what material need the Member State adduce in support of its grounds for justification?

The ECJ gave its judgment, although in some respects, in particular in relation to discrimi- **10.07** nation, it could be argued that this was less than helpful.[7] In dealing with the first two questions, the ECJ ruled that an award of compensation for a breach of the right not to be unfairly dismissed does indeed constitute pay within the meaning of Art 119 of the EC Treaty (Art 157 of the TFEU). The ECJ also ruled that the conditions determining whether an employee is entitled, where he has been unfairly dismissed, to obtain compensation also fall within the scope of Art 119 of the Treaty. The ECJ went on to say, however, that the conditions determining whether an employee is entitled, where that person has been unfairly dismissed, to obtain reinstatement or re-engagement fall within the scope of the Equal Treatment Directive.

With regards to the questions relating to discrimination posed by the House of Lords, the **10.08** ECJ in its ruling did not particularly help.

As to the question regarding what the legal test is for establishing whether a measure adopted **10.09** by a Member State has such a disparate impact as between men and women that it may amount to indirect discrimination, the ECJ said that in order to establish whether a measure adopted by a Member State has disparate effect as between men and women to such a degree as to amount to indirect discrimination the national court must verify whether the statistics available indicate that a 'considerably smaller percentage' of women than men is able to fulfil the requirement imposed by that measure. In other words, the answer to the question simply begged a further question, 'What is meant by considerably smaller'?

In respect of the question as to when the test is to be applied, the ECJ stated that it is for the **10.10** national court, taking into account all of the legal and factual circumstances, to determine the point in time at which the legality of a rule is to be assessed.

Finally, in respect of the last question, what are the legal conditions for establishing objective **10.11** justification of a measure for the purposes of indirect discrimination? The ECJ stated that it is for the Member State, as the author of the allegedly discriminatory rule, to show that the said rule 'reflects a legitimate aim of its social policy, that that aim is unrelated to any discrimination based on sex, and that it could reasonably consider that the means chosen were suitable for attaining that aim'.

In its judgment the ECJ did give a view on the percentages involved in this particular case. The **10.12** ECJ said that although it is for the national court to determine whether the statistics indicate that a considerably smaller percentage of women than men is able to satisfy the condition required, they strongly suggested that a 'snap shot' approach would not necessarily be appropriate. In other words, it may not be appropriate to simply take a point in time, examine the statistics and determine whether, at that point in time, there was discrimination. In particular, the ECJ said that sex discrimination could be apparent if the statistical evidence 'revealed a

---

[7] [1999] IRLR 253, ECJ.

lesser but persistent and relatively constant disparity over a long period between men and women who satisfy the requirements of, in this case, two years employment'. What the ECJ seemed to be saying is that where there is a, perhaps obvious, large disparity in the statistics between men and women, then that disparity may be relatively short-term but still amount to sex discrimination. But even where the disparity between men and women is relatively small, if that disparity has persisted over a long period and has been relatively constant then that too may amount to evidence sufficient to show sex discrimination. Of course, such a test still begs the question what is meant by relatively smaller or to use the words of the ECJ a 'lesser but persistent and relatively constant disparity'. Fortunately, the ECJ gave some assistance on the facts of the case. The ECJ said that in the present case in 1985, the year in which the requirement of two years' service was introduced, 77.4 per cent of men and 68.9 per cent of women fulfilled that condition. Over the period 1985 to 1991 the average ratio of male to female was 10:9. The ECJ did not think that these figures evidenced a considerable disparity. They did emphasise, however, that it is for the national court to establish whether the 1985 statistics concerning the respective percentages of men and women fulfilling the requirement of two years' service are relevant and sufficient for resolving this particular case.

10.13 The case finally found its way back to the House of Lords and judgment was given on 17 February 2000.[8]

10.14 The House of Lords held that the applicants had shown that, at the time of their dismissal in 1991, the two-year qualifying period to bring an unfair dismissal complaint had a disparately adverse impact on women so as to amount to indirect discrimination contrary to Art 119 (now Art 157 of the TFEU) of the EC Treaty. Adopting the language of the ECJ, the House of Lords said that in a case of indirect discrimination, the obligation is to avoid applying unjustifiable requirements having a 'considerable disparity of impact'. The House of Lords commented that the approach adopted by the European Court is similar to that provided in s 1(1)(b) of the Sex Discrimination Act 1975, now absorbed into s 19 of the EA 2010, i.e. indirect discrimination. That is to say that a considerable disparity can be more readily established if the statistical evidence covers a long period and the figures show a persistent and relatively constant disparity and, in such a case, a lesser statistical disparity may suffice to show that the disparity is considerable than if the statistics cover only a short period or if they present an uneven picture. In other words, the concept of 'considerable' would not seem to relate to the size of the disparity but the fact that it has persisted over a long period of time.

Conclusion

10.15 So here we have, arguably, some confusion. It may be possible to show a disparity in the statistics between men and women who can comply with a particular requirement. If there is a disparity, then the question is whether it is considerable. It would now seem to be the case that if the statistics indicate a large percentage difference (although 'large' is never defined) then it does not matter that that disparity may not have persisted for any great length of time; the mere size of the disparity at the particular time will amount to a considerable disparity and therefore to indirect sex discrimination simply because the disparity is a big one. On the other hand, where the disparity is relatively smaller (although again that is entirely undefined), provided that it has persisted over a period of time and has been constant (again that is not defined) the disparity may also be 'considerable'.

---

[8] [2000] IRLR 263, HL.

For the applicants in this case, of course, the sting in the tail was that although they had **10.16** succeeded in showing that there was a considerable disparate adverse impact on women so as to amount to indirect discrimination, the House of Lords also held that the Secretary of State had discharged the burden of showing that the extension of the qualifying period was justified by factors which were objective and unrelated to discrimination based on sex. One final point for the sake of completion is that the House of Lords did say that since the requirements of EU law must be complied with at all relevant times, the retention of a measure which has a disparately adverse impact may, over time, become unjustified. For example, the benefits hoped for may not materialise. Therefore the onus is on the Government to review the position periodically. The greater the disparity of impact, the greater the diligence which can be reasonably expected of the Government, according to the House of Lords. The response of employment tribunals was to strike out all unfair dismissal claims which were being held in abeyance awaiting the outcome of the *Seymour-Smith* litigation unless the applicants could show good reason why that should not be the case. As a postscript, however, the BIS Consultation Paper: *Resolving Workplace Disputes* (January 2011) proposes once more to lift the qualifying period back to two years. No doubt the above arguments will re-surface. Indeed, the paper invites comments as to whether the proposal would be perceived as disproportionally impacting on women and ethnic minorities.[9]

The meaning of dismissal for unfair dismissal purposes is contained in s 95 of the ERA 1996, and **10.17** redundancy dismissals can fall within the categories listed. Our discussion of the concept of dismissal in Chapter 2 therefore, has some overlap here. Section 95(1) of the ERA 1996 states that:

> . . . an employee is dismissed by his employer if (and, subject to subsection (2), only if):
> (a) the contract under which he is employed is terminated by the employer (whether with or without notice),
> (b) he is employed under a limited-term contract and that contract terminates by virtue of the limiting event without being renewed under the same contract, or
> (c) the employee terminates the contract under which he is employed (with or without notice) in circumstances in which he is entitled to terminate it without notice by reason of the employer's conduct.

As mentioned in Chapter 2, another common misconception is that a termination of employ- **10.18** ment through voluntary redundancy is not a dismissal. However, employment tribunals are reluctant to deprive individuals of their rights to claim unfair dismissal merely because they have, in some sense, agreed that the reason for termination is redundancy and have volunteered to opt for a redundancy package. Some employers have sought to argue that voluntary redundancy is akin to consensual termination rather than dismissal. However, the principle is well established that a person who volunteers for redundancy is dismissed within the meaning of s 95(1) of the ERA 1996. The leading case is *Burton Allton & Johnson Ltd v Peck*.[10]

That is not to say that distinctions cannot be drawn in this difficult area. In *Morley v C T Morley* **10.19** *Ltd*[11] the EAT held that when an employee director volunteered for redundancy he had been dismissed. This is in contrast to the Court of Appeal's decision in *Birch and Humber v University of Liverpool*,[12] in which the university offered staff early retirement with the express warning

---

[9] At p 55.
[10] [1975] ICR 193.
[11] [1985] ICR 499.
[12] Ibid., 470.

that if not enough individuals volunteered there would be compulsory redundancies. Birch and Humber volunteered for early retirement and then sought to claim that they had been dismissed. The employment tribunal agreed that they had been dismissed but the Court of Appeal reversed this decision. Early retirement was consensual termination and did not amount to a dismissal on the facts; it appeared that, in this case, the volunteer was not forced to leave even if the university agreed to the early retirement following an individual's request. In other words, the ultimate decision lay with the individual and not with the university.

10.20   In *Walley v Morgan*[13] Mr Morgan, a farm worker, persuaded his employer to dismiss him by reason of redundancy in order that he could claim a redundancy payment. The employer agreed. Ultimately, when the case was litigated, this arrangement was found to be a dismissal and not consensual termination.

10.21   It is worth considering the case of *Scott v Coalite Fuels & Chemicals Ltd*,[14] in which Mr Scott was given a choice between accepting dismissal by reason of redundancy or opting to take early retirement. The difference between the two was in the financial package, which would be more beneficial on early retirement. Not surprisingly, Mr Scott elected to take early retirement. Subsequently he left on that basis, but then sought to claim a redundancy payment and the issue arose as to whether he had been dismissed. The EAT was divided. The majority said that it would not overturn the employment tribunal's decision that there was consensual termination. However, the minority view was that, in reality, the employer had decided that Mr Scott's employment would terminate and it was only the method of termination that employer and employee were discussing. In those circumstances there was a dismissal.[15]

10.22   It is also of note that, by virtue of volunteers for redundancy being deemed to have been dismissed by reason of redundancy, such volunteers are to be included in the number of employees whom the employer proposes to dismiss by reason of redundancy for the purposes of the statutory consultation regime under s 188 of the TULR(C)A 1992.

10.23   Such was the case in *Optare Group Limited v Transport and General Workers Union*,[16] in which volunteers for redundancy were sought, applied for, and their applications accepted. In this case, three such applications were accepted and 17 employees were at risk of compulsory redundancy. The tribunal at first instance was required to determine whether the employer could be said to be proposing to dismiss as redundant 20 employees for the statutory consultation procedures to apply. The tribunal's decision, upheld by the EAT, concluded that the reason the employees volunteered was because they had been invited to do so and were deemed to have been dismissed, thus triggering the provisions of TULR(C)A. See also the cases discussed in Chapter 2.

Defending an unfair dismissal case

Reason

10.24   In a claim for unfair dismissal it is for an employer to prove that the dismissal was by reason of redundancy: redundancy is one of the potentially fair reasons for dismissal under s 98 of the ERA 1996.

---

[13] [1969] 4 ITR 122.
[14] [1988] IRLR 131.
[15] See also *Gateshead Metropolitan Borough Council v Mills* (EAT 610/92) and *Renfrew District Council v Lornie*, 23 June, 1995, Court of Session.
[16] UKEAT/0143/07.

However, where an applicant is seeking to argue that he was dismissed (or selected for redundancy) for trade union reasons (see below) then the burden of showing that reason in fact falls upon the applicant rather than on the respondent, thus reversing the normal rule (*Smith v The Chairman and Other Councillors of Hayle Town Council*[17]). Section 154 of the TULR(C)A 1992 states that the qualifying period does not apply to the dismissal of an employee if it is shown that the reason is an inadmissible reason (and being in this case a trade union reason)—see also the section on other inadmissible reasons discussed below. **10.25**

Smith was followed by the EAT in the case of *Driver v Cleveland Structural Engineering Co Ltd*.[18] Of course, if the applicant does overcome this hurdle, then that will be the end of the matter because if the tribunal is convinced that the reason (or principal reason) for dismissal was an inadmissible one (see below) it must then go on to make a finding of unfair dismissal. **10.26**

Reasonableness

Finally, assuming dismissal is not automatically unfair, the employment tribunal must be satisfied that the employer acted reasonably in relying on redundancy as a reason for dismissal. **10.27**

Establishing the reason for dismissal

Normally in redundancy cases, establishing the reason for dismissal does not prove problematic. An employment tribunal will not usually investigate whether or why there was a redundancy situation unless this is effectively challenged by an applicant. Furthermore, an applicant cannot claim that the employer acted unreasonably in opting to make redundancies (*Moon v Homeworthy Furniture (Northern) Ltd*[19]). **10.28**

If the issue as to whether there was a redundancy is challenged, then it is open for the tribunal to find that, in the circumstances, the employer has failed to establish the reason. It should also be noted that there is no presumption that, simply because a tribunal has found that a genuine redundancy situation existed, it necessarily follows that the tribunal must find that the particular dismissals were made for that reason. **10.29**

In *Timex Corporation v Thompson*,[20] an employment tribunal had found on the evidence that there was a redundancy situation. During the hearing the employer had stated that Mr Thompson had been selected for dismissal because he lacked an engineering qualification which the other two candidates for redundancy dismissal held. However, it also said that it had been influenced by Mr Thompson's poor performance. The tribunal said, *inter alia*, that the employer had not established the reason for the dismissal. The employer appealed, arguing that the evidence of redundancy was clear and that therefore, in the absence of compelling proof of some other reason, the employment tribunal ought to have found that redundancy or reorganisation was the reason for dismissal. The EAT, in rejecting this argument, said that there was no such presumption. **10.30**

In giving the judgment of the EAT, Browne-Wilkinson J said: **10.31**

> Even where there is a redundancy situation, it is possible for an employer to use such a situation as a pretext for getting rid of an employee he wishes to dismiss. In such circumstances the

---

[17] [1978] IRLR 413.
[18] [1994] IRLR 636.
[19] [1976] IRLR 298; see also *Hollister v National Farmers' Union* [1979] ICR 542 and *James W Cook & Co (Wivenhoe) Ltd v Tipper* [1990] ICR 716; cf. *Ladbroke Courage Holidays Ltd v Cisten* [1981] IRLR 59.
[20] [1981] IRLR 522.

reason for dismissal will not necessarily be redundancy. It is for the industrial tribunal in each case to see whether, on all the evidence, the employer has shown them what was the reason for dismissal, that being the burden cast on the employer by section 57(1) of the 1978 Act [now s 98(1) of the ERA 1996].

10.32   Conversely, in the case of *Hyde v Britvic* [21] the applicant, a sales representative, lost his driving licence and subsequently, for a brief period, worked for the employer in an administrative job. After a time the employers moved from their base in Solihull to Cheltenham. The applicant was dismissed. The employer asserted that the applicant was dismissed as a result of the loss of his licence but the tribunal found, on the evidence, that the real reason for the dismissal was redundancy as a result of the cessation of work by the employer at Solihull.

10.33   The true reason for a dismissal was also considered by the EAT in the case of *Manchester College of Arts and Technology v Smith and Others*.[22] The EAT highlighted that claimants may succeed in challenging the reason for their dismissal in one of two ways. First, they may challenge the genuineness of the redundancy situation, leading the tribunal to consider the alternative reason put forward on behalf of the claimant. Second, even accepting the business case for redundancies, the claimant may successfully establish that the redundancy was not the true reason for their dismissal.

10.34   The EAT gave guidance on the reason for dismissal and timing of the termination of employment in the case of *West Kent College v Richardson*.[23] The EAT held that for a reason to be an admissible reason for dismissal it had to remain constant throughout the 'process of dismissal'. That process begins with the moment of notice and ends with termination, and lasts throughout the period in between. In this case, Mr Richardson was given notice on 29 March 1996 that he was to be made redundant and that his employment would terminate on 31 August 1996. During the notice period, sufficient teaching hours became available to justify his retention. However, the college failed to offer him alternative employment. Mr Richardson complained of unfair dismissal and indeed that his dismissal was for a trade union reason contrary to s 152(1)(b) of the TULR(C)A 1992. The employment tribunal found that at the expiry of the notice period sufficient work was available to justify the college retaining Mr Richardson, that he was not redundant, and moreover that the true reason for his dismissal was his union activities. The college appealed.

10.35   The EAT, upholding the appeal, stated that in assessing the reason for dismissal it was not appropriate to look only at the date of the expiry of the notice. The tribunal should have made a finding as to the reason for dismissal when the notice was given and then 'traced its retention or otherwise' during the period between the giving of notice and the termination date. The EAT in making this finding relied upon the decision of the Court of Appeal in *Parkinson v March Consulting Limited*,[24] in which Evans LJ stated at 284:

> When the employment is terminated by reason of notice given in accordance with the terms of the contract of employment, then in my judgment the employer's reason for the dismissal

---

[21] COIT 2055/134 (unreported).

[22] UKEAT/0460/06.

[23] [1998] ICR 511.

[24] [1997] IRLR 308. The EAT might also have considered as relevant the Court of Appeal's decision in *Alboni v Ind Coope Retail Ltd* [1998] IRLR 131, in which the Court states that in determining the reasonableness of an employer's decision to dismiss, what occurs during the period between the giving of notice and the date of termination is relevant to the tribunals assessment.

has to be determined, not only by reference to his reason when the dismissal occurs but also by reference to his reason for giving the prior notice to terminate.

Thus it is arguable that if at the date notice is given there is a redundancy situation but that **10.36** situation no longer pertains at the date the notice expires, the employment tribunal can find that the reason for dismissal is not redundancy, notwithstanding the fact that that was the reason notice was given in the first place.

B. The Standard of Reasonableness Expected of Employers

In accordance with s 98(4) of the ERA 1996, an employment tribunal must determine **10.37** whether the employer acted reasonably in treating the redundancy as a sufficient reason for dismissing the employee. It should also take into account the size and administrative resources of the employer and have regard to equity and the substantial merits of the case. The test of reasonableness has been somewhat simplified by the repeal of the statutory dispute procedures which were created by the Employment Act 2002 and which were repealed by the Employment Act 2008 with effect from 6 April 2009. The statutory disputes procedures therefore no longer apply to the law of unfair dismissal and whether the employer has behaved reasonably or unreasonably depends on the test in s 98(4).

In the mainstream of unfair dismissal law, the statutory disputes procedures have, in effect, **10.38** been replaced by the 2009 ACAS code of practice on discipline and grievance. As with previous ACAS codes of practice, breach of the code does not make a dismissal automatically unfair but it has to be taken into account by the employment tribunal in determining the question of fairness. In the mainstream of unfair dismissal law, with particular reference to discipline and grievance cases, unreasonable breach of the code can result in an uplift of unfair dismissal compensation in the case of employers breach by 25 per cent and a reduction, in the case of breach by an employee (for example, for failure to follow a grievance procedure) by up to 25 per cent.[25]

However, the ACAS code of practice expressly does not apply to dismissals by reason of **10.39** redundancy, nor to the dismissal that arises by failure to renew a limited-term contract. The status of the code (and the compensation adjustment under s 207A of the Trade Union and Labour Relations (Consolidation) Act 1992 (TULR(C)A 1992)) in relation to redundancy dismissals is that it is strictly not relevant. Nonetheless, it is hard to believe that an employment tribunal will not be influenced by the provisions of the code in terms of good practice and procedure in relation to redundancy dismissals.[26]

In the absence of the code of practice, the law and practice in relation to fair redundancy **10.40** dismissals is to be found in the case law, which we examine below.

There is, however, an ACAS advisory booklet, *Redundancy Handling* (October 2010), which **10.41** contains good advice in relation to the fairness of redundancy dismissals. This content may indeed be relied upon by advocates for employees in the employment tribunal, although as

---

[25] TULR(C)A 1992, s 207A.
[26] An employment tribunal has already held that the ACAS code applies to 'some other substantial reason' dismissals (ERA 1996, s 98 (a) (b)) (though such dismissals are not expressly excluded from the code, as in the case of redundancy dismissals: see *Cummings v Siemens Communications Ltd* (ET/3500013/10).

this document does not have a status of a code of practice it is not in any way *required* to be taken into account by an employment tribunal. Its content nonetheless mirrors law and good practice.

10.42   The ACAS booklet stresses a number of key issues in unfair redundancy procedure as follows:

- consideration of alternatives (for example, pay cuts and other adjustments and voluntary redundancy);
- establishing the right pool for selection for redundancy;
- consultation;
- establishing fair selection criteria;
- making sure the selection itself is not unfair;
- avoiding automatically unfair selection by avoiding prohibited grounds for selection;
- the search for alternative employment;
- time off to look for new work or for training.

Alternatives to redundancy

10.43   As an initial step, a tribunal will be concerned to see whether the employer considered alternatives to redundancy prior to implementing compulsory redundancies.[27]

10.44   One of the main ways that employers avoid compulsory redundancies is to seek alternative employment for employees in danger of being dismissed, and this is discussed further below. Other ways of avoiding compulsory redundancies include redeployment, reallocation of work, a general reduction in hours, a ban on overtime, natural wastage, early retirement and, of course, voluntary redundancy.[28]

10.45   Each of these courses of action will impose different difficulties upon the employer. For example, abolishing overtime or otherwise changing hours (for example, altering shift patterns) may involve a change in existing employees' terms and conditions, with its concomitant effect on the contractual relationship. It may not be simple to implement such a change, particularly in a large organisation.

Objectivity of assessment

10.46   The test of reasonableness underwent a brief revolution. For many years it was clear that the test to be applied was an objective one, with the employment tribunal being urged to avoid substituting its own decision for that of the employer. This was made clear by Lord Denning MR in the Court of Appeal case of *British Leyland (UK) Ltd v Swift*,[29] a case concerned with

---

[27] A feature of the 2010 recession has been a willingness both by employers and employees to embrace an alternative to redundancy. These have included recruitment freezes, deferment of new joiners (particularly trainees in professional firms), secondment (again, particularly from professional service firms to clients), early retirement, sabbaticals, reduction of hours, and reduction of remuneration in some way. The realisation may be that: (1) redundancies are costly—as it is some time before the benefits of redundancies are realised (the Chartered Institute of Personnel and Development (CIPD) has estimated that redundancies may cost up to £16,000 per employee when one takes into account disruption of the business, capital cost of redundancies, and recruitment costs when the upturn happens, or more precisely, £16,375 per employee according to its chief economist, John Philpott, <http://www.cipd.co.uk/pressoffice/_articles/050108costofredundancy.htm>); (2) realism by employees; and (3) the perceived need to retain workers for the upturn. In many senses, the staff attrition that we saw in the 1980s has been avoided, although job losses have still been heavy. The Comprehensive Spending Review has also meant heavy job losses in the public sector.

[28] See also the duty in relation to the collective consultation process in s 188 of the TULR(C)A.

[29] [1981] IRLR 91.

dismissal for misconduct. In that case the employment tribunal decision had included the statement, '. . . a reasonable employer would, in our opinion, have considered that a lesser penalty was appropriate'. In commenting upon this, Lord Denning said:

> I do not think that this is the right test. The correct test is: was it reasonable for the employers to dismiss him? If no reasonable employer would have dismissed him, then the dismissal was unfair. If a reasonable employer might reasonably have dismissed him, then the dismissal was fair. It must be remembered that in all these cases there is a band of reasonableness, within which one employer might reasonably take one view; another quite reasonably take a different view. One would quite reasonably dismiss the man, the other would quite reasonably keep him on. Both views may be quite reasonable. If it was quite reasonable to dismiss him, then the dismissal must be upheld as fair even though some other employers may not have dismissed him.

Clearly, in redundancy cases the employer would be most often concerned with defending its decision to select for redundancy, but the same principle applied: would a reasonable employer reasonably have selected the particular employee for redundancy in the same circumstances? **10.47**

Perhaps the most often-quoted statement of the test of reasonableness was contained in the judgment of Browne-Wilkinson J in the EAT in the case of *Iceland Frozen Foods Ltd v Jones*.[30] In considering the application of what was then s 57(3) of the EPCA 1978 (now ERA 1996, s 98(4)), Browne-Wilkinson J said: **10.48**

> Since the present state of the law can only be found by going through a number of different authorities, it may be convenient if we should seek to summarise the present law. We consider that the authorities establish that in law the correct approach for the industrial tribunal to adopt in answering the question posed by section 57(3) of the 1978 Act is as follows:
>
> (1) The starting point should always be the words of section 57(3) [98(4)] themselves;
> (2) In applying the section an industrial tribunal must consider the reasonableness of the employer's conduct, not simply whether they (the members of the industrial tribunal) consider the dismissal to be fair;
> (3) In judging the reasonableness of the employer's conduct an industrial tribunal must not substitute its decision as to what was the right course to adopt for that of the employer;
> (4) In many (though not all) cases there is a band of reasonable responses to the employee's conduct within which one employer might reasonably take one view, another quite reasonably take another;
> (5) The function of the industrial tribunal, as an industrial jury, is to determine whether in the particular circumstances of each case the decision to dismiss the employee fell within the band of reasonable responses which a reasonable employer might have adopted. If the dismissal falls within the band the dismissal is fair; if the dismissal falls outside the band it is unfair.[31]

Although this was not a redundancy case, the principles were followed in a number of cases dealing with redundancy. In particular, the Court of Appeal approved Browne-Wilkinson J's analysis in *Hereford and Worcester County Council v Neale*[32] and again in *Morgan v Electrolux* **10.49**

---

[30] [1982] IRLR 439.
[31] For a full discussion on the range of reasonable responses test see Andy Freer, GMB, 'The range of Reasonable Responses Test—from Guidelines to Statute' (1998) *27 ILJ* 4.
[32] [1986] IRLR 168.

Ltd.[33] However, this orthodoxy was said simply to be wrong in the case of *Haddon v Vandenbergh Foods Limited*.[34] Arguably the facts of this case were somewhat extreme, but the result could have amounted to a sea change in the approach of the employment tribunals to the question of reasonableness in unfair dismissal cases. The employer invited Mr Haddon for drinks in order to celebrate 15 years' employment and to receive a good service award. He was required to attend at 5.15pm and there was to be a presentation at 5.30pm with a buffet supper to finish at 7.30pm. Mr Haddon was actually scheduled to work on the day of the award from 2pm until 10pm. Prior to the presentation Mr Haddon spoke to his manager about working arrangements for the day in question. He was told that he could leave early to change and to collect his wife, who would be attending the award ceremony with him. However, he was also told that he would be required to return to work after the ceremony as the employer was short staffed due to a high level of sickness. As a matter of interest, Mr Haddon spoke to a different manager, who told him that it was unusual to ask people to return to their shift after such an event because alcohol was provided both before and during the meal.

10.50   However, Mr Haddon was told to resolve the issue with his direct line manager. Mr Haddon did not do so.

10.51   On the day in question Mr Haddon and his wife attended the ceremony and were offered alcohol. At that point he decided that he would not return to work. He did not return to work and was dismissed for what was described as disobedience. His defence was that he did not take his manager's request that he return to work seriously. He also alleged inconsistency because others who had not returned to their shifts were not dismissed.

10.52   The employment tribunal hearing the claim said that most people would regard Mr Haddon's dismissal as 'harsh in the extreme'. The conclusion of the tribunal was that there had been a

---

[33] [1991] IRLR 89.

[34] [1999] IRLR 672. It should be noted that before this case was decided the band of reasonable responses test had already been the subject of much criticism over the years as amounting to an unwarranted gloss on the terms of the statute. The argument has been that the test allows a harsh dismissal to be fair and looks at 'fair dismissals' rather than 'just dismissals'. This argument was taken up by H Collins in his book, *Justice in Dismissal: The Law of Termination of Employment* (OUP, 1992) in Chapter One 'Harsh but Fair'. Collins states '. . . . The law of Unfair Dismissal, which was heralded as protecting employees' job security, as even giving workers property rights in their jobs, [has] become sterilised to such an extent that it endorses and legitimises harsh disciplinary treatment of employees and only deters wholly unreasonable, irrational and arbitrary dismissals.' It is only when the employer's decision steps outside what Collins refers to as 'this charmed and manipulable circle' that an Employment Tribunal will regard the dismissal as unreasonable and therefore unfair. Collins illustrates this thesis with a particularly harsh case, *Matthewson v R B Wilson Dental Laboratories Ltd* [1988] IRLR 512. In his case Matthewson was employed as a dental technician working as one of three chrome finishers responsible for polishing metal dentures. In December 1987 during his lunch break, he purchased a small amount of cannabis for his personal use, was arrested, and charged with being in possession of drugs. He was subsequently convicted and fined. When he returned an hour late from lunch he informed one of the company's directors that he had been arrested and admitted that he had been in possession of a small piece of cannabis. He was dismissed. The employers had never stated that they had any policy in relation to drugs, Mr Matthewson had never received the company handbook which stated that an employee would be dismissed with payment in lieu of all remuneration entitlement should he, or she, be convicted by a court of law of an offence which, although not connected with the company, gave reasonable doubt as to the individual suitability for employment in the company's type of business. The handbook gave as examples theft, indecent behaviour, or assault. Furthermore there had been no attempt to discuss the matter with Matthewson. Nevertheless, the majority of the employment tribunal took the view that the dismissal fell within the band of reasonable responses open to any reasonable employer. The EAT upheld the decision saying 'the majority's conclusion that, on the information before the employers at the time of dismissal, the decision to dismiss the appellant fell within the band of reasonable responses which a reasonable employer might have adopted was based on methods of fact and could not have been held to have been perverse'.

clear instruction to Mr Haddon to return to work and even though the employer could have handled the matter better and perhaps made the instruction clearer and even though Mr Haddon's absence from work for the very short time left on the shift made no difference to productivity, the tribunal found the dismissal to be fair.

The EAT set out the tribunal's decision at length. Having set out that there was a very short time left on the shift and that the instruction was not clear, the tribunal went on to consider whether the instruction to return to the shift was a reasonable one. The tribunal recognised that many people would not find such an instruction to be reasonable but the tribunal had reminded themselves that they should not substitute their view for the views of the employer. The bottom line was that the tribunal could not say that it was unreasonable for the employer to require Mr Haddon to return to his shift. The tribunal then said this: **10.53**

> It falls then for us to consider whether dismissal falls within the range of reasonable responses. Once again it is not for us to say what we would have done or would not have done, but if dismissal is to fall outside the range, we have to ask whether no reasonable employer would have dismissed in these circumstances.

The tribunal concluded that it would not be possible for them to say that dismissal was outside the range of reasonable responses. They found this conclusion with some reluctance and despite saying that it was a decision that many reasonable employers would not have taken.

On behalf of Mr Haddon, his representative made a forceful argument that the range of reasonable responses test is a fundamentally erroneous approach to unfair dismissal and the EAT were persuaded by this argument. In particular, the EAT seemed to sympathise with the view that the test made it too difficult for an employee to win in any misconduct case. A number of authorities were considered on the correct test to apply and the EAT seemed to be particularly persuaded by some words of the Court of Appeal in the case of *Gilham & Others v Kent County Council (No. 2)*.[35] The Court of Appeal said at 243: **10.54**

> The wording of [s 98(4)] is straightforward and easy to understand, and I do not myself think that it helps to try and analyse it further, save only this, that a tribunal in applying the section must not ask themselves what they would have done, but must ask themselves how a reasonable employer would have acted.

The EAT in *Haddon* said: **10.55**

> In our view the approach taken in *Gilham* is to be followed. The statute is clear and unambiguous . . .we respectfully suggest that tribunals now return to the task in hand which is to apply [s 98(4)] without embellishment, and without using mantras so favoured by the lawyers in this field.

The EAT also stated: **10.56**

> . . . the question for the tribunal is the reasonableness of the decision to dismiss in the circumstances of the particular case having regard to equity and the substantial merits. Because the tribunals are applying an objective test, that is, a test of reasonableness, it is not sufficient for them simply to say 'well, we would not have dismissed in those circumstances'. They must recognise that, however improbable, their own personal views may not accord with reasonableness. Just asking 'what would I have done' is not enough. However, it is neither reasonable nor realistic to expect the objective question to be asked and answered without the members

---

[35] [1985] ICR 233.

of the tribunal having first asked 'what would we have done'. And provided that they do not stop there, we see nothing wrong with that approach.

10.57   In other words, it is appropriate for a tribunal to ask itself what it would have done as individuals and the EAT said it is likely that what the tribunal themselves would have done will often coincide with its judgment as to what a reasonable employer would have done. The EAT said that providing the tribunal applies the test of reasonableness, it is its duty both to determine its own judgment and to substitute it for the employer's where appropriate.

10.58   The EAT went on to raise a further issue. It said that it is quite possible that there will be cases where a decision to dismiss and a decision not to dismiss on the same facts would be reasonable. It does not follow that because dismissal would be reasonable every other possible sanction would be unreasonable. However, there is a clear indication from the EAT that these will be marginal cases. The EAT said specifically:

> The mantra 'the band or range of reasonable responses' is not helpful because it had led tribunals into applying what amounts to a perversity test, which, as is clear from *Iceland* itself, was not its purpose. The moment that one talks of a 'range' or 'band' of reasonable responses one is conjuring up the possibility of extreme views at either end of the band or range. In reality, it is most unlikely that in an unfair dismissal case involving misconduct the tribunal will need to concern itself with the question of whether the deployment of each of the weapons in the employer's disciplinary armoury would have been reasonable. Dismissal is the ultimate sanction. There is, in reality, no range or band to be considered, only whether the employer acted reasonably in invoking that sanction.

10.59   The danger, said the EAT, was that tribunals testing the fairness of the dismissal would refer to the extreme examples rather than the majority of 'normal' cases. Thus, in one fell swoop the range of reasonable responses test was apparently no more. On the face of it, this seems perfectly reasonable because the statute is clear and unambiguous and the range of reasonable responses test is a gloss on that statute. However, that test has been approved by the Court of Appeal in *British Leyland v Swift*[36] and the EAT itself in *Iceland Frozen Foods Limited*. Furthermore, the range of reasonable responses test was applied by the Court of Appeal in *British Gas v McCarrick*[37] and in Scotland by the Inner House of the Court of Session in the case of *Gair v Bevan Harris Limited*.[38]

10.60   As a result, many commentators said that the *Haddon* case rested on fragile ground and would not survive long into the future. Such commentators were considerably bolstered by the view of Lindsay J, who commented on the *Haddon* case in *Midland Bank Plc v Mr J Madden*.[39] In this case, Mr Madden was employed as a lending officer who had worked for Midland Bank since 1986. He was dismissed on 24 October 1997 on the ground of gross misconduct—this being the misappropriation of three of the bank's customer's debit cards. Those cards were subsequently fraudulently used, resulting in a loss to the bank of almost £3,000.

10.61   In a hearing at the employment tribunal sitting in London (North) in 1998 the unanimous decision of the tribunal was that Mr Madden had been unfairly dismissed. He was awarded

---

[36] [1981] IRLR 91.
[37] [1991] IRLR 305.
[38] [1983] IRLR 368.
[39] EAT/1107/98 (unreported), 7 March 2000.

compensation of £11,300. The bank appealed on three grounds. They were that the tribunal substituted its own view for that of the employer, that the tribunal had applied a standard of proof of beyond reasonable doubt to the investigation process, and that the tribunal had not correctly approached the question of whether the bank had carried out a reasonable investigation. The employment tribunal had referred itself to the well-known case of *British Home Stores v Burchell*.[40] There was a good deal of argument revolving around *Haddon* at the EAT; the EAT saying that it would not ordinarily comment at length on another EAT case but that it felt it was appropriate to set out its views on *Haddon* at some length.

The EAT then looked at the facts of *Haddon* and discussed both the statutory test and related case law. The EAT then went on to discuss what it called the controversial areas. The area we are concerned with here is whether the so-called 'band of reasonable responses' test is appropriate or whether, as in *Haddon*, the test is simply to be whether dismissal was 'reasonable'. In *Haddon* there was criticism of the so-called 'mantra' of 'the band of range of reasonable responses' and that this was unhelpful because it had led to tribunals applying what amounted to a perversity test. The EAT in *Midland Bank* said quite clearly that 'it is not, in our view, within the province of the EAT, but only of some higher court, to outlaw reference to the band'.[41] **10.62**

The EAT pointed out that a reference to a range of responses or to a range of reasonable responses went back at least as far as 1980 in the decision of the EAT in *Rolls Royce v Walpole*[42] and even in the earlier case of *N C Watling & Co v Richardson*,[43] when the EAT said: **10.63**

> It has to be recognised that there are circumstances where more than one course of action may be reasonable.

The EAT also remarked that the Court of Appeal used this concept again in *British Leyland* and it was used by the EAT itself in *Iceland Frozen Foods*. Indeed, as the EAT pointed out, in *Haddon* it is said that the approach taken in *Gillam* is to be followed. In the present case, the EAT said that it accepts that but that there is nothing in *Gillam*, either express or implied, which disapproves of reference, in an appropriate case, to a band of reasonable responses. On the contrary, says the EAT. In *Gillam* Griffiths LJ held that: **10.64**

> A tribunal in applying the section must not ask themselves what they would have done, but must ask themselves how a reasonable employer would have acted.

The EAT in *Midland Bank* concluded this point by saying at para 38: **10.65**

> Given this history we think it is not open to any court short of the Court of Appeal to deny reference to 'a band of reasonable responses', not only as a guide but, as it is expressed to be, as a determinative test.

The position was settled by the Court of Appeal in the *Midland Bank* case[44] (re-named *HSBC* and conjoined with *Foley v Post Office*), in which the band of reasonable responses test was reasserted in determining the reasonableness or unreasonableness of a dismissal.[45] **10.66**

---

[40] [1978] IRLR 379.
[41] Judgment of the Lindsay J, para 32.
[42] [1980] IRLR 343.
[43] [1978] ICR 1049.
[44] [2000] 1 CR 1283.
[45] See also *Sheffield Health and Social Care NHS Foundation Trust v Crabtree* (EAT/0331/09).

Tribunals are sometimes tempted to challenge the way employees have been selected for redundancy, in particular the way in which employers have assessed employees against criteria for selection. In *Semple Fraser LLP v Daly*,[46] the EAT criticized the employment tribunal for, in effect, re-marking the scores of two employees at risk of redundancy and, thereby, finding the employee selected for redundancy had been dismissed unfairly. But this was the wrong way to approach it. Even if different scores could have been reached by another employer, that did not demonstrate that this employer had acted unreasonably. The band of reasonable responses test applied, and only if the employer had acted outside the band of reasonable responses could dismissal be unfair.

Redundancies and unfair dismissal under section 98(4) of the ERA 1996

10.67   In determining whether any particular redundancy dismissal is fair within the meaning of s 98(4) of the ERA 1996, employment tribunals will take note of what is considered good industrial relations practice and, in particular, will consider the standards set out by the EAT in the seminal case of *Williams v Compair Maxam Ltd*.[47]

10.68   Browne-Wilkinson J, in giving judgment for the EAT, set out the position as follows:

> . . . there is a generally accepted view in industrial relations that, in cases where the employees are represented by an independent union recognised by the employer, reasonable employers will seek to act in accordance with the following principles:
>
> (1) The employer will seek to give as much warning as possible of impending redundancies so as to enable the union and employees who may be affected to take early steps to inform themselves of the relevant facts, consider possible alternative solutions and, if necessary, find alternative employment in the undertaking or elsewhere.
>
> (2) The employer will consult with the union as to the best means by which the desired management result can be achieved fairly and with as little hardship to the employees as possible. In particular, the employer will seek to agree with the union the criteria to be applied in selecting the employees to be made redundant. When a selection has been made, the employer will consider with the union whether the selection has been made in accordance with those criteria.
>
> (3) Whether or not an agreement as to the criteria to be adopted has been agreed with the union, the employer will seek to establish criteria for selection which so far as possible do not depend solely upon the opinion of the person making the selection but can be objectively checked against such things as attendance record, efficiency at the job, experience, or length of service.
>
> (4) The employer will seek to ensure that the selection is made fairly in accordance with these criteria and will consider any representations the union may make as to such selection.
>
> (5) The employer will seek to see whether instead of dismissing an employee he could offer him alternative employment.
>
> The lay members stressed that not all of these factors are present in every case since circumstances may prevent one or more of them being given effect, but they would expect these principles to be departed from only where some good reason is shown to justify such a departure. The basic approach should be that as much as is reasonably possible should be done to mitigate the impact on the workforce of the redundancy situation and to demonstrate that the selection has been made fairly.

---

[46]   1 EATS/0045/09
[47]   [1982] IRLR 83.

It should be emphasised that the principles set out in the *Compair Maxam* case do not **10.69** amount to rules of law which, if not adhered to, would necessarily make a dismissal unfair (see, for example, the EAT on this point in *Rolls-Royce Motors Ltd v Dewhurst*[48]). However, it should also be noted that the *Compair Maxam* case does set out what is widely recognised as being good practice. It should also be remembered that, in certain circumstances, consultation must take place with employee representatives (whether they are recognised trade unions or elected representatives) under TULR(C)A 1992, s 188, and in any event agreement should be sought as to the procedure to be followed with such representatives (see Chapter 11). It will be noted that the EAT in *Williams v Compare Maxam*[49] placed emphasis, for the purposes of unfair dismissal, on consultation with a trade union. Doctrinally, however, the test of unfair dismissal and whether there has been a breach of s 188 of the TULR(C)A 1992 are separate and distinct. Breach of s 188 of the TULR(C)A 1992 does not lead to unfair dismissal automatically. Remedies for breach of s 188 are contained in ss 189–192 of the 1992 Act.[50] However, the EAT has recently held in *Morgan v Welsh Rugby Union*[51] that the principles in *Williams* are more apt in cases of selection of employees to be made redundant from an existing group. Where, instead, an employer has to appoint to new roles after a reorganization, 'the employer's decision must of necessity be forward looking. It is likely to centre on the ability of the individual to perform in the new role.' Judge Richardson likened this kind of exercise to an interview process. This may, he considered, involve 'a substantial element of judgment'. 'The employer is entitled, at the end of the process, to appoint a candidate which it considers able to fulfil the role.' This illustrates that the factors in *Williams* are not principles of law, but standards of behaviour.

The importance of procedure has been stressed time and again in cases dealing with these **10.70** issues, but probably most importantly by the House of Lords in *Polkey v A E Dayton Services Ltd*.[52] In particular, Lord Bridge of Harwich stated in that case:

> . . . an employer having prima facie grounds to dismiss for [redundancy] . . . will in the great majority of cases not act reasonably in treating the reason as a sufficient reason for dismissal unless and until he has taken the steps, conveniently classified in most of the authorities as 'procedural', which are necessary in the circumstances of the case to justify their course of action . . . In the case of redundancy, the employer will not normally act reasonably unless he warns and consults any employees affected or their representative, adopts a fair basis on which to select for redundancy and takes such steps as may be reasonable to avoid or minimise redundancy by redeployment within his own organisation. If an employer has failed to take the appropriate procedural steps in any particular case, the one question the industrial tribunal is not permitted to ask in applying the test of reasonableness imposed by s 57(3) [of the EPCA 1978] is the hypothetical question whether it would have made any difference to the outcome if the appropriate procedural steps had been taken. On the true construction of section 57(3) this question is simply irrelevant. It is quite a different matter if the tribunal is able to conclude that the employer himself, at the time of the dismissal, acted reasonably in taking the view that, in the exceptional circumstances of the particular case, the procedural steps normally appropriate would have been futile, could not have altered the decision to dismiss and therefore

---

[48] [1985] IRLR 184.
[49] [1982] IRLR 83.
[50] *Hammonds LLP v Mwitta* (EAT/0026/10). On the other hand, earlier case law suggests that an employment tribunal may wish to take this into account (see *Mugford v Midland Bank* [1997] IRLR 208; *Hough and APEX v Leyland DAF Ltd* [1991] IRLR 194.
[51] [2011] IRLR 376.
[52] [1987] IRLR 503.

could be dispensed with. In such a case the test of reasonableness under section 57(3) may be satisfied.

(For s 57(3) of the EPCA 1978, read s 98(4) of the ERA 1996.)

10.71 Lord Mackay of Clashfern said:

> This appeal raises an important question in the law of unfair dismissal. Where an industrial tribunal has found that the reason for an applicant's dismissal was a reason of a kind such as could justify the dismissal and has found that there has been a failure to consult or warn the applicant . . . should the tribunal consider whether, if the employee had been consulted or warned before dismissal was decided on, he would nevertheless have been dismissed? . . . the subject matter for the tribunal's consideration is the employer's action in treating the reason as a sufficient reason for dismissing the employee. It is that action and that action only that the tribunal is required to characterise as reasonable or unreasonable . . . it is what the employer did that is to be judged, not what he might have done. On the other hand, in judging whether what the employer did was reasonable it is right to consider what a reasonable employer would have had in mind at the time he decided to dismiss as the consequence of not consulting or not warning . . . if the employer could reasonably have concluded in the light of the circumstances known to him at the time of dismissal that consultation or warning would be utterly useless he might well act reasonably. Failure to observe the requirement[s] of . . . consultation or warning will not necessarily render a dismissal unfair. Whether in any particular case it did so is a matter for the industrial tribunal to consider in the light of the circumstances known to the employer at the time he dismissed the employee.

10.72 It is to be noted that exceptional cases where consultation would be 'futile' (*per* Lord Bridge) or 'utterly useless' (*per* Lord Mackay) were envisaged by the House of Lords. But these are exceptional and will rarely apply. They comprise, however, the so-called '*Polkey* exception', referred to later in this chapter.

Size and administrative resources

10.73 The employer's size and administrative resources will undoubtedly have an impact upon an employment tribunal's decision. Indeed, they are to be taken into account expressly according to s 98(4)(a) of the ERA 1996. This aspect may not be something that is easy to quantify, but it is probably safe to say that in practice the larger the undertaking in question the more likely it is that a tribunal will expect formal procedures to be followed and, furthermore, to be followed rigorously.

10.74 However, if an employment tribunal finds that procedural steps have been omitted altogether and attempts to excuse that because, for example, the employer's undertaking is small, that may be an error of law.

10.75 In *De Grasse v Stockwell Tools Ltd*[53] Mr De Grasse was dismissed by reason of redundancy. There was no warning or consultation. In giving its decision the employment tribunal found that, because the employer was a small company there was no need for it to undertake early warning or consultation in a redundancy case. The dismissal was held to have been fair. Mr De Grasse appealed against this decision and, in giving the judgment of the EAT, Tucker J reviewed the authorities. In particular, the EAT held that while the size of the undertaking may affect the nature or formality of the consultation process, it cannot excuse the lack of any consultation at all. However informal the consultation may be, said the EAT, it should ordinarily take place.

---

[53] [1992] IRLR 269.

Consultation and other procedural matters are discussed further below. It is sufficient at this juncture to note that in redundancy cases procedural factors are of great significance and it is unwise to omit any procedural step. In summary, whilst less formal procedures may be excused in a small undertaking, some procedure must still be followed. Conversely, a large employer will generally be expected to achieve higher standards.[54]   **10.76**

We shall now turn to look at the particular elements of a redundancy procedure in more detail.   **10.77**

C. The Warning and Consultation Process

Where there are to be collective redundancies, consultation must take place in accordance with the TULR(C)A 1992 (see Chapter 11). This section is concerned with individual consultation, and it should be particularly noted that the fact that there may be a recognised trade union or elected representatives with whom consultations have taken place in a collective redundancies situation, does not obviate the need for the employer to consult directly with each individual employee who may be affected by that redundancy situation.[55]   **10.78**

Early warning of impending redundancies and consultation with individuals are basic requirements of a fair redundancy procedure. Without warning and consultation the procedure is highly likely to be unfair, except in very exceptional circumstances.   **10.79**

Giving warning to employees

Early cases did not suggest that warning and consultation were particularly important.[56] However, with the increasing importance placed upon procedures in general, in more recent times there has been a much greater emphasis on the need to be rigorous with regard to warning employees of their impending redundancy. One issue that has caused some concern with regards to early warning is how far the employer can go without breaking the employee's contract in suggesting that there will be a dismissal. Here, too, there is some overlap with the law on redundancy payments.[57]   **10.80**

In the case of *Secretary of State for Employment v Greenfield*[58] Mr Greenfield had worked for a company for 29 years, which subsequently went into receivership. All of the employees were told they would be made redundant but no date was set. Mr Greenfield found another job and he asked the receiver for voluntary redundancy. The receiver stated that Mr Greenfield would not be given voluntary redundancy but he would be made redundant in due course. Mr Greenfield left in any event and when the whole workforce was made redundant a few weeks later, claimed a redundancy payment. Before the employment tribunal it was held that when the receiver told Mr Greenfield he would be made redundant the employer had evinced an intention to repudiate the employment contract and therefore Mr Greenfield was entitled   **10.81**

---

[54] It is to be noted that it will be unreasonable for an employer wholly to delegate selection and consultation to a third party, such as the company to whom an employee has been seconded (*Atlantic Power & Gas Ltd v More.* (EAT/1125/97)).

[55] See, for example, the cases of *Mugford v Midland Bank* [1997] ICR 399 and *Candy & Others v The London Borough of Lewisham.*

[56] See, for example, *Noble v David Gold & Son Ltd* [1980] IRLR 252.

[57] See Chapter 2 for a further discussion of the problems in this area.

[58] EAT, 18 May 1990.

to claim constructive dismissal. The Secretary of State (who, in the circumstances, was responsible for making the redundancy payment) appealed. The EAT said that a mere warning of impending redundancy did not constitute a breach of contract, nor could it amount to a dismissal, actual or constructive.

10.82   Clearly, therefore, warnings should be given where there may be redundancies. Commercially, there is a line to be drawn between the need to warn employees of the possibility of redundancy and the need to ensure that the period between the warning and the actual redundancies is not so great that, for example, key staff are lost to other employers or low morale unnecessarily affects output. The employer is entitled to take such matters into account when considering the timing of the warning and the consultation processes in respect of potential redundancies. These are also, therefore, proper matters to put before an employment tribunal when attempting to justify the particular procedure followed. However, it is clear that it is not sufficient merely to pay lip service to the idea of warning (and consultation).

10.83   The potential difficulties in failing to warn an employee can be seen clearly in the case of *Argos Electronics Ltd v Walsh*.[59] In this case, Mr Walsh was asked to take over the duties of the quality assurance manager on a trial basis whilst he continued to do his work as technical manager. Mr Walsh concluded after a period of time that he could not carry out both functions and asked to be returned to his original duties as technical manager. Argos agreed to this and recruited a new quality assurance manager. Once Mr Walsh returned to the job of technical manager he realised that he had less work to do than had been the case before and eventually, as a result of the insufficient work, the management informed him that he would be dismissed by reason of redundancy. The redundancy took immediate effect and Mr Walsh claimed unfair dismissal. The employment tribunal was satisfied that the reason for dismissal was redundancy, since the company ceased or anticipated ceasing the job of technical manager. The tribunal went on to state that management could have foreseen the possibility of the technical manager's post becoming redundant at a future date when they transferred Mr Walsh to carry out the duties of the quality assurance manager as well as his own duties. The tribunal took the view that a reasonable employer would have warned Mr Walsh of the probable consequences when he temporarily transferred jobs. This lack of warning meant that Mr Walsh had put himself in a position where his employment was to come to an end in the near future. If he had been warned about this, he may have thought twice about returning to the job of technical manager. Consequently the lack of an early warning made the difference between his staying in employment (as quality assurance manager/technical manager) or being made redundant from his job as technical manager. Mr Walsh's dismissal was therefore ruled unfair.

10.84   The employer appealed to the EAT, but the EAT took the view that the tribunal's decision was proper and could not be overturned. It agreed that management was in a position to see what the results of the changes in the company would be, and therefore agreed that early warning might well have made the difference between Mr Walsh losing his job by reason of redundancy or staying in employment.

10.85   The EAT has also underlined a distinction between warning and consultation. In *Rowell v Hubbard Group Services Limited*[60] Mrs Rowell was dismissed as redundant in November 1992. On 16 October of that year the managing director of the company had sent a letter to

---

[59] EAT 184/89. 7 March 1990.
[60] [1995] IRLR 195.

all employees warning them of impending redundancies and setting out the criteria upon which selection for dismissal would be based. Mrs Rowell received another letter on 13 November which informed her that her employment was being terminated due to redundancy. That letter reiterated the criteria upon which selection was based. The letter gave details of what she would be paid and also invited her to discuss any issues with the managing director or another manager.

Mrs Rowell complained to the employment tribunal that she had been unfairly dismissed. The **10.86** tribunal found that the procedure followed by the employer was fair, referring itself to *Polkey*. The tribunal said that the requirements that the employee be warned of the likelihood of redundancy and given ample opportunity for consultation had been adequately met on the basis of the letters of 16 October and 13 November. Mrs Rowell appealed. The EAT allowed the appeal and substituted a finding of unfair dismissal. In giving its judgment the EAT said:

> The letter warning her of impending redundancies consisted neither of consultation nor of an invitation to consult and the letter inviting her to discuss matters was written after the decision had been taken to terminate her employment.

It is important to recognise the distinction between warning an employee that they may be redundant and consulting with them about that redundancy (which will include consultation about selection and alternative employment—see below).

The EAT in the case of *Elkouil v Coney Island Limited*[61] took a contrary view and suggested that **10.87** the duty to warn employees is not a separate duty from the duty to consult. It was stated that:

> . . . the process by which an employee is dismissed for redundancy necessarily should include, if it is to be done properly, a consultation process. That consultation process should commence with a warning that the employee is at risk. There are not two separate processes…the two parts, warning and consultation, are part of the same single process of consultation which begins with the employee being given notice that he is at risk.

The EAT in this case also emphasised the policy behind the need for employees to be given **10.88** as much warning as possible, which is to allow them to consider alternatives to mitigate the need for redundancies and allow them to find alternative employment. In the case of *Elkouil* the compensation for failing to warn was increased to 10 weeks' pay on the basis that, had he been warned, the employee could have started seeking new employment some 10 weeks earlier than he in fact could.

It is clear, however, that whilst the duty to warn employees may form part of the consultation **10.89** process, the duty to consult requires much more than just a warning.

Consultation with individual employees

The starting point for consideration of this issue is the judgment of Browne Wilkinson J in the **10.90** case of *Freud v Bentalls Ltd*.[62] Mrs Freud had been dismissed by reason of redundancy, and there had been no warning or consultation. The employment tribunal directed itself that:

> . . . the only question for the tribunal was whether the dismissal had been fair in view of the failure at the first opportunity to warn the applicant, or to consult, or indeed to refer the matter to the trade union to which the respondent knew that the applicant belongs.

---

[61] [2001] UKEAT/0520/00.
[62] [1982] IRLR 443.

10.91 In considering whether the employer should have warned Mrs Freud of the possibility of redundancy, the employment tribunal said that the employer must be allowed to conduct its business in a reasonable way, and undue or too early publication that its press office was closing might have done its business harm, and indeed deprived the applicant of prospects of continued employment by the employer had business improved. The tribunal, therefore, could not find authority nor indeed any common-sense reason for finding that the dismissal due to redundancy was unfair. Mrs Freud appealed.

10.92 On appeal, however, the EAT said that consultation was one of the foundation stones of modern industrial relations practice. Browne-Wilkinson J said:

> In the particular sphere of redundancy, good industrial relations practice in the ordinary case requires consultation with the redundant employee so that the employer may find out whether the needs of the business can be met in some way other than by dismissal and, if not, what other steps the employer can take to ameliorate the blow to the employee. In some cases . . . the employee may be able to suggest some reorganisation which will obviate the need for dismissal; in virtually all cases the employer if he consults will find out what steps he can take to find the employee alternative employment either within the Company or outside it . . . therefore good industrial relations practice requires that, unless there are special circumstances which render such consultation impossible or unnecessary, a fair employer will consult with the employee before dismissing him.

10.93 The EAT was careful to say that it was not stating that good industrial relations practice always requires consultation. It was well aware that there may be circumstances that render consultation impracticable, for example where there was such a catastrophic cash flow problem that it was essential for the survival of the business that immediate steps to reduce the wages bill were taken. What the EAT was saying was that a reasonable employer would have to show some special reason why there had been a failure to consult.

10.94 The approach which tribunals follow may best be summed up in the words of Lord Bridge in the House of Lords in *Polkey* (see above): '. . . in the case of redundancy, the employer will normally not act reasonably unless he warns and consults any employees affected or their representative . . .'. Many cases since *Polkey* have emphasised the importance of consultation.[63]

10.95 It is also important to note how the courts assess the content of consultation, before moving on to consider exceptions to the rule. In the Divisional Court in *R v British Coal Corporation and Secretary of State for Trade & Industry ex parte Price & Others*[64] Glidewell LJ said:

> It is axiomatic that the process of consultation is not one in which the consulter is obliged to adopt any or all of the views expressed by the person or body whom he is consulting. I would respectfully adopt the tests proposed by Hodgson J. in *R v Gwent County Council, ex parte Bryant*, reported, as far as I know, only at [1988] Crown Office Digest 19, when he said:
> 'Fair consultation means:
> (a) consultation when the proposals are still at a formative stage;
> (b) adequte information on which to respond;
> (c) adequate time in which to respond;
> (d) conscientious consideration by an authority of the response to consultation'.
> Another way of putting the point more shortly is that fair consultation involves giving the body consulted a fair and proper opportunity to understand fully the matters about which it

---

[63] However, a failure to consult may be remedied by allowing the employee to appeal by way of a full re-hearing (*Lloyd v Taylor Woodrow Construction* [1999] IRLR 782).

[64] [1994] IRLR 72.

is being consulted, and to express its views on those subjects, with the consultor thereafter considering those views properly and genuinely.

It is this standard, whether collective or individual consultation, which an employer will be **10.96** expected to meet or at least attempt to meet, and if it does not then the employer will have to explain the reasons for any shortcomings and, if those explanations are not accepted as being sufficient to explain the employer's failings, the employer should expect no less than a finding of unfair dismissal. What flows from that may depend on the extent of the shortcomings in the consultation process.[65]

The so-called 'Polkey exception'

We referred above to the so-called '*Polkey* exception', assembled from the opinions of Lords **10.97** Bridge and MacKay, where consultation is either 'futile' or 'utterly useless'. The cases discussed below suggest that some caution is necessary in relying on it.

There has been some debate as to whether an employer, wishing to rely on the *Polkey* **10.98** exception had to show to the tribunal that, prior to taking the decision to dismiss, a conscious decision was taken to omit the procedural step which might otherwise give rise to a finding of unfairness; or whether the employer could simply rely on the argument that, regardless of whether it considered omitting that procedural step, it could still rely on the argument that the step was 'futile' or 'useless'. The matter has now been settled in the Court of Appeal, in which the latter argument has succeeded. In other words, the employer need not have consciously decided beforehand to omit a particular procedural step (for example, early warning or consultation in a redundancy case) in order to rely on the argument that that procedural step, had it been followed, would have made no difference.[66]

In *Heron v Citylink-Nottingham*,[67] an employment tribunal held that there were exceptional **10.99** circumstances, which meant that lack of consultation did not render the dismissal of an employee unfair. It said that the exceptional circumstances were twofold: the need for immediate decisions to be made about the dismissal, and the fact that the only person who could be made redundant was the applicant.

This was challenged on appeal, and the EAT had to decide whether those findings were **10.100** supported by the evidence and, if they were, whether they could be regarded as circumstances justifying the failure to consult. The EAT held that neither of the reasons given and relied upon by the tribunal as constituting exceptional circumstances were capable of being so regarded. A finding that the requirement to consult was obviated by the need for immediate decisions can be supported only if the circumstances made it necessary for the employers to dismiss the employee when they did and at no later date.

On the facts, the EAT found that, in this particular case, although the employer's financial **10.101** position had been deteriorating over the few months prior to the dismissal of the applicant, there was no evidence that anything had occurred on or shortly before Mr Heron was dismissed that made it necessary for him to be dismissed at that particular time. The EAT was of the view that another week would have made little difference and consultation could have taken place. Within that week there may have been a change in the fortunes of the company,

---

[65] *Mafunanya v (1) Richmond Fellowship (2) Mr A Hanley* (EAT/0449/03).
[66] See *Duffy v Yeomans & Partners Ltd* [1994] IRLR 642.
[67] [1993] IRLR 372.

or the employee himself may have come up with suggestions to preserve his position, and so forth. The point is that lack of consultation meant that none of this occurred. It will be seen, therefore, that there will need to be truly exceptional reasons for failing to consult in a redundancy situation.

10.102   In *De Grasse* (above) the EAT said that, notwithstanding the fact that s 98(4) of the ERA 1996 specifically refers to 'the size and administrative resources of the employer's undertaking' as factors to be considered by a tribunal in determining whether a dismissal was fair or unfair, even a small undertaking could not excuse a total absence of procedure. The size of the undertaking might well affect the formality of the consultation process in a redundancy situation but could not excuse lack of any consultation at all.

10.103   In the case of *KGB Micros Ltd v Lewis*[68] the EAT stressed the importance of consultation where the selection criteria lacked objectivity, because in such a case '. . . genuine consultation by an employer with an open mind . . .' might well make a difference to the outcome of the redundancy process. See also the decision in *Ferguson v Prestwick Circuits*,[69] in which the EAT said that 'it is clear that good industrial practice requires that, wherever possible, there should be consultation'.

10.104   Further examples of the importance of consultation have been seen in a number of cases: see, for example, *Rolls-Royce v Price and Others*[70] (importance of individual consultation notwithstanding consultation with trade unions); *Robertson v Magnet Ltd (Retail Division)*[71] (where the EAT overturned a majority tribunal decision that exceptional circumstances were present to enable a fair procedure to have been followed, despite the fact there was no individual consultation. In this case, the EAT preferred the approach whereby compensation is limited in such circumstances—see below); and *Campbell and Others v Dunoon & Cowal Housing Association Ltd*[72] (reduction in compensation where lack of consultation was the principal reason for unfairness).

10.105   In considering consultation in this context, the case of *Clews and Others v Liverpool City Council*[73] is of some interest. The applicants were supervisors in a security force operated by the council. In early 1991 the council decided that workforce reductions were necessary by way of redundancy, and consultation commenced with trade unions.

10.106   The council's plans for redundancies created industrial unrest, which included a strike and wide-scale picketing. Up to dismissal, consultation had been attempted between the council and the unions. This had broken down because of the industrial action, and arrangements were made for individual applicants to be seen by the personnel officer. The employment tribunal took the view that the consultation procedure was not satisfactory but that this was not a normal case. The tribunal referred to the fact that it was obliged to consider the employer's reasonableness 'in the circumstances', as contained in the wording of s 98(4) of the ERA 1996. The tribunal believed that although the consultation procedure was not perfect, and perhaps not even satisfactory, it was reasonable 'in the circumstances'.

---

[68] EAT 573/90, 25 March 1991.
[69] [1992] IRLR 268.
[70] [1993] IRLR 203.
[71] [1993] IRLR 512.
[72] [1993] IRLR 496.
[73] EAT 463/93. 4 May1994.

The EAT agreed with the employment tribunal. It said that the consultation process fell **10.107** short of what would normally be expected of a large employer and, in particular, that the consultation conducted with individuals was open to criticism. However, it was for the tribunal of fact, i.e. the employment tribunal, to weigh in the balance the need for the consultation against all of the circumstances facing the employer. The EAT could find no fault with the tribunal's reasoning.

It has also been suggested that the more nebulous the criteria to be used in assessing any **10.108** particular employees for redundancy, the greater the need for consultation. In *Graham v ABF*[74] the criteria of 'quality of work, efficiency in carrying it out and the attitude of the persons evaluated to their work' were adopted. Mr Graham was selected principally on the basis that he had a poor attitude to work, which the company justified because he was involved in a number of incidents where he had used obscene and abusive language to other employees. Mr Graham was dismissed and claimed unfair dismissal, principally on the ground that 'attitude to work' was an inherently unfair criterion for redundancy selection. He also complained that he had been denied an opportunity to consult before dismissal. The tribunal said that whilst attitude to work was an unusual criterion it was nevertheless fair (particularly in this case as it had been agreed with the union).

Mr Graham appealed and the EAT held that, notwithstanding that 'attitude to work' is **10.109** highly relative, involving personal and subjective judgements, it did not feel it could over-turn the employment tribunal's decision that such a criterion was capable of founding a fair selection for redundancy. However, it should be noted that in giving the EAT's judgment Waite J expressed the hope that 'so nebulous a criterion will not be found again in the negotiated agreements for redundancy selection' (see also *KGB Micros Ltd v Lewis* above).

The latitude of the employment tribunals to determine cases on matters of fact in this area has **10.110** been stressed in a number of cases. See, for example, *Arora v Coopers & Lybrand*[75] in which the EAT held that it would normally be a question of fact and degree for the employment tribunal to consider whether consultation with the employee was so inadequate as to render the dismissal unfair. This means that cases in this area should be treated as indicative or at best guidance. In *King and Others v Eaton Limited*[76] an employment tribunal held that the dismissal of four employees was unfair, stating that 'there was no consultation worthy of the name with any of the employees'. The employers successfully appealed and the EAT found that there had been no individual consultation but that there had been extensive consultation with the unions. The employees appealed and the Court of Session, allowing the appeal and restoring the decision of the employment tribunal, held that the EAT had erred in concluding that the employer had consulted extensively with the trade unions before dismissing the individuals on the grounds of redundancy. Although there were a number of meetings with the union, there was no justification for the EAT's conclusion that there was extensive consultation regarding the selection for redundancy, because discussions with the union only took place after the employer's proposals had been formulated. The union had not been given adequate time to respond and therefore there was no meaningful consultation in the sense meant by Glidewell LJ in *ex parte Price* (above). Since there was no consultation with individual employees and no proper consultation with the union, the EAT could not find that dismissals were fair.

---

[74] [1986] IRLR 90.
[75] Unreported, 1998.
[76] [1995] IRLR 75.

Mugford v Midland Bank

10.111   The EAT in *Mugford v Midland Bank*[77] summarised the position as follows:

(1)   Where no consultation about redundancy has taken place with either the trade union or the employee the dismissal will normally be unfair, unless the Industrial Tribunal find that a reasonable employer would have concluded that consultation would be an utterly futile exercise in the particular circumstances of the case.

(2)   Consultation with the trade union over selection criteria does not of itself release the employer from considering with the employee individually his being identified for redundancy.

(3)   It will be a question of fact and degree for the industrial tribunal to consider whether consultation with the individual and/or his union was so inadequate as to render the dismissal unfair. A lack of consultation in any particular respect will automatically lead to that result. The overall picture must be viewed by the tribunal up to the date of termination to ascertain whether the employer has or has not acted reasonably in dismissing the employee on the grounds of redundancy.

10.112   In considering consultation and selection, tribunals and the higher courts do have regard for the practicalities of consultation. However, it will not be a simple matter for an employer to convince a tribunal that there has been sufficient consultation where, for example an individual's selection is not discussed with them in some detail. In *John Brown Engineering Limited v Brown and Others*[78] an employment tribunal held that Mr Brown and his colleagues were unfairly dismissed on the ground that there had been no proper consultation about selection because although the employer had used a points system for assessing individuals, and although that had been agreed with the union, individuals were not given their particular scores and therefore, even though the redundancy process contained an appeal against selection, the individuals had no material on which to base an appeal to challenge their selection. The employment tribunal held that in those circumstances the appeals procedure was a sham, there was no consultation, and the dismissals were unfair. On appeal the employers argued that to have consulted individually with those selected would have been to call into question the validity of the marking system, which would have been invidious. The employers seemed to be arguing that once the selection criteria had been agreed with the union, that was as far as consultation needed to go. Not surprisingly, the EAT agreed with the employment tribunal and dismissed the appeal.

10.113   The tribunal had not erred in holding that the employer had unfairly selected the employees for redundancy. The EAT reiterated that a fair redundancy selection process requires that individual employees have the opportunity to contest selection either by themselves or through their representatives. The Court was not going as far as to say that league tables of staff should be published, but merely that the employees must be given some basis on which to challenge their selection. In *King* (above) it is reiterated that it is not necessary for employees to know the scores of other staff against whom they were assessed in order to establish a fair selection process. It is perfectly reasonable to expect an employee to question their own marks on an objective basis. For example, if an employee is scored low because of their attendance they could argue that attendance records are incorrect or that there is an explanation as to why they had a particularly difficult period in relation to attendance at work at so on. It is not necessary for that employee to see their colleagues' scores to do that.

---

[77] [1997] IRLR 208.
[78] [1997] IRLR 90.

In *Alexander v Brigden Enterprises Limited*,[79] whilst considering for the purposes of the case   **10.114**
the then applicable statutory procedures, the EAT determined that the information to be provided to an employee must include the selection criteria and the assessment of the employee
against those criteria.

In *Davies v Farnborough College of Technology*[80] the EAT held that the employee simply   **10.115**
needed the opportunity to challenge the information held by the employer and 'that may
involve the giving of the particular marks, or it may not'.

The EAT, however, held in *Pinewood Repro Ltd t/a County Print v Page*[81] that fair consultation   **10.116**
during redundancy involves giving an employee an explanation as to why he has been marked
down in a scoring exercise. In this case, through conversations with the trade union, it was agreed
that the scoring matrix headings were to be attendance, quality, productivity, abilities, skills,
experience, disciplinary record, and flexibility. Employees were told that staff at risk would be
selected for redundancy via a point-scoring matrix system, a copy of which was sent to the
employees concerned. The employee was informed that it was likely that he would be selected
for redundancy and was invited to a meeting to discuss the position. Prior to this meeting the
employee had not received his actual scores, but he did prepare a list of questions for the meeting,
which included the questions, 'Why was I chosen from a pool of three?' and 'Can I see the scoring sheets for the selected criteria?' At the meeting he was given a copy of his personal scores, but
the employment tribunal found that the company made no attempt to explain how his scores
had been arrived at, the employer simply saying that the scores were 'reasonable and appropriate'. It was held that without the markers giving some indication of how the scores had been
arrived at it was not possible for the employee to advance arguments against the scores. This
made the dismissal unfair. It was noted that authorities such as *Eton v King* prevented a tribunal
carrying out a 'microscopic' analysis of the scoring system or points awarded but, nonetheless, it
is open for a tribunal, said the EAT, to decide whether the employee in a particular case has been
given a fair and proper opportunity to understand fully the matters about which he is being
consulted and to express his views on the subjects and 'with the consultor thereafter considering
those properly and genuinely and that may well include being given sufficient information to be
able to challenge the scores given to him in the completion of the redundancy exercise'.

In relation to consultation and alternative employment several cases have stressed the need   **10.117**
for consultation. In *Marche v John Lewis Plc*[82] an employment tribunal had determined that
John Lewis Plc had acted reasonably in treating redundancy as a sufficient reason for
dismissal and dismissed Mrs Marche's claim for unfair dismissal. Mrs Marche had worked
for the company since 1979, rising to the position of senior contracts assistant in the furnish-
ing department. The department was making a loss and the company embarked upon a
reorganisation which affected 10 employees, of which one was to be made redundant. Mrs Marche
was in fact told that she would be redeployed and a number of interviews with senior managers
and personnel officers followed. Three openings were discussed with Mrs Marche but none
of these jobs were suitable and she was made redundant. The employment tribunal found
that Mrs Marche had not been unfairly dismissed on the basis that she had been adequately
consulted. Mrs Marche appealed and the EAT rejected the appeal. It is accepted that in

---

[79] [2006] IRLR 422.
[80] [2008] IRLR 14.
[81] EAT/0028/10.
[82] Unreported, 1997.

exceptional circumstances consultation or some other procedural step may be curtailed or dispensed with. However, in the present case there appeared to be sufficient consultation, particularly on the question of alternative employment, bearing in mind the number of meetings and opportunities that were discussed with Mrs Marche. The tribunal had not erred in law in finding the dismissal fair. Finally, under this heading consider the case of *Helen McMullen v Hayes Manor School*.[83] The employment tribunal dismissed Helen McMullen's complaint of unfair dismissal. Ms McMullen was employed at Hayes Manor School from September 1992. In July 1995 she was told that her position as head of drama would be redundant from 31 August 1995. She remained employed by the school, covering for absent colleagues and she was also head of year. In April 1996 the school decided to reduce their heads of year from seven to four and all heads of year were asked to apply for the four positions. In July 1996 Ms McMullen was told that she had not been successful and that there would be no job for her from December of that year, as a result of which she would be made redundant. The tribunal determined that dismissal was by reason of redundancy and that the procedure followed was reasonable in all the circumstances.

10.118   The EAT held that there had been no consultation at all in relation to the question of alternative employment. There was no clear express finding by the tribunal that it had been reasonable for the employer to dispense with consultation on the ground that consultation as to alternative employment would have been futile or useless. Ms McMullen's appeal was allowed.

D.   The Selection Process

General

10.119   It is probably in the area of selection that most employers find difficulty in escaping unfair dismissal liability. The importance of selection was made clear by the EAT in *Williams v Compair Maxam Ltd* (above), where it was said that the employer must establish criteria for selecting employees for redundancy that, so far as possible, do not depend solely upon the opinion of the person making the selection but can be objectively checked against such things as attendance records, efficiency at the job, experience, or length of service. The employer must then ensure that selection is made fairly in accordance with these criteria, which must also be objectively applied.

10.120   In *Compair Maxam* the EAT quoted extensively from the decision in *Greig v Sir Alfred McAlpine & Son (Northern) Ltd*,[84] in which it was stated:

> . . . in considering the reasonableness of a redundancy dismissal where a selection has to be made between those who are to be retained and those who are to be dismissed, the most important matter upon which the employer has to satisfy the tribunal is that he acted reasonably in respect of the selection of the particular employee. That normally involves two questions, namely whether the employer adopted reasonable criteria for selection, and whether those reasonable criteria were reasonably and fairly applied in respect of the individual.

It should be noted that this section in *Greig* no longer correctly emphasises the burden of proof which, under s 98(4) of the ERA 1996 is neutral, but nevertheless the statement does

---

[83] Unreported, 1999.
[84] [1979] IRLR 372.

show the principles of good employment practice, which an ordinary tribunal does and should adopt in testing the fairness of a redundancy dismissal.

It is also clear that there may be more than one fair method of selecting for redundancy. **10.121** In *Green v A & I Fraser (Wholesale Fish Merchants) Ltd*,[85] the EAT was asked to decide an appeal from a majority industrial tribunal decision. In relation to the question of reasonableness, it said:

> As has been said in a number of recent cases this is a situation in which one employer may act in a certain way and act perfectly reasonably and another employer in identical circumstances may act in the opposite way and still act perfectly reasonably. There is in short what has been described as a band of reasonableness and the actings of an employer will only be unfair if it is shown that they fell without that band. In the present case we have a classic example of the situation where two reasonable employers might follow a different course of action. That is exemplified by the fact that the industrial tribunal found themselves divided on the matter.

In other words, there is almost always going to be more than one method of redundancy selection. The issue for the employer will be whether the procedure which is in fact adopted can be justified as reasonable in relation to the situation in which the employer finds himself.

As the EAT has pointed out in the past, an employer seeking to argue that redundancy dis- **10.122** missals were fairly implemented will have to convince the court and adduce evidence as to:

(a) what person, or body of persons, took the decision to dismiss particular employees;
(b) what information it or they took into account in reaching that decision; and
(c) upon what criteria it or they assessed whatever information was taken into account.

In the absence of such evidence, a tribunal may well find the dismissals unfair.[86]

For these reasons it is difficult to lay down clear guidelines on, for example, redundancy selec- **10.123** tion criteria. Each case will turn on its own facts. It is convenient, in line with the approach taken in *Greig*, to subdivide this section into a consideration of the choice of the correct pool for redundancy selection and an analysis of specific criteria which may be adopted. The section on criteria may conveniently be further subdivided into two issues, first, what criteria may be used and, second, the application of those criteria to any specific set of circumstances.

Pool of selection

As an initial step, the employer must be sure that the employees to be made redundant are **10.124** chosen from the correct group of employees. According to the decision in *Cowen v Haden Carriers Ltd*,[87] this group may not be limited to those actually doing the work that is ceasing or reducing.

Indeed, if under their contracts the employees doing this work can be required to do other **10.125** work, and such work is available, they may not even be redundant at all (see the discussion in Chapter 3). It was noted in *Cowen* that this interpretation (which comes from the Court of Appeal decisions in *Nelson v BBC*[88] and *Nelson v BBC (No. 2)*[89]) caused tremendous

---

[85] [1985] IRLR 55.
[86] See *Bristol Channel Ship Repairers Ltd v (1) O'Keefe and Others and (2) G N Lewis* [1977] IRLR 13.
[87] [1982] IRLR 314.
[88] [1977] IRLR 148.
[89] [1979] IRLR 346.

difficulties for employers. If no such other work is available then there may be redundancies; but even in these circumstances it does not automatically follow that the workers who are directly affected (i.e. those who are actually doing the work which is ceasing or diminishing) should be dismissed. They may claim that the basis of selection should be such that other employees should be selected instead of them and that they should be given those jobs. The impact has been limited following the decision on the definition of redundancy in the case of *Murray v Foyle Meats Ltd*[90] and indeed the approach was disapproved in *Safeway Stores Plc v Burrell*.[91] The EAT in *Burrell* held that the decision in *Nelson* was simply authority for the proposition that where a redundancy situation arises and a potentially redundant employee is directed to transfer to other work within the scope of his contract and the employee refuses to transfer, the reason for the dismissal is not redundancy.

10.126   The EAT in *Burrell* also found that the EAT's decision in *Cowen*, that there was nothing in the legislation requiring analysis of an employee's contract, was 'plainly and obviously correct'. However, the EAT in *Cowen* had felt bound by *Nelson*. Although the Court of Appeal in *Cowen* had overturned the EAT's ultimate decision, the EAT in *Burrell* commented, 'we prefer to view the decision of the Court of Appeal in that case as being correct in the result' but noted that it had lead 'unhappily' to the development of the contract test and that the 'applicant/employee terms and conditions of employment are irrelevant to the questions raised by statute'.

10.127   The correct pool from which selection is to be made is primarily a matter for the employer to determine. Employees will have difficulty challenging this, provided the employer has acted logically and reasonably. As is suggested above, the pool may not be limited to employees doing the same work. Where there is a degree of flexibility within the workforce (as is often the case in modern industries), the employee will need to ensure that all of those persons capable of doing, and capable of being required to do, different jobs are included in the pool, and that the pool is not artificially limited to those employees who are carrying out the functions that are ceasing or reducing.

10.128   It must be stressed that s 98(4) of the ERA 1996 does not actually require a consideration, for redundancy purposes, of similarly placed employees. Nevertheless, as has been said, if the employer unreasonably limits the pool of selection, that may itself lead to unfairness. In *Thomas & Betts Manufacturing Ltd v Harding*,[92] the employment tribunal held that Mrs Harding's dismissal was unfair because, although she was employed in making fittings, she could have been found work as a packer, even though that may have meant dismissing a recently recruited packer. This decision was upheld by the EAT.

10.129   The employer appealed to the Court of Appeal on the basis that the employment tribunal had erred in law in holding that Mrs Harding should have been offered alternative work as a packer. The Court of Appeal dismissed this appeal, and in so doing Eveleigh LJ said, '. . . I would reject the contention put forward in this case that the employer is under no obligation, as a matter of law, to look elsewhere among his employees, other than those employed in similar positions'. The Court of Appeal was very clear that the choice of the correct pool was a matter for the employer acting reasonably to determine, and the reasonableness of the employer's act is a matter for an employment tribunal to determine, based on principles of common sense.

---

[90] See Chapter 3.
[91] UKEAT/168/96.
[92] [1980] IRLR 255.

It is difficult and indeed undesirable to lay down any rules of law in this particular area, and   **10.130**
case law is, therefore, useful only for general guidance at best. The position in regards to
identifying the appropriate pool was outlined by Rimer J in *Kvaerner Oil and Gas Limited v
Parker and Others*,[93]

> . . . the starting point is, and must always be, whether or not the Tribunal was correct to con-
> clude that the dismissals were unfair by reference to the considerations set out in section 98 (4)
> of the 1996 Act. But in approaching that exercise it is important to underline that the authori-
> ties show that different people can quite legitimately have different views about what is or is not
> a fair response to a particular situation and the fact that A considers that solution X is the fair
> one, whereas B favours solution Y, does not mean that one or another of them must be adopting
> an unfair solution. In those situations there will be a band of potential responses to a particular
> problem and it may be that both of solutions X and Y will be well within that band.

In *Powers and Villiers v A Clarke & Co (Smethwick) Ltd*[94] the employer had used the criteria   **10.131**
of 'last in, first out' amongst two separate pools: class one drivers and class three drivers.
Mr Powers and Mr Villiers argued that class one and class three drivers should have been
treated as one pool, which would have meant that on the application of 'last in, first out' they
would not have been selected.[95] There were differences in basic pay between class one and
class three drivers, differences in shift working, and other differences between the two classes.
It was agreed that there was some flexibility between drivers and some movement between
class one and class three. Mr Powers and Mr Villiers drew the court's attention to *Thomas &
Betts Manufacturing Ltd* (above) which had suggested a broader approach than the employers
had used in selecting the pool in their case. However, the EAT said that *Thomas & Betts
Manufacturing Ltd* involved employment of an unskilled nature and a high degree of flexibility could therefore be expected. In the case of Mr Powers and Mr Villiers the court pointed
out that only class one drivers could drive articulated vehicles and any flexibility was strictly
limited. In other words, the employers were not acting wholly unreasonable in treating both
classes as separate pools from which to select employees for redundancy.

Also relevant is *Green v A & I Fraser (Wholesale Fish Merchants) Ltd* (above), in which the   **10.132**
EAT agreed that the pool for selection was properly limited to the company's lorry drivers,
despite the fact that a mechanic had shorter service than Mr Green and was retained. The
EAT again pointed to the fact that the work involved was skilled and it is a question of fact
for the industrial tribunal to determine whether the pool chosen was correct. The EAT
would not interfere with the tribunal's decision. (See also *Babar Indian Restaurant v Rawat*,[96]
in which the EAT, upholding the tribunal's decision, found that it was reasonable for the
owners of a restaurant to treat it as a separate business from their other businesses of a frozen
food concern and an offsales shop.) There were separate records and accounts and the tribunal's finding of fact could not be challenged.

In *Highland Fish Farmers Ltd v Thorburn and Another*[97] the EAT said that in carrying out a   **10.133**
redundancy exercise an employer should begin by identifying the group of employees from
whom the redundancies will be made. It is members of the chosen pool who will need to be

---

[93] EAT/0444/02.
[94] [1981] IRLR 483.
[95] This was a case considered under the now repealed s 59(1)(b) of the EPCA 1978, but the principles are of
some general application.
[96] [1985] IRLR 57.
[97] EAT 1094/94, 9 March 1995.

warned and consulted and from which selection will be made. In choosing the correct pool the employer must act reasonably. In this case, the company owned a number of fish-farming sites employing in total about 50 people. Two of the sites were relatively close together (about 40 minutes' travelling time apart) and they shared some facilities. The sites were treated as distinct working units by the company, and the applicants were employed on one site exclusively. It was subsequently decided by the company to close the site at which the applicants worked, thus creating three redundancies. The company also needed to make five other redundancies and chose those from amongst various other sites.

10.134   The employment tribunal had found that the geographical proximity between the two sites in question (notwithstanding the fact that there was a 40-minute drive between the two) meant that a reasonable employer would have considered all of the employees employed on both sites as one pool. The principal issue before the EAT, therefore, was whether the tribunal was entitled to find that the employers acted unreasonably when they treated one site separately from the other. The employer argued that it was not unreasonable for it to look at each site separately and consider that the correct pool in each case was that of the employees employed at that particular site. The EAT said that the argument had some force but it could not interfere with the tribunal's decision because it was a matter of fact for the tribunal to determine whether the employer's approach had been reasonable. The tribunal had not erred in law, nor acted perversely. The EAT therefore refused to uphold the appeal.

10.135   An example of the principle that, provided the employer acts reasonably the fact that the pool could have been different from the one chosen will not necessarily give rise to an unfair dismissal claim, can be seen in the case of *Lenting & Others v Bristow Helicopters Limited*.[98] Bristow Helicopters wished to reduce the number of its helicopter pilots. It went through a multi-stage process. First, certain categories of pilots were excluded from the pool for selection. A second sifting process took place, from which co-pilots were excluded. A third process took place where the pool for redundancies was limited to those pilots who were of normal retiring age. It was only then that the criterion for selection was applied (last in, first out in this case). Two pilots were selected as redundant and the employment tribunal found both dismissals to be unfair. The EAT allowed the company's appeal, as did the Court of Session. The Court of Session confirmed the EAT's reasoning that the company could arrive at the pool it did provided it could justify the process as reasonable. In this case, the reason was a business concern, i.e. the need to achieve a balanced pilot compliment, which was fair in the circumstances. There was no unfairness in limiting the pool to pilots who had reached normal retirement age.

10.136   The EAT in *Hendy Banks City Print Limited v Fairbrother and Others*[99] upheld the tribunal's decision that the pool had been unreasonably selected and thus the employees had been unfairly dismissed. The claimants in this case had formed part of the respondent's finishing department and had been skilled employees performing work described as 'perfect binding'. The tribunal held that 'those who worked in the Finishing Department should have been part of the pool and that it had been unfairly restricted to the "perfect binders"'. The EAT held that there had been good reasons for the tribunal coming to the conclusion that the pool selected was not one within a reasonable band for selection and upheld the decision. The EAT highlighted the various factors which it considered were good reasons for this conclusion which included, *inter alia*, that the claimants were the most experienced employees,

---

[98]   Unreported, 1998.
[99]   EAT/0691/04.

they covered all aspects of finishing work, they spent only a third of their time on the perfect binding machine, and that they were multi-skilled workers.

Summary

One may summarise the rules on identification of the pool as follows.

10.137

Essentially the matter is one of an issue of managerial prerogative and in this regard the tribunal must not substitute its own view for that of the employer. The 'band of reasonable responses' test will apply and any decision by the employer on identification of the pool that is within the band of reasonable responses should not result in unfairness.

As the EAT stated in *Blatchford Solicitors v Burger*[100]

10.138

> . . . the question in every case is, as *Prowse -Wilkinson J said in B L Cars v Lewis* paragraph 15, was the selection one which a reasonable employer could have made? To regard the [in this case] lifo principle alone as wholly inadmissible is to substitute the tribunal's view for that of a reasonable employer. Equally it is not open to the tribunal to substitute its view as clearly appropriate criterion, here the relevant competence of the candidates for selection, itself a subjective criterion (*C F Williams v Compair Maxam* [1982] IRLR 83) for the objective criterion of length of service.[101]

Nonetheless, it has been held by the EAT that a dismissal may be unfair on the basis of a failure to consult about or to consider all the possibilities concerning the identification of the pool.[102]

The immediate instinct is to focus on employees carrying out work of the kind which is perceived as diminishing. But consideration should also be given to including other employees whose jobs are similar to or interchangeable with those employees. As the EAT stated in *Bansi v Alpha flight Services*:[103]

10.139

> . . . the pool cannot be limited to persons actually doing the work for which the requirement has diminished but should include those can potentially do such work. However it is for the employer to select the appropriate skills it wished to retain.

Certainly an employer should take into account any pre-existing agreement concerning use of a pool. The ACAS booklet, *Redundancy Handling*, and case law comments also suggest that consulting about the pool with employee representatives is a reasonable thing to do.[104] Whether it is appropriate from an industrial relations point of view or for unfair dismissal purposes for an employer to consider 'bumping' another employee out of his or her job (which that employee may have been performing perfectly satisfactorily to date) is a question of fact in each case. There is no absolute obligation to 'bump'.[105] The issue is what a reasonable employer would do in the circumstances. In particular, did the employer's decision fall within the band of reasonable responses available to a reasonable employer?[106] It is, on the other hand, wrong for an employer to always assume *automatically* that the pool should only include the employee holding the position that it has decided to remove from its structure.[107]

10.140

---

[100] EAT/207/00.
[101] See also the view of the EAT in *Drake International Systems Limited (T/A Drake Distribution Services) v O'Hare* (EAT/0384/03/TM).
[102] *Fulcrum Pharma (Europe) Limited v Bonaserra* (EAT/0198/10).
[103] EAT/0652/03.
[104] See also *Fulcrum Pharma (Europe) Limited v Bonaserra* (EAT/0198/10).
[105] *Byrne v Arvin Meritor LVS (UK) Limited* (EAT/239/02).
[106] *Lionel Leventhal Limited v North* (EAT/0265/04).
[107] *Fulcrum Pharma (Europe) Limited v Bonaserra* (EAT/0198/10).

10.141 In conclusion, employers do have a discretion as far as the pool is concerned but a dismissal may be unfair if an employer cannot show it has given the issue proper consideration (which includes, as stated, consultation).

Selection criteria

10.142 As mentioned above, the EAT in *Williams v Compair Maxam* said that a reasonable employer should attempt to establish selection criteria which do not depend solely upon the opinion of the person who is selecting employees for redundancy but which can be checked objectively against things such as attendance records, efficiency at the job, experience, or length of service. Added to that might also be factors such as disciplinary records and other objective evidence of an employee's performance in the work place.

10.143 *Compair Maxam* also suggested that where there is a recognised trade union, selection criteria should be drawn up in consultation, and if possible by agreement, with that union (and presumably now also with any elected representatives of the affected workforce[108]). Once selection criteria are agreed and in place they must be applied fairly and selection made in accordance with them.

'Attitude' and other subjective criteria to avoid

10.144 Many employers have, in the past, attempted to use subjective criteria such as 'attitude'. On the whole this is a dangerous area for the employer to stray into because of the difficulty in justifying the opinion given about the particular employee selected for redundancy on such a basis. However, it must be stressed that if 'attitude' means, for example, numbers of warnings about performance or conduct, then obviously it would be something that could be checked objectively against the employee's personal record. Consequently, it will be seen that the heading which is given to the particular chosen criteria is not as important as the substance of the criteria to be used. Other instances of unsatisfactorily subjective criteria include an employee's buy-in to 'company values'[109] and 'range of influence, empathy, self insight and the ability to win hearts and minds'.[110]

Length of service and discrimination issues

10.145 A criterion which has been in and out of favour at varying times is length of service (or, as is often described, 'LIFO' (last in, first out)). Current thinking suggests that length of service should *not* be the only criterion an employer should use. With the potential for this criterion to be both discriminatory against women, who statistically have shorter service, and discriminatory on the grounds of age, employers must be cautious in their approach.

10.146 In *Suflex Ltd v Thomas*[111] the EAT said that in some industries problems being encountered in what they described as 'modern conditions' are acute and 'the relevance of the concepts of "last in, first out" in selecting for redundancy is becoming outdated'. However, the EAT has since suggested that to eliminate length of service totally from the decision to dismiss an employee as redundant could well found a criticism of unfairness, although, of course, every case will depend on its own facts (see *Westland Helicopters Ltd v Nott*[112]). In *Westland* the EAT

---

[108] See Chapter 11.
[109] *Howard v Siemens Energy Services* (ET/ 2324423/2008).
[110] *Abbey National Plc v Chagger* [2009] IRLR 86, EAT; [2010] IRLR 47, CA.
[111] [1987] IRLR 435.
[112] EAT 342/88, (11 October 1989).

also suggested that a fair system taking into account length of service might be achieved where the employer includes length of service as just one selection factor amongst several.

The Court of Appeal in Northern Ireland upheld a finding that an employer had not acted unlawfully in removing length of service as a redundancy selection criterion in this case on the basis that it would have had a disproportionate affect on recently hired Roman Catholics and would have undermined the company's affirmative action programme. In *Hall & others v Shorts Missile Systems Limited*[113] Shorts Missile Systems Limited (SMS), a division of Short Brothers Plc, was bound by a negotiated redundancy selection procedure with the Confederation of Ship Building and Engineering Unions. This agreement stated that where a redundancy situation becomes unavoidable it would be the company's policy to retain in its employment the most efficient personnel and when selecting for redundancy the company would take into account quality of work, productivity, attitude, ability to work unsupervised, housekeeping, disciplinary record, and length of service. Each employee had an annual assessment in respect of each criteria and were awarded marks up to a total possible maximum of 900. Length of service was dealt with by allowing four points per year of complete service.

10.147

Short Brothers was a Protestant-dominated firm. The fair employment legislation was the motive for increasing the proportion of Roman Catholics in the Short Brothers company and the company had some success in this area. By definition, however, Catholics within the organisation at the time of the redundancy situation had less service on average than Protestants.

10.148

Use of the length-of-service criteria would therefore, it was argued, have discriminated against those recently appointed Roman Catholics, and the company decided to reduce the number of points awarded to length of service to two per year rather than four per year. SMS, a division of Short Brothers, could not reach that agreement with its union locally and decided to abandon the criterion of length of service entirely. Protestants who were dismissed claimed that their dismissal was unfair and discriminatory. The Fair Employment Tribunal in Northern Ireland disagreed. The dismissals were neither unfair nor discriminatory.[114]

10.149

In summary, an employer may have good reason for not wishing to use 'last in, first out' as the only or main criterion for selection. This may be because individuals who are selected on this basis are the younger and perhaps more flexible employees; they are usually paid less than employees who have been within the organisation longer; and it may leave the employer with an ageing workforce many of whom could be coming up to retirement and whose skills it may be difficult to replace. On the other hand, in practice, many redundancy agreements still contain provisions to the effect that selection will be made on the basis of 'last in, first out' since this has traditionally been popular with trade unions. It was formerly the case that if the dismissal of an individual was in breach of a customary arrangement or agreed procedure then that dismissal was automatically unfair under s 59(1)(b) of the EPCA 1978. However, that provision was repealed by the Deregulation and Contracting Out Act 1994 and applied to dismissals taking effect after 3 January 1995. Whilst this gives employers more flexibility to manoeuvre, it should nevertheless be remembered that breach of an agreed procedure may be taken into account in assessing the fairness of a dismissal.

10.150

---

[113] EOR 72 1997, p 39.
[114] See below for a fuller discussion on redundancy and discrimination.

10.151 Length of service as a criterion within a selection matrix was analysed by a Court of Appeal in *Rolls-Royce Plc v Unite the Union*.[115] Proceedings had been commenced in the High Court to determine whether use of this criterion in a redundancy selection procedure constituted unlawful age discrimination contrary to the Employment Equality (Age) Regulations 2006 (now the Equality Act 2010). Whilst it had been acknowledged by the parties that unless justified, its use constituted unlawful indirect age discrimination, the question arose as to whether its use could be justified as a proportionate means of achieving a legitimate aim under reg 3(1) (Equality Act 2010, s 13 (2)), and/or whether it fell within reg 32 (Equality Act 2010, Sch, 9, para 10) amounting to an award of a benefit and whether the purpose of the use of length of service as a criterion could be said to be fulfilling a business need.

10.152 The High Court was asked to determine these questions, although no dispute had yet arisen. The High Court, with misgivings, agreed to do so and concluded that both questions could be answered affirmatively.

10.153 On appeal to the Court of Appeal it was held that use of length of service as a criterion was indirectly discriminatory, but Wall LJ outlined that the inclusion of length of service as a criteria was a proportionate means of achieving a legitimate aim. He held that:

> ... the legitimate aim is the reward of loyalty and the overall desirability of achieving a stable workforce in the context of a fair process of redundancy selection. The proportionate means is in my judgment, amply demonstrated by the fact that the length of service criterion is only one of a substantial number of criteria measuring employee suitability for redundancy and that it is by no means determinative.

10.154 In considering reg 32, (Equality Act 2010, sched 9, para 10) Wall LJ identified that its use did constitute a benefit and that 'a length of service criterion of more than 5 years does *reasonably* fulfil the business need of the company... of having a loyal and stable workforce'. The important point about this case, however, is that length of service was just one of a number of criteria employed. If LIFO is to be used, we would comment that it would be prudent to include this as part of a bundle of criteria, rather than the sole criterion.

Equality law and other potentially unlawfully discriminatory criteria

10.155 We have touched on the dangers of length of service as a criterion, as it will inevitably be indirectly discriminatory on the grounds of age, a protected characteristic under the Equality Act 2010. Caution must also be exercised to avoid indirect discrimination on account of any other of the Act's protected characteristics, i.e. disability,[116] gender re-assignment, marriage and civil partnerships,[117] race,[118] religion or belief, sex,[119] sexual orientation, or pregnancy and maternity.[120]

10.156 Care must therefore be taken, when developing selection criteria and applying the criteria for selection for dismissal, to exclude absences on account of illness amounting to disability— or

---

[115] [2009] EWCA Civ 387.

[116] *British Sugar Plc v Kirker* [1998] IRLR 624; *Kent County Council v Mingo* [2000] IRLR 90.

[117] *Simon v David Altman & Co* (ET/2202664/98).

[118] *Fletcher v Federal Mogul Aftermarket UK Limited* (ET, unreported, 1999); *Wilson v Pimlico Village Housing Cooperative* (ET/2300490/98).

[119] *C F Brooke v London Borough of Haringey* [1992] IRLR 478.

[120] *Kaur v PKG Manufacturing Limited* (ET/2504584/97); *Price v Salycae Systems Limited* (ET/1302205/98); *Tootle v Kew Park Hire Limited* (ET/2100203/98; *William B Morrison & Son Limited v Sarah Jane Healey* (ET, unreported, 1999); *McGuigan v T G Baynes & Sons* (EAT, unreported, 1999).

indeed to include in the criteria considerations that would adversely impact on a disabled employee.[121] In *Beynton v Saurus General Engineering Limited*[122] the EAT confirmed that before dismissing a disabled person as redundant it is incumbent upon the employer to find out from the employee what the real affects of the disability might be and to find out what the up-to-date medical position is. It is a fairly obvious point that the now archaic (and potentially unlawful) practice of selecting part-time employees before full-time employees should be avoided as this will be indirect sex discrimination against female workers, who are the highest population of part-time workers.[123] Selection of fixed-term employees gives rise to similar problems. Fixed-term employees should not be selected first, on account of their employment status alone.[124]

Finally, in the use of attendance as a criterion, absences through, for example, maternity leave must obviously be discounted. In the latter regard, however, care must be taken not to over-compensate for such employees' absence lest a male in the same selection pool is discriminated against on grounds of sex. Thus, in *Eversheds LLP v De Belin*[125] an employment tribunal considered the case of property solicitors employed by Eversheds who were at risk of redundancy. One of the criteria, relating to financial performance, concerned the lawyers' 'lock-up' (the amount of unbilled work in progress for a client). Mr De Belin scored lowest on this criterion, with 0.5. Ms Reinholz, who was on maternity leave (and therefore had no lock-up) was awarded a *notional* score of 2. This made the crucial difference. Overall Mr De Belin scored 27 points and Ms Reinholz scored 27.5. **10.157**

It was held that the employer had over-compensated for Ms Reinholz's absence. This was unlawful sex discrimination as far as Mr De Belin was concerned. The employer should have chosen a historical period relating to lock-up when Ms Reinholz was actually at work so that a proper score could be attributed to her. This case was subsequently upheld by the EAT.[126] **10.158**

The additional danger for an employer (and material advantage to an employee) in arguing an unlawfully discriminatory reason for selection for redundancy is the possibility of an additional discrimination-based claim alongside an unfair dismissal claim. This carries with it a potentially uncapped claim for compensation for unlawful discrimination as well as the (capped) claim for unfair dismissal compensation. An expensive example of this is the litigation in *Chagger v Abbey National Plc*.[127] Chagger was of Indian origin, employed by Abbey National Plc, and made compulsorily redundant. He claimed that his selection for redundancy was on racial grounds. An employment tribunal awarded him compensation for the totality of his claims for unfair dismissal and race discrimination, both of which were successful, in the total sum of £2,794,962.27[128] (plus interest). Mr Chagger won his claim for unfair dismissal because the dismissal was contrary to the (now repealed) statutory procedure contained in s 98A of the ERA 1996, and his race claim on the basis that the employer had not discharged the reverse burden of proof on it. The Court of Appeal held **10.159**

---

[121] *British Sugar Plc v Kirker* [1998] IRLR 624.
[122] Unreported, 1999.
[123] See also Part-time Workers (Prevention of Less Favourable Treatment) Regulations 2000 SI 2000/1551.
[124] See *Whiffen v Milham Girls School* [2001] IRLR 468, CA. See also The Fixed Term Employees (Prevention of Less Favourable Treatment) Regulations 2002 (SI 2002/2034).
[125] ET Case No. 1804069/09.
[126] EAT/0352/10.
[127] [2010] IRLR 47 (CA); [2009] IRLR 86 (EAT).
[128] Partly distorted by the uplift made to compensation under the 2002 Act (now repealed).

that compensation in such a case could be reduced to reflect the chance that Mr Chagger would have been dismissed for redundancy in any event (see the argument on *Polkey* in unfair dismissal law, below). But future loss should not be limited to the period during which the claimant would have remained in employment with the employer. In the present case, the employment tribunal correctly assessed compensation on the assumption that Mr Chagger would have remained with Abbey throughout his career in financial services unless he chose to obtain another ground on an equivalent salary. It also held that Abbey could be liable for losses resulting from the fact (if proven) that Mr Chagger was unlawfully stigmatised by future employers who were unwilling to employ him because he had taken legal action against Abbey.

10.160   In short, the risk of an allegation of unlawful discrimination arising from selection for redundancy must always be borne in mind and the selection process must therefore be scrupulous with regard to equality issues. We have also drawn attention to the attraction to a claimant of combining a discrimination claim with a claim for unfair dismissal. Compensation for unlawful discrimination is unlimited, and a discrimination claim can be employed where an individual lacks the necessary qualifying period of employment to bring an unfair dismissal claim, as the former requires no qualifying period of service. For further detail about discrimination claims, including issues of remedies (e.g. compensation for injury to feelings, aggravated damages, etc.) and burden of proof, a specialist work should be consulted. For the practitioner, *Harvey on Industrial Relations and Emploment Law* is the starting point.[129]

Personal considerations

10.161   In making a selection for redundancy it may be important to take into account an individual's personal circumstances.[130] In the case of *The Earl of Bradford v Jowett*,[131] Mr Jowett had moved from County Durham to Shropshire to take up a job as an assistant to a Mr Owen. Mr Jowett and Mr Owen fell out and Mr Jowett took up the job undertaken by a Mr Botwood, who then became Mr Owen's assistant. When a redundancy situation arose Mr Jowett (who had longer service than Mr Botwood) was made redundant instead of Mr Botwood. The person who selected Mr Jowett had it in mind that if Mr Jowett and Mr Owen could have continued working together Mr Botwood would have been selected for redundancy rather than Mr Jowett. Mr Jowett was never informed of this fact. It became clear during the hearing that if Mr Jowett had been informed of this he would have made up his disagreement with Mr Owen rather than risk dismissal.

10.162   The employment tribunal, in finding the dismissal unfair, had taken into account Mr Jowett's domestic situation (he had recently relocated to his present job). The EAT confirmed that such a consideration did fall to be taken into account and personal circumstances may not simply relate to a particular employee's domestic situation, as was the case in *Jowett*.[132]

---

[129] See Division L. See also *Hammonds LLP v Mwitta* (EAT/0026/10) and *Rowse-Piper v Anglian Windows Ltd and Ors* [2010] EWCA Civ 428.

[130] See *Forman Construction Ltd v R Kelly* [1977] IRLR 468.

[131] [1978] IRLR 16.

[132] In Germany, where urgent genrational reasons trigger the possibility of dismissal and no alternative employment can be found, the employer has to factor in social grounds in selection (*sozial ausurahl*). For an account of this phenomenon. See Stephanie Konnett (2005) ICCLR, pp. 431–44.

Attendance

If an employer is intending to use attendance in order to determine selection for redundancy, **10.163**
it is important that the reasons for poor attendance are examined. In *Paine and Moore v
Grundy (Teddington) Ltd*,[133] May J said:

> In general terms, if employers are going to rely upon what we will describe briefly as an
> attendance record criterion in redundancy cases, we think that it is desirable that they should
> seek to ascertain the reasons for the absences which made up the attendance record of the
> particular employees concerned and, for instance, if an employee happens still to be absent at
> the time that the redundancies have to be put into effect, they should try to find out when that
> employee is likely to return to work. We think that this is merely a particular application of the
> much more general principle of industrial relations that employers should do all that is reason-
> able to ensure that they have in their possession as full information as is reasonable about their
> employees and the relevant situation before coming to any decision, for instance to dismiss on
> the grounds of redundancy.[134]

'Efficiency'

'Efficiency' has been held to be relevant in redundancy selection, although employers should **10.164**
be careful in assessing employees against objective criteria in attempting to determine relative
levels. It will certainly be the case that, where there are marginal differences between employees
in terms of efficiency, a tribunal may well feel that length of service should tip the balance in
favour of longer-serving employees.[135]

Greater experience on certain machinery has also been found to have been a fair criterion for **10.165**
selection.[136]

A specimen selection matrix may be found at Appendix 2.[137] **10.166**

Applying the selection criteria

It was pointed out in *Williams v Compair Maxam* that the application of the selection criteria **10.167**
should be carried out fairly. In *BL Cars Ltd v Lewis*[138] the EAT said that, in approaching the
question of whether a selection was one that a reasonable employer could have made, an
employment tribunal will have to consider not only the criteria that were adopted but
whether the employers had demonstrated that they had fairly applied those criteria to the
particular redundancy. The EAT went on to say that a typical case involving a large employer
would require an employer to show that in selecting a particular individual it had compared
him or her in relation to length of service, the job, and skills (and other criteria) with those
others who might be made redundant (i.e. the others in the pool of selection). The EAT went
on to say that in the ordinary case, although not always, that would require evidence from
the person who made the selection, indicating on what basis that selection was made (and for
the consequences of failing to do this at the appropriate juncture (see below)).

---

[133] [1981] IRLR 267.
[134] cf. *Byrne v Castrol (UK) Ltd* (EAT 429/96, unreported). However, it will not necessarily be unreasonable
to take into account absences caused by accidents at work (*Bartholomew v The Mayor & Burgess of the London
Borough of Haringey* (EAT 627/90, unreported). Special considerations arise where absence is due to pregnancy,
maternity leave, or disability, where leave on such grounds should be positively disregarded.
[135] See, for example, *Farthing v Midland Household Stores Ltd* [1974] IRLR 354.
[136] *Abbotts and Standley v Wesson-Glynwed Steels Ltd* [1982] IRLR 51.
[137] This is for guidance only.
[138] [1983] IRLR 58.

10.168 In the case of *Protective Services (Contracts) Ltd v Livingstone*[139] the EAT upheld the employment tribunal's decision that an employee had been unfairly selected for redundancy because the employer had failed to show how the selection criteria were applied. In that case the employer had argued that Mr Livingstone had been measured against other employees in relation to skill levels, reliability, timekeeping, compliance with company rules, and ability to drive. The employer claimed that Mr Livingstone's skill levels were not top-of-the-range but nearer the bottom. The employer further stated that although he had reasonable skills in preparation, his skill level in terms of finishing was low, his work rate was average, and his timekeeping reliability was said to be only fair. Mr Livingstone disputed this analysis but the tribunal said that it was not necessary for him to do so. The tribunal said that the employer's explanation as to how Mr Livingstone was selected was not good enough. It was surprised that somebody who had been promoted to the post of foreman was not considered to have the edge over labourers in respect of most of the redundancy selection criteria. This anomaly could not be resolved because no evidence had been given to the tribunal as to how Mr Livingstone's ability rated in comparison with those of other employees who had been retained. The tribunal said that the process of selection was 'unsystematic, haphazard and unreasonably hasty'. Mr Livingstone was found to have been unfairly dismissed.[140]

10.169 The employer appealed but the EAT would not interfere with the tribunal's decision that, although the employer had set out the selection criteria, it had failed to show that they had been properly applied.

10.170 Since then, cases on selection have tended to focus upon the extent to which the employer has an obligation to show to the tribunal that the information upon which it relied was accurate. In *Eaton Ltd v King and Others*,[141] the EAT said that the obligation of the employer is to show that the method of selection was fair in general terms and was applied reasonably. The employer does not have to prove the accuracy of the information upon which selection was made. That decision of the EAT has been expressly endorsed by Millett LJ in *British Aerospace Plc v Green and Another*.[142] The Court of Session duly upheld the EAT in *Eaton Ltd v King*[143] (although the employees' appeal succeeded on another ground, that of a defect in the consultation procedure—in that regard see the important case of *Pinewood Repro Ltd t/a County Print v Page*,[144] as discussed above).

10.171 And to be borne in mind is the injunction from higher courts to tribunals that they must not get involved in an exercise amounting to a re-scoring of scores already arrived at by the employer. A recent application of this approach may be found in *Semple Fraser LLP v Daly*.[145] In this case, there was a pool of two in a redundancy selection process. Daly was given the lower score. The employment tribunal found the dismissal to be unfair in circumstances where they had re-marked the scores of Daly and the other employee. On the re-scoring exercise by the employment tribunal equal scores were arrived at and the tribunal therefore concluded that Daly must have been unfairly dismissed. It was held that this was entirely the wrong approach. The employment tribunal in accordance with the principle in *Iceland Frozen*

---

[139] EAT 269/91, 18 October 1991.
[140] See also *Pinewood Repro Ltd t/a County Print v Page* (EAT/0028/10).
[141] [1995] IRLR 75.
[142] Ibid., 433, CA.
[143] [1996] IRLR 199.
[144] EAT/0028/10.
[145] EAT/0045/09.

Foods Limited v Jones[146] could not substitute its own view for that of the employer. Furthermore, rarely would it be appropriate for an employment tribunal to embark on a detailed scrutiny of a criteria they used for scoring or the application of those criteria to the particular circumstances of the claimant and others in the same pool. There is a band of reasonable responses open to an employer and tribunals are warned against becoming 'embroiled in a re-marking exercise'. Even if different scores could have been reached by another employer, this did not demonstrate that this particular employer acted unreasonably.

In the light of a 'glaring inconsistency', however, the tribunal should be prepared to step in. **10.172** Such was the case in *Northgate HR Limited v Mercy*.[147] The tribunal at first instance had highlighted what it considered to be an inconsistency in the scoring of Mr Mercy but found there to have been no bad faith in the selection process and held that he had not been unfairly selected.

The EAT's decision in this respect, upheld subsequently by the Court of Appeal, held that it **10.173** was not necessary for there to have been any finding of bad faith, 'the lawful basis for intervention would be where a glaring inconsistency, whether as a result of bad faith or simple incompetence, evidenced a decision which was outside the band of reasonableness'.

The position was summarised by the EAT in *Inchcape Retail Limited v Symonds*,[148] in which **10.174** it was stated that:

> . . . once the criteria are fixed, the scope for complaint by a redundant employee is quite narrow. But there can be challenges where objective factors come into play and simple mistakes can be corrected . . . it would be unreasonable to dismiss a worker whose scores were based on demonstrably wrong figures. However, absent of an allegation of actual bias in a manager, criticism of a points allocation for work performance or job knowledge would be difficult to make in fact and law.

The right to appeal

Some redundancy selection procedures contain a right to appeal against selection. In particular, **10.175** this may be the case where the procedure has been agreed with a trade union recognised by the employer. Failure to allow an employee to appeal against his or her selection for redundancy will not render a redundancy dismissal in itself unfair (*Robinson & Others v Ulster Carpet Mills Ltd*[149]), but it can be taken into account, especially if it is in breach of an agreement. The ACAS advisory booklet, *Redundancy Handling*, also recommends an appeals procedure.

E. Alternative Employment

Failure to look for alternative employment for potentially redundant employees may make **10.176** an otherwise fair redundancy dismissal unfair. What are reasonable efforts to find alternative employment is a question of fact for the employment tribunal.[150] This does not mean having

---

[146] [1982] IRLR 439.
[147] [2008] IRLR 222.
[148] UKEAT/0316/09.
[149] [1991] IRLR 348. See also *Taskforce (Finishing and Handling) Ltd v Love* (EATS/0001/05).
[150] *Stanco Exhibition Plc v Wright* (EAT/0291/07); *Garricks v Nolan* [1980] IRLR 259.

to create a job that is not there or of which there is no need. In *Merseyside v Taylor*[151] the EAT (O'Connor J) stated:

> It cannot be right that, in such circumstances, an employer can be called upon by the law to create a special job for an employee however long-serving he may have been. On the other hand, each case must depend upon its own facts.

10.177 But there is no doubt that significant importance is attached to consideration of alternative employment. The high-water mark of this aspect of redundancy procedure was the case of *Vokes Ltd v Bear*.[152] In this case, the works manager was made redundant without any attempt to see whether he could be found another job within the group, which consisted of some 300 companies. At the time of his dismissal it was established that at least one of the companies in the group had been advertising for persons to fill senior management positions shortly after Mr Bear's dismissal. Mr Bear claimed unfair dismissal and an industrial tribunal decided that the dismissal was indeed unfair. The employer appealed to what was then the National Industrial Relations Court (NIRC) on the grounds that the tribunal should have only taken into account circumstances that related to or surrounded the redundancy. In other words, it was argued that the employer's failure to mitigate the consequences of an otherwise fair dismissal by failing to look for alternative employment was irrelevant to the question of fairness. The NIRC rejected this argument and the appeal. Sir Hugh Griffiths said:

> Having decided that the employee was dismissed by reason of redundancy the tribunal then turned to consider whether nevertheless his dismissal was unfair by virtue of the provisions of [s 98(4) of the ERA 1996]. The tribunal held that it was unfair because no attempt whatever had been made to see if the employee could have been fitted into some other position in the group before he was dismissed. The evidence showed that the Tilling Group consisted of some 300 companies and there was evidence that at least one of those companies was advertising for persons to fill senior management positions shortly after the employee's dismissal. The Tilling Group apparently had no centralised machinery for providing services to all the companies in the group and it was argued before the tribunal and before this court that in all the circumstances it would have been impracticable to have made any enquiries within the group to see if there was another position that the employee might fill. The tribunal would have none of this argument. They [*sic*] said:
>
> 'We do not think that such enquiries were impracticable. We think that some enquiries should have been made to see whether it was possible to help someone like [the employee] whose services had proved satisfactory to his employers in every respect. We think [the employer's] failure to consider the question of finding some other position for [the employee] in the group made the dismissal unfair.'
>
> We find ourselves in full agreement with the way in which the tribunal expressed themselves. It would have been the simplest of matters to have circulated an inquiry through the group to see if any assistance could be given to the employee in the very difficult circumstances in which he would shortly find himself.

This decision appeared to impose a very onerous responsibility on employers to seek alternative employment for redundant employees. Although the principle invoked was subsequently approved by the Court of Appeal, there have been, since the original decision, some attempts to restrict its scope.

---

[151] [1975] IRLR 60.
[152] [1973] IRLR 363.

The modern view

The current view, therefore, is that the employer must take reasonable steps, though not   **10.178**
every conceivable step, to find alternative employment for an employee who may otherwise
be dismissed by reason of redundancy. (See, for example, the decisions in *Quinton Hazell Ltd
v Earl*[153] and *British Shoe Machinery Co Ltd v Clarke*.[154]) This more limited view can also be
seen in the case of *Barratt Construction Ltd v Dalrymple*.[155] At first instance the employment
tribunal decided that the dismissal was unfair for (amongst other reasons) failure on the part
of the employer to look for alternative employment in other companies within the group
(amongst other reasons). The employer appealed and the EAT stated that the employment
tribunal had exceeded its function in stating that the employer should have looked for
employment in other legally independent companies within the group.

As a result of this view, employers have been tempted not to look for alternative employment   **10.179**
in other group companies. This approach was bolstered by the decision of the EAT in *MDH
Ltd v Sussex*,[156] in which it was held that it was an error of law for a tribunal to hold that it was
obliged to treat the *Vokes* case as establishing any legal principle which it was bound to follow.

In *Euroguard Ltd v Ryecroft*[157] the scope of the duty to seek alternative employment has   **10.180**
apparently been widened once again. The facts of the case are of importance. Mr Ryecroft
was employed as a personnel officer by GTS Ltd. GTS had two subsidiaries: Euroguard Ltd
and CIT Ltd. Mr Ryecroft's letter of employment was signed on behalf of GTS by its
personnel director. Twelve months after his appointment, Mr Ryecroft received a letter from
the same personnel director on GTS notepaper offering him the job of personnel officer with
Euroguard. Mr Ryecroft accepted the position. In 1991 it was necessary for the group to
make redundancies and it was determined that of the three personnel officers within the
group one should be made redundant. Mr Ryecroft was chosen as the only conceivable
candidate and was made redundant in September 1991. His notice period was extended to
allow the company to investigate the possibility of alternative employment, and at the time
Mr Ryecroft was made redundant CIT was seeking to recruit a senior personnel officer.
Mr Ryecroft expressed interest in the position and Euroguard obtained an interview for him
with CIT. Mr Ryecroft did not get the job and his employment with Euroguard ended on
23 October 1991. The dismissal was written on Euroguard notepaper but it was signed by
the personnel director of GTS.

Mr Ryecroft claimed unfair dismissal and an employment tribunal found his dismissal unfair   **10.181**
on the ground that Euroguard had failed to make sufficient effort to consider Mr Ryecroft
for any posts for which they might reasonably have believed him to have been suitable. The
tribunal said that Euroguard had a duty to consider Mr Ryecroft fairly and objectively with
a view to determining whether or not he was the best candidate for any particular job. The
company appealed to the EAT on the ground that Euroguard and CIT were independent
companies. They argued that one company's failure to properly deal with an application for
employment could not give rise to a finding of unfair dismissal against another company.
Mr Ryecroft argued that Euroguard had control and/or responsibility in relation to CIT.

---

[153] [1976] IRLR 296.
[154] [1977] IRLR 297.
[155] [1984] IRLR 385.
[156] [1986] IRLR 123.
[157] (S) EAT 842/92.

10.182 In considering all of the issues, the EAT held that, in certain circumstances it may be appropriate for an employer to consider whether alternative employment in another company within a group of companies is appropriate. In Euroguard it was found that both Euroguard and CIT were subsidiary companies of GTS, GTS and Euroguard had a common board of directors, and the companies co-operated at board, marketing, and operational levels. Therefore, as a fact it was found that Euroguard was able to influence GTS. The EAT concluded that the employment tribunal had been entitled, in the circumstances, to find that Mr Ryecroft's dismissal was unfair. The appeal was dismissed.

10.183 Whilst the *Euroguard* case did not take us back to the *Vokes* position, it does appear that in certain circumstances it will be necessary for employers to consider alternative employment within another group company based upon the degree of control it has over those other companies.[158]

10.184 The level of information to be provided to an employee when offering suitable alternative employment was considered by the EAT in *Fisher v Hoopoe Finance Limited*.[159] The EAT held that the employer should inform the employee of the financial prospects of the position available but that lack of interest from an employee and whether it was reasonably practical to provide such information may be factors to consider in reducing the compensation awarded. The issue of opening up positions to the workforce was considered by the EAT in *Ralph Martindale and Co Limited v Harris*,[160] in which the tribunal had highlighted that good industrial relations practice required a company to establish whether those at risk of redundancy were suitable for the new role before opening up the new role to further applicants. The EAT upheld the tribunal's decision. Finally, the EAT has stated that the principles of conciliation and suitable alternative employment apply to both voluntary and compulsory redundancies.[161]

F. Remedies

General

10.185 There are three possible remedies for unfairly dismissed employees: reinstatement, re-engagement, and compensation. On the face of it, it was Parliament's intention that reinstatement or re-engagement be the primary remedy in unfair dismissal cases. Despite this, it is clear that for whatever reasons re-employment orders are rare. The vast majority of tribunal claims are related to unfair dismissal. Indeed, in 2008/2009 there were 52,711 unfair dismissal claims brought in the tribunal. Out of 3,935 cases upheld by the tribunal, reinstatement or re-engagement was awarded in just seven cases, which represents just 0.1 per cent of unfair dismissal cases proceeding to a hearing.

---

[158] Where there are a limited number of alternative positions, in selecting those employees to whom they should be offered, an employer need not follow the guidelines set out in *Williams v Compair Maxam Ltd* above (*Thompson v Akzo Coatings Plc* (EAT 1117/94 & 1037/95, unreported)). However, an employer must be careful not to discriminate in determining to whom such employment should be offered.

[159] UKEAT/0043/05. The EAT in *Akzo Coatings Plc v Thompson* (EAT/0117/94) expressed the view that an employment tribunal does have to slavishly apply the *Williams v Compair Maxam* approach to the possibility of alternative employment in the same way that it should do in relation to selection for a dismissal by reason of redundancy.

[160] UKEAT/0166/07.

[161] *Kilgallon v Pilkington United Kingdom Limited* (EAT/0771/03), approving *Cole v Hackney LBC* (EAT/973/99).

Section 112 of the ERA 1996 sets out that, where the grounds of the complaint are well founded: **10.186**

> The tribunal shall—
> (a) explain to the complainant what orders may be made under section 113 and in what circumstances they may be made, and
> (b) ask him whether he wishes the tribunal to make such order.
> If the complainant expresses such a wish, the tribunal may make an order under section 113.

In *Pirelli General Cable Works Ltd v Murray*[162] the EAT accepted that, on a straightforward reading of what is now s 112 of the ERA 1996, it is clear that the tribunal was impelled to consider remedies, first by asking whether a reinstatement order should be made, and only then (if it should not) can it, second, go on to consider whether re-engagement should be ordered. If neither of those are appropriate remedies only then can the tribunal go on to consider what compensation should be awarded to the applicant. **10.187**

However, in *London Transport Executive v Clarke*[163] it was held that the interpretation given to what is now s 112 of the ERA 1996 in the *Pirelli* case would not necessarily apply each time this aspect of the law was considered. This view was also held in the case of *Cowley v Manson Timber Ltd*,[164] in which the applicant, having been made redundant, was awarded only minimal compensation and complained to the EAT that the tribunal had failed to advise him of his other possible remedies and had therefore failed to fulfil its obligation under, again what is now, s 112 of the 1996 Act. In giving its decision to dismiss the appeal, the EAT said that it did not follow that a failure to act in accordance with the procedural requirements set out in the Act would necessarily render a tribunal's decision invalid in each case. The EAT went on to say that since neither reinstatement nor re-engagement were ever genuine possibilities the tribunal's failure to follow the requirements of the Act did not make its decision invalid in this particular case. **10.188**

It is very difficult to square the EAT's reasoning in *Cowley* with the clear words of s 112 of the ERA 1996. Nevertheless, this position does appear to summarise the current state of the law in this area. Employers faced with having to defend an unfair dismissal claim should therefore be prepared to give evidence about reinstatement and re-engagement and note that failure for a tribunal to consider this may result in an appeal.[165] **10.189**

We now consider the three possible remedies in more detail. Reinstatement and re-engagement are considered together (and are together referred to in this subsection as 're-employment'). **10.190**

Reinstatement and re-engagement

Reinstatement means returning the employee to the original job from which he was dismissed. Consequently, in a case where unfair dismissal following a redundancy is found on any ground other than the fact that there was no genuine redundancy, a claim for reinstatement should in principle, fail (see re-engagement, below). In a genuine redundancy the job effectively (if not actually) will have disappeared. **10.191**

---

162 [1979] IRLR 130.
163 [1990] ICR 532.
164 EAT 115/92 (unreported), 1994.
165 *Constantine v McGregor Cory Limited* (EAT/236/99).

10.192   Section 116(1) of the ERA 1996 says that, in considering whether to order reinstatement, a tribunal must consider:

    (i)   whether the complainant wishes to be reinstated;

    (ii) whether it is practicable for the employer to comply with an order for reinstatement; and

    (iii) whether the complainant caused or contributed to some extent to the dismissal, whether it would be just to order his reinstatement.

10.193   An order for re-engagement means an order whereby the successful complainant is taken on by the employer, or a successor, or associated employer of the employer, in employment 'comparable to that from which he was dismissed or other suitable employment'.[166]

Considerations in making an order

10.194   Section 116(3) of the ERA 1996 states that, in considering re-engagement, a tribunal must take into account:

    (i)   any wish expressed by the complainant as to the nature of the order to be made;

    (ii) whether it is practicable for the employer or (as the case may be) a successor or associated employer to comply with an order for re-engagement;

    (iii) whether the complainant caused or contributed to some extent to the dismissal; and

    (iv) whether it would be just to order his re-engagement and if so on what terms.

10.195   Section 115(2) ERA 1996 states that in making an order for re-engagement an employment tribunal must specify the following:

    (a) the identity of the employer;

    (b) the nature of the employment;

    (c) the remuneration for the employment;

    (d) any amount payable by the employer in respect of any benefit which the complainant might reasonably be expected to have had but for the dismissal, including arrears of pay, for the period between the date of termination of employment and the date of re-engagement;

    (e) any rights and privileges, including seniority and pension rights, which must be restored to the employee; and

    (f) the date by which the order must be complied with.

10.196   Setting out these terms in an order for re-engagement is mandatory and failure to do so will allow an appeal.[167] Moreover, in a case of re-engagement, unless the successful complainant contributed to his or her dismissal, the order must be on terms that, so far as is reasonably practicable, are as favourable as an order for reinstatement.[168]

10.197   Section 116(5) of the ERA 1996 makes it clear that where the employer has engaged a permanent replacement for the dismissed employee, a tribunal must not take that into account in determining whether it is practicable to order re-employment unless one of two exceptional circumstances applies. These circumstances are: first, the employer can show that it was not practicable for the dismissed employee's work to be done without taking on a permanent replacement; and, second, a reasonable period of time had elapsed before the replacement had been taken on without having heard from the dismissed employee that

---

[166] ERA 1996, s 115(1).
[167] See *Stena Houlder Ltd v Keenan* (S) EAT 272/93.
[168] ERA 1996, s 116(4).

he wished to be re-employed, and when the employer engaged the permanent replacement it was no longer reasonable for him to arrange for the dismissed employee's work to be done except by a permanent replacement.

In considering the issue of practicability the leading case is the Court of Appeal decision in **10.198** *Port of London Authority v Payne and Others*.[169] The Court of Appeal held that before an order for (in this particular case) re-engagement is made, an employment tribunal must make a determination as to whether it is practicable for the employer to comply with such an order. At that stage such a determination would only be provisional, and the final conclusion as to practicability is made when the employer finds whether he can in fact comply with the order in the period prescribed. At this second stage, where an order for re-engagement is made but not complied with by the employer, the burden of proof rests firmly on the employer to show that it was not practicable to carry the order into effect.

The Court of Appeal found support for this two-stage approach in a number of cases and in **10.199** particular referred to *Timex Corporation v Thompson*;[170] *Freemans Plc v Flynn*;[171] *Boots Co Plc v Lees-Collier*,[172] *Mabirizi v National Hospital for Nervous Diseases*;[173] *Cold Drawn Tubes Ltd v Middleton*;[174] and *Rao v Civil Aviation Authority*.[175]

For example, the approach for considering practicability was set out in the guidance of the **10.200** EAT given by Wood J in *Rao* and is, in essence, as follows:

(a) Orders for reinstatement or re-engagement under s 113 of the ERA 1996 are primary remedies for unfair dismissal.

(b) Such orders are discretionary: see ERA 1996, sub-ss 112 and 113.

(c) The only fetter on that wide discretion is that a tribunal must take into account the considerations set out respectively in s 116(1) and (2) of the ERA 1996.

(d) In both subsections in (c) above the word 'practicable' is used rather than 'possible' or 'capable'. At that stage an employment tribunal is not required to reach a conclusion on practicability; that need only be decided if the provisions of s 117 of the ERA 1996 become relevant. But the 1996 Act specifically requires that the employment tribunal shall take into account practicability for the employer to comply with the order. An employment tribunal must use its experience and common sense, looking at what has happened in the past and what could reasonably be anticipated for the future, always maintaining a fair balance as to what is just and reasonable between the parties.

(e) It is always unwise to seek to define rules for different factual situations, but factors that have influenced decisions in the past are:

 . . . the fact that the atmosphere in the factory is poisoned . . . the fact that the employee has displayed her distrust and lack of confidence in her employers and would not be a satisfactory employee on reinstatement . . . a change in policy which reinstatement would undermine . . . insufficient employment for the employee . . . and, possibly, where parties are in close relationships at work . . .

---

[169] [1994] IRLR 9.
[170] [1991] IRLR 522.
[171] [1984] IRLR 486.
[172] [1986] IRLR 485.
[173] [1990] IRLR 133.
[174] [1992] IRLR 160.
[175] Ibid., 203.

10.201 Many have argued that if re-employment is to be the principal remedy in the employment tribunal, then legislative change will be necessary to achieve this. The difficulty can be seen if one looks at the case of *Wood Group Heavy Industrial Turbines Limited v Crossan*.[176] In this case Mr Crossan was dismissed for gross misconduct. Allegations had been made by his colleagues that he had used and dealt in drugs at work. Timekeeping offences were also taken into account.

10.202 Mr Crossan alleged that the witnesses against him were simply out to get him. The employment tribunal determined that the dismissal was unfair on the basis that the company had failed to conduct a reasonable investigation and had not followed a fair procedure. The tribunal went on to say that there was no animosity between Mr Crossan and those who had given evidence against him and ordered re-engagement. The company appealed. In allowing the appeal the EAT said that it would not be 'practical to order re-engagement against the background of the finding that the employer genuinely believed in the substance of the allegations'. The EAT went on to say that in a case where mutual trust and confidence is broken it would be rare for there to be an order for re-employment. Lord Johnstone said:

> [It was] difficult to see how the essential bond of trust and confidence that must exist between an employer and an employee, inevitably broken by such investigations and allegations can be satisfactorily repaired by re-engagement.

10.203 In other words, the prudent employer who dismisses an employee for gross misconduct and wishes to avoid any possibility of re-employment (should the employment tribunal find in the employee's favour), will assert during the disciplinary process that they no longer have any trust or confidence in the employee and that this essential bond has been shattered. However, on the other side of the coin it is something of a quirk of the law here that an implied term which, for all practical purpose, exists to protect employees in circumstances where their employer behaves unreasonably or capriciously should now be used against them in terms of a remedy for that unreasonable or capricious behaviour. The line of thought running through the *Crossan* case also means that it will be virtually impossible for an employee who successfully claims constructive dismissal to obtain a re-employment order. Almost by definition constructive dismissal will lead to a finding of breach of trust and confidence. On the other hand, it is at least arguable that the two-part test of practicability set out above does at least give an opportunity to see whether, notwithstanding the allegation of a breakdown of trust and confidence, it is practicable to reintegrate the employee into the organisation. The mere fact that trust and confidence broke down some time prior to the employment tribunal hearing does not mean that at the time of the hearing reinstatement is impossible, or at least not reasonably practicable. It may well be. There may have been staff changes and other aspects of reorganisation of the business. The tribunal could award re-engagement on terms which meant that the individual could be put back into the organisation such that he or she no longer has significant contact with those who dismissed him and so forth. If, having re-employed the individual it turns out that the employer finds it impossible to continue that relationship, then it is open for them to go back to tribunal and argue that re-employment was not reasonably practicable for that reason, i.e. trust and confidence had been and remains destroyed. The EAT's decision in *Crossan* would seem to make that possibility unlikely.

---

[176] [1998] IRLR 680.

As has already been mentioned, re-employment orders are rare. It should be noted that an **10.204** employment tribunal is extremely unlikely to order re-employment where it finds that the dismissal was technically unfair but that the employee would have been dismissed even if a fair procedure had been followed. In a sense, in such a case there is no basis for ordering re-employment. However, the converse may also be true, i.e. that an employment tribunal is much more likely to consider re-employment where it finds that there was no genuine redundancy, or where perhaps there was a good chance that if a proper procedure had been followed the particular individual would not have been dismissed.

If a re-employment order is made following a finding of unfair dismissal, the order will **10.205** require that the complainant receives a sum of money to compensate him for any loss suffered between the date of termination and the date of re-employment. In making such an order the tribunal will take into account any pay in lieu of notice received by the applicant, any sums earned by way of mitigation, and any *ex gratia* payment made to the complainant.

Compensation

Following a successful complaint of unfair dismissal the complainant may be entitled to a **10.206** basic award and/or a compensatory award. In certain circumstances of non-compliance by an employer with a re-employment order, he may also be entitled to an additional award. These awards are each described below.

Basic award

The basic award is identical to a statutory redundancy payment in respect of its calculation,[177] **10.207** except for the following:

(1) If the complainant is dismissed for redundancy and unreasonably rejected an offer of suitable alternative employment, or if he is dismissed for redundancy and he had his contract renewed or has been re-engaged, then the basic award will be two weeks' pay.[178]
(2) Where selection for redundancy is for an inadmissible reason under s 100(1)(a) or (b) of the ERA 1996 (health and safety reasons), s 101A(d) (dismissal of a candidate or representative who performed or proposed to perform representative functions pursuant to the Working Time Regulations), s 102(1) (dismissal of trustee of an occupational pension scheme), under s 103 (dismissal of employee representative in relation to collective redundancies or transfers of undertakings) or s 157 of the TULR(C)A 1992 (trade union membership or activities), the minimum basic award is currently £5,000 (ERA 1996, s 120(1)).

Unlike a statutory redundancy payment, the basic award in an unfair dismissal complaint **10.208** may be subject to deductions in certain circumstances, as follows:

(1) Where the complainant has been dismissed for redundancy and has received a statutory redundancy payment, this will be offset against the basic award. Obviously, in most circumstances the whole of the basic award will be wiped out.
(2) Under s 122(4)(b) the basic award is also reduced by any other payments made by the employer to the employee on the grounds that the dismissal was by reason of redundancy. This would suggest that any *ex gratia* award or, for example, any contractual redundancy payment can count against the basic award in these circumstances. It is

---

[177] See Chapter 8.
[178] See ERA 1996, sub-ss 121, 138, 141(1), (2) and (3).

suggested here that if an employer wishes the amount of any payment, other than a statutory redundancy payment, made to the employee who is dismissed by reason of redundancy to be offset then such a payment should be made expressly on the grounds that the dismissal is by reason of redundancy and not for any other reason.

(3) Under s 122(1) of the ERA 1996, where a tribunal finds that the complainant has unreasonably refused an offer of employment by the employer which, if accepted, would have had the effect of reinstating the complainant in his employment in all respects as if he had not been dismissed, the tribunal shall reduce the amount of the basic award by an amount that it considers just and equitable in the circumstances. It should be noted, however, that this section of the 1996 Act is very strict: if the offer does not put the complainant in exactly the same position as he was in before the dismissal (so as to treat him as though he had never been dismissed), no reduction is permitted at all.

(4) The tribunal has the power to reduce the basic award where the conduct of the complainant was such that the tribunal considers it just and equitable to do so. This includes any conduct discovered after dismissal, provided the conduct relates to the period before dismissal or, if dismissal was with notice, before notice was given. Note, however, that in redundancy cases this will not apply unless the reason for selection was one of those specified in s 100(1)(a) and (b), 101A(d), 102(1), or 103, in which case the reduction may apply but only to so much of the basic award as is payable in those circumstances.[179]

10.209 Finally, it falls to be considered whether any other payments made to the employee on termination of employment could be set off against the basic award. In redundancy cases this will rarely be an issue, since if a complainant was genuinely redundant and is claiming unfair dismissal he would be well advised to put in a claim for a redundancy payment if none has been made. Assuming the redundancy is genuine, a tribunal will award the redundancy payment, in which case, if the employee then went on to win the claim for unfair dismissal, the amount of the redundancy payment would be offset against the basic award following the rules set out above.

10.210 In general, any other payments made to a complainant will not be set off against the basic award (except as described under point (2) above) unless it can be shown that it was clearly intended that such payment should include an element for that liability. Consequently employers are advised, in agreed settlements, to state that any sums paid to the employee are in full and final settlement of all claims, and then to set out what claims are covered (including a basic award). Employers should not rely upon the general statement that a payment is made 'in full and final settlement of all claims'.

Compensatory award

10.211 The purpose of the compensatory award is to give to the successful complainant an amount of money that compensates him for financial loss as a result of the unfair dismissal. The tribunal must not make an award to the complainant out of any sympathy for the predicament in which he finds himself.[180] In redundancy cases in particular the tribunal must avoid the temptation to 'top up' a redundancy payment.

10.212 The general scheme which applies to calculating the compensatory award is that the employment tribunal can award an amount which, in the words of s 123 of the ERA 1996, the tribunal

---

[179] ERA 1996, sub-ss 122 (2) and (3).
[180] See *Clarkson International Tools Ltd v Short* [1973] IRLR 90 and *Lifeguard Assurance Co Ltd v Zadrozny* [1977] IRLR 56.

considers 'just and equitable in all the circumstances having regard to the loss sustained by the complainant in consequence of the dismissal insofar as that loss is attributable to action taken by the employer'. This is subject to a maximum limit for the compensatory award which, at the time of writing, is £68,400.00. This applies in all cases except those set out below.

It is to be noted that the award must be both just and equitable. Consequently, the award of **10.213** compensation will be limited where it is just and equitable to limit it. To put it another way, if the complainant does not deserve to receive a substantial award even though his financial loss may be substantial, it is incumbent upon the tribunal to ensure that justice is seen to be done. In *W Devis & Sons Ltd v Atkins*[181] Viscount Dilhorne said:

> Section [123 of the ERA 1996] does not . . . provide that regard should be had only to the loss resulting from the dismissal being unfair. Regard must be had to that but the award must be just and equitable in all the circumstances, and it cannot be just and equitable that a sum should be awarded in compensation when in fact the employee has suffered no injustice by being dismissed.

This judgment has been relied upon by employers who have failed to take particular pro- **10.214** cedural steps but who have sought to argue before an industrial tribunal that such a step would not have made any difference in any event. The argument is not one where, because the outcome of the procedure would have been the same despite the fact that a particular element was missing, the procedure should be held to have been fair, but rather one where the procedure that was actually followed was fair in the circumstances. In other words, it is not forgiving an unfair procedure but deciding that a procedure from which one or more of the 'normal' steps is missing was, in any event, a fair procedure.

The success or failure of this argument will depend considerably upon the reason for the **10.215** omission. For example, if one of the crucial requirements missing was objective selection criteria, the employee is more likely to be successful in arguing that if a proper procedure had been followed he would not (or may not) have been dismissed; normal compensation rules will be applied if such an argument is successful. On the other hand, if there was simply a lack of warning or consultation but the employer is successful in arguing that that warning or consultation would still have resulted in the particular employee's dismissal, then it may be possible to limit the award of compensation to the period during which, for example, consultation should have taken place; this may be as little as one or two weeks' pay.

In a redundancy case, as in other cases, it falls upon an employment tribunal when assessing **10.216** the compensatory award to determine the period over which the award should be made. There are, in principle, three situations that the tribunal has to consider following a successful complaint of unfair dismissal, all of which affect the period and hence the compensatory award, as follows:

(1) The complainant would not have been dismissed. This will involve the tribunal calculating for what period compensation should be awarded into the future and is discussed below.
(2) Employment would have ceased in any event. This is likely to lead to a nil award of compensation or a very limited award. In practice, tribunals will find it quite difficult to establish that a complainant whom it found had been unfairly dismissed would have in any event been dismissed. This may occur in a redundancy case where the fault is purely procedural and where the tribunal can say that such a fault made no difference. If, in

---

[181] [1977] IRLR 314.

those circumstances, dismissal would have occurred at the same date on which it in fact occurred, compensation should be nil. It is also possible that (for example, in a case where the tribunal determines that there was a lack of consultation that would have made no difference) the award is for a period over which consultation should have taken place; that may mean the award is limited to only a few weeks' pay. Such a finding would be in line with the House of Lords decision in *Polkey*. Such a principle has been applied in a number of cases—for example the case of *Abbotts and Standley* (above) and *Mining Supplies (Longwall) v Baker*.[182]

(3) Dismissal might anyway have occurred. This involves the tribunal in an assessment of whether, on the balance of probabilities, the complainant would or would not have been dismissed had the employer acted fairly. In *Polkey* Lord Bridge said as follows:

> If it is held that taking the appropriate steps which the employer failed to take before dismissing the employee would not have affected the outcome, this will often lead to the result that the employee, though unfairly dismissed, will recover no compensation or, in the case of redundancy, no compensation in excess of his redundancy payment.

10.217 An example of the position set out in point (1) above was seen in the case of *Continental Tyre Group Limited v Mrs I Holman*.[183] In this case, the employer appealed against an employment tribunal's decision that, having been unfairly dismissed, Mrs Holman had a 100 per cent chance of being offered a new position with the company. Mrs Holman was dismissed without warning or consultation in June 1996 following a need for a reduction in secretarial staff. She had been secretary to the marketing director. Her job and that of the managing director's secretary were to be merged. The dismissal was clearly unfair. The tribunal said that if the company had acted fairly Mrs Holman would have been retained in their employment on the basis that, had a proper procedure been followed the company would have discovered either that at the date of Mrs Holman's dismissal the secretary who retained the post of joint secretary to the marketing director and managing director was shortly to leave, in which case Mrs Holman, the only other candidate, would have got the job, or alternatively she should have been given the post of a temporary secretary until the joint secretary left. The EAT upheld the tribunal's decision. One interesting footnote to the case is that at the appeal the employer sought to argue that even if they had followed the fair procedure suggested by the employment tribunal, Mrs Holman would not have got the job because the managing director did not like her. Somewhat scathingly the EAT point out that it is not appropriate that, when assessing the chance that an unfairly dismissed employee would have been retained, the employer should be allowed to rely on what amounted to an allegation that if they had not committed the unfairness which led to the finding of unfair dismissal, they would nevertheless have committed some other unfairness, in this case not appointing Mrs Holman because of the MD's personal dislike of her.

10.218 In relation to situation (3) above, most employment tribunals find in practice that if there is an important procedural step missing from a redundancy procedure then the dismissal has been unfair. And as we have explained above, *Polkey* means that the 'no difference' rule is not available to the employer at the merits stage. However, it is then open for the employer to argue at the remedies hearing that, if the employee would have been dismissed in any event, either no compensation should be paid (i.e. the dismissal would have taken place at the same

---

[182] [1988] IRLR 417.
[183] Unreported, 1997.

time in any event) or that compensation should at least be limited to a specified period (e.g. a reasonable period for consultation).[184]

An example of the application of this principle can be seen in the case of *Campbell & Others v Dunoon & Cowal Housing Association Ltd*,[185] in which the tribunal had made a reduction in the compensatory award of 75 per cent on the basis that although the employees had been unfairly dismissed because of a lack of consultation there was a 75 per cent chance that if the proper procedure had been followed they would still have been dismissed. On appeal the Court of Session noted that the tribunal could have made a 100 per cent reduction on the basis that dismissal would definitely have occurred, but in the event it had made a 75 per cent reduction using a broad assessment and on the basis that it could not be certain that consultation would definitely have led to dismissal. **10.219**

Particular issues in discrimination cases

The Court of Appeal in *Chagger v Abbey National Plc & Another*[186] considered this approach further. The employee had been selected for redundancy from a pool of two and brought proceedings claiming unfair dismissal and racial discrimination. Having been found to have been unfairly dismissed and discriminated against, appeals arose in respect of the remedy awarded. The Court of Appeal held that compensation for a discriminatory dismissal should be assessed taking into account whether the dismissal would have occurred in any event. In this case there had been a redundancy situation and thus the question was remitted to the tribunal to consider the prospects of dismissal if there had been no discrimination. As discussed above, however, the discrimination head of compensation meant future loss was not limited to the period the employee would have remained in employment with Abbey and damages for unlawful stigmatisation by future employers were (in theory) available. **10.220**

One footnote worth mentioning from this discussion is the correct series of deductions where a compensatory award is being made. This has been the subject of much debate. The position was clarified by the Court of Appeal in *Digital Equipment Co Limited v Clements (No. 2)*,[187] in which the Court of Appeal held that the order of deductions should be: first the total loss should be calculated, second, the percentage reduction should be applied (on the basis that the individual is only entitled to a just and equitable award under s 123(1) of the ERA), thirdly the amount of any redundancy payment in excess of the basic award should be deducted (s 123(7) of the ERA) and finally, and if necessary, the statutory cap should be applied. **10.221**

It should be noted that the onus is on the employer to show that dismissal would have occurred in any event.[188] The EAT in *Software 2000 Limited v Andrews and Others*,[189] outlined the following principles which had emerged from the case law: **10.222**

(1) In assessing compensation the task of the tribunal is to assess the loss flowing from the dismissal, using its common sense, experience, and sense of justice. In the normal case

---

[184] See, for example, *Mining Supplies (Longwall) Ltd v Baker* [1988] IRLR 417; *Boulton and Paul Ltd v Arnold* [1994] IRLR 532; *Steel Stockholders (Birmingham) Ltd v Kirkwood* [1993] IRLR 515; and *Smith v Adwest Engineering Ltd* [1994] 508 IRLB 14.

[185] [1993] IRLR 496.

[186] [2010] IRLR 47.

[187] [1998] ICR 258.

[188] See *Forth Estuary Engineering Ltd v Litster* [1986] IRLR 59 and *Britool Ltd v Roberts* [1993] IRLR 481.

[189] [2007] IRLR 568.

that requires it to assess for how long the employee would have been employed but for the dismissal.

(2) If the employer seeks to contend that the employee would or might have ceased to be employed in any event had fair procedures been followed, or alternatively would not have continued in employment indefinitely, it is for him to adduce any relevant evidence on which he wishes to rely. However, the tribunal must have regard to all the evidence when making that assessment, including any evidence from the employee himself. (He might, for example, have given evidence that he had intended to retire in the near future.)

(3) However, there will be circumstances where the nature of the evidence which the employer wishes to adduce, or on which he seeks to rely, is so unreliable that the tribunal may take the view that the whole exercise of seeking to reconstruct what might have been is so riddled with uncertainty that no sensible prediction based on that evidence can properly be made.

(4) Whether that is the position is a matter of impression and judgment for the tribunal. But in reaching that decision the tribunal must direct itself properly. It must recognise that it should have regard to any material and reliable evidence which might assist it in fixing just compensation, even if there are limits to the extent to which it can confidently predict what might have been; and it must appreciate that a degree of uncertainty is an inevitable feature of the exercise. The mere fact that an element of speculation is involved is not a reason for refusing to have regard to the evidence.

(5) An appellate court must be wary about interfering with the tribunal's assessment that the exercise is too speculative. However, it must interfere if the tribunal has not directed itself properly and has taken too narrow a view of its role.

(6) Having considered the evidence, the tribunal may determine:

    (a) that there was a chance of dismissal but less than 50 per cent, in which case compensation should be reduced accordingly;

    (b) that employment would have continued but only for a limited fixed period. The evidence demonstrating that may be wholly unrelated to the circumstances relating to the dismissal itself, as in the *O'Donoghue* case;

    (c) employment would have continued indefinitely.

10.223 *O'Donoghue* refers to *O'Donoghue v Redcar & Cleveland Borough Council*,[190] where the Court of Appeal held that an employee, unfairly dismissed on the grounds of her sex would have been dismissed six months later for misconduct.

10.224 It must also be noted that, following the Employment Act 2008, s 98A has since been repealed.

10.225 Once an employment tribunal has made its decision on a compensatory award, it must set out in its decision details of the heads of compensation (*Norton Tool Co Ltd v Tewson*[191]). In practice, employment tribunals calculate loss in two stages. First, a tribunal will calculate loss between the date of dismissal and the date of the remedies hearing. Second, if appropriate, the tribunal will calculate future loss. The first calculation can be relatively accurate since it is based on what has in fact occurred in relation to the complainant's former employment (so that, for example, any increases in pay or benefits that have

---

[190] [2001] IRLR 615.
[191] [1973] 1 All ER 183.

occurred will be known and should be included in the calculation). Inevitably, however, the second stage is more speculative in that it involves the tribunal in an assessment of both, over what period of time future loss should be awarded, and an assessment of what might occur with regard to increases in pay and benefits during that period. At the second stage, account must be taken of the complainant's employment position and, if he is still unemployed at the date of the remedies hearing, his prospects of obtaining employment in the future.

Section 123 of the ERA 1996 provides that compensation should include any expenses **10.226** reasonably incurred by the complainant in consequence of the dismissal and loss of any benefits he might reasonably expect to have had but for the dismissal (save for the contingent right to a redundancy payment) but is limited to pecuniary loss.[192] Consequently, arising out of the above, an employment tribunal can be expected to consider the following heads of compensation:

(a) loss of salary from dismissal to the remedies hearing;
(b) future loss of salary;
(c) loss of benefits;
(d) loss of pension rights;
(e) loss of statutory rights;
(f) expenses incurred as a result of the dismissal; and
(g) loss arising from manner of dismissal if this makes it more difficult for the employee to find a new job (*Norton Tool* (above)).

Additional award

If an order for re-employment is not complied with and the employer cannot show that it **10.227** was not practicable to comply with it, then in addition to receiving compensation the complainant will also receive an additional award.[193] The amount of the additional award is between 26 and 52 weeks' pay (introduced by the ERA 1999, which also abolished the special award).

This award is not intended to cover sums already covered by the compensatory award but, on **10.228** the other hand, it is not meant to be a sum awarded simply to cover loss suffered as a result of the failure to re-employ. Nevertheless, a tribunal will take into account whether the employer has deliberately refused to re-employ the applicant (in which case an award nearer the top end would be justified) or whether there was a genuine belief that, for example, trust and confidence had broken down.[194]

The tribunal has a very wide discretion with regard to the amount of the additional award **10.229** and the issues of mitigation and set-off (discussed above) apply in the same way to an additional award as they do to the compensatory award.[195]

[192] *Dunnachie v Kingston-upon-Hull City Council* [2004] UKHL 36.
[193] ERA 1996, s 117.
[194] See, for example, *Mabiritzi v National Hospital for Nervous Diseases* [1990] IRLR 133.
[195] See *Mabiritzi v National Hospital for Nervous Diseases* [1990] IRLR 133 and *Motherwell Railway Club v McQueen* [1989] ICR 418.

G. Automatically Unfair Dismissal

10.230   Section 105 of the ERA 1996 states as follows:

An employee who is dismissed shall be regarded for the purposes of this part as unfairly dismissed if —

(a) the reason (or, if more than one, the principal reason) for the dismissal is that the employee was redundant,

(b) it is shown that the circumstances constituting the redundancy applied equally to one or more other employees in the same undertaking who held positions similar to that held by the employee and who have not been dismissed by the employer, and[196]

(c) it is shown that any of sub-sections 2A to 7K applies.

10.231   Dismissal by reason of redundancy will be automatically unfair in the following circumstances:

(1) an employee has been selected for redundancy because he has carried out or has proposed to carry out activities in connection with preventing or reducing risks to health and safety at work, where that employee has been designated by the employer to carry out such activities (ERA 1996, s 100(1)(a));[197]

(2) an employee, being a representative of workers on matters of health and safety at work or a member of a safety committee, in accordance with arrangements established under or by virtue of any enactment or by reason of being acknowledged as such by the employer, has been selected for redundancy because he performed or proposed to perform any functions as such a representative or a member of such a committee;[198]

(3) an employee has been selected for redundancy because he took part or proposed to take part in consultation with the employer pursuant to the Health & Safety (Consultation with Employees) Regulations 1996 or took part or proposed to take part in the election of representatives of employee safety within the meaning of those Regulations whether the employee was to be a candidate or otherwise;[199]

(4) an employee has been selected for redundancy in circumstances where there was no safety representative or Committee (or there is but it was not reasonably practicable to raise the matter with them) and he brought to the employer's attention by reasonable means circumstances connected with his work which he reasonably believed were harmful or potentially harmful to health and safety;[200]

---

[196] Where an employee holds a unique position within the undertaking, therefore, he is unlikely to be able to claim under this section, although his dismissal may otherwise be unfair on general principles. Section 235(1) of the ERA 1996 defines 'position' to comprise of the status, nature of work, and terms and conditions of the employment of an employee, taken as a whole. The fact that in practice an employee performs a less onerous role in order to allow him to carry out his trade union duties should be disregarded for the purpose of determining what that employee's position is for the purposes of applying s 153 of the TULR(C)A 1992 (*O'Dea v ISC Chemicals Ltd t/a Rhone-Poulenc Chemicals* [1995] IRLR 599).

[197] However, such employees are not entitled to be treated more favourably than other employees, so that performance of these duties should be ignored in the selection process (*Smiths Industries Aerospace and Defence Systems v Rawlings* [1996] IRLR 656). Indeed, a dismissal may be reasonable even if in selecting which employees to dismiss an employer takes no account of the fact that performance of these duties has hindered the employee's ability to comply with criteria relating to qualifications (*Herbert v Air UK Engineering* (EAT 575/97, unreported).

[198] ERA 1996, s 100(1)(b).

[199] Ibid., (1)(ba).

[200] Ibid., (1)(c).

(5) an employee has been selected for redundancy because he left, or proposed to leave, or refused to return to his place of work or any dangerous part of his place of work in circumstances of danger that the employee reasonably believed to be serious and imminent and that he could not reasonably have been expected to avert;[201]

(6) an employee has been selected for redundancy because he took or proposed to take appropriate steps to protect himself or other persons from danger in circumstances that he reasonable believed to be serious and imminent;[202]

(7) an employee has been selected for redundancy because he is a protected shop worker or betting worker and refused to work on a Sunday or being an opted out worker gave or proposed to give an opting out notice to the employer;[203]

(8) an employee has been selected for redundancy because he refused or proposed to refuse to comply with the requirements which the employer imposed or proposed to impose upon him in contravention of the Working Time Regulations 1998;[204]

(9) an employee has been selected for redundancy in circumstances where he refused or proposed to refuse to forego a right conferred on him by the Working Time Regulations 1998;[205]

(10) an employee has been selected for redundancy because he failed to sign a workforce agreement for the purposes of the Working Time Regulations 1998 or to enter into or agree to vary or extend any other agreement with his employer which is provided for in the Working Time Regulations 1998;[206]

(11) an employee has been selected for redundancy because he was a representative of members of the workforce for the purposes of Schedule I of the Working Time Regulations 1998 or was a candidate in an election in which any person elected would be such a representative and he performed or proposed to perform any functions or activities as such a representative or candidate;[207]

(12) an employee has been selected for redundancy because he is permitted to participate in education or training by s 27 or 28 of the Education and Skills Act 2008, and he exercised or proposed to exercise that right;[208]

(13) an employee has been selected for redundancy because he is a trustee of a relevant occupational pension scheme;[209]

(14) an employee has been selected for redundancy and the reason is that the employee was a representative for the purposes of collective redundancies or transfers of undertakings under the TULR(C)A 1992 or TUPE or was candidate in an election in which any person elected will be such a representative and performed or proposed to perform functions or activities as such an employee representative or candidate;[210]

(15) an employee has been selected for redundancy in circumstances where the reason is that the employee took part in an election of employee representatives for the purposes of collective redundancies under the TULR(C)A 1992 or TUPE;[211]

---

[201] Ibid., (1)(d).
[202] Ibid., (1)(e).
[203] Ibid., s 101.
[204] Ibid., A(a).
[205] Ibid., (b).
[206] Ibid., (c).
[207] Ibid., (d).
[208] Ibid., B.
[209] Ibid., s 102(1).
[210] Ibid., s 103(1).
[211] Ibid., (2).

(16) an employee has been selected for redundancy because that person made a protected disclosure under Part IVA of the ERA 1996;[212]

(17) an employee has been selected for redundancy because he has brought proceedings against the employer to enforce a 'relevant statutory right', or has alleged that the employer has infringed such a right.[213] The 'relevant statutory rights' are:

 (a) any right conferred by the ERA 1996;[214]

 (b) an infringement of an employee's right to minimum notice pursuant to section 86 of the ERA 1996;[215]

 (c) any infringement of the following rights under the TULR(C)A 1992:[216]

   (i) the right not to suffer deduction of unauthorised or excessive subscriptions;[217]

   (ii) objection to contributing to a political fund;[218]

   (iii) inducements relating to union membership or activities;[219]

   (iv) inducements relating to collective bargaining;[220]

   (v) action short of dismissal on grounds relating to union membership or ctivities;[221]

   (vi) time off and payment for carrying out trade union duties;[222]

   (vii) time off for union learning representatives;[223]

   (viii) time off for trade union activities.[224]

 (d) any infringement of rights conferred by the Working Time Regulations, Sea Merchant Shipping (Working Time: Inland Waterway) Regulations 2003, Sea Fishing Vessels (Working Time: Sea-fisherman) Regulations 2004, or the Cross-border Railway Services (Working Time) Regulations 2008;

 (e) an infringement of rights conferred by TUPE;

(18) an employee has been selected for redundancy because action was taken with a view to enforcing or securing the benefit of the right of the employee to a specified rate of pay under the National Minimum Wage Act 1998;[225]

(19) an employee has been selected for redundancy because his employer was prosecuted for an offence under section 31 of the National Minimum Wage Act 1998 as a result of action taken by or on behalf of that employee to enforce rights under that Act;[226]

(20) an employee has been selected for redundancy because he qualifies, will or might qualify for the National Minimum Wage or for a particular rate of National Minimum Wage under the National Minimum Wage Act 1998;[227]

---

[212] Ibid., A, inserted by the Public Interest Disclosure Act 1998, sub-ss 5 and 18(2).
[213] Ibid., s 104(1)(a) and (b).
[214] Ibid., (4)(a).
[215] Ibid., (b).
[216] Ibid., (c).
[217] TULR(C)A, s 68.
[218] Ibid., s 86.
[219] Ibid., s 145A.
[220] Ibid., B.
[221] Ibid., s 146.
[222] Ibid., s 168 and 169.
[223] Ibid., s 168A.
[224] Ibid., s 170.
[225] ERA 1996, s 104A(1)(a).
[226] Ibid., (b).
[227] Ibid., (c).

(21) an employee has been selected for redundancy because action was taken or proposed to be taken by or on behalf of the employee to enforce rights or secure benefits under s 25 of the Tax Credits Act 2002;[228]

(22) an employee was selected for redundancy because a penalty was imposed on the employer or proceedings for a penalty were brought against the employer under the Tax Credits Act 2002;[229]

(23) an employee was selected for redundancy in circumstances where he is entitled or will be or may be entitled to working tax credit;[230]

(24) an employee was selected for redundancy because the employee made or proposed to make an application for flexible working, exercised a right or proposed to exercise a right in respect of the flexible working requirements, brought proceedings against the employer or alleged the existence of circumstances which would constitute a ground for bringing proceedings;[231]

(25) an employee was selected for redundancy for reasons in relation to pension enrolment;[232]

(26) an employee was selected for redundancy in relation to an application or enforcement of rights to study or train under section 63D of the ERA;[233]

(27) an employee was selected for redundancy in relation to the Employment Relations Act 1999 (Blacklists) Regulations 2010;[234]

(28) that the employee has asserted or exercised functions or rights under certain aspects of the below mentioned legislation:

    (a) The Transnational Information and Consultation of Employees Regulations 1999;[235]

    (b) The Part-time Workers (Prevention of Less Favourable Treatment) Regulations 2000;[236]

    (c) The Fixed-term Employees (Prevention of Less Favourable Treatment) Regulations 2002;[237]

    (d) The European Public Limited-liability Company Regulations 2004;[238]

    (e) The Information and Consulation of Employees Regulations 2004;[239]

    (f) The Occupational and Personal Pension Schemes (Consultation by Employers and Miscellaneous Amendment Regulations) Regulations 2006;[240]

    (g) to be accompanied or to accompany another in accordance with the Employment Equality (Age) Regulations 2006;[241]

---

[228] Ibid., B(i)(a).

[229] Ibid., (b).

[230] Ibid., (c).

[231] Ibid., C.

[232] Ibid., D.

[233] Ibid., E.

[234] Ibid., F.

[235] s 105 7D.

[236] s 105 7E.

[237] s 105 7F.

[238] s 105 7G.

[239] s 105 7H.

[240] s 105 7I.

[241] s 105 7IA (subject to the Employment Equality (Repeal of Retirement Age Provisions) Regulations 2011(SI 2011/1069)).

(h) The European Cooperative Society (Involvement of Employees) Regulations 2006;[242]

(i) The Companies (Cross Border Mergers) Regulations 2007.[243]

Additional points in relation to dismissal on grounds of assertion of statutory right

10.232   The important points to note here are as follows:

(1) the employee must have actually brought proceedings against the employer to enforce a relevant statutory right (see above);[244] or

(2) the employee must have alleged that the employer had infringed a right that is a relevant statutory right; and

(3) it is immaterial for either (1) or (2) above whether the employee actually has the right or not and whether it has been infringed or not, provided that the claim to the right and the claim that it has been infringed are made in good faith;[245] and

(4) the employee need not have told the employer precisely what is being claimed—section 104(3) of the ERA 1996 says merely that the employee must make it 'reasonably clear' to the employer which right is being claimed to have been infringed.[246]

Selection for redundancy on grounds related to trade union membership or activities

10.233   There are also automatically unfair trade union reasons under s 152 read with s 153 of the TULR(C)A 1992. The reasons are that the employee has been selected for redundancy wholly or principally because:

(1) he was, or proposed to become, a member of an independent trade union;[247] or

(2) he had taken part or proposed to take part in the activities of an independent trade union at an appropriate time;[248] or

(3) he had made use or proposed to make use of trade union services at an appropriate time;[249] or

(4) he had failed to accept an offer made in contravention of section 145A or 145B;[250] or

(5) he was not a member of any trade union, or of a particular trade union, or of one of a number of particular trade unions, or had refused or proposed to refuse to become or remain a member.[251]

10.234   Whether or not selection is for one of the stated reasons will be a matter of fact to be determined by an employment tribunal in any particular case.

10.235   There is no qualifying period of employment for bringing a complaint of unfair dismissal under s 153 of the TULR(C)A 1992 (selection for redundancy on union grounds) by virtue of s 154 of that Act.

---

[242] s 105 71.
[243] s 105 7K.
[244] Ibid., (1)(a) and (b).
[245] Ibid., (2)(a) and (b).
[246] Ibid., (4).
[247] TULR(C)A, s 152(1)(a).
[248] Ibid., (b).
[249] Ibid., (ba).
[250] Ibid., (bb).
[251] Ibid., (c).

In *Dundon v GPT Ltd*,[252] Mr Dundon was dismissed by GPT on the ground of redun- **10.236**
dancy. Mr Dundon had been an active trade unionist for many years and was a union
representative, spending about 10 per cent of his time acting in that role. But when he
became a senior representative, both he and GPT recognised that he would need to
spend more time on union activities. Difficulties arose because the company believed
that Mr Dundon was spending too much time on these union activities and it eventually
entered into an agreement with him under which he agreed to spend at least half of his
time at work. Subsequently a redundancy situation arose. Employees were selected on the
basis of quality and quantity of work, co-operation, attendance and timekeeping, special
knowledge and experience, and length of service. It was made clear to those carrying out
assessments that employees were not to be penalised because of union duties. Mr Dundon's
quantity of work was assessed as very poor. Despite the agreement he had entered into
with GPT, he was in fact spending less than 20 per cent of his time on the employer's
business.

Mr Dundon appealed against his selection and the assessors were asked to look again at his **10.237**
selection. They were told that they should allow for a reasonable amount of time for the
union activities rather than assess him on the actual quantity of work he undertook. The
selection was confirmed and Mr Dundon was dismissed. Mr Dundon claimed unfair
dismissal. The employment tribunal rejected his claim that he had been unfairly selected for
redundancy by reason of his trade union activities. The tribunal said that although his union
activities were 'relevant to his selection', GPT had not deliberately selected him because he
was a union activist. They did find, however, that he was unfairly dismissed because he
should have been assessed on the amount of time he actually spent at work rather than
the amount of time he was supposed to spend at work according to the agreement he had
entered into with the company.

Mr Dundon appealed. The EAT held that the tribunal was wrong to find that Mr Dundon **10.238**
had not been selected by reason of trade union activities on the basis that the employers had
not acted deliberately or maliciously in selecting him because of those activities. The EAT
said that:

> An employer does not have to be motivated by malice or a deliberate desire to be rid of a trade
> union activist in order to fall within the provisions now set out in sections 152(1)(b) and 153
> of TULR(C)A 1992.

The EAT said that the tribunal's finding was that the feature of the employee's working life **10.239**
that made the employers select him for redundancy was his poor work because he was
spending too much time on trade union duties and this was the same as saying they
selected him for the direct reason that he was spending too much time on trade union
duties. In other words, there was no separation between the assessment of the work and
the fact that he was carrying out trade union duties; they were in essence two sides of the
same coin.[253]

The ERA made a number of changes to the TULR(C)A 1992, giving workers further rights in **10.240**
relation to trade union issues. Set out below are the rights and relevant statutory references.

---

[252] [1995] IRLR 403.
[253] See also *Herbert v Air UK Engineering* (EAT 575/97, unreported).

10.241   If an employee is dismissed as redundant for any of the reasons set out in para 161(2) of Sch A1 to the TULR(C)A 1992, then such a dismissal is automatically unfair for the purposes of Pt X of the ERA 1996 (by virtue of para 162 of Sch A1 to the TULR(C)A 1992).

10.242   The reasons under para 161(2) of Sch A1 are:

(1)   the employee acted with a view to obtaining or preventing recognition of a union under the statutory recognition procedures;

(2)   the employee indicated that he supported or did not support recognition of a union by the employer under statutory recognition procedures;

(3)   the employee acted with a view to securing or prevent the ending of bargaining arrangements under the statutory procedure;

(4)   the employee indicated that he supported or did not support the ending of bargaining arrangements under the statutory procedure;

(5)   the employee influenced or sought to influence the way in which votes were to be cast by other workers in a ballot arranged under the statutory recognition procedure;

(6)   the employee influenced or sought to influence other workers to vote or to abstain from voting in a ballot in relation to statutory recognition/de-recognition;

(7)   the employee voted in such a ballot;

(8)   the employee proposed to do, failed to do or proposed to decline to do any of the things referred to above.

10.243   However, it should be noted that by virtue of para 161(3) of Sch A1 a reason cannot fall within para 161(2) of Sch A1 if the employee's act or omission is unreasonable.

10.244   By virtue of s 105(7C) of the ERA 1996 if an employee is dismissed as redundant and the principal reason is one of those mentioned in s 238A(2) of the TULR(C)A 1992 then such a dismissal will be automatically unfair.

10.245   The reasons in s 238A(2) are that the employee took protected industrial action provided that the dismissal takes place within a period of eight weeks beginning with the day on which the employee started to take the protected industrial action or, the dismissal takes place after the end of that eight-week period and the employee had stopped taking protected industrial action before the end of the eight-week period. Alternatively, a dismissal in these circumstances which takes place after the end of the eight-week period can still be unfair even if the employee had not stopped taking protection industrial action before the end of the eight-week period provided that the employer, in the words of the statute 'had not taken such procedural steps as would have been reasonable for the purposes of resolving the dispute to which the protected industrial action relates'.

10.246   The steps referred to above include:

(i)   whether the employer or a union had complied with procedures established by any collective or other agreements;

(ii)   whether the employer or the union offered or agreed to commence or resume negotiations after the start of the protected industrial action;

(iii)   whether the employer or a union unreasonably refused, after the start of the protected industrial action, a request that conciliation services be used; and

(iv)   whether the employer or the union unreasonably refused, after the start of the protected industrial action, a request that mediation services be used in relation to procedures to be adopted for the purpose of resolving the dispute.

(v) whether there was an agreement to use either of the services mentioned in (iii) and (iv) above.

In determining whether an employer has behaved 'reasonably', the tribunal cannot have regard to the merits of the dispute.

Dismissal on grounds related to pregnancy or childbirth; suspension on maternity grounds, maternity leave, parental leave or time off for dependants

The Employment Relations Act 1998 introduced new provisions into the ERA 1996 relating to maternity leave, parental leave, and what might be termed emergency leave. Following that the Government introduced the Maternity and Parental Leave, etc. Regulations 1999 pursuant to powers given to it under the amended ERA 1996. **10.247**

The rights are as follows. **10.248**

According to reg 10 of the Maternity and Parental Leave, etc. Regulations 1999 where, during an employee's ordinary maternity leave or additional maternity leave it is not practicable for her to continue to be employed because of redundancy then, where there is a 'suitable available vacancy'[254] the employee is entitled to be offered alternative employment with the employer or a successor or associated employer under a new contract of employment which complies with reg 10(3).

The offer must be made before the termination of the employee's existing contract. **10.249**

According to reg 10(3) the new contract of employment must be such that: **10.250**

(i) the work to be done under the new contract is of a kind which is both suitable in relation to the employee and appropriate for her to do in the circumstances; and

(ii) the provisions of the contract as to the capacity and place in which the individual is to be employed and as to the other terms and conditions of her employment cannot be substantially less favourable to her than in relation to the job which is redundant.

Regulation 20 sets out the unfair dismissal provisions and in essence states that if an employee is dismissed for the purposes of Pt X of the ERA 1996, then that will be automatically unfair if the reason or the principal reason is either: **10.251**

(i) that the employee is redundant and reg 10 (see above) has not been complied with; or

(ii) the reason or principal reason for dismissal is one of the reasons set out in reg 20(3) (see below).

Furthermore, by virtue of reg 20(2) an employee who is dismissed shall also be regarded as unfairly dismissed for the purposes of Pt X of the ERA 1996 if: **10.252**

(i) the reason for the dismissal is that the employee was redundant;

(ii) it is shown that the circumstances which constituted the redundancy applied to others in the same undertaking who held similar positions to that held by the employee but who have not been dismissed; and

(iii) it is shown that the reason for which the employee was selected for dismissal was one of the reasons set out in reg 10(3).

---

[254] Regulation 10(2).

10.253   The reasons set out in reg 10(3) are as follows:

    (i) the employee is pregnant;

    (ii) the employee has given birth to a child;

    (iii) a relevant requirement or relevant recommendation has been applied to her as set out in s 66(2) of the ERA 1996 (suspension on maternity grounds);

    (iv) the fact that the employee sought to take or availed herself of the benefits of ordinary maternity leave or additional maternity leave;

    (v) the fact that the employee took or sought to take parental leave or time off for dependants under s 57A of the ERA 1996;

    (vi) the fact that the employee failed to return after a period of ordinary or additional maternity leave where the employer did not notify of the date on which the period in question would end and she reasonably believed the period had ended or the employer gave her less than 28 days' notice of the date on which the period in question would end, and it was not reasonably practicable for her to return on that date;

    (vii) the fact the employee undertook, considered undertaking, or refused to undertake work in accordance with reg 12(A);

    (viii) the fact that the employee declined to sign a workforce agreement for the purposes of the Maternity and Parental Leave, etc. Regulations 1999;

    (ix) the fact that the employee being a representative of members of the workforce for the purposes of entering into workforce agreements or was a candidate in an election in which on being elected such a person would become such a representative, performed or proposed to perform any function or activities as such a representative or candidate.

10.254   In relation to non-compliance with reg 10, a dismissal here is only automatically unfair if it brings the ordinary or additional maternity leave period to an end. Likewise, a dismissal is only automatically unfair in relation to the fact that the employee has given birth to a child[255] if that brings to an end the ordinary or additional maternity leave period.

10.255   Furthermore, there will be no automatic unfair dismissal where the woman accepts an offer of suitable alternative employment or, alternatively, unreasonably refuses an offer of suitable alternative employment.

---

[255] Regulation 20(3)(b).

PART IV

INFORMATION AND CONSULTATION

11

INFORMATION AND CONSULTATION ON MULTIPLE REDUNDANCIES

A. Introduction	11.01	D. Special Circumstances	11.66
B. General Scope	11.05		
C. The Impact of European Law on Information/Consultation Obligations	11.11		

> [Making workforce reductions]…is undoubtedly the most downbeat form of workplace change that HR and managers will have to manage in their careers. But, done properly, in a generally consultative manner, it does not have to lead to the negative employment relations fall out that is so commonly associated with redundancy situations.
>
> ACAS Policy Discussion Paper: Collective Consultation on Redundancies (858a)[1]

A. Introduction

11.01 Council Directive (EEC) 75/12 of 17 February 1975 on the approximation of the laws of the Member States relating to collective redundancies requiring Member States to implement a regime for the information to and consultation with employee representatives was one of the first employment directives of the EC.[2] It was amended by Council Directive (EC) 92/56 and eventually consolidated into Council Directive (EC) 98/59 of 20 July 1998 on the approximation of the laws of the Member States relating to collective redundancies.[3]

11.02 UK law transposing the 1975 Directive was originally contained in s 99 *et seq* of the Employment Protection Act 1975. As detailed below, this original UK legislation was flawed in material respects and necessitated correction via the Transfer of Undertakings (Protection of Employment) (Amendment) Regulations 1995 and the Collective Redundancies and Transfer of Undertakings (Protection of Employment) (Amendment) Regulations 1999.

---

[1] See <http://www.acas.org.uk/CHttpHandler.ashx?id=2629&p=0>.
[2] Council Directive (EEC) 75/129 [1976] OJ L39/40. For detailed commentary, see MR Freedland, 'Employment protection: redundancy procedures and the EEC' (1976) *ILJ* 24–34.
[3] [1998] OJ L225/16.

UK law is now contained in Chapter II of the Trade Union and Labour Relations (Consolidation) Act 1992 as amended:

> The general duty of the employer under section 188 of the Trade Union and Labour Relations (Consolidation) Act 1992 is that, where he is proposing to dismiss as redundant 20 or more employees at one establishment within a period of 90 days or less, he shall consult about the dismissals all appropriate employee representatives of any of the employees who may be affected by the proposed dismissals or may be affected by measures taken in connection with those dismissals.

11.03 The consultation has to be in good time and in any event where the employer is proposing to dismiss 100 or more employees, at least 90 days, and in all other cases, at least 30 days before the first dismissal takes effect.

11.04 Where there is an independent trade union recognised by the employer in respect of a category of employees there is a required single channel of communication with trade union representatives. In other cases consultation must be with elected employee representatives. Consultation has to include ways of avoiding dismissals, reducing the numbers of employees to be dismissed, and mitigating the consequences of the dismissals. It must also be undertaken by the employer with a view to reaching agreement with the appropriate representatives.[4] For the purposes of consultation, s 188 (4) prescribes the delivery of specified information in writing (see below).

B. General Scope

11.05 Originally, the definition of redundancy in UK legislation for the purposes of information and consultation obligations was exactly the same as the definition of redundancy for the purposes of the ERA 1996 and individual redundancy payment entitlement. But, following the successful complaint made by the EC Commission about the shortcomings in UK legislation detailed below, the definition was later widened to bring it in line with the wider definition in what is now Art 1.1(a) of the 1998 Directive.

For the purposes of information and consultation over multiple redundancies, s 195 of the TULR(C)A 1992 states as follows:

> (1) In this Chapter references to dismissal as redundant are references to dismissal for a reason not related to the individual concerned or for a number of reasons all of which are not so related.

11.06 Section 195 of the TULR(C)A, therefore, applies to dismissals for economic or reorganisational reasons *as well as* for traditional redundancy reasons. Dismissals, therefore, to effect change in contracts of employment for economic or organisational reasons clearly fall under s 195 triggering the consultation obligations, even if such reorganisational dismissals would not ordinarily fall under the definition of redundancy in what is now the ERA. Thus, economically related 'some other substantial reason' dismissals (ERA 1996, s 98(1)(b)) in employment law will now attract the application of TULR(C)A 1992, s 195 (as long as 20 or more dismissals are being proposed).[5]

Examples of some other substantial reason dismissals on reorganisational or similar grounds which would, it is suggested, be dismissals for a reason unconnected to the individual

---

[4] TULR(C)A 1992, s 188(2).
[5] *GMB v MAN Truck & Bus Ltd* [2000] IRLR 636.

concerned are *Hollister v MFU*;[6] *RS Components Ltd v Irwin*;[7] *Trebor Bassett Ltd v (1) Saxby (2) Boorman*;[8] *Richmond Precision Engineering Ltd v Pearce*;[9] *St John of God (Care Services) Ltd v Brookes*;[10] *Catamaran Cruisers Ltd v Williams*;[11] *Selfridges v Wayne*;[12] and *GMB v Man Truck and Bus UK Ltd*.[13]

The width of s 195 does not affect the traditional definition of redundancy for redundancy payments liability which remains, as before, limited. **11.07**

Most voluntary redundancies will count as proposed dismissals for the purposes of informa- **11.08** tion and consultation obligations. This was held by the EAT in *Optare Group Ltd v Transport and General Workers Union*.[14] And it has been further held that an employer may be proposing redundancies while actively considering alternatives to redundancy. In *Scotch Premier Meat Limited v Burns*,[15] following the loss of a major order the company decided to sell its business as a going concern or, alternatively, as a development site. The latter would entail redundancies. Applications for voluntary redundancy were invited. A number of employees accepted and the remainder were dismissed. A complaint was made about failure to inform and consult appropriate employee representatives. It was held that the employers were proposing to dismiss as redundant 20 or more employees within the meaning of the legislation notwithstanding that as an alternative they were considering selling the business as a going concern.[16]

The duty to inform and consult may also apply even if the employer is offering alternative **11.09** employment. In *Hardy v Tourism South East*[17] an employer proposed to close its main office and to offer employees re-deployment at another site 100 miles away. The employer disputed that it was proposing to dismiss 20 or more employees as redundant. The issue was whether the employer's proposal had the effect of terminating the existing contract of employment, albeit that a new contract at a new location was being offered. This would depend upon the terms of the employment contract. Thus, if there were no mobility clause in the employment contract the correct construction would be that the employer would be proposing to terminate the existing employment contract at the original site with an offer of a new contract at a new location, in which case the employer would be proposing to dismiss as redundant, in this case, 20 or more employees.

Finally, it must be remembered that non-renewal of a fixed-term contract is a dismissal and if the **11.10** reason for the non-renewal is redundancy the information and consultation obligations apply. This is sometimes forgotten in establishments where a large number of workers are employed under fixed-term contracts, many of which fail to be renewed due to lack of external funding.

---

[6] [1979] IRLR 542.
[7] [1974] 1 All ER 41; [1973] ICR 535; [1973] IRLR 239, NIRC.
[8] EAT 658/91.
[9] [1985] IRLR 179, EAT.
[10] [1992] ICR 715; [1992] IRLR 546.
[11] [1994] IRLR 386, EAT.
[12] IRLB, December 1995, p 13 (EAT).
[13] [2000] IRLR 636.
[14] [2007] IRLR 931. See also *Graff Diamonds Ltd v Boutwright* (EAT/0148/10). Although to be contrasted with cases where there are terminations by mutual agreement (particularly where no compulsory redundancies are proposed, as in the case of *Birch and Humber v University of Liverpool* [1985] IRLR 165, as discussed in Chapter 2).
[15] [2000] IRLR 639.
[16] The case is also further authority for the fact that voluntary redundancies will, in general, attract the information and consultation obligations.
[17] [2005] IRLR 242.

Universities are a case in point. However, if, for example, there are 20 or more proposals not to renew fixed-term contracts within a period of 90 days or less, the obligations will apply. A recent example is *Lancaster University v The University and College Union*.[18]

C. The Impact of European Law on Information/ Consultation Obligations

11.11 As hinted above, UK legislation on information and consultation on multiple redundancies has had a chequered career. It became clear that UK law, as originally drawn in the Employment Protection Act 1975 (s 99 onwards) fell short of what was required in Community law.

11.12 On 21 October 1992 the Commission of the European Communities brought infringement proceedings against the UK for breach of Directive 75/129. The complaints were that domestic legislation was in breach by:

(a) failing to provide for the designation of employee representatives where this did not occur voluntarily in practice;

(b) limiting the scope of its legislation designed to implement the Directive to a less wide range of dismissal situations than that foreseen by the Directive;

(c) failing to require an employer who was contemplating collective redundancies to consult employees' representatives with a view to reaching an agreement and in relation to the matters specified in the Directive; and

(d) failing to provide for effective sanctions in the case of failure to consult employees' representatives as required by the Directive.

11.13 Some of these matters were addressed by the changes to the TULR(C)A 1992 made by the Trade Union Reform and Employment Rights Act 1993 (TURERA 1993), but not all. The principal matter outstanding was the failure to provide for effective designation of employee representatives. In *EC Commission v United Kingdom*,[19] in infringement proceedings brought by the EC Commission against the UK for breach of the Directive, all of these complaints were upheld. As mentioned, TURERA 1993 had addressed all complaints prior to this ruling, save for the worker representative point. As recognition of trade unions in the UK was, at the time, entirely voluntary, the ECJ ruled that there was no effective transposition by the UK of the obligation to make employers consult with worker representatives if this was confined to consultation with recognised trade union representatives. Amending legislation therefore followed by way of the Collective Redundancies and Transfer of Undertakings (Protection of Employment) (Amendment) Regulations 1995, improved upon by the Collective Redundancies and Transfer of Undertakings (Protection of Employment) (Amendment) Regulations 1999.[20]

---

[18] EAT/0278/10.

[19] [1994] ICR 664; [1994] IRLR 412, ECJ.

[20] A Bryson and J Forth trace the decline in trading in membership and influence in 'Trade Union Membership 1999–2009', National Institute of Economic and Social Research, discussion paper no. 362, September 2010. See also J Achur, 'Trade Union membership 2009', *BIS*, 2010. Achur recorded that union density for employees in 2009 was 27.4%, trade union membership falling broadly as the same rate as total employment union density in the private sector was 15.1% and in the public sector 56.6%. Workers covered by collective agreements have remained more or less constant over recent years. The 2004 Workplace Employee Relations Survey (WRERS) suggested unions were recognised for collective bargaining in 30% of workplaces. Whilst the statutory recognition procedure introduced in Sch A1 to the Trade Union and Labour Relations (Consolidation) 1992 resulted in some recognition gains (see AL Bogg, 'Representation of employees and

'Contemplating' dismissals and 'proposal to dismiss'

One example of the disparity between the terms of the Directive and UK law is the difference **11.14** in wording between the Directive and s 188 of the 1992 Act. Under the Directive the obligations are triggered when redundancies are *contemplated*. Under the 1992 Act the obligations are triggered when there is a '*proposal*' to dismiss. It has been consistently argued that *contemplating* is earlier in time than *proposing*. Some authorities suggest that there is no difference between the two terms.[21] However, most authorities conclude that there is a difference between the wording and the difference cannot be reconciled.[22] It has been ruled, therefore, that because of the clear diversions in wording between European law and UK law, it is not possible to interpret the domestic legislation in line with the European legislation.[23]

However, some of the heat has been taken out of this debate in the sense that under the terms **11.15** of s 188 as presently drafted, consultation has to take place 'in good time' (the legislation previously referred to consultation commencing 'at the earliest opportunity').

Furthermore, by virtue of the European Court decision in *Junk v Kühnel*[24] the employer **11.16** must have consulted with appropriate representatives and have completed the process of consultation, or at least made a bona fide attempt to achieve an agreed solution, before the employer reaches any final decision to dismiss or issue notice of dismissal, and the court in *Junk* stated that the Directive, in effect, imposes an obligation to negotiate.

Finally, in the recent case of *UK Coal Mining Ltd v National Union of Mine Workers* **11.17** *(Northumberland Area) and Another*,[25] Elias J held that the difference in wording between 'proposed' and 'contemplate' did not prevent the consultation obligation under s 188 extending to consultations over closures of plants leading to redundancies in a closure context where it is recognised that dismissals will inevitably or almost inevitably result from the closure. (Elias J noted the decisions in *R v British Coal Corporation and Secretary of State for Trade and Industry ex parte Vardy*[26] and *MSF v Refuge Assurance plc*[27] to the effect that the incompatibility between the wording could not be reconciled—although he had some reservations about that conclusion.)

The ECJ subsequently delivered a decision in *Akavan Erityisalojen Keskusliddo AEK ry v* **11.18** *Fujitsu Siemens Computers Oy*.[28] In this case, the ECJ, in considering when the obligation to consult arises, noted, in agreement with the UK Government, that should the duty to consult occur prematurely, this could lead to results that would be contrary to the aim of the Directive by creating employee uncertainty and reducing employer flexibility. On this basis, the ECJ

---

collective bargaining within the firm; voluntarism in the UK', report to the XVII International Congress of Comparative Law, July 2006). The Labour Force Survey of trade union membership and recognition 1997–1998 estimated that in 1998 approximately 8 million, or 35%, of employees were covered by collective bargaining over pay. Achur in 2009 estimated that across all sectors about one-third of all UK employees had stated their pay and conditions were affected by a collective agreement. Collective agreements covered approximately one-fifth of the private sector employees, with public sector workers evidencing a density of 68.1%.

[21] *Hough v Leyland DAF Limited* [1991] ICR 696.
[22] See *R v British Coal Corporation and Secretary of State for Trade and Industry ex parte Vardy* [1993] IRLR 104.
[23] Under the principle in *Litster v Forth Dry Dock & Engineering Co Ltd* [1989] 1 All ER 1134.
[24] [2005] IRLR 310.
[25] [2008] IRLR 4.
[26] [1993] IRLR 104.
[27] [2002] IRLR 324.
[28] [2009] IRLR 944.

held that the consultation procedure should be commenced by the employer 'once a strategic or commercial decision compelling him to contemplate or plan for collective redundancies has been taken'. The ECJ did, however, highlight that commencement of consultation is not dependent upon the provision of all the necessary information which must be supplied to workers' representatives under the Directive and cannot therefore be delayed on this basis.

11.19   As the employer in question in this case was a subsidiary company, the ECJ was also required to consider whether the obligation arises when the parent company contemplates collective redundancies and whether the affected subsidiary needs to be identified in order to trigger the start of consultation. In this regard, the ECJ ruled that, whether or not collective redundancies are contemplated by a parent company or the undertaking which employs the workers concerned, it is always the undertaking that employs the workers that is obliged to commence consultation and it is not therefore possible to start consultation until the subsidiary has been identified. This may consequently lead to a delay between the obligation arising and the actual commencement of consultation.

11.20   Overall the decision is far from crystal clear, but it could be argued that the ECJ decision is consistent with the UK wording of 'proposal', notwithstanding the difference in wording in the directive between 'proposing' and 'contemplating' (discussed above).

> This lack of clarity was, however, identified in *United States of America v Nolan*,[29] where the Court of Appeal referred the issue of when consultation should begin to the European Court. The Court said that, after consideration of the decision in *Akavan*, it could be argued that *UK Coal* had interpreted the consultation obligation as being more extensive than prescribed by the Directive. The Court of Appeal said thus:

>> . . . the Court has of course had careful regard to the USA's express unwillingness for any such reference to be made; and it recognises that it is not the court of last resort and so is not obliged to make a reference. The Court is, however, also sensitive to the consideration that the issue upon which it requires guidance is so important not just to the disposition of this litigation but also to industrial practice generally: employers need to understand the nature of their consultation obligations. If the Court were to venture a view on the true interpretation of [*Akavan*] and decide the question of principle accordingly, its decision would be binding unless and until the Supreme Court were to hold otherwise in this or another case; and there can be no certainty that its decision in this case, whichever way it went, would be taken to the Supreme Court. In short, the Court regards the point as too important for it to risk adopting the wrong interpretation of the decision in [*Akavan*].

'Proposal' and 'decision'

11.21   Finally, it is clear at least that a 'proposal' to dismiss may occur at an earlier stage than a 'decision' to dismiss, thus triggering the obligations at an earlier point. In *Leicestershire County Council v UNISON*[30] a proposal to make employees redundant was taken by officers of the council a month before the proposal was formally ratified by a political decision of the council's employment committee. It was held by the EAT (subsequently upheld by the Court of Appeal) that a proposal to dismiss for the purposes of s 188 had been made by the council officers notwithstanding the need for its subsequent political ratification, thus triggering the information and consultation obligations at the earlier point in time.

---

[29]   [2010] EWCA Civ 1223.
[30]   [2005] IRLR 920 (EAT); [2006] IRLR 810 (CA).

The concept of 'establishment'

Information and consultation under the TULR(C)A has to take place in respect of redun-   **11.22**
dancies proposed at the one establishment. What an 'establishment' is seems to be a question
of fact for the employment tribunal. Until recently guidance included the view that an establishment must denote some degree of permanence, perhaps of building, administration,
centralisation of records, and tools and equipment.[31] However, the European Court has
examined the concept of 'establishment' for the purposes of what is now Directive 98/59 and
'establishment' for the purposes of TULR(C)A must be considered in the same way.

In *Rockfon A/S v Specialarbejderforbundet i Danmark* [32] the facts were that Rockfon was part   **11.23**
of the multinational group Rockwool International which comprised, in total, four companies.
The group had a centralised personnel department in a company called Rockwool A/S.
Rockfon dismissed 24 workers out of its workforce of 162. For determining when the consultation provisions were triggered Denmark adopted the scheme in the Directive which provided
that if dismissals occurred over a period of 30 days (as was the case in *Rockfon*) consultation
provisions applied where workers to be dismissed were:

- at least 10 in establishments normally employing more than 20 and less than 100 workers;
- at least 10 per cent of the number of workers in establishments normally employing at least
  100 but less than 300 workers;
- at least 30 in establishments normally employing 300 workers or more.

If Rockfon A/S was itself an establishment, clearly the consultation provisions were triggered   **11.24**
because the redundancies exceeded 10 per cent. Rockfon contended, however, that it was the
Rockwool *group* which constituted the establishment and, since the group employed more
than 300 workers, consultation would only have been required if in excess of 30 workers
were to be dismissed.

Danish law defines an establishment as a unit which, *inter alia*, has a management and which   **11.25**
can independently effect large-scale dismissals. The district court held that Rockfon was an
establishment because the joint personnel department had only a consultative role and
Rockfon itself had the power to carry out dismissals. The matter was referred to the European
Court. The European Court held that Art 1(1)(a) of the Directive did not preclude two or
more interrelated undertakings in a group, neither or none of which has a decisive influence
over the other or others, from establishing a joint recruitment and dismissal department so
that dismissals on ground of redundancy in one of the undertakings could take place
only with that department's approval. 'Establishment' for the purposes of the Collective
Redundancies Directive must be understood as designating the unit to which the workers
made redundant are 'assigned to carry out their duties'. It was not necessary to construe
establishment as meaning a unit endowed with a management which could independently
effect collective redundancies. That would be incompatible with the aim of the Directive
because it would allow companies belonging to the same group to try and make it more

---

[31] See *Barley v Amey Roadstone Corpn Ltd* [1977] ICR 546, [1977] IRLR 299, EAT; *Barratt Developments (Bradford) v Union of Construction, Allied Trades and Technicians* [1978] ICR 319, [1977] IRLR 403, EAT; *Clarkes of Hove Ltd v Bakers' Union* [1979] 1 All ER 152, [1978] ICR 1076, CA; *E Green & Sons (Castings) Ltd v Association of Scientific, Technical and Managerial Staffs* [1984] ICR 352, [1984] IRLR 135, EAT.
[32] [1996] ICR 163; [1996] IRLR 168, ECJ.

difficult for the Directive to apply to them by conferring the power to take decisions concerning redundancies onto a separate decision-making body.

11.26 By analogy with the law on whether an employee is employed in an undertaking for the purposes of the Acquired Rights Directive 2001/23 the European Court held:

> An employment relationship is essentially characterised by the link existing between the employee and the part of the undertaking or business to which he is assigned to carry out his duties. Therefore 'establishment' in art 1(1)(a) must be interpreted as meaning depending on the circumstances the unit to which the workers made redundant are assigned to carry out their duties.

11.27 In the UK the Employment Protection Act 1975, s 99 (subsequently consolidated into the TULR(C)A, s 188) originally provided for minimum periods of consultation, of 30 days where between 10 and 100 workers were to be made redundant in any establishment, and 90 days where the numbers in any establishment were 100 or more. However, s 188, as originally drawn, provided for the consultation where even a single redundancy was to be effected in any establishment. The Collective Redundancies and Transfer of Undertakings (Protection of Employment) (Amendment) Regulations 1995 altered the redundancy consultation regime in s 188 by raising the minimum threshold for redundancies to 20 or more redundancies in any period of 90 days. Therefore, the effect of the *Rockfon* decision, although well-intentioned, has been to make it more difficult for worker representatives to establish that consultation requirements should be triggered. If 'establishment' is to be defined narrowly as a unit to which the employee is 'assigned' this is likely to be much smaller in practice than an establishment, as previously interpreted by UK tribunals and courts. The irony of *Rockfon* then is that while the decision may be helpful in Member States which use a percentage test for employee thresholds triggering consultation, it rebounds to the disadvantage of employees in the UK, and will assist employers in some cases, especially as the 1995 Regulations lifted the threshold for establishments to a minimum of 20 employees.

11.28 In *Athinaiki Chartopoiia AE v Panagiotidis*[33] the concept of establishment was considered once more by the ECJ. In this case Athinaiki Chartopoiia had three separate production units in three different locations in Greece: a unit for the manufacture of writing paper, printing paper, mechanical paper, chipboard, and aluminium sulphate; a second unit for the manufacture of soft kitchen paper, toilet paper, and bags; and a third unit for the processing of soft paper. Each of the units had distinct equipment and a specialised workforce, and a chief production officer. Decisions concerning operating expenditure, purchase of materials and product cost were taken at the company's head office.

11.29 In July 2002 the company decided to close down the first unit, dismissing almost all of the 420 workers employed there. It began consultation with workers' representatives. When agreement was not reached, the Minister for Labour extended the consultations for a further 20 days. However, the company proceeded to terminate the contracts of the employees concerned before this extended consultation period expired. In proceedings brought by the workers challenging the lawfulness of the collective redundancies, the company claimed that the production unit in question was an independent unit and therefore fell within a derogation from the collective redundancy provisions allowed under Greek law. This was rejected by the Thrace Court of Appeal, which held that the dismissals were invalid. On appeal the

---

[33] [2007] IRLR 284.

Supreme Court of Cassation referred the issue of whether the independent unit was an establishment to the ECJ for a preliminary ruling. The ECJ held that the production unit in question came within the concept of 'establishment' for the purposes of Directive 98/59.

The Court held that 'establishment' in the context of an undertaking may consist of a **11.30** distinct entity having a certain degree of permanence and stability, which is assigned to perform one or more given tasks and which has a workforce, technical means, and a certain organisational structure allowing for the accomplishment of those tasks. The entity in question need not have any legal autonomy, nor need it have economic, financial, administrative, or technical autonomy, in order to be regarded as an 'establishment'. In addition, it is not essential for the unit in question to be endowed with a management that can independently effect collective redundancies. Nor must there be a geographical separation from the other units and facilities of the undertaking. In the present case, the unit in question had distinct equipment and a specialised workforce; its operation was not affected by that of other units; it had a chief production officer who ensured that the work was carried out properly, was responsible for supervision of the entire operation of the unit's installations, and ensured that technical questions were solved. Those factors gave such a unit the air of an 'establishment' for the purposes of the application of Directive 98/59. The fact that decisions concerning the operating expenditure of each of those units—the purchase of materials and the costing of products were taken at the company's headquarters where a joint accounts office was set up—was irrelevant in this regard. Guidance in this case is consistent with and elaborates on the Community law on the concept of establishment laid down by the *Rockfon* case.

Finally, the provisions of the Act apply only to one employer. So, if a number of associated **11.31** employers genuinely operate at the same establishment, each employer's redundancy programme has to be considered separately and the number of redundancies proposed as a whole by separate (even though associated) employers at this establishment cannot be aggregated for the purpose of enlarging the consultation period.[34]

Also, as a general rule, within one employer each batch of redundancies has to be considered separately. Thus, section 188 (3) states:

> . . . in determining how many employees an employer is proposing to dismiss as redundant no account shall be taken of employees in respect of whose proposed dismissals consultation has already begun.

As the learned editors of *Harvey on Industrial Relations and Employment Law* point out,[35] this **11.32** can have some odd results. For example, if an employer proposes 21 dismissals and it commences consultation and, in a second later batch proposes a further 10 dismissals, s 188(3) means that consultation about the further 10 does not need to take place. Put the other way round, however, if the employer originally proposes 10 dismissals and then decides that a further 20 are necessary there is a duty to consult about all 30. The original 10 are not discounted since consultation did not begin in respect of those proposed dismissals.[36]

---

[34] *Transport and General Workers' Union v Nationwide Haulage Ltd* [1978] IRLR 143, IT.
[35] Para [2551].
[36] See s 118 (3).

11.33 An employer might be tempted artificially to stagger his redundancy programme in order that he might implement redundancies in small consecutive groups, thus in each case attracting less onerous information and consultation periods in respect of each group of dismissals. It is submitted that if this is plainly a sham the employment tribunal could look behind this arrangement and decide that the redundancy programme was connected. But the statutory scheme is regrettably not entirely safe from possible abuse by unscrupulous employers and from dubious fragmentation exercises.[37]

Employee representatives

11.34 By s 188(1B) of the TULR(C)A, for the purposes of information and consultation, the appropriate representatives of affected employees are trade union representatives if the employees are of a description in respect of which an independent trade union is recognised by the employer.

11.35 In any other case, the employer may chose between:

(a) employee representatives appointed or elected by the affected employees otherwise than for the purposes of s 188 who (having regard to the purposes for and the method by which they were appointed or elected) have authority from those employees to receive information and to be consulted about proposed dismissals on their behalf; or

(b) employee representatives elected by the affected employees for the purposes of s 188 in an election satisfying the requirements of s 188A(1).

11.36 The question of whether non-members of a trade union are 'employees of a description in respect of which a trade union is recognised by the employer' has been addressed by the Court of Appeal in Northern Ireland in the case of *Northern Ireland Hotel and Catering College (Governing Body) and North Eastern Education and Library Board v National Association of Teachers in Further and Higher Education*.[38] The Court decided that the statutory obligation on an employer to consult a trade union (in accordance with the Industrial Relations (Northern Ireland) Order 1976, art 49(1)) relates to an employee of a description or category in respect of which the union is recognised, whether or not that employee is a member of that particular union. On the facts, the respondent union was recognised by the employers in respect of the relevant category of employees, in this case college lecturers, and the court held that the union should have been consulted with regard to the proposed redundancies of two lecturers who were not members of the respondent union. The union should have been consulted because it was recognised by the employers in respect of employees 'of a description' whom it proposed to dismiss, i.e. college lecturers.[39]

Recognition

11.37 As stated, the rights under the TULR(C)A, s 188 apply both to elected employee representatives and recognised independent trade union representatives. Where an employer recognises a trade union, however, he *must* inform/consult with trade union representatives. The question of recognition is therefore highly significant. Recognition can arise in several ways.

---

[37] See *Transport and General Workers Union v Nationwide Haulage Ltd* [1978] IRLR 143, above.

[38] [1995] IRLR 83, NI CA.

[39] Cf. *Makro Self Service Wholesalers Ltd v Union Shop, Distributive and Allied Workers* (EAT, 828/93), in which the EAT held that the insertion into a staff handbook of a clause about trade union membership did not amount to an extension of the recognition agreement to cover managerial staff).

It can arise from a collective agreement (but in that case it does not of course matter whether the agreement itself is legally enforceable).[40] It can arise informally and it can even be implied from a previous course of dealing.[41] According to the cases, the question is a mixed one of fact and law.[42]

Recognition has to be recognition 'for the purpose of collective bargaining', i.e. in relation to one or more of the matters specified in s 178(2) and (3) of the TULR(C)A. It has been held that for the purposes of recognition this must be recognition of negotiating rights as opposed to merely representational or consultation rights. However, it seems that the granting of partial negotiation rights to a trade union would be sufficient to count as recognition. Recognition has to be 'to any extent' and therefore if there is a partial recognition covering say only one or two of the matters set out in s 178(2) this will count for the purposes of the rights to consultation and notification over redundancies.   **11.38**

The requirements for election of employee representatives

Under s 188A(1) of the TULR(C)A, the requirements for the election of employee represen-   **11.39**
tatives under s 188(1B) above are that:

(a) the employer has to make such arrangements as are reasonably practical to ensure that the election is fair;

(b) the employer has to determine the number of representatives to be elected so that there are sufficient representatives to represent the interests of all the affected employees having regard to the number and classes of those employees;

(c) the employer has to determine whether the affected employees should be represented either by representatives of all the affected employees or by representatives of particular classes of those employees;

(d) before the election the employer has to determine the term of office of employee representatives so that it is of sufficient length to enable information to be given and consultations under section 188 to be completed;

(e) the candidates for election as employee representatives have to be affected employees on the date of the election;

(f) no affected employee may be unreasonably excluded from standing for election;

(g) all affected employees on the date of the election are entitled to vote for employee representatives;

(h) the employees entitled to vote may vote for as many candidates as there are representatives to be elected to represent them or, if there are to be representatives for particular classes of employees, may vote for as many candidates as there are representatives to be elected to represent their particular class of employee; and

(i) the election is conducted so as to secure that so far as is reasonably practicable, those voting do so in secret and the votes given at the election are accurately counted.

---

[40] *Amalgamated Society of Boilermakers, Shipwrights, Blacksmiths and Structural Workers v George Wimpey ME & Co Ltd* [1977] IRLR 95, EAT.

[41] *National Union of Gold, Silver and Allied Trades v Albery Bros Ltd* [1978] ICR 62, [1977] IRLR 173, EAT; affd [1979] ICR 84, [1978] IRLR 504, CA.

[42] *National Union of Tailors and Garment Workers v Charles Ingram & Co Ltd* [1978] 1 All ER 1271, [1977] ICR 530, [1977] IRLR 147, EAT; cf. *Transport and General Workers' Union v Dyer* [1977] IRLR 93, EAT.

11.40 Finally, where, after an election of employee representatives, satisfying the above requirements, one of those elected ceases to act as an employee representative and any of those employees are no longer represented, they have to elect another representative by an election satisfying the above requirements (s 188A(2)).

The obligation to consult and to complete consultation before issuing notices of dismissal: *Junk v Kühnel*

11.41 Consultation has to begin in good time (previously, consultation had to begin 'at the earliest opportunity'. The Government took the opportunity, when enacting the Collective Redundancies and Transfer of Undertakings (Protection of Employment) (Amendment) Regulations 1995, to substitute 'in good time', the actual words used by the Collective Redundancies Directive) and in any event within a minimum specified period.

11.42 Thus, if the employer proposes to dismiss as redundant 100 or more employees at one establishment within a period of 90 days or less the consultation period must begin at least 90 days before the first of those dismissals takes effect. Where an employer proposes to dismiss as redundant 20 or more employees at one establishment within a period of 90 days or less the period of consultation must commence at least 30 days before the first of those dismissals takes effect.

11.43 The wording of the UK legislation focuses on a period worked back from when the first of the dismissals 'takes effect'. Taken literally, the focus is not on consultation before notice of dismissal is issued but rather when that dismissal notice takes effect. It is questionable whether an employer may rely with confidence on what the legislation appears to say. Indeed, insofar as the wording tricks the employer into thinking that he can issue notices of dismissal in parallel with the running of the consultation period he will be wrong, as the consultation process must be concluded *before* the first dismissal notice can be issued. This was clarified in the highly important case of *Junk v Kühnel*[43] in the ECJ.

11.44 Here the European Court made it plain that a notice of dismissal for redundancy under the Redundancies Directive can only be given once the consultation process with workers' representatives has been concluded. As stated, under UK law, the obligation is to consult representatives of the workforce in good time and at least 30 or 90 days before the first redundancy 'takes effect', depending on the numbers involved. The ECJ in *Junk* stated that the Directive 'imposes an obligation to negotiate'. So, if the workforce or union representatives claim that there are still counter proposals to be evaluated and considered and that, therefore, the consultation process is still continuing, the employer may risk legal liability by issuing any of the notices of dismissal. Such dismissal notices would be premature and the dismissals in breach of the Directive.

11.45 In one sense the European Court was saying nothing new by stipulating that, as the purpose of the consultation process is, *inter alia*, to avoid dismissals and reduce the numbers affected, consultation cannot take place on any meaningful basis if notices of dismissal have already been issued. This does not mean to say that employers are strictly obliged to wait 30 or 90 days, as the case may be, after the start of the consultation process before they can issue dismissal notices. But a very strong argument can be raised by employee representatives in the future that the full 30- or 90-day period (or something like it) might have to be allowed

---

[43] [2005] IRLR 310.

before notices of dismissal are issued because of the ECJ's strong views about the quality of consultation to be entered into; that is to say, a consultation obligation tantamount to an 'obligation to negotiate'.

The Collective Redundancies (Amendment) Regulations 2006,[44] reg 3, effective from **11.46** 1 October 2006 now makes it clear that, as far as the duty on employers to inform the Secretary of State about collective redundancies is concerned, the notification of 30 days or 90 days (depending on the size of redundancies) must also be made to the Secretary of State before any notice of dismissal has been issued. Interestingly, the Government took the view that it was not necessary to make a similar amendment to s 188 itself to make it clear in the wording of s 188, to give effect to *Junk*, that the 30-days or 90-days consultation must begin before the first notice of dismissal has been issued by the employer. Instead, the Government took the view that the words 'in good time' in s 188 mean that employment tribunals will be compelled to construe this in line with *Junk* and therefore employers will still have to commence consultation over the appropriate period before any notice of dismissal has been issued. The Department of Trade and Industry (DTI) (now The Department for Business Innovation and Skills (BIS)) subsequently posted new guidance,[45] in which it is stressed that the information and consultation obligations under Pt IV of the 1992 Act must be completed before notices of dismissal are issued by the employer.

Consultation only on the proposed redundancies or also on the reasons behind those redundancies?

In *UK Coal Mining Ltd v National Union of Mineworkers (Northumberland Area) and* **11.47** *Another* [46] it was held that the obligation to consult over avoiding the proposed redundancies inevitably involves engaging with the reasons for the dismissals and that in turn requires consultation over the reasons for the closure. It is strictly the proposed dismissals that are the subject of consultation, and not the closure itself. It follows that if an employer planned a closure but believed that redundancies would nonetheless be avoided, there would be no need to consult over the closure decision itself, at least not pursuant to the obligations under the 1992 Act. In the context of closure, however, that is likely to be a very exceptional case. Where the closure and dismissals are inextricably linked, the duty to consult over the reason arises. As will be seen below, the Court of Appeal in *United States of America v Nolan* [47] has referred the whole issue of timing of consultation to the European Court, given the uncertainty over the compatibility of *UK Coal Mining* with the ECJ decision in *Akavan Erityisalojen Keskuslidda AEK ry v Fujitsu Siemens Computers oy* [48] and the relative opacity of *Akavan* itself. The account of *UK Coal Mining* below is subject to the outcome of the referral in *Nolan*.

In this case, the trade unions, the NUM, and the British Association of Colliery Manage- **11.48** ment (BACM) pursued a claim for a protective award against UK Coal Mining following the company's announcement that it would close Ellington Colliery in January 2005. In a formal letter under s 188 and in other communications UK Coal Mining stated that the

---

[44] SI 2006/2387.
[45] *Redundancy Consultation and Notification–Guidance*) (URN No 06/1965) at: <http://www.berr.gov.uk/employment/employment-legislation/employment-guidance/page13852.html>.
[46] [2008] IRLR 4.
[47] [2010] EWCA Civ 1223.
[48] [2009] IRLR 944.

decision to close the colliery was taken for safety reasons following the penetration of water underground. As such the company sought to rely upon a special circumstances defence and dismissed the majority of the 329-strong workforce before the expiry of the 90-day statutory consultation period.

11.49   An employment tribunal sitting in Newcastle found that as a fact the purported safety reason for the closure put forward by UK Coal Mining was untrue and that the economic viability of the mine was the main reason for the closure. As a consequence, the tribunal ordered a maximum protective award of 90 days and held that as UK Coal Mining had deliberately provided a false reason for the redundancy proposals, it could not rely upon the special circumstances defence. UK Coal Mining appealed and the issue arose whether there was an obligation to consult on a decision to close the mine itself.

11.50   Earlier authority [49] suggested that consultation did not oblige the employer to consult about the reason for proposed redundancies. This, the employed argued, extended to mean that the employer is not obliged to consult about the reason for closures. Also, in *R v British Coal and Secretary of State for Industry ex parte Vardy* [50] Glidewell LJ had observed, *obiter*, that s 188 did not require consultation about reasons for redundancy, including whether a mine would close. Elias J held that the *obiter* comments of Glidewell LJ in *Vardy* were no longer good law in view of subsequent changes to the statutory wording.

11.51   The ratio of *UK Coal Mining* is therefore:

- Previously, *Vardy* had been accepted as binding authority for the proposition that an employer was not obliged to consult on the reasons for redundancy. This proposition no longer holds good.
- In the vast majority of cases involving a site closure, employers are now obliged to consult with representatives of the workforce regarding the closure decision itself.
- Only in a 'very exceptional case' where an employer planned a closure but believed that redundancies would be avoided would there be no need to consult on the reasons for the closure itself.
- In the context of a closure situation, employers will generally now be obliged to begin consulting with the workforce at a much earlier stage than they may have done before.
- As to situations not involving a closure, the following may be suggested. While the facts of the *UK Coal Mining* case related specifically to a site closure, there remains a question as to whether this decision could have further ramifications with respect to consultation obligations in other restructuring exercises that do not involve a site closure. As the obligation under s 188(2) is to consult about ways to avoiding the dismissals, employers who do not begin to consult with the workforce representatives until such time as they have fully formulated a decision that redundancies will occur will run the risk of successful claims for protective awards. In assessing such claims, tribunals will inevitably have to consider the state of mind of the employer and how far it has gone down the decision-making process at the point in time at which consultation commenced. Employers who only start consultation after formulating a decision will be taking a risk as it may then be too late for them to consult about ways of avoiding the dismissals.

---

[49] *Securicor Omega Express Ltd v GmB* [2004] IRLR 9 and *Middlesbrough Borough Council v TGWU* [2002] IRLR 332.
[50] [1993] IRLR 104.

UK Coal Mining Limited v NUM was applied in *United States of America v Nolan*,[51] when a **11.52** US army base in Hampshire was closed. The EAT considered that failure to consult about the reasons for the closure in the light of *UK Coal Mining Limited v NUM* was a failure to begin consultations 'in good time' as required by the legislation. The EAT also confirmed that *UK Coal Mining Limited v NUM* applies not only to commercial decisions but also to decisions which have a public policy element. Thus:

> ... there is no warrant in section 188 for drawing such a distinction: the obligation to consult applies to both public sector and private sector employees. Redundancies in the public sector may well result from decision taken for political and other non-commercial reasons. These reasons are not excluded from the consultation requirements of section 188.

As discussed, the Court of Appeal in *Nolan*[52] subsequently referred the issue of timing of **11.53** consultation to the European Court and the effect of the decision of the Court in *Akavan* on *UK Coal Mining Limited v NUM*. However, in considering the United State's argument that consultation obligations could not apply as such to a sovereign state received no sympathy from the Court of Appeal. The sovereign state's interests were fully protected by its ability to claim sovereign immunity (of which the United States failed to do in this case). Furthermore, it considered, *obiter*, that a decision not to consult over an operational decision of military sensitivity might allow the sovereign state to rely on the s 188(7) 'special circumstances defence' (which again was not pleaded in the case).

The information required to be disclosed

For the purposes of consultation required by the TULR(C)A the employer has to disclose in **11.54** writing to appropriate representatives the following information:

(a) the reason for his proposals;
(b) the numbers and descriptions of employees whom it is proposed to dismiss as redundant;
(c) the total number of employees of any such description employed by the employer at the establishment in question;
(d) the proposed method of selecting the employees who may be dismissed;
(e) the proposed method of carrying out the dismissals with due regard to any agreed procedure including the period over which the dismissals are to take effect; and
(f) the proposed method of calculating the amount of any redundancy payments to be made (otherwise than in compliance with an obligation imposed by or by virtue of any enactment) to employees who may be dismissed.[53]

This information has to be given to each of the appropriate representatives by delivery **11.55** to them or sent by post to an address notified by them, to the employer or, in the case of representatives of a trade union, sent by post to the union at the address of its head or main office (TULR(C)A, s 188(5). In *National and Local Government Officers' Association v London Borough of Bromley*,[54] it was argued by the union that consultation did not begin until the information had reached the relevant official, notwithstanding that it had hitherto been delivered to a person at the union's offices. This was rejected by the EAT, which held that delivery to a person at the offices with apparent authority to receive was enough.

---

[51] [2009] IRLR 923.
[52] [2010] EWCA Civ 1223.
[53] TULR(C)A, s 188(4) as amended by TURERA, s 33.
[54] EAT 671/91, *IDS Brief* 497, July 1993, p 15.

The question of whether information is adequate to enable proper consultation to begin is a question of fact.[55] In *GEC Ferranti Defence Systems Ltd v MSF* [56] and *MSF v GEC Ferranti (Defence Systems) Ltd (No. 2)*,[57] it was held, on the facts, that the information requirement was not satisfied by the employer giving to the union a copy of Form HR1 (notification to the now Department for Business Innovation and Skills).

Quality of consultation required

11.56 It is important to note that the provisions of the TURERA considerably improved the quality of the consultation obligations. This was to improve conformity with European law. For example, previously, s 188(6) of the TULR(C)A only required the employer during the course of consultation to consider any representations made by the union and to reply to those representations and, if he rejected any of those representations, to state the reasons. This was replaced by the TURERA, and the requirement during the course of consultation is now consultation about ways of:

(a) avoiding dismissals;
(b) reducing the number of employees to be dismissed; and
(c) mitigating the consequences of the dismissals.[58]

11.57 It has been held, in *Middlesbrough Borough Council v TGWU*,[59] that these requirements are disjunctive. Each must be complied with. In this case, the council was suffering from financial problems and it resolved that redundancies had to be made. The unions were informed. Thereafter consultation took place about reducing the number of employees to be dismissed and mitigating the consequences of dismissals. The employer had not genuinely consulted under heading (a), i.e. about ways of avoiding dismissals in the first place. The employer was therefore in breach of s 188(2).

11.58 Furthermore, to underpin this, s 188(2) of the TULR(C)A provides that consultation has to be 'undertaken by the employer with a view to reaching agreement with the appropriate representatives'. Again, this was inserted by the TURERA (as amended by the 1995 and 1999 Regulations) to make TULR(C)A comply with the terms of the Directive, which always did require an employer to consult with a view to reaching an agreement.[60]

Special circumstances

11.59 If there are 'special circumstances' which render it not reasonably practicable for the employer to comply with any of the requirements of the supply of information and consultation the employer has to take all such steps towards compliance with that requirement as are reasonably practicable in the circumstances. It is for the employer to prove in any tribunal proceedings complaining of infringements of the section that there were such 'special circumstances' which rendered it not reasonably practicable for him to comply with any requirement of TULR(C)A, s 188, and, also, that he took all such steps towards compliance with that

---

[55] *Spillers-French (Holdings) Ltd v Union of Shop, Distributive and Allied Workers* [1980] ICR 31; [1979] IRLR 339, EAT.
[56] [1993] IRLR 101, EAT.
[57] [1994] IRLR 113.
[58] TULR(C)A, s 188(2).
[59] [2002] IRLR 332.
[60] In *Securicor Omega Express Ltd v GMB* (EAT/0877/02) the EAT stressed that the consultation has additionally to be fair and meaningful and not a sham.

requirement as were reasonably practicable in these circumstances. If the employment tribunal is satisfied that there were special circumstances and that steps as described above were taken, it may find there was no infringement of the provisions by the employer. But special circumstances are not easy to establish and it should not be assumed that this defence will easily be satisfied.[61] As has been discussed (above) in *Middlesbrough Borough Council v TGWU*,[62] the council complied with s 188(b) (consultation about reducing the numbers to be dismissed, and s 188(c) (consultation about mitigating the consequences of dismissals) but not s 188(a) (ways of avoiding the dismissals). The EAT held that it was impossible to conceive of circumstances that could be special which excuse non-compliance with s 188(2)(a) when the employer had time, and did, consult over the subject matter of s 188(2)(b) and (c).

Where the employer has invited the election of employee representatives, and the invitation was issued long enough before the time when consultation is required to begin, the employer is treated as complying with the requirements if he begins consultation as soon as is reasonably practicable after the election of representatives.[63] If, after the employer has invited affected employees to elect representatives, the affected employees fail to do so within a reasonable time, the employer has to give to each affected employee the information required by s 188(4).[64] **11.60**

In one sense, the 'special circumstances' defence is controversial: it has no parallel in the Directive and, therefore, arguably, for this reason, TULR(C)A, s 188 is in breach of the Directive. However, it is provided that where the decision leading to the proposed dismissal is that of a person controlling the employer (directly or indirectly), failure on the part of that person to provide information to the employer shall not constitute special circumstances, rendering it not reasonably practicable for the employer to comply with such a requirement.[65] **11.61**

Complaints to an employment tribunal

Where an employer has failed to comply with a requirement of s 188 of the TULR(C)A (information/consultation) or s 188A (requirements for election of employee representatives) a complaint may be presented to an employment tribunal on that ground: **11.62**

(a) in the case of a failure relating to the election of employee representatives, by any of the affected employees or by any of the employees who have been dismissed as redundant;

(b) in the case of any other failure relating to employee representatives by any of the employee representatives to whom the failure related;

(c) in the case of failure relating to representatives of a trade union, by the trade union; and

(d) in any other case, by any of the affected employees or by any of the employees who have been dismissed as redundant.[66]

---

[61] TULR(C)A, s 188(7). See *Clarks of Hove v Bakers' Union* [1978] ICR 1076, CA.

[62] [2002] IRLR 332.

[63] TULR(C)A, s 188(7A).

[64] TULR(C)A, s 188(7B).

[65] TULR(C)A, s 188(7) (inserted by TURERA, s 34(1), (2)(c). As explained below, in a group of companies it will therefore be obvious that it is the 'employer' that has to discharge the information and consultation obligations. If the subsidiary is the employer it will have to discharge the obligations, irrespective of control by the parent. In *Akavan Eritysalojen Keskusliito A EK Ry v Fujitsu Siemens Computers Oy* [2009] IRLR 944, the European Court held that when the parent company of a group of undertakings adopts decisions likely to have repercussions on the jobs of workers within that group, it is, as stated, for the subsidiary whose employees may be affected by the redundancies, in its capacity as their employer, to commence consultations with employee representatives. But, held the Court, it is not possible to start such consultations until such time as the subsidiary has been identified.

[66] TULR(C)A, s 189(1).

11.63 If, on such a complaint, a question arises as to whether or not any employee representative was an appropriate representative for the purposes of s 188 it is for the employer to show that the employee representative had the authority to represent the affected employees.[67] On a complaint regarding a failure relating to the election of employee representatives, it is for the employer to show that the requirements as to the election of representatives have been satisfied.[68]

11.64 It is clear that where there is a recognised trade union or elected employee representatives, as the case may be, only the representatives may bring the claim.[69]

11.65 This approach as to who is the proper claimant for a breach of the information and consultation provisions is borne out by the European Court decision on information and consultation on collective redundancies in Case C-12/08 *Mono Car Styling SA v Dervis Odemis*.[70]

D. Special Circumstances

11.66 As has already been discussed, there is a 'special circumstances' defence for the employer. We have already suggested that this may infringe the Directive. However, on the assumption it will be applied (although, giving the legislation a purposive interpretation, it may have a very limited meaning) the law seems to be as follows. It is unwise to generalise about the sort of facts which might give rise to special circumstances such as insolvency (e.g. receivership), sudden reduction of the order book, and so forth. The circumstances must be special in each case. In other words, an insolvency or perhaps a sudden falling off of orders might be a special circumstance in one case but not another.

11.67 In *Shanahan Engineering Ltd v UNITE the Union*[71] it was held that:

> The tribunal must keep three stages in mind. (1) were there special circumstances? (2) did they render compliance with section 188 (1A), (2) and (4) not reasonably practicable? (3) if so, did the employer take all such steps towards compliance with these provisions as were reasonably practicable?

It is important that, notwithstanding 'special circumstances', the employer can demonstrate compliance with condition (3) above.

11.68 A case commonly cited to illustrate the narrowness of the special circumstances defence is *Clarks of Hove Ltd v Baker's Union*.[72] In that case, the company had been in financial difficulty for some time and had long been seeking assistance but eventually all avenues proved to be impossible. In the meantime the company underwent serious losses. It was decided that the company should cease trading immediately and 300 employees were summarily dismissed. A receiver was appointed very shortly thereafter. It was held that while it was not reasonably practicable to comply fully with the information and consultation provisions, since the proposal to dismiss and the actual dismissals were simultaneous, there were no special circumstances absolving the company totally from the duty to inform and consult. In view of the industrial tribunal, special circumstances were 'something out of the ordinary run of events'.[73]

---

[67] TULR(C)A, s 189(1A).
[68] Ibid., (1B).
[69] See *Nolan v United States of America* [2009] IRLR 923; *Northgate HR Limited v Mercy* (EAT/0046/06).
[70] [2009] 3 CMLR 1589.
[71] EAT/0411/09. See also *Clarks of Hove Ltd v The Bakers Union* [1978] IRLR 366, *per* Geoffrey Lane LJ.
[72] [1979] 1 All ER 152; [1978] ICR 1076, CA.
[73] Ibid.

These might include, according to the industrial tribunal, the destruction of the plant, a general trading boycott, or a sudden withdrawal of supplies from the main supplier.[74] The industrial tribunal decided that insolvency of itself was not a special circumstance. This decision was approved by the Court of Appeal and has considerable weight.[75]

This principle is underpinned by two further cases. In *Re Hartlebury Printers Ltd (In Liquidation)*[76] it was held that there was no principle that s 188 does not apply to a case where the employer is a company in administration and the administrator proposes the dismissals. In addition, an administration order does not of itself render it impracticable for an employer to comply with the consultation requirements. Therefore, that a company is in administration is not of itself a 'special circumstance' within the meaning of TULR(C)A, s 188(8), rendering it not reasonably practicable for the employer to comply with those consultation requirements. Further, in *GMB v Rankin and Harrison*[77] it was held that the shedding of employees in order to make a sale of a business more attractive (the company was in receivership) is not something special to a particular case but is a common fact in any form of receivership or insolvency. Similarly, that the business could not be sold and that there were no orders are again common features of insolvencies and not special circumstances.   **11.69**

The European Court has also held in *Claes and Others v Landshanki Luxembourg SA, In Liquidation*[78] that Directive 98/59 applies to a termination of activities of an establishment by judicial decision ordering its dissolution and winding up on grounds of insolvency until the legal personality of an establishment whose dissolution and winding up have been ordered ceases to exist. The obligations to inform and consent apply to the residual management of the insolvement enterprise, or its liquidator.   **11.70**

However, exceptionally, if there is genuine uncertainty as to whether, for example, the employer might lose a vital contract, or when a contract might end and so there is a genuine difficulty in predicting when redundancies might have to be proposed, this could amount to special circumstances if inaction over the period of uncertainty postponed the start of consultation and thereby caused a breach of the TULR(C)A.[79] We have already noted (see above) one modification to the availability of the special circumstances defence made by the TURERA.   **11.71**

If the complaint is well-founded, the tribunal makes a declaration to that effect and it may also make a protective award (TULR(C)A, s 189(2)). This is an award covering such employees as may be specified in the award, being employees who have been dismissed or whom it is proposed to dismiss as redundant and in respect of whose dismissal or proposed dismissal the employer has failed to comply with s 188.[80] It is an order for a payment of remuneration to these employees for a protected period.[81] The protected period is a period   **11.72**

---

[74] Ibid.
[75] Further illustrations of the courts' approach can be found in *Association of Pattern Makers and Allied Craftsmen v Kirvin Ltd* [1978] IRLR 318, EAT; *Union of Shop, Distributive and Allied Workers v Leancut Bacon Ltd* [1981] IRLR 295, EAT; *Armour (Hamish) v Association of Scientific, Technical and Managerial Staffs* [1979] IRLR 24, EAT.
[76] [1992] ICR 559; [1992] IRLR 516.
[77] [1992] IRLR 514, EAT.
[78] Combined cases C-235 to C-239/10.
[79] See the circumstances in *Hartlebury Printers Ltd (In Liquidation)* [1992] IRLR 516. See also *Union of Textile Workers v FA Morris Ltd (In Liquidation)* (EAT 484/91).
[80] TULR(C)A, s 189(3).
[81] TULR(C)A, s 189(4).

not exceeding 90 days[82] (a lesser maximum of 30 days in the case where the minimum consultation was 30 days only was abolished by the Collective Redundancies and Transfer of Undertakings (Protection of Employment) (Amendment) Regulations 1999). This is a maximum and it is possible that a smaller (or nil) award may be made by the tribunal even though the employer has breached the provisions. This will depend on what the tribunal determines to be just and equitable in all the circumstances, having regard to the seriousness of the employer's default in complying with the requirements of the provisions.[83] Thus, in *Sovereign Distribution Services Ltd v Transport and General Workers Union*[84] it was stressed that the purpose of s 188 was to ensure consultation took place even where an employer thought it would serve no purpose. So, where an employer sent out dismissal notices on the same day redundancies were first notified and where no written information was given, contrary to s 188, a significant award was made. The paragraph which follows elaborates on the penal nature of the protective award.

No cap on the amount of a week's pay

11.73   There is no statutory cap on the amount of a week's pay for the purposes of a protective award, unlike in the case of a redundancy payment.

11.74   The reason why there is no cap on the amount of a week's pay for the purposes of a protective award is because s 190(5) of the TULRe(C)A 1992 provides that Ch II of Pt IX of the Employment Rights Act 1996 applies with respect to the calculation of a week's pay for the purposes of the protective award. This comprises ss 220 to 229 of the Employment Rights Act 1996. Within that grouping of sections it is s 227 which provides for the maximum amount of a week's pay for certain purposes. But this is only[85] for the purposes of calculating an award of compensation under s 63J(1)(b); an award of compensation under s 80I(1)(b); a basic award of compensation for unfair dismissal, and an additional award of compensation for unfair dismissal; an award under s 112 (5); or finally, the redundancy payment. A protective award under s 190 of the 1992 Act is not included within the list of employment protection rights to which the cap applies. A recent dramatic example of the absence of the cap on the amount of a week's pay for the purposes of a protective award is *Canadian Imperial Bank of Commerce v Beck*,[86] where the protective award of 90 days in the case of one individual amounted to £45,000, the claimant's basic salary being £125,000.00.[87]

---

[82] Ibid.

[83] Ibid., (b).

[84] [1990] ICR 31; [1989] IRLR 334, EAT.

[85] Section 227(1).

[86] EAT/0141/10/RN.

[87] Although the EAT refused to count in, for the purposes of the amount of his actual pay, his substantial bonus of £775,000. The same situation applies *mutatis mutandis* in a case under the Transfer of Undertakings (Protection of Employment) Regulations 2006 in respect of an award for failure to inform and consult under reg 13 of TUPE. Some doubt had arisen whether a cap applied for the purposes of a week's pay on information and consultation awards under TUPE because of the wording of reg 16(4). But in *Zaman v Kozee Sleep Products Limited t/a Dorlux Beds UK* (EAT/0312/10) the EAT considered that, as a matter of construction, because s 227 of the Employment Rights Act 1996 also omits reference to information and consultation awards under TUPE, a cap on the amount of a week's pay did not apply to awards for failure to inform and consult under TUPE in the same way that it does not apply in the case of protective awards in respect of failure to inform and consult on redundancies.

Penal effect of protective award

There has been, moreover, a significant case decided by the Court of Appeal that emphasises **11.75** the punitive effect of s 188 of the TULR(C)A. The purport of this case is that an employment tribunal must start off with the idea of awarding the maximum award available, namely 90 days, and it will be for the employer to argue that this should be less. The effect of this litigation cannot be underestimated.

In *Susie Radin Ltd v GMB*[88] the EAT approved the decision of an employment tribunal **11.76** when it made an award for breach of TULR(C)A, s 188 relative to a protective period of 90 days. In so doing, the EAT tacitly approved the punitive nature of s 194 and agreed that the purpose of the provisions of s 188 *et seq* were to emphasise that an employer must comply with the information and consultation requirements. The implication is that the employment tribunal should start off with the maximum 90-day protective award available and adjust it as to what is just and equitable in the circumstances. In the *Radin* case the EAT stated 'other tribunals may have made a lesser award but on what was called the "jury point" the award made by the tribunal was one which could properly be considered just and equitable in the circumstances'. The EAT also emphasised the very limited circumstances in which the appeal tribunal could interfere with an employment tribunal's finding on this point.

The Court of Appeal laid down more emphatically the rules for employment tribunals in **11.77** deciding whether to make a protective award. Peter Gibson LJ stated:

1. The purpose of the award is to provide a sanction for breach by the employer for the obligations in TULR(C)A, s 188: it is not to compensate the employees for loss which they have suffered in consequence of the breach.
2. The ET has a wide discretion to do what is just and equitable in all the circumstances but the focus should be on the seriousness of the employer's default.
3. The default may vary in seriousness from the technical to a complete failure to provide any of the required information and to consult.
4. The deliberateness of the failure may be relevant, as may be the availability to the employer of legal advice about its obligations under s 188.
5. How the ET assesses the length of the protective period is a matter for the ET, but an appropriate approach in a case where there has been no consultation is to start with the maximum period and reduce it only where there are mitigating circumstances justifying a reduction to an extent to which the ET considers appropriate.

A subsequent decision, *(1) Smith (2) Moore v Cherry Lewis Ltd (In Receivership)*[89] elaborates **11.78** further on the nature and purpose of the sanction of the protective award and discusses the effect of the guidance in *Susie Radin Ltd v GMB* when the employer is insolvent. In this case the employees, Smith and Moore, were employed by the company in receivership as cutters at its factory in Hinkley. On receivership, the employees, including the claimants, were dismissed. No union was recognised for collective bargaining purposes and nor were any employee representatives elected. There was no consultation with anyone about redundancies until they were actually announced on appointment of the receiver. The receiver wrote a letter terminating employment contracts forthwith and advising employees of entitlement to claim reimbursement of outstanding monies from the DTI (as it then was) under the relevant provisions of the ERA 1996. In the absence of a trade union or elected employee

---

[88] [2004] EWCA Civ 180; [2004] IRLR 400.
[89] [2004] ICR 893.

representatives, the claim was presented by the affected employees. The tribunal easily found that there was a breach of s 188.

11.79 In *Cherry Lewis*, the employment tribunal chairman had in mind the guidance of the Court of Appeal in *Susie Radin*. There had been a complete failure to provide any of the required information and to consult. Nor had the employer put forward any mitigating circumstances. However, the employment tribunal chairman considered that it was not just and equitable to make a protective award. As the company was in receivership it was rare for the company to be able to make any payment to creditors in full or for ordinary creditors to receive any sort of dividend. Accordingly, the making of a protective award, whilst it would compensate employees, would be completely ineffective as a sanction against the employer. The company would not be affected in any way by the sanction. The only person affected by the imposition of a sanction from the failure to consult would in these circumstances be the Secretary of State for Industry and the Redundancy Payments Fund. For that reason the employment tribunal declined to make a protective award.

11.80 The employees argued that the effect of the chairman's decision was to remove the only sanction which is provided for in cases of insolvency of the employer and that this would contravene the requirement for provision of a sanction imposed by reference to the relevant EC directives.

11.81 The EAT in *Cherry Lewis*, however, inferred from the Court of Appeal's analysis in *Susie Radin* that the sanction under TULR(C)A, s 189 is meant to be punitive and to have a deterrent effect. Its effectiveness ought to be judged at the time when the failure to provide the required information and to consult about proposed redundancies occurs and not at a later stage when the redundancies are actually implemented and when a complaint is presented to the tribunal: 'The sanction of a protective award in these cases aims to enforce the statutory requirement of consultation and to dissuade employers from failing to comply with their statutory duties to provide information and to consult.'

11.82 In the present case the chairman had declined to make a protective award solely on the grounds that he considered it to be 'completely ineffective as a sanction against the employer'. The EAT in *Cherry Lewis*, however, considered that the chairman in so deciding had failed to focus on the seriousness of the employer's default in failing to comply with the duty of consultation. He took into account irrelevant factors, namely the employer's insolvency, its inability to pay, and the likelihood that the Government would have to step into the employer's shoes.

> The Chairman was, in this way, considering sanction in a retributive rather than punitive or a dissuasive sense and, approaching it in that way, he concluded that the imposition of a financial debt upon a company which continued in existence, even if insolvent, did not amount to a sanction. This approach, in my view, is erroneous. It fails to apply the guidance of the Court of Appeal in the *Radin* case and it contravenes the requirement for the provision of the sanction imposed by reference to the relevant EC Directives. The aims of the legislation would be seriously undermined in cases where the employer was about to enter into insolvency if the Chairman's reasoning were adopted.

Instead of remitting the matter to the employment tribunal the EAT made what it thought was the appropriate order which, as in the *Radin* case, was a protective award of 90 days' pay.

11.83 As is discussed below, the reasoning in the *Susie Radin* litigation, on the protective award to be made for breach of TULR(C)A, s 188 has been carried over to the assessment of compensation under reg 15 of TUPE for breach of the provisions of reg 13 of TUPE (see *Sweetin v Coral Racing Ltd*[90] and the discussion below).

Subsequently, the EAT in *Todd v Strain*[91] (Underhill J (P) presiding) considered that it would be wrong to apply the *Susie Radin* test 'mechanically'. In a case concerning information/consultation under TUPE, Underhill J considered that *Susie Radin* was aimed at a situation where the employer had done nothing at all and it was wrong to award the maximum compensation in circumstances where (as in *Todd v Strain*) some (though inadequate) information had been given and the measures requiring consultation were of very limited significance. In that case the award of 13 weeks' pay (the maximum) was reduced to seven weeks.

In *Lancaster University v The University and College Union*[92] the EAT, in a redundancy consultation case confirmed that the employment tribunal had been correct in adopting a 'top down' approach under *Susie Radin,* placing a serious breach at the top end and looking for mitigation from the employer. This was a case in the university sector where large numbers of fixed-term contracts were not renewed in a cycle attracting the information and consultation provisions of the 1992 Act. In the past the employer, with the apparent consent of the trade union, had not engaged in the full process under s 188. The employer had merely sent out lists of contracts coming to their end and had consulted individually with employees. It was held that the employment tribunal was right to accept as mitigation that the union had for many years effectively condoned the practice of the university in sending out those lists and it was only when there was a change of personnel in the union requiring strict adherence to the statutory procedures that the university was taken by surprise and in the words of the EAT had been 'lulled into a sense of false security'. It was not unreasonable for the employment tribunal to take that aspect into account. **11.84**

Commencement of protective award

There has been some confusion as to when the protected period (and hence the payment under the award) commences.[93] The better view seems to be that it commences on the date on which the first dismissal to which the complaint related was proposed to take effect, not when it actually occurred or, in the case of proposed dismissals that have not yet been implemented, the date of the employment tribunal award.[94] **11.85**

Protective award

Under s 190 of the TULR(C)A, if the employment tribunal has made a protective award under s 189 the employee included in the description of employees to which the award relates is then entitled to be paid remuneration by the employer for the protected period, as **11.86**

---

[90] [2006] IRLR 252.
[91] EATS/0057/09.
[92] EAT/0278/10.
[93] *E Green & Sons (Castings) Ltd v Association of Scientific, Technical and Managerial Staff* [1984] ICR 352; [1984] IRLR 135, EAT. cf. *GKN Sankey Ltd v National Society of Metal Mechanics* [1980] ICR 148; [1980] IRLR 8, EAT. See also *General and Municipal Workers' Union (Managerial, Administrative, Technical and Supervisory Association Section) v British Uralic Ltd* [1979] IRLR 413; *National Union of Teachers v Avon County Council* [1978] ICR 626, [1978] IRLR 55, EAT; *Transport and General Workers' Union v R A Lister & Co Ltd* (1986) IRLIB 21 May 1989, p 11, EAT.
[94] *Transport and General Workers' Union v Ledbury Preserves (1928) Ltd* [1986] ICR 855; [1986] IRLR 492, EAT, preferring *E Green & Sons (Castings) Ltd v Association of Scientific, Technical and Managerial Staffs* over *GKN Sankey Ltd v National Society of Metal Mechanics.* However, this is a matter of some controversy and there are arguments in favour of the commencement date being after the first dismissal actually took place.

specified in the award. The rate of remuneration payable under the award is a week's pay for each week of the protected period and, if remuneration has to be calculated for less than one week, the amount of a week's pay is reduced proportionately. It used to be the case that an employer could reduce his liability under the protective award by setting off any payments made to an employee under his contract of employment or by way of damages for breach of that contract in respect of the period falling within the protected period. In other words, for example, he could set off wages or a payment in lieu of notice. One of the complaints of the EC Commission about the UK's implementation of the Directive was the failure to provide an adequate remedy. Under the principle in *Von Colson and Kamann v Land Nordrhein-Westfalen*[95] a remedy must be effective. The TURERA therefore abolished the right of the employer to set off payments under the contract or damages for breach of contract falling under the protected award and TULR(C)A, s 190(3) was repealed.

11.87 There are surviving provisions for reduction of the protective award. For example, an employee ceases to be entitled to remuneration under the award when he is fairly dismissed by his employer during the period of the protected award for a reason other than redundancy (TULR(C)A, s 191(1)(a)), or in a case where the employee unreasonably terminates his contract of employment over this period (TULR(C)A, s 191(1)(b)). Also, in dismissal cases, the employer may make the employee an offer before the ending of his employment under the old contract to renew his contract or to re-engage under a new contract so that the renewal or re-engagement will take effect before or during the protected period. If the terms and conditions of the new contract do not differ from the old contract or, if they do, the offer constitutes an offer of suitable employment in relation to the employee (TULR(C)A, s 191(2)), then, if the employee unreasonably refuses the offer, he is not entitled to any remuneration under a protective award in respect of any period during which, but for the refusal, he would have been employed. This latter point is subject to the enjoyment of a trial period on the part of the employee and the provisions concerning the trial period here mirror the provisions concerning a trial period in the redundancy payments provisions of the ERA (see above) (TULR(C)A, s 191(3)–(7)).

11.88 An employee who is not paid remuneration under a protective award may complain to an employment tribunal. If successful he is entitled to an order that the employer pays him the amount of remuneration which the employment tribunal finds is due under the award (TULR(C)A, s 192).

Notification to the Secretary of State

11.89 Until 1984, an employer intending to dismiss any employee by reason of redundancy had to give advance information of that dismissal to the then Department of Employment under the Redundancy Rebate Regulations. The Redundancy Rebate Regulations 1984 (SI 1984/1066) then abolished that requirement and thereafter the sole advance notification provisions to a government department (the employer is now obliged to notify the Insolvency Service of BIS, which has taken over the functions of the DTI and The Department for Business, Enterprise and Regulatory Reform (BERR)[96] pursuant to TULR(C)A, s 193. The correct format is form HR1, which is reproduced at Appendix 8.

11.90 Under s 193 of the TULR(C)A, as amended, the duty to notify the Secretary of State arises where 100 or more employees are to be made redundant within a period of 90 days or less or

---

[95] [1984] ECR 1891, ECJ.
[96] Form HR1, which currently carries the banner of the Insolvency Service Redundancy Payments Directorate.

where 20 or more employees at one establishment are to be made redundant within such a period. The period of notification is, respectively, 90 days and 30 days.[97] The Government has amended TULR(C)A, s 193 by the Collective Redundancies (Amendment) Regulations 2006 (SI 2006/2387), effective from 1 October 2006, which obliges, expressly, an employer to notify the Secretary of State at least 90 days or 30 days, as the case may be, before any notice of dismissal has been issued. This is to ensure that the provisions comply with the ECJ ruling in Case C-188/03 *Junk v Kühnel*.[98] A copy of the notice under s 193 has to be given to the appropriate representatives.[99] A special circumstances defence similar to that under s 188 may apply.[100] If there is default under the section, it is provided that the Secretary of State may take criminal proceedings.[101] The duty to notify under s 193 applies whether or not the employer has recognised any trade union and whether or not there are other employee representatives.

The inter-relationship between collective obligations to inform and consult and liability to individual employees for unfair dismissal

In law it has always been the case that s 188 is independent from the question of fairness of dismissal of an individual employee (see Chapter 10). Certainly, a failure to consult for the purposes of s 188 cannot render, *per se*, an individual dismissal unfair.[102] This was recently confirmed by the EAT in *Hammonds LLP v Mwitta*.[103] Nonetheless, failure to consult a recognised trade union/employee representative or indeed, an individual, may be one factor (not necessarily conclusive) in deciding the fairness or otherwise of an individual dismissal. This should be so whether or not s 188 actually applies and may be regarded simply as good industrial relations practice.[104]   **11.91**

The inter-relationship between the Information and Consultation of Employees Regulations 2004 and Information and Consultation Requirements on Multiple Redundancies

The Information and Consultation of Employees (ICE) Regulations 2004,[105] which implement Council Directive (EC) 2002/14 of 11 March 2002[106] establishing a general framework for informing and consulting employees in the EC, clarify the relationship between information and consultation requirements under the ICE Regulations and the requirements under s 188 of the TULR(C)A. Regulation 20 (5) makes it clear that the obligation to inform and consult representatives under the standard information and consultation provisions of the ICE Regulations on 'decisions likely to lead to substantial changes in a work organisation or in contractual relations' cease to apply where the employer is already under a duty under s 188 and the employer has notified the information and consultation representatives under the ICE Regulations in writing that he will be complying with his duty under s 188 instead of under the ICE Regulations.   **11.92**

---

[97] TULR(C)A, s 193(1), (2).
[98] [2005] IRLR 310, ECJ.
[99] TULR(C)A, s 193(6).
[100] Ibid., (7) (as amended by the TURERA).
[101] TULR(C)A, s 194.
[102] *Hollister v National Farmers Union* [1979] ICR 542, CA; *Ladbroke Courage Holidays Ltd v Asten* [1981] IRLR 59, EAT; *Hough v Leyland DAF Limited* [1991] ICR 696 (EAT).
[103] EAT/0026/10.
[104] *Williams v Compair Maxam* [1982] ICR 156; *Grundy (Teddiungton) Limited v Plummer* [1983] ICR 367.
[105] SI 2004/3426.
[106] [2002] OJ L80/29.

Part V

CONTRACTUAL SCHEMES

12

CONTRACTUAL REDUNDANCY SCHEMES

A. General	12.01	D. Unfair Dismissal Law:	
B. Enforceability	12.54	Proceduralism Revisited	12.81
C. Contractual Redundancy Schemes and Age Discrimination	12.70		

A. General

On an individual employment law level, this book is mainly concerned with statutory **12.01**
employment rights such as statutory redundancy payments and unfair dismissal law.
However, as we mentioned in the introduction, there is a common, but not by any means
universal, pattern of extra-statutory redundancy arrangements struck between employers and
employees or their representatives.[1]

Some of the extra-statutory arrangements in existence are contractual and some non- **12.02**
contractual. Either way, they can often substantially enhance basic employment protection

---

[1] *IDS Study 586*, Redundancy Terms (September 1995), on which this section draws heavily, surveyed 14
major organisations and the extra-statutory redundancy arrangements they had in place at the time of its
publication: ABB Rail Vehicles, Automobile Association, Clarks International, Dairy Crest, Digital Equipment
Corporation, Driver and Vehicle Licensing Agency, Greene King, London Docklands Development
Corporation, National Westminster Bank, Nestlé Rowntree, Norwich Union, Rumbelows, Shoefayre, and
TSB. Those surveyed provide a useful cross-section of industry practice. A later study (*IDS Studies Plus*,
'Managing Redundancy', Spring 1999) surveyed practice and procedure, in particular in relation to eight com-
panies: British Steel (sections, plates, and commercial steels), Fujitsu Micro Electronics, National Grid
Company, Transco, British Nuclear Fuels, Eagle Star Insurance, Pace Micro Technology, and Royal and Sun
Alliance. Enhanced redundancy payments under contractual schemes are summarised on pp 10–11 of the
study. It gives some indication of the then practice in major corporates in the UK. The study also revealed that
in addition to enhanced payments, contractual schemes also include consultation procedures, selection criteria,
redeployment policies, outplacement facilities, and, particularly in relation to financial services, transitional
arrangements in respect of fringe benefits such as subsidised mortgage arrangements and concessional terms for
staff life assurance and non-life insurance. IDS HR Studies also feature periodic analyses of company-specific
schemes (<http://www.idshrstudies.com/app/smg/gbn/main>–subscription required.) The economic analysis
of extra-statutory arrangements may be found in a number of studies, for example, in relation to specific industries (the 1984 Redundant Mineworkers Payments Scheme: V Wass, 'Who controls selection under "voluntary"
redundancy? The case of the Redundant Mineworkers Scheme II (1996) *British J of Industrial Relations* 249–
265) and more generally: AL Booth, 'Extra-statutory redundancy payments in Britain' (2009) *British J of
Industrial Relations* 401–418. At the same time, previously generous public sector redundancy schemes may be
trimmed in line with the Comprehensive Spending Review 2010 (<http://www.guardian.co.uk/politics/interactive/
at/19/comprehensive-spending-review-cuts/2010>).

rights, either through the munificence of the employer or through collectively bargained and hard-won agreements. The applicability of such schemes may also vary depending on whether the redundancy is voluntary or compulsory. A redundancy agreement regarding selection can regulate (and make less flexible) the method of identification of those who should be dismissed. A redundancy scheme concerning payment could also considerably enhance the basic statutory entitlement—which is an important issue, as we mention in our introduction, because of the inadequacy of the statutory scheme. Also, extra-statutory schemes can cover such issues as counselling and outplacement services, redeployment policies, and continuation of benefits following redundancy.[2]

12.03 It has not been possible to quantify how many employments are governed by extra-statutory redundancy schemes, but we feel the subject is an important one. We do not purport to include a comprehensive coverage of the area, but we nonetheless concentrate on some key practical issues.

Sources of the rules concerning redundancy schemes

12.04 Extra-statutory redundancy schemes can be contained (less commonly) in individual contracts of employment, in company handbooks, in collective agreements, or simply in the policy of the employer in applying a scheme in practice. There can also be enhancement specified in respect of pension rights upon redundancy under certain pension schemes. We discuss these sources as follows.

The contract of employment

12.05 If a redundancy scheme, whether it relates to payment or to criteria for selection, is contained in the employment contract, an employee is protected to the greatest extent possible. If the arrangements are infringed, he will have a claim for breach of contract, enforceable in the manner suggested below. However, in our experience, it is rare for extra-statutory schemes to be contained in contracts of employment themselves.

Company handbooks

12.06 Some company handbooks may contain a redundancy scheme of one sort or another. Company handbooks are quite likely to be part of the contract, although not necessarily, and the handbook itself must be construed in each case to determine whether there is a contractual right of enforcement. The leading case on the subject is now *Keeley v Fosroc International Ltd*,[3] in which it was held that a provision in an employer's staff handbook detailing a right to an enhanced redundancy payment could be apt for incorporation into the individual employment contract. The Court accepted that where a contract of employment expressly incorporates a document such as a collective agreement (see below) or a staff handbook, it does not necessarily follow that all of the provisions in the agreement or handbook as the case may be are apt to be terms of the employment contract. Some provisions in their contextual setting, may be declarations of an aspiration or a policy falling short of

---

[2] See *IDS Study 586*, 'Redundancy Terms' (September 1995), pp 6 and 7. For a study of the negotiation of a redundancy agreement in Western Australia, see RE Fells, 'Negotiating a redundancy agreement', *Economic Activity*, July 1986, p 10. A survey of Dutch social plans (industry or company redundancy agreements) showed such agreements place more emphasis on maintaining an individual's employability and finding alternative work than on severance compensation: see *IDS Employment Europe 463*, July 2000, p 18.

[3] [2006] EWCA Civ 1277.

a contractual promise. However, the fact that the document is presented to employees as a collection of 'policies' does not necessarily preclude their having contractual effect if, by their nature and language, they are apt to be contractual terms. It is important to consider these documents in their respective contexts, the incorporating words, and the provisions in question. The Court stated:

> Highly relevant, in any consideration, contextual or otherwise, of an 'incorporated' provision in an employment contract, is the importance of the provision to the overall bargain, here, the employees remuneration package—what he undertook to work for. A provision of that sort, even if couched in terms of information or explanation, or expressed in discretionary terms, may still be apt for construction as a term of his contract (provided it is not in conflict with other contractual provisions . . . . Provision for redundancy, notwithstanding statutory entitlement, is now a widely accepted feature of an employee's remuneration package and as such, is particularly apt for incorporation by reference, as the judge recognised in the following passage in paragraph 45 of its judgment:
>
> 'The payment of enhanced redundancy payments was a well-known fact of employment life in the group and, given the frequently with which redundancy exercises were conducted, clearly an important factor in particular to higher-paid and longer-serving employees. . .'.
>
> Equally, if not more important, is the wording of a provision under question in an incorporated document containing contractual terms. If put in clear terms of entitlement, it may have a life of its own, not to be snubbed out by context immediate or distant in the document of which it forms part. Where the wording of the provision, read on its own, is clearly of a contractual nature and not contradicted by any other provision in the documentary material constituting the contract, context is not all.'

In the present case it was material that the handbook used the word 'entitled' and the location of the enhanced redundancy payment details was in the 'employee benefits and rights' part of the handbook. Clearly this was quite different from a procedural, aspirational, or discretionary matter. Finally, it was not fatal that the enhanced redundancy payment provision was conditional on 'details' being found elsewhere. The provision was not void for uncertainty as it identified the means of reference by which the appropriate payment could be calculable when the time came. **12.07**

Conversely, if the employer uses language which is inconsistent with contractual intention, this may negative any possibility of contractual effect. Employers frequently precede the narrative of any staff handbook with words to the effect that, for example, 'this does not form part of your contract of employment'. This would be, it seems, quite a strong indicator against contractual intent. However, in *Peries v Wirefast Ltd*[4] the EAT refused to accept, in principle, that such a 'mantra' (in that case the words 'this is not part of your contract') could prevent the term of the handbook from having contractual status if there were other, countervailing factors.[5] This decision, should, perhaps, be treated with some caution, and as exceptional.[6] **12.08**

---

[4] EAT/0245/06.

[5] Judge Pugsley stated: 'We . . . base [that principle] on the experience of both members both [lay] members who have years of experience of the practical application of the general principles of employment law'. For that reason it may not be the strongest authority on the point. See also *Cameron v Digital Equipment Co Ltd* [2001] EWCA Civ 1751; *Breakspear v Colonial Financial Services (UK) Ltd* [2002] EWHC 1456; *Carter v Ludwig Institute for Cancer Research* [2007] EWHC 1672. See also, however, *Harlow v Artemis International Corporation Limited* [2008] EWHC 1126, where use of the words '*ex gratia*' in relation to a payment was not conclusive (but set against consideration of the documents and texts published by the employer).

[6] For another case in this area, involving the appropriate interpretation of various documents, see *Powermarque Limited v Sykes* (EAT/0954/03/MH).

Collective agreements[7]

12.09   Empirical evidence shows that the involvement of trade union representatives increases the chances of improved redundancy terms whether relating to redundancy selection criteria or improved redundancy payments. The invaluable WERS 2004 Survey[8] found that where consultation had occurred with the union or non-union employee representatives about redundancy, 86 per cent of such consultations covered selection criteria and 59 per cent covered redundancy payments. In two-thirds of cases there had been consultation regarding options for reducing the number of redundancies.

12.10   In 10 per cent of cases such consultation had led to reduction in the numbers made redundant, in 6 per cent changes in the selection criteria had occurred, and in 5 per cent redundancy payments had been increased. According to the WERS Survey 'outcomes appeared, therefore, to be a little more favourable from the employee perspective where representatives were engaged in the consultations'.[9]

12.11   Enforceability of collectively bargained terms has two dimensions, one collective and one individual. On a collective level, collective agreements are not usually enforceable between the parties, namely the trade union and the employer. Under s 179 of the TULR(C)A 1992 collective agreements are conclusively presumed not to have been intended to be legally enforceable between the parties unless the agreement is in writing and contains a provision which (however expressed) states that the parties do intend that the agreement shall be a legally enforceable agreement. This provision has been held to be a substantive rather than procedural matter so that, where the legal presumption applies, any agreement arrived at between the parties will not simply be an unenforceable contract, as one might expect, but not even a contract at all.[10] In labour law this refinement will, for most purposes, be academic; it is enough that the contract is not enforceable to exclude legal action on the collective agreement.

12.12   On the other hand, if the statutory conditions concerning enforceability are satisfied, then the agreement is conclusively presumed to be a legally enforceable agreement.[11] A contrary presumption applies to collective agreements entered into between 1 December 1971 and 15 September 1974. Such agreements were presumed to be legally enforceable unless there was a provision to contrary effect. This was the period of the Industrial Relations Act 1971, legislation that met with considerable resistance by trade unions. As a result, the norm

---

[7]   Under s 178 of the TULR(C)A 1992, 'collective agreement' means 'any agreement or arrangement made by or on behalf of one or more trade unions and one or more employers or employers' associations' and relating to one or more of the following, namely: 'terms & conditions of employment or the physical conditions in which any workers are required to work; engagement or non-engagement or termination or suspension of employment or the duties of employment, of one or more workers; allocation of work or the duties of employment between workers or groups of workers; matters of discipline; a worker's membership or non-membership of a trade union; facilities for officials of trade unions; and, machinery for negotiation or consultation and other procedures relating to any of the preceding matters, including the recognition by employers or employers' associations of the right of a trade union to represent workers in such negotiation or consultation or in the carrying out of such procedures'. In *Edinburgh Council v Brown* [1999] IRLR 208 the EAT held that the deliberations of a local authority's joint consultative committee and its subsequent recommendations to the council could properly be regarded as bargaining or negotiations to achieve a collective agreement.

[8]   B Kersley, C Alpin, J Forth, A Bryson, H Bewley, G Dix, and S Oxenbridge, *Inside the Workplace: Findings from the 2004 Workplace Employment Relations Survey* (Routledge, 2006).

[9]   p 203.

[10]   *Monteresso Shipping Co Ltd v International Transport Workers' Federation* [1982] ICR 675.

[11]   TULR(C)A 1992, s 179(2).

became for collective agreements to include what is referred to by some commentators[12] as a 'TINALEA' clause ('this is not a legally enforceable agreement'). It is thus almost unheard of to find a 1971/1974 agreement which failed to rebut the presumption of enforceability. And, in fact, it would be rare even now for a collective agreement struck between an employer and a trade union to satisfy the current conditions regarding enforceability, even though unions are more willing than traditionally to resort to the courts to enforce legal rights.

Therefore our focus shifts to whether terms from the collective agreement may be directly enforceable by the employees intended to be under its coverage. There are two main hurdles to be cleared by employees. The first is the question of bridging between collective agreement and individual contracts and the second is the appropriateness of terms of the collective agreement for incorporation into the individual contract. **12.13**

As far as bridging is concerned, this can be by mechanism of an express term in the individual contract, or by custom and practice in relation to union–employer bargaining.[13] An example of bridging in the context of redundancy agreements occurred in *Lee v GEC Plessey Telecommunications*,[14] where it was held that the statement of terms and conditions issued by the employer referring to 'provisions of relevant collective agreements' was deemed to have incorporated the relevant provisions into individual employment contracts. In *Henry and Others v London General Transport Services Ltd*[15] the Court of Appeal held that, in principle, a tradition of collective negotiation between employers and the recognised trade union could be sufficient to establish a custom and practice that fundamental changes, including a reduction of pay, could be incorporated into individual contracts by virtue of such collective bargaining. **12.14**

Aptness for incorporation of the collectively bargained term

Perhaps a more difficult question with regard to collective agreements is the appropriateness of terms for inclusion into the individual contract. The basic test is the distinction between collective terms and individual terms. The traditional dividing line is that drawn by Scott J in *National Coal Board v National Union of Mineworkers*,[16] between terms in a collective agreement that are designed and intended to govern a relationship between the employer and the union, and those that are designed and intended to benefit individual employees.[17] The question is therefore whether a part of the agreement is 'apt' for information (individual) or 'inapt'. Scott J considered that terms relating to pay and hours of work would be 'apt'. A conciliation agreement, for example, would be 'inapt'. In *Scottish Courage Brewing Limited v Berry*[18] the EAT (Silber J presiding) regarded terms as to redundancy payments as being 'apt' for incorporation into the individual employment contract. **12.15**

---

[12] e.g. Elias, Napier and Wallington, *Labour Law: Cases and Materials* (1980), p 85.
[13] See *Edwards v Skyways Ltd* [1964] 1 All ER 494; *Land v West Yorkshire Metropolitan County Council* [1979] ICR 452 revised, [1981] ICR 334 CA (on a different ground); *Singh v British Steel Corporation* [1974] IRLR 131; *National Coal Board v Galley* [1958] 1 All ER 91; *Gascol Conversions Ltd v Mercer* [1974] ICR 420.
[14] [1993] IRLR 383.
[15] [2002] IRLR 472.
[16] [1986] IRLR 439.
[17] See also *Young v Canadian Northern Railway Co* [1931] AC 83; *British Leyland (UK) Ltd v McQuilken* [1978] IRLR 245; *Tadd v Eastwood and Daily Telegraph Ltd* [1983] ICR 320, aff'd [1985] ICR 132 (on different grounds); *Gallagher v Post Office* [1970] 3 All ER 712; *Camden Exhibition and Display Ltd v Lynott* [1966] 1 QB 555.
[18] EAT/0079/04.

12.16 Finally, it should be added that it is settled law that, if a term has been incorporated into the individual employment contract via a collective agreement and the employer resiles from the collective agreement, this does not necessarily affect the term in the individual employment contract. A collective agreement can, therefore, continue to be the source of the contractual term in question even if the collective agreement no longer exists.[19] This was applied in *Framptons Ltd v Badger*.[20] In this case, employees' rights to enhanced redundancy pay were contained in a collective agreement which set an end date for its operation. When the collective agreement ended, the employer contended that as a result, the enhanced redundancy terms came to an end at the same time. The EAT rejected the employer's argument. The collective agreement can continue to be the source of individual rights which have found their way into the individual employment contract even if the collective agreement has been withdrawn from or, as in this case, expired, thus:

> … the terms of a collective agreement may continue to operate and bind the parties of the individual contract even where the collective agreement has been brought to an end and indeed even after the employer has withdrawn recognition from the union. In each case it is necessary to construe the terms of the individual contract to determine whether the collective agreement continues to have that normative effect even if it has ceased to be in operation.

> … there will be a very strong presumption that the parties to the individual contract will have intended that terms should continue to be derived from the collective agreement even after that agreement has ceased to have effect if the consequence of not doing so is that there will be no binding contractual terms at all.[21]

12.17 The EAT pointed out that there could of course be collective agreements which were not intended to confer rights beyond the limited period, for example, in relation to special enhanced redundancy terms for a particular redundancy exercise. But if the context is otherwise, terms of employment (including redundancy terms) which are negotiated through a collective agreement and incorporated into the individual contract do not fall away by virtue of the employer's withdrawal from the agreement or its expiry.

A redundancy agreement struck by an employer with unions can obviously deal with a number of matters. We deal with these under the three principal (but not exhaustive) headings of long-term planning, redundancy selection, and redundancy pay.

Long-term planning

12.18 This kind of subject matter in a collective agreement is likely to be viewed as of a collective or procedural nature and so not apt for incorporation into an individual contract. In *British Leyland UK Ltd v McQuilken*,[22] McQuilken was employed in the engineer experimental department in Glasgow. In 1976 the company entered into an agreement with the unions concerning discontinuation of the department in Glasgow. The agreement provided that employees would be interviewed by a member of the personnel department with a view to establishing a list of employees who wished to take up the option of either re-training or redundancy. Then in 1977 the policy was changed and the employees were told they would have a choice of transferring to Bathgate, Preston, or to another site within Glasgow. McQuilken was expressly told that the company would have work for him. He sought

---

[19] *Robertson v British Gas Corporation* [1983] ICR 351.
[20] EAT/0138/06.
[21] *Per* Elias J.
[22] [1978] IRLR 245.

information through his union about his future but was given none; no interview took place, nor was a list drawn up. He then resigned and claimed a redundancy payment. The case partly turns on whether he had been dismissed expressly or constructively because of mere uncertainty as to the future. However, it was held that this could not amount to either an express dismissal in law or a constructive dismissal[23] and on this basis the claim was held to fail. But the other issue was whether the company's failure to implement the collective agreement regarding the planned reorganisation itself amounted to a constructive dismissal. It was held, however, that the terms of a collective agreement are not necessarily to be regarded as incorporated within an individual contract of employment. In this case, the collective agreement was a long-term plan dealing with policy rather than with the rights of individual employees under their contracts of employment. Thus the failure by the employers to interview the employee in accordance with the collective agreement with a view to determining whether he wished to be re-trained did not amount to a breach of the employment contract.

Selection: normative or procedural?

Commonly, unions and employers will agree selection criteria for dismissal by reason of redundancy. Under the principles in *Williams v Compair Maxam Ltd*[24] and many other cases,[25] employers are also encouraged to do this for unfair dismissal purposes in order to persuade an employment tribunal as to procedural regularity and fairness. The question here, however, is whether the collectively agreed selection criteria can be incorporated into the individual contract, and thus be normative rather than procedural.   **12.19**

It may be thought that it is at least arguable that agreed selection criteria should be incorporated into the individual contract. In *Alexander v Standard Telephones and Cables Ltd (No. 1) and (No. 2)* this was held not to be the case, although it is to be stressed that the case in part depends upon its own facts.   **12.20**

In the *Alexander* litigation the employees were employed by STC Submarines Systems. Their statement of employment terms indicated that their main terms of employment were in accordance with the collective agreement negotiated at plant level with the union. This included a provision that 'in the event of compulsory redundancy selection will be made on the basis of service within the group'; employees in a linked action had similar expectations. In 1988, a rationalisation was declared and it was proposed to make certain individuals redundant. The unions maintained that the 'last in, first out' arrangements in the collective agreement should apply. The company insisted that it needed to retain workers whose skills and flexibility were most suitable in the current circumstances. Negotiations fell through and redundancy dismissals were effected in breach of the collectively agreed selection criteria.   **12.21**

In *Alexander v Standard Telephones and Cables Ltd (No. 1)*,[26] and in the context of an interlocutory application by the individuals for an *ex parte* injunction restraining the employers from implementing the dismissal notices until 'last in, first out' arrangements had been   **12.22**

---

[23] See *Morton Sundour Fabrics Ltd v Shaw* [1967] ITR 84 (Chapter 2).
[24] [1982] ICR 151.
[25] See also *Polkey v AE Dayton Services Ltd* [1988] ICR 142; *Holden v Bradville Ltd* [1985] IRLR 483; *Graham v ABF Ltd* [1986] IRLR 90; *Sykes v Hereford and Worcester County Council* [1989] ICR 800; *Huddersfield Parcels v Sykes* [1981] IRLR 115; *Freud v Bentalls Ltd* [1983] ICR 77; *Walls Meat Co Ltd v Selby* [1989] ICR 601) *Langston v Cranfield University* [1998] IRLR 172.
[26] [1990] IRLR 55.

complied with, Aldous J held that there was in fact a serious issue to be decided as to whether the contracts included a term that 'last in, first out' would be applied. Considering *National Coal Board v National Union of Mineworkers* and the distinction between those terms designed to cover the relationship between the employer and the union (on the one hand) and those designed and intended to benefit individuals (on the other), Aldous J decided that the individuals had an arguable case that the provisions in the collective agreement providing for 'last in, first out' were part of their contracts of employment. (On the facts, the injunctive relief applied for was refused on the basis of traditional case law, which declines an employee such relief save in exceptional circumstances (see below).)

12.23 In *Alexander v Standard Telephones and Cables Ltd (No. 2)*[27] the action was continued at full trial, with the employees' claim reduced to a claim for damages for breach of contract. Hobhouse J considered that the seniority provisions in the collective agreement were not expressly or impliedly incorporated into individual contracts of employment. The learned judge held that it was necessary to consider the character of the document concerned and the relevant part of it and whether it was apt to form part of the individual contract. None of the other clauses in the collective agreement was, in the opinion of the learned judge, apt to be incorporated into the individual contract of employment. Thus it would require some cogent indication that a particular clause was to have a different character in order to be incorporated. On the facts, the clauses in question on which the employees relied, when considered within the context of the joint consultation scheme of the procedure agreements as a whole, were not sufficiently cogently worded to support the inference of incorporation into the individual contracts of employment. Many would disagree with this decision if it laid down a statement of general principle. However, the case does, to a considerable extent, hinge on the facts of the case, the wording of the collective agreement, and the circumstances in question. It is therefore suggested that it cannot be conclusively presumed that a redundancy selection procedure is incapable of transposition from a collective agreement to an individual employment contract.

12.24 However, this authority was added to by *LTI Ltd v Radford*,[28] where it was held that a tribunal was entitled to take the view that redundancy terms concerning selection procedures in a collective agreement were not intended to have normative effect and were intended to apply between the employer and the trade unions only. The employer is the famous manufacturer of 'black cab' London taxis, which was the employer's sole product. A new model was introduced in 1997, which was to be introduced by the more modern techniques with a reduction in demand for traditional skills. The employer entered into a number of joint collective agreements with various trade unions for collective bargaining purposes. Redundancies were announced in 1998 and the employer wished to introduce selection terms which included employee skills. After negotiation, the employer conceded that skills for this purpose would be looked at in the context of the job undertaken in the particular trade category in which an employee worked, and not on a wider basis.

12.25 Mr Radford was selected for redundancy and alleged departure from the redundancy selection scheme negotiated in the collective agreement. The employment tribunal considered that the terms relating to redundancy were not part of the day-to-day activities between

---

[27] [1991] IRLR 286.
[28] EAT/164/00.

employers and employees and were not therefore by implication to be taken to have been incorporated into the employment contract. The EAT agreed. It took the view that the provisions were not intended to have normative effect. The redundancy procedures were contained in a separate part of the employer's employment documentation in an appendix entitled 'Company policy and procedure for handling redundancies', away from the substantive terms relating to terms, pay, and conditions. In a broad statement the EAT stated:

> A procedure for redundancy selection is more akin to 'the stuff of' a collective agreement than that of an individual contract of employment . . . .

12.26 In *Kaur v MG Rover Group Ltd*[29] the Court of Appeal reversed an EAT decision on the question of whether a statement in a collective agreement that there would be no compulsory redundancies was a term incorporated into the individual employment contract.

12.27 Mrs Kaur was employed under standard terms and conditions of employment which provided that:

> . . . employment with the company is in accordance with and, where appropriate, subject to . . . collective agreements made from time to time with the recognised trade unions representing employees within the company.

Collective agreements were agreed between the employer and trade unions applicable to the company's Longbridge plant under the names 'Rover Tomorrow–The New Deal' and 'The Way Ahead', dated respectively 1991/1992 and 1997. The first agreement indicated that reductions in manpower would be achieved otherwise than through compulsory redundancies. 'The Way Ahead' stated, in its 'job security' section: 'THERE WILL BE NO COMPULSORY REDUNDANCY'. In rejecting the employee's claim that because her employment contract referred to the collective agreements and because the collective agreements contain the principle that there would be no compulsory redundancies, she had the contractual right not to be made compulsorily redundant. The Court applied the principles set out by Hobhouse J in *Alexander v Standard Telephones and Cables Ltd (No. 2)*[30] referred to above. Thus, where a document is expressly incorporated by general words it is still necessary to consider, in conjunction with the words of incorporation, whether any particular part of that document is apt to be a term of the contract. It took the view that in the present case, the commitment and the collective agreement that there would be no compulsory redundancy was not intended to be incorporated and was not apt for incorporation. Examining the words in their context, they were expressing an aspiration rather than a binding contractual term. It also took the view that the general wording was more consistent with a commitment to work with trade unions to avoid compulsory redundancies than with a direct promise which could be relied upon by individual employees.

12.28 In *Malone v British Airways Plc*[31] the Court of Appeal ruled that certain provisions concerning staffing levels contained in staff agreements and manuals, and in particular section 7.1 of the Work Scheduling Agreement which stated: 'All services will be planned to the current industrially agreed complements for each aircraft type. Future crew complements will continue to take into account in-flight product and cabin crew rest requirements', was not apt for incorporation. Smith LJ was influenced by the commercial consequences of importing

---

[29] [2005] IRLR 40.
[30] [1991] IRLR 286.
[31] [2010] EWCA Civ 1225.

a term of this nature enforceable by a single employee. Thus: 'when one considers . . . the disastrous commercial effect of holding section 7.1 to be individually enforceable, one is driven to the conclusion that the parties could not have intended such a consequence'. The undertaking was meant to be an undertaking by the employer towards cabin crew employees collectively intending to protect jobs and partly to protect crews, collectively, against excessive work demands. 'Thus it was intended, to be binding only in honour, although it created a danger that, if breached, industrial action would follow.'

12.29 Other cases may be more arguable and where the wording of the collective agreement and the statement of terms and conditions or employment contract give a different impression of contractual intent, the position may be different.

12.30 Thus, in *Anderson v Pringle of Scotland Ltd*,[32] a redundancy procedure had been agreed in a collective agreement with GMB union. The employee's statement of terms and conditions of employment issued to him in compliance with statutory requirements made no express reference to those redundancy procedures. But clause 2 of the statement said 'the terms and conditions of your employment are in accordance with and subject to the provisions of the agreement' between the employers and GMB. The Court of Session held that this was effective to incorporate the whole of that agreement into the employment contract so that the selection criteria for a redundancy in the agreement were to be treated as provisions having individual contractual force between the employee and his employer.

Redundancy pay

12.31 It may seem, in the framework of deciding what is apt and what is not, that pay should be considered to be a term apt for incorporation from the collective agreement into the individual contract. And, in fact, the decided cases conform to this analysis.[33] In *Lee v GEC Plessey Communications*[34] the employees were long-serving production employees at the company's Beeston plant. In 1985 the collective agreement negotiated by the unions provided for enhanced redundancy payments. The employers issued a statement of terms and conditions that expressly incorporated general instructions, notices, and versions of collective agreements. A later statement of terms and conditions came into force in 1990 and made no reference to incorporation of collective agreements. Later in 1990 the employers purported to withdraw the enhanced redundancy terms when redundancies were announced without the benefit of the enhanced severance terms. Legal action ensued and a deal was struck between the company and the unions whereby it was agreed that the existing redundancy terms would be applied to the current redundancies but not to any redundancies made subsequent to 31 May 1991. After that date any enhanced redundancy terms would be the subject of negotiations.

---

[32] [1998] IRLR 64.

[33] In *Edinburgh Council v Brown* [1999] IRLR 208, the EAT held that the policy in a collective agreement of a local authority to make a re-grading of a successful applicant for re-grading retrospective to the date the application was made was incorporated in the employee's contract of employment by virtue of an express reference in his statement of terms and conditions to the effect that 'from time to time variations in your terms and conditions of employment will result from negotiations and agreements with a specified union or unions and these will be separately notified to you or otherwise incorporated in the documents to which you have reference'. Mr Brown was sent a copy of the minutes of the meeting between the joint consultative committee and the employer at which this decision was made and it was thereby incorporated into his employment contract. See also *(1) Toach (2) Hayto v British United Shoe Machinery Ltd*, EAT, 18 May 1998.

[34] [1993] IRLR 383.

Mr Lee was made redundant in July 1991 and he claimed the benefit of the 1985 terms, **12.32**
worth £26,643. It was held that he was entitled to a declaration that he was eligible for the
enhanced severance payment; that the 1985 collective agreement had created severance
terms which were apt for incorporation into the individual contract of employment; that a
withdrawal from that agreement by the employer—even with agreement of the union—
could not affect the individual contract of employment; and that the unions could not be
regarded as acting as agents for the employees concerned in respect of the original litigation.
Accordingly, Mr Lee was successful.

There is a long line of authority preceding *Lee* to the effect that a collective agreement can **12.33**
provide the source of a term for the individual contract, and the term would not be affected
by the unenforceability of the collective agreement itself,[35] nor by the unilateral termination
of the collective agreement.[36]

Custom and practice

Apart from incorporation from collective agreements, another difficult issue is whether a **12.34**
redundancy agreement, applied only by custom and practice, can form part of the employment agreement between the employer and the employee.

The question is not an easy one and it is clear that mere unilateral management action cannot, **12.35**
of itself, constitute custom and practice giving rise to contractual effect. In *Duke v Reliance
Systems Ltd*[37] the EAT considered whether a normal retirement age had been established in
the particular employment. In considering whether any policy with regard to the retiring age
had been communicated to employees or whether there was any evidence of notorious
practice with regard to the retirement age, Browne-Wilkinson J stated:

> A policy adopted by management unilaterally cannot become a term of the employees'
> contracts on the grounds that it is an established custom and practice unless it is shown that
> the policy has been drawn to the attention of the employees or has been followed without
> exception for a substantial period.[38]

In 1996 the EAT handed down guidance in the case of *Quinn v Calder Industrial Materials* **12.36**
Ltd,[39] a decision which has been influential as a point of guidance and a building block for
other rulings on the subject. Here, employees were dismissed by their employer by reason of
redundancy in July 1994 and they claimed extra-statutory redundancy compensation. In 1987
the group had issued a policy document to all subsidiary companies concerning guidelines on
extra-statutory redundancy payments. The terms of the policy were not communicated to
employees or the unions, although the terms were generally known. On each of the four occasions between 1987 and 1994 when redundancy occurred, enhanced payments as set out
under the policy had been made. It was a fact, however, that the payment was not necessarily
made automatically but required a decision from higher management on each occasion.
Employees dismissed in 1994, denied the enhanced redundancy payments, claimed that entitlement to the enhanced payments had been incorporated through custom and practice.

---

[35] *Marley v Forward Trust Group Ltd* [1986] ICR 891.
[36] *Morris v Bailey* [1969] 2 Lloyd's Rep 215; *Burroughs Machines Ltd v Timmoney* [1977] IRLR 404; *Gibbons v
Associated British Ports* [1985] IRLR 113; *Marley v Forward Trust Ltd* [1986] ICR 891.
[37] [1982] IRLR 347.
[38] At p 452.
[39] [1996] IRLR 126.

12.37 An employment tribunal, hearing the case under its breach of contract jurisdiction (see below), rejected the claim. It considered that the employees had failed to establish that the policy had been drawn to their attention by management or that it had been followed without exception for a substantial period. Thus, although the employees had expected to receive the enhanced payments, they were not contractually entitled to them. On appeal to the EAT in Scotland, the EAT held that the tribunal had correctly concluded that the employers were not in breach of their individual contracts of employment in failing to make the payments.

12.38 In making this decision, the EAT laid down the following guidelines by way of questions for consideration in future cases:

(i) Has the policy been drawn to the attention of the employees by the management?
(ii) Has the policy been followed without exception for a substantial period?
(iii) What are the other circumstances of the case?

12.39 The EAT considered the test applied in *Duke*, referred to above, stating:

> In a case such as the present, the factors to which Browne-Wilkinson J referred are likely to be among the most important circumstances to be taken into account, but they have to be taken into account along with all the other circumstances of the case. Thus, for example, in our view, the question is not whether the period for which a policy has been followed is 'substantial' in some abstract sense, but whether, in relation to the other circumstances, it is sufficient to support the inference that that policy has achieved the status of the contractual term. Again, with regard to communication, the question seems to us not so much whether the policy has been made or become known directly to the employees or through intermediaries, but whether the circumstances in which it was made or has become known support the inference that the employers intended to become contractually bound by it.

12.40 The question of whether a policy has been applied for a period has to be looked at in the circumstances of whether it can support an inference that the policy has achieved the status of contractual terms. The question of whether the employees know about the policy is not the key issue; rather, the key issue is whether the circumstances in which it was made or had become known supported the inference that the employers intended to be contractually bound by it. On the facts of *Quinn*, the terms were not contractually binding: seven years was the period over which the policy had been applied but only ever on four occasions, and even then a decision had to be made in relation to each occasion.

12.41 Clearly, an employer is at risk if he consistently applies a practice of giving extra-statutory redundancy pay. If he wishes conclusively to avoid the possibility of a contractual expectation, he should, at the very least, indicate that, on each occasion, this is *ex gratia*.

Cases following *Quinn*

12.42 The case of *Quinn* has been applied and elaborated upon in a number of subsequent decisions. In *Pendragon Plc v Pellowe*,[40] Mrs Pellowe commenced employment with Lex Vauxhall in November 1994 as a purchase ledger clerk. On 1 October 1997 the business in which she was employed was transferred to Pendragon under the TUPE Regulations. As a result, she transferred to Pendragon on the same terms as she enjoyed with Lex. On 14 November, Pendragon dismissed her by reason of redundancy and paid up her statutory redundancy entitlement. She then brought a claim for breach of contract in the employment tribunal,

---

[40] EAT, 15 July 1999.

alleging that under her employment contract with Lex she was entitled to an enhanced redundancy payment. The question was whether, therefore, she transferred to Pendragon on Lex terms, which had included with Lex, a right to an enhanced redundancy payment. An employment tribunal dismissed the claim. The applicant called an employee from the accounts department, who gave evidence that over the 10 years during which she had performed her duties there had been more than 100 redundancies and in every case, payment was made in accordance with a ready reckoner table stating entitlements more favourable than the basic statutory minimum. There was no specific reference to redundancy entitlement in the employment contract, although the employee handbook referred to compensation being paid on redundancy where it was not possible to find suitable alternative employment. The employment tribunal chairman, however, found that the document setting out the enhanced redundancy payment scales was not intended for mass circulation; it was an instruction manual for members of management only and although every redundant employee had received a payment during the Lex era, there was no express contractual term giving rise to an entitlement.

On appeal, Mrs Pellowe submitted that automatic payment of enhanced redundancy pay- **12.43** ment by Lex without an individual decision being taken for over 20 years, with reference to compensation being paid in the handbook, meant that an implied contractual term by custom and practice had arisen. However, the EAT said that the documents formed part of a policy and no more. There was no evidence that Mrs Pellowe had accepted employment on the basis of enhanced redundancy payments being a term of her employment contract. The management manual had not been formally distributed to the workforce. The appeal was therefore dismissed.[41]

As a further example, in *Reynolds v London Borough of Haringey*[42] a local education authority's **12.44** redundancy policy had become incorporated into the employee's employment contract by custom and practice on the basis that the policy, which was notorious, had been applied to every case of redundancy over the previous 18 years, during which there had been some 100 instances. In *Marsland v Shropshire Mental Health NHS Trust*[43] the EAT considered that a term of this nature in a collective agreement, on the facts, was neither expressly or by impli- cation incorporated into the employment contract, nor was there any sufficient evidence of custom and practice so as to incorporate that term into the contract.

The area was treated to a review by the Court of Appeal in *Albion Automotive Ltd v Walker.*[44] **12.45** This was an appeal by an employer from an employment tribunal decision to the effect that 22 employees of Albion who had been made redundant were contractually entitled to enhanced redundancy terms on their redundancy. The employment tribunal had decided that, by custom and practice, the enhanced redundancy terms had become part of the employees' contracts. The employees were employed at Albion's Farington site. This site was originally bought by Volvo in March 1989 and acquired by Albion in October 1995 on a

---

[41] Nothing illustrates the vagaries of litigation more than the outcome of another case, *LRG (Enfield) Ltd v Smith* (EAT/344/97), where a different division of the EAT found that the same or presumably similar Lex redundancy arrangements were contractual. When LRG acquired a dealership in Waltham Cross from Lex, it acquired the Lex redundancy terms. The tribunal was unconvinced that the evidence put forward before it was sufficient to rebut the impression that the scheme was contractual.

[42] EAT, 10 January 2000.

[43] EAT/764/96. See also *Jefferies v Powerhouse Retail Ltd* (EAT/1328/95).

[44] [2002] EWCA Civ 946.

business purchase. Between 1990 and 1994 there were six redundancy exercises involving the site. On the first occasion enhanced redundancy terms were negotiated, as the report suggests, against a background of industrial and political action. The terms were that each employee, on redundancy, would receive 12 weeks' pay at £1,000 per annum of service. On this occasion 292 employees were made redundant on these terms and in subsequent exercises, 177, 200, 70, 32, and 12 employees respectively, each received these terms. In 1996, after Albion acquired the site, five employees were made redundant but did not receive enhanced terms. Apparently, the employees received legal advice but did not take legal action.

12.46 The exercise, the subject of the present case, occurred in January 1999. On this occasion it was put to the employer by the employees' representatives that the enhanced redundancy entitlement should apply. The employer, however, indicated that it would only pay statutory redundancy pay. The enhanced payments were not made and the employees claimed the enhanced payments before the employment tribunal. They succeeded. According to the tribunal, the terms had become contractual by custom and practice.

12.47 Peter Gibson LJ, giving the judgment of the court, approved the analysis of Counsel[45] that the considerations, in the light of *Duke* and *Quinn*, are that there are likely to be a number of factors to consider in deciding whether a policy originally instituted unilaterally by management has become contractual by custom and practice. These were:

(a) whether the policy was drawn to the attention of employees;
(b) whether it was followed without exception for a substantial period;
(c) the number of occasions on which it was followed;
(d) where the payments were made automatically;
(e) whether the nature of communication of the policy supported the inference that the employers intended to be contractually bound;
(f) whether the policy was adopted by agreement;
(g) whether employees had a reasonable expectation that the enhanced payment would be made;
(h) where the terms were incorporated in a written agreement;
(i) whether the terms were consistently applied.

12.48 Counsel then highlighted a number of factors in the employment tribunal decision or in the evidence put before the tribunal which met these criteria. Thus:

(1) the terms negotiated in 1990 were the outcome of extensive and high-profile negotiations and, as the employment tribunal found, it was likely that these had the approval of the parent company;
(2) the terms were subsequently applied to further redundancy exercises with little or no consultation with the parent company;
(3) the availability of the enhanced redundancy terms had been drawn by the employer to the attention of all employees in writing at the time of each redundancy exercise and the terms of the policy were well known to all employees at the Farington site;
(4) the policy had been followed for an extensive period of time and it affected, in total, 750 employees, amounting to three-quarters of the workforce;

---

[45] Tim Brennan QC.

(5) the policy was followed for six redundancy exercises and it was intended to be followed in two further exercises which had been announced but not followed through. Payment of enhanced terms was found, on these occasions, to be automatic or virtually automatic from the employer's view point;

(6) all employees had a reasonable expectation that the enhanced redundancy payments would be made;

(7) the policy was reduced to writing both by the trade unions for employees at the site and by the employer;

(8) the employees had an actual understanding that there were enhanced redundancy terms of contractual effect;

(9) the contemporaneous documentation from the employer which referred to terms currently in operation were consistent with an agreed formula being in existence contractually for compensating employees made redundant.

Cases occupying the 'middle ground'[46] will, as has been put by the leading work,[47] be arguable. Some examples, following *Quinn* and *Albion*, are as follows.

In *Warman International Ltd v Wilson*,[48] Warman needed to effect compulsory redundancies **12.49** in 1983. The union wanted 'last in, first out' selection. Warman wished to apply selection criteria to retain what it considered to be better employees in the interest of the business. In the end the employer's criteria were accepted by the unions in return for redundancy payments enhanced by a half-week's pay for each completed year of service. In 1987 a further redundancy round took place. The same enhancement was given by the employer—this time voluntarily. Between 1991 and 1993 there was a rolling programme of redundancy dismissals and, again, the same enhancement was made. This was repeated in 1999. In February 2000 Mr Wilson alone was dismissed by reason of redundancy. He was offered no redundancy enhancement. Mr Wilson claimed the payment before the employment tribunal when he argued that because the enhanced payments had been made on four previous occasions, they should be made on the present, fifth occasion. The employer's practice had become contractual. However, it was material that in relation to the 1983 redundancies it was agreed that the enhanced payments would only apply to that particular redundancy exercise and were not to be taken as representing future company policy. That was made clear to a meeting of shop stewards in 1983 and minutes of the meeting concerned were in evidence before the tribunal. However, the lay members of the employment tribunal considered that a practice had arisen sufficient to convert it into a contractual right. The chairman dissented.

The EAT considered that the chairman of the employment tribunal was right to express the **12.50** view that he did, that the test in *Quinn v Calder* did not support Mr Wilson's case. There was nothing in Mr Wilson's contract, or any other written document he had ever received, about redundancy pay and he did not claim that any oral agreement had been made with him. Therefore, the *Quinn* test for implication of a term by custom and practice was material. The first redundancy package was negotiated to secure the employer's redundancy criteria and was described as a local agreement relevant to that exercise. On the evidence, the employer

---

[46] *Harvey on Industrial Relations and Employment Law*, Division A, para 285.
[47] Ibid.
[48] EAT/1383/00.

had made a conscious decision whether or not to apply enhancements on subsequent occasions. As the EAT stated:[49]

> To be binding, the provision of enhanced redundancy would have to become, by repeated operation, or by recognition, an obligation upon the employer which the employee was entitled to expect. If, on each and every occasion that payment had been made it was expressed to be for that occasion only, the effect of that qualification would be to deny the practice as setting any precedent. It would be to deny the very existence of the custom and practice upon which the claim for incorporation depended. Similarly, the trade union's recorded expression of 'hope' for enhanced redundancy payments, coupled with their denial of any continuing agreement as to the criteria of selection, in 1991 are inconsistent with both those matters already being concluded by agreement. One would be entitlement, and the other, the quid pro quo.
>
> … where entitlement to payment is denied, even repeatedly, although the payment itself is ultimately conceded (for a variety of different reasons on different occasions) it does not, by payment under protest, become an entitlement for future occasions. From the payer's point of view, the fact of payment, if made under protest, does not create an obligation to pay on a future occasion.[50]

12.51   In *Solectron Scotland Ltd v Roper*[51] the boot was on the other foot. An employer, who inherited enhanced redundancy terms on a TUPE transfer argued that, post-transfer, custom and practice was such that the redundancy terms were negatived by custom and practice. The TUPE transfer of the factory in question was from BT. Employees enjoyed redundancy compensation terms as part of their employment contracts. On the transfer the transferee gave an undertaking that the BT terms and conditions would continue. It was accepted that TUPE applied. During the 1990s there were several redundancy exercises when different terms and conditions were negotiated in respect of those being made redundant. In 2000 there was another TUPE transfer to the appellant, Solectron Scotland Ltd. About a year after the transfer there were further redundancies. On these redundancies the employees claimed that because of the two previous TUPE transfers they were entitled to enhanced redundancy terms in accordance with the BT terms and conditions. Solectron argued that the original BT terms were no longer contractually binding as a result of custom and practice.[52] The employment tribunal found in favour of the employees. Amongst other matters, the decision on that point was appealed. The EAT found that the employment tribunal was correct in concluding that the redundancy terms still formed part of the employees' employment contracts and had not been removed by custom or practice. The EAT accepted that a custom or established practice applied with sufficient regularity could become the source of an implied contractual term. Such a practice must be 'reasonable, notorious and certain'. We have seen that employees cannot assume that mere regularity of conduct will, of itself, give rise to custom and practice which will crystallise into a contractual term. Here the

---

[49] Mr Recorder Langstaff QC.

[50] In *Moore and Others v Simoco Europe Ltd* (debarred) (EAT/0725/02) in remitting the case to an employment tribunal the EAT did not find as conclusive (albeit that it was an important factor) the fact that a 50% uplift had occurred in each one of 20 earlier redundancy exercises involving 3,000 to 5,000 employees. It was not conclusive of there being a contractual term, although it was plainly a relevant factor to be taken into account.

[51] [2004] IRLR 4.

[52] The case also concerned another important point for the purposes of interpretation of TUPE as to whether, in settling redundancy claims by a compromise agreement, such compromise agreements were valid given the basic rule that the provisions of TUPE cannot be contracted out of (it was held that a compromise agreement settling a dismissal claim even if following a TUPE transfer could be perfectly valid).

employers were facing an uphill task. They were seeking to displace an existing contractual right by custom and practice. The EAT rejected the notion that the contractual terms had been displaced by custom and practice.

> In this case, there is in truth no custom at all. The employers have not considered themselves to be bound by any specific term. Had they done so they could not have set different terms for each redundancy exercise, albeit only varying in part. Nor could the term be limited by the redundancies being effected within a specific timeframe. Nor could it be within the employer's power to determine and vary the terms. The custom and practice relied upon is neither certain (since the terms vary) nor reasonable (since it depends upon the will of the employer), nor notorious (since there is no consistent application of any of these terms). The appellants are not in fact seeking to rely upon custom to define terms; rather, they are relying upon the relatively short practice of fixing terms for volunteers by reference to payments other than those in accordance with the BT terms, purely in order to defeat a contractual claim to those BT terms.

The EAT was doubtful whether custom and practice could, in principle, vary express existing **12.52** contractual rights.

> We doubt whether a custom can ever have that effect. Even if it can, in our view, it would need very long established practice indeed before it could be inferred that a party had, by implication, accepted the rights conferred by custom at the expense of more favourable rights.

In *William Pentland Stenhouse v First Edinburgh Ltd*,[53] although the facts before the EAT **12.53** were scanty, the gist of the employees' claim was that enhanced terms had been followed, on a number of voluntary redundancy exercises, thus entitling the employees to those terms upon a compulsory redundancy on closure of the employer's paint shop at his Dalkeith premises. In upholding the employment tribunal decision to the effect that the evidence did not establish the necessary degree of incorporation by custom and practice the EAT stated that:

> It is well settled that such must be so clear and obvious and existing practice that in effect the parties both knew that they had to adhere to it and did not consider it necessary so to state.[54]

B. Enforceability

Injunctions

If there is a redundancy procedure in the contract of employment, whilst there may be an **12.54** argument for damages for breach of it (see below) an employee might want to consider seeking an injunction (or in Scotland, an interdict) to restrain the redundancy selection in breach of it. In England the chances do not seem to be good. As mentioned above, in *Alexander v Standard Telephones and Cables Ltd*,[55] individuals asked for an *ex parte* injunction restraining the employers from implementing dismissal notices until 'last in, first out' arrangements had been complied with. Aldous J refused the injunctions on the basis of traditional case law, which declines employees an injunction save in exceptional circumstances. According to the learned judge, the injunction could only be granted if confidence

---

[53] EATS/0017/04.
[54] Lord Johnston.
[55] [1990] IRLR 55.

was subsisting in the employment relationship, and whilst it might seem odd in a redundancy case where the employee is not at fault to raise this as a relevant issue, the learned judge considered that the principle was applicable because *ex-hypothesi* the employer had more confidence in those employees retained than those selected for redundancy. This, with respect, seems a fatuous argument, but the case is the leading authority on the point in England.

12.55   A different approach has, however, been taken in Scotland. In *Anderson v Pringle of Scotland Ltd* [56] the Court of Session saw no reason why a redundancy procedure should not be enforced by interim interdict. Pringle was to make 290 employees redundant. An agreement with the GMB union included a redundancy procedure providing for 'last in, first out'. The employers decided to depart from that scheme and use a different set of criteria for selection. Mr Anderson was selected for redundancy on this basis, but he would not have been selected on the basis of 'last in, first out'. Mr Anderson sought an interdict against the employers breaking the redundancy procedure. Although the employer argued that the proper remedy could only be in damages there was no reason, in principle, considered the Court of Session, why there should be an absolute bar against an interdict to enforce the mechanism of dismissal. In contrast to the position taken by the High Court in *Alexander* there was no lack of trust and confidence in the employee and implicitly if not expressly dealing with the argument of trust and confidence raised in *Alexander*, Lord Prosser said:

> . . . if there were any question of mistrust, the position would no doubt be very different; but at least on the material before me I am not persuaded that there is any true analogy between [the employers] preference for other employees and the need for confidence which is inherent in the employer/employee relationship.

Lord Prosser went on to say that 'it may be very inconvenient or difficult for the [employer] to abide by the priorities that they have agreed to; but they can hardly call it unfair to be held to their own bargain'.

Compensation

12.56   A contractual redundancy scheme, as its classification suggests, is enforceable by way of the law of contract. Recovery would be by proceedings in the County Court or High Court, depending on the value. Claims for breach of contract which arise from or are outstanding at the termination of employment may also be pursued in the employment tribunals, provided that the value does not exceed the current maximum jurisdictional limit of £25,000. [57] In many (although obviously not all) employment cases the enhanced redundancy payment will not exceed £25,000 and a claim in the employment tribunal is apt. An example of this is *Quinn v Calder Industrial Materials Ltd* [58] and other cases discussed in this chapter. [59]

12.57   A claim for non-payment of a redundancy payment cannot be made under Pt II of the ERA 1996 because, by virtue of s 27(2)(d) of that Act, any payment by reference to a worker's redundancy is excluded from the definition of 'wages' for the purposes of the Act.

---

[56] [1998] IRLR 64.
[57] Employment Tribunals Extension of Jurisdiction (England and Wales) Order 1994; Employment Tribunals Extension of Jurisdiction (Scotland) Order 1994.
[58] See above.
[59] See also *Powermarque Limited v Sykes* (EAT/0954/03/MH).

Most claims by virtue of a contractual scheme will be for the quantum of payment itself. But **12.58**
contractual schemes can, as discussed above, provide the apparent right to fair treatment, e.g.
selection in a certain mode such as 'last in, first out'. How could this be enforced? We have
already mentioned that in *Alexander v Standard Telephones and Cables Ltd (No. 1)* the learned
judge at interlocutory stage refused injunctive relief to restrain the alleged breach of contract by
the employer in not following a 'last in, first out' procedure. But if the arrangement is contractual (and see the discussion above as to whether this might be the case) surely a claim for damages for breach of contract would be available. In *Alexander v Standard Telephones and Cables
Ltd (No. 2)*, however, Hobhouse J viewed the employee's claim for damages rather unsympa-
thetically and considered the employee's rights under his contract of 'limited value'. Even if the
employees in *Alexander* had a claim for breach of contract (which was, according to the learned
judge, moot) the employee's claim was limited to the notice period to which he was entitled
under the employment contract. This is questionable; the measure of damages for breach of
contract is what would have happened had the contract been performed under its terms and, if
it had, would the employee have been dismissed? If not, general damages for loss of job security
would seem only fair. In cases of breach of disciplinary procedure the courts are beginning to
recognise the principle that damages for breach of contract arising out of a procedurally defective dismissal are available, at the very least, to compensate for the period of employment lost
over which the disciplinary process would have taken place.[60] It is perhaps curious why this
should not be the case concerning contractual procedures regarding redundancy security.[61]

Contractual redundancy rights and transfers of undertakings

It is germane to the issue of enforceability as to whether contractual redundancy schemes will **12.59**
transfer from transferor to transferee for the benefit of the employee upon a transfer of an
undertaking under the TUPE Regulations.[62] The EAT in *Jefferies v Powerhouse Retail Ltd*[63]
confirmed that a contractual enhanced severance or redundancy payment will transfer to a
transferee under reg 4 of the TUPE Regulations. In the same case, however, the EAT confirmed
that only contractual rights will transfer to a transferee. In the *Jefferies* case itself, the scheme
was non-contractual (see the discussion of *Quinn v Calder Industrial Materials Ltd* above[64]).

Regulation 10 of the TUPE Regulations 2006 disapply regs 4 and 5 (transfer of employment **12.60**
contracts and liabilities and transfer of collective agreements, respectively) to so much of a
contract of employment or collective agreement as relates to an occupational pension scheme
within the meaning of the Pensions Schemes Act 1993. However, this exclusion does not
apply to provisions of an occupation pension scheme which do not relate to benefits to old
age, invalidity, or survivors. In other words, any matter unrelated to old age, invalidity, or
survivors' benefits can transfer under TUPE. The chief example in the UK is certain public
sector pension scheme provisions which provide for redundancy payments/pension enhancement

---

[60] *Gunton v Richmond on Thames London Borough Council* [1980] ICR 755; *Dietman v Brent London Borough
Council* [1988] ICR 842; *Boyo v Lambeth London Borough Council* [1994] ICR 72; see also *Gregory v Philip
Morris Ltd* (90) ALR 455; *Wheeler v Philip Morris Ltd* (97) ALR 282; *Nicholson v Heaven and Earth Gallery Pty
Ltd* (126) ALR 233; McMullen (1995) ILJ 353–363.
[61] See, e.g., *Edwards v Chesterfield Royal Hospital NHS Trust* [2010] EWCA Civ 571—damages beyond the
notice period for breach of an express term (there a disciplinary procedure). (At the time of writing, to be heard
by the Supreme Court on 22 June 2011.)
[62] The Transfer of Undertakings (Protection of Employment) Regulations 2006 (S1 2006/246); formerly
the Transfer of Undertakings (Protection of Employment) Regulations 1981 (S1 1981/1794).
[63] EAT/1328/95.
[64] [1996] IRLR 126. See also *LRG (Enfield) Ltd v Smith* (EAT/34497).

upon the attainment of a certain age. The legal question is whether these benefits relate to old age or whether they are out with the exclusion. After a view in the UK in the EAT in *Frankling v BPS Public Sector Ltd* [65] that such provisions were essentially still retirement benefits, even though accelerated and enhanced, the European Court ruled that this kind of provision is not one related to old age and therefore not covered by the exclusion in TUPE or the Acquired Rights Directive.

Beckmann

12.61 The landmark decision of the European Court was *Beckmann v Dynamco Whicheloe MacFarlane Ltd*.[66] In this case, Katia Beckmann worked for the North West Regional Health Authority, contributing to the National Health Service (NHS) superannuation scheme. There was a TUPE transfer to Dynamco Whicheloe MacFarlane (DWM). Subsequently Mrs Beckmann was dismissed by DWM by reason of redundancy. What were her rights under s 45 of the Whitley Council conditions of service? She was entitled to an enhanced lump sum redundancy payment. The transferee, DWM, did not dispute that this had transferred from the NHS. However, under s 46, there was payable, under the NHS superannuation scheme, an early retirement pension and a payment of a lump sum upon attainment of a certain age (which Mrs Beckmann had reached) upon a dismissal by reason of redundancy. DWM argued that this was excluded by reg 10. Mrs Beckmann argued that it was not a payment by reason of old age (retirement) but was outside the exemption and therefore it transferred.

12.62 The European Court held that any exception to transfer of undertakings must be narrowly construed. In that connection it is only benefits paid from the time when an employee reaches the end of his (or her) normal working life as laid down by the general structure of the pension scheme in question that are excluded. Benefits payable earlier than the normal retirement age (e.g. early retirement benefits) are transferred to a transferee even if they are calculated by reference to the rules for calculating normal pension benefits.

12.63 The second argument on behalf of DWM was that the benefits payable under the Whitley Council paragraph were payable pursuant to regulations made by the Secretary of State and not the employer, and therefore they could not be transferred from a transferor employer to a transferee employer. Here the Court again ruled in favour of the employee. The benefits concerned transferred regardless of the fact that those obligations derived from a statutory instrument.

12.64 The case has potentially far-reaching consequences. The referral concerned was about the transferability of enhanced retirement benefits payable on early retirement by reason of redundancy to employees leaving public sector schemes (such as the NHS) to join private employers. But the decision seems to go wider. It refers to all early retirement benefits intended to enhance the conditions of early retirement payable before the end of the normal working life.

12.65 In Case C-4/01 *Martin v South Bank University* [67] the European Court followed *Beckmann*, and combined, *Martin* and *Beckmann* have a far-reaching effect. In *Martin v South Bank University* three employees were employed as nursing lecturers at Redwood College

---

[65] [1999] IRLR 212.
[66] [2002] IRLR 578.
[67] [2004] IRLR 74.

of Health Studies (part of the NHS). Their employment was governed by Whitley Council conditions. These included enhanced retirement pensions and other compensation in the event of a termination by reason of redundancy. Redwood College became part of South Bank University in 1994. Staff were offered new contracts of employment. But it was made clear that they would not be able to continue in the NHS pension scheme. They were offered admission to the Teachers Superannuation Scheme (TSS), which they accepted. The TSS scheme did not include the redundancy enhancements provided for by the NHS pension scheme. When offered early retirement in 1997 they claimed that they were entitled to the more favourable NHS terms of early retirement instead of the South Bank University terms. After an opinion in their favour from Advocate-General Abler the Court ruled as follows:

(1) Rights contingent upon dismissal or on the grounds of early retirement by agreement with the employer fall within the rights and obligations referred to in Article 3(1) of Council Directive 77/187/EEC of 14th February 1977 on the approximation of the laws of the Member States relating to the safeguarding of employees' rights in the event of transfers of undertakings, businesses, or parts of businesses.

(2) Early retirement benefits and benefits intended to enhance the conditions of such retirement paid in the event of early retirement arising by agreement between the employer and the employee to employees who have reached a certain age such as the benefits at issue in the main proceedings are not old age, invalidity, or survivors' benefits under supplementary company or inter-company pension schemes within the meaning of Article 3(3) of Directive 77/187.

Article 3 of that Directive is to be interpreted as meaning that obligations arising upon the granting of such early retirement resulting from the contract of employment, an employment relationship or a collective agreement binding the transferor as regards the employees concerned are transferred to the transferee subject to the conditions and limitations laid down by the Article, regardless of the fact that those obligations derive from statutory instruments or are implemented by such instruments and regardless of the practical arrangements adopted for such implementation.

(3) Article 3 of Directive 77/187 precludes the transferee from offering the employees of a transferred entity terms less favourable than those offered to them by the transferor in respect of early retirement and those employees from accepting those terms, where the terms are merely brought into line with the terms offered to the transferee's other employees at the time of transfer, unless the more favourable terms offered by the transferor arose from a collective agreement which is no longer legally binding on the employees of the entity transferred having regard to the conditions set out in Article 3(2).

(4) Where in breach of the public policy obligations imposed by Article 3 of Directive 77/187 the transferee offered employees of the entity transferred early retirement less favourable than that to which they were entitled under their employment relationship with the transferor and those employees accepted such early retirement, it is for the transferee to ensure that those employees are afforded early retirement on the terms to which they were entitled under their employment relationship with the transferor.

Thus, to no surprise, the early retirement benefits that had also been under consideration in **12.66** the *Beckmann* case were held to be rights that transferred under TUPE and nor did the employees waive those rights by joining the less favourable pension scheme put forward by the transferee.

12.67   In *Whitewater Leisure Management Ltd v Franklin*[68] a contractor failed successfully to challenge liability for inheriting a local authority-enhanced redundancy payments scheme. In this case, the EAT, at a preliminary hearing, rejected the case of a contractor acquiring a Direct Service Organisation (DSO) business from a local authority that the blanket application by the authority of its enhanced redundancy payments scheme did not bind it as a transferee. The London Borough of Brent, via its direct service organisation, provided leisure facilities under the name of Forward Leisure. The business of Forward Leisure was transferred to Whitewater in December 1995. In March 1996 the applicant was dismissed by reason of redundancy. Under the local authority terms and conditions, the employee was entitled to a contractual enhanced redundancy payment. Naturally, this was claimed from Whitewater. Whitewater resisted liability to make the enhanced payment. Whitewater argued that the Court of Appeal decision in *Allsop v North Tyneside Metropolitan Borough Council*[69] meant that blanket application of an enhanced redundancy payments scheme was *ultra vires* the local authority and therefore not binding on the transferee of the employees of that authority.

12.68   An employment tribunal rejected this contention, relying in particular on the Local Government (Compensation for Redundancy and Premature Retirement) Regulations 1984, reg 5, which allowed Brent to disapply the statutory limit on a week's pay for the purposes of calculating an enhanced redundancy payment. But Whitewater argued that the provisions of reg 5 did not allow a blanket policy to operate an enhanced scheme. Instead, it said, an authority had discretion to make an increased redundancy payment within limits, and only when a person was actually dismissed. It contended that a blanket policy in advance of such dismissals was *ultra vires*. However, this was rejected by the EAT. In *Allsop*, the issue was that the local authority made enhanced redundancy payments in excess of the higher figure based on the actual weekly wage of the employee for which provision was expressly made in the Local Government (Compensation for Redundancy and Premature Retirement) Regulations 1984, reg 5. Brent, although applying a blanket policy of enhanced payments, did not exceed the terms of the Regulations in the amount of such payments. The *Allsop* case was therefore not relevant. There was nothing to prevent a blanket policy of applying a particular enhanced redundancy scheme to all of an authority's employees who were dismissed by reason of redundancy. Such payments were *intra vires* and therefore valid and also contractual as to the transferee and bound *Whitewater*.

12.69   Finally, the European Court, in *Renato Collino and Louisa Chiappero v Telecom Italia SpA*[70] has confirmed that a severance payment calculable by seniority is a matter which transferred to a transferee under the terms of Art 3 of the Acquired Rights Directive 77/187.

C. Contractual Redundancy Schemes and Age Discrimination

12.70   As most contractual redundancy schemes are based on variables including age and length of service these are potentially discriminatory on grounds of age in the advent of the Employment Equality (Age) Regulations 2006, the rules under which are now to be found in the Equality Act 2010 (EA 2010), age being a protected characteristic under s 5 of that Act.

---

[68] EAT/964/98.
[69] [1992] ICR 639.
[70] Case C-343/98 [2000] IRLR 788. This issue will be revisited when the European Court hears the reference to it in *Scattalon v Ministerio dell' Università e della Ricerca* (Case C-108/10).

However, para 13 of Sch 9 to the EA 2010 exempts enhanced redundancy payment schemes from age discrimination provided certain conditions are followed. Basically, to secure exemption the contractual redundancy schemes must mirror in most respects the statutory redundancy payment scheme which the Government decided, itself, was justifiable in its existing, seniority-based format. To secure exemption from age discrimination a contractual redundancy scheme must be calculated exactly in accordance with the scheme in ss 162(1) to 162(3) of the Employment Rights Act 1996; that is to say, the mode of calculation of a statutory redundancy payment. But the contractual scheme can be adjusted as follows whilst retaining the exemption.

First, the cap on a week's pay can be removed or adjusted.[71] Second, the amount allowed for **12.71** each year of employment such as one-and-a-half weeks' pay, one week's pay, or half a week's pay, depending on the age of the employee, under the statutory scheme can be multiplied by a figure of more than one.[72] Finally, once either or both of those measures have been taken the overall figure produced by the calculation can be increased by multiplying it by a figure of more than one.[73] It is therefore important that all contractual redundancy schemes are reviewed to ensure compliance and tracking with the statutory scheme as varied above. Otherwise, the scheme will be *prima facie* unlawful and will require objective justification under s 13(2) of the EA 2010, which provides that the protected characteristic of age may be justified if the discriminatory treatment can be shown to be a proportionate means of achieving a legitimate aim.

A number of cases where the Sch 13 exemption did not apply to a redundancy scheme and **12.72** where the onus fell on the employer to justify the age discrimination are instructive. In *MacCulloch v Imperial Chemical Industries Plc*[74] the employer's redundancy scheme was, on the facts, generous, and had been in force since 1971. Payments under the scheme, according to the judgment, were 'conditioned by two factors'. First, the payment increased depending on length of service (although length of service beyond 10 years was not rewarded). Second, the size of the redundancy payment was also increased with age. Miss MacCulloch was almost 37 years old when she was dismissed by reason of redundancy, having a length of service of seven years and eight months. Under the scheme she was entitled to a little over 55 per cent of her gross annual salary. In comparison, however, a person aged between 50 and 57 with 10 or more years of service was entitled to 175 per cent of his gross annual salary. It was conceded that the provisions of the scheme constituted direct age discrimination and therefore the question was whether this direct discrimination could be justified under what is now s 13(2) of the EA 2010.

The employment tribunal considered that it had to determine whether the scheme could be **12.73** treated as a proportionate means of achieving legitimate aims. In this case these aims were to reward loyalty, to give larger financial payments to older workers because they were more vulnerable in the job market and to encourage older workers to leave, thereby making available space for more junior employees, to avoid compulsory redundancies, and to make it easier to manage change. The tribunal considered that the scheme was a proportionate means of achieving those aims. It relied on the generosity of the scheme and the fact that it had been in force for 35 years with broad consensus. The EAT (Elias J (P) presiding) considered that

---

[71] EA 2010, Sch 9, para 5(a).
[72] Ibid., (b).
[73] Ibid., para 6.
[74] [2008] IRLR 846 noted by M Sargeant (2009) MLR 628–647; Wynn-Evans (2009) ILJ 113–121.

the Employment Tribunal had not applied the principle of proportionality correctly. The tribunal, said the EAT, had to carry out the exercise of balancing the reasonable needs of the business against the discriminatory effects on the claimant. In the words of the EAT:

> . . . the principle of proportionality requires an objective balance to be struck between the discriminatory effect of the measure and the needs of the undertaking. The more serious disparate adverse impact, the more cogent must be the justification for it. It is for the employment tribunal to weigh the reasonable needs of the undertaking against the discriminatory effect of the employer's measure and to make its own assessment of whether the former outweighs the latter.
>
> In circumstances where the direct discrimination is reflected in general laws or policies, the discriminatory effect of the measure will necessarily be greater than where a rule is cast in apparently neutral terms but has indirect discriminatory adverse effects. To that extent, direct discrimination may be harder to justify.
>
> In carrying out the proportionality exercise, it will be necessary to bear in mind that any change in the differential between the claimant's payment and the sum paid to her comparator will necessarily have an impact on the structure of the scheme as a whole. Whilst the proportionality test must focus on the extent of the disadvantage, the balancing exercise will have to have regard to the impact which a different scheme would have on the whole range of employees.
>
> The fact that the laws are fixed and do not vary with individual circumstances is a feature of the scheme which itself needs justifying, although in practice that will not be difficult for such a scheme since transparency and equality and treatment are important principles in their own rights. In assessing justification for such a scheme it is not necessary or appropriate to focus on the matter specifically referable to the individual but not shared by others of the same age or length of service.
>
> It cannot, however, be assumed that just because a scheme in broad terms achieves certain business objectives that this necessarily establishes the justification for those differentials. A most careful appraisal is required in order to justify a discrimination. The tribunal's decision must demonstrate that such an appraisal has taken place.

12.74 It seems that in relation to enhanced redundancy schemes that do not meet the Sch 9 exemption satisfying proportionality, the exercise of analysing justification will be a difficult and challenging issue for employers.[75]

12.75 In *Galt v National Starch and Chemical Limited*[76] the employees received enhanced redundancy payments. The package, which was negotiated to ensure an orderly closure of the company's Warrington site, involved three week's gross pay for each year of service for affected employees under the age of 40 and four week's gross pay for each year for employees aged over 40. Although it was held that the enhanced scheme had a 'broad correspondence' with the statutory scheme, it did not comply with the requirements of Sch 9 and therefore the company conceded that the claimants had been treated less favourably than other employees by reason of their age. It fell to decide whether the treatment afforded was a proportionate means of achieving a legitimate aim and therefore justified. The company's position with regard to the legitimate aim being pursued was that unless acceptable proposals were made

---

[75] See A Baker, 'Proportionality and employment discrimination in the UK (2008) *ILJ* 305–328. And as Wynn-Evans (2009) ILJ 113, 120 states: 'one of the problems prescribed by the proportionality test is its inevitable fact sensitivity which renders specific first instance decisions of limited value'. See also Sargeant (2009) MLR 628, 633–634.

[76] ET/2101804/07.

to the employees there was a possibility of industrial unrest. The purpose of offering the enhanced terms was to avoid that unrest and bring an orderly and satisfactory closure of the Warrington site. The employment tribunal accepted that this was a legitimate aim. The question was whether the less favourable treatment of the claimants was a proportionate means of achieving that aim. It was put forward that older workers ought to be favoured financially because they would find it harder to find new employment. However, the company was unable to provide evidence to substantiate that assertion. The tribunal considered that for the purposes of arguing that the treatment was a proportionate means of achieving a legitimate aim, the age discrimination must be intended to have a particular consequence and that consequence must be the legitimate aim. In this case, it could not be said that favouring the older workers under the scheme was something that the company had considered would be likely to reduce the possibility of industrial unrest, not least because they had not consciously addressed that discrimination. In other words, the disparate treatment was a consequence of the actions of the company—it was not constructed of itself to meet the legitimate aim concerned.

In contrast, in *Loxley v BAE Systems (Munitions & Ordinance) Limited*,[77] the EAT considered **12.76** that tapering down of benefits at a certain age could, potentially, be justified. In this case, an enhanced redundancy scheme directly discriminated on grounds of age because of a tapering provision which applied to employees who had reached the age of 57, and because those over 60 received no enhanced payment at all (the rationale being that they were able to take benefits under the employer's pension scheme at the age of 60). The reason for the tapering and tail off was that otherwise employees close to retirement would have had a windfall had they been entitled to take the full redundancy payment. In other words, they would have been better off being made redundant than if they had simply worked until retirement. The employment tribunal held that the tapering provisions had a legitimate aim in preventing older employees close to retirement from obtaining a windfall and that in Mr Loxley's case the means adopted by the employer were proportionate. The EAT, disagreeing with the way that the employment tribunal had approached the issue of proportionality, nonetheless considered that preventing a windfall can be a legitimate aim of a redundancy scheme. To answer that question the tribunal has to consider whether the treatment of the claimant achieves that legitimate objective and is proportionate to any disadvantage which he suffers. Thus (*per* Elias J):

> We recognise that there are many employers who adopt redundancy schemes of this kind. We do not say for one moment that it may not be justified to exclude those who are entitled to immediate benefits from their pension fund from the scope of a redundancy fund. Moreover, in such circumstances tapering provisions of a kind adopted in this case will, we suspect, be very readily justified. They would be necessary to ensure equity as between those close to retirement and those in retirement receiving pensions. However, it is not in our view inevitable and in all cases justified, for those entitled to an immediate receipt of a pension to be excluded from the redundancy scheme. Ultimately it must depend on the nature of both schemes.
>
> There can surely be no doubt that the fact that an employee is entitled to immediate pension benefits will always be a highly relevant factor which an employer can properly consider when determining what redundancy rights, if any, the employee ought to receive. No doubt in some, perhaps many, cases it will justify excluding such an employee from the redundancy scheme altogether.

---

[77] [2008] IRLR 853.

To answer that question the tribunal [has] to ask whether the treatment of the claimant in this case has exclusion from the scheme—achieves a legitimate objective and is proportional to any disadvantage which he suffers.

12.77　As in *Galt*, there had been consultation with trade unions concerning whether the treatment was proportionate and, as was the case in *Galt*, the EAT considered that trade union approval does not render what would otherwise be an unlawful scheme lawful, but some significance is to be attached to the fact that a trade union and an employer have agreed a scheme which they consider fair. That is not to say that such consultation will be conclusive, because, as the EAT pointed out, the parties might be influenced consciously or subconsciously by traditional assumptions related to age and any justification relied upon by the employer must be 'subject to critical appraisal'.

12.78　The views of the EAT in *Loxley* were relied upon by a different division of the EAT in *Kraft Foods UK Limited v Hastie*.[78] In this case, in a contractual redundancy scheme, there was a cap preventing employees recovering more than they would have earned had they remained in employment until their retirement age. When applied to the claimant it reduced the amount he would otherwise have received by some £14,000. The employment tribunal held that the cap was discriminatory, disproportionately impacting on those approaching retirement age, and was not justifiable. The EAT (Underhill J (P) presiding) considered that the employment tribunal's rejection of the 'windfall justification' could not be accepted. It took the view that the object of the scheme was to compensate employees who took voluntary redundancy for the loss of earnings that they had a legitimate expectation of receiving if their employment had continued.[79] The EAT drew 'strong support' from the observations of Elias J in *Loxley*.[80]

12.79　A counter point to the 'no windfall' justification is the argument that the employee should not be disproportionately disadvantaged and that any pension terms considered to be in lieu of the termination payment are adequate (see *Loxley,* above). This appears to be clear from the ECJ decision in Case C-499/08 *Ingeniørforeningen i Danmark v Region Syddanmark*.[81] In this case, the law on salaried employees in Denmark allowed an employee who had been employed for 12, 15, or 18 years, respectively to a termination payment equivalent to one, two, or three months' salary, respectively. Compensation was denied to employees entitled to an old-age pension from a scheme they joined before the age of 50. Andersen was 63 at the date of termination, and as he was entitled to draw a pension, he was refused compensation. The exclusion applied even if the employee did not wish to retire at that point and even if the amount of the pension would be reduced as a result of bringing forward the retirement date. Andersen did not want to retire early and wished to re-enter the labour market. The ECJ held

---

[78] EAT/0024/10/ZT.

[79] Relying on the statement in *Harvey on Industrial Relations and Employment Law* (para e [9]) that 'the British view of a redundancy payment is that it is in the nature of compensation to the employee for loss of his job; that is to say for the loss of his expectation of continued employment. It is, so to speak, the price he receives for the compulsory purchase of his existing employment.' See also comments by Lord Woolf in *Mairs v Haughey* [1994] 1 AC 303.

[80] In a different context the EAT (Underhill J (P) presiding held in *Woodcock v Cumbria Primary Care Trust* (EAT/0489/09) that a redundant chief executive who was dismissed without full consultation in order that his notice period expired before the date on which he would have qualified for an enhanced redundancy payment could not claim age discrimination. His treatment was a proportionate means of bringing about a legitimate aim of avoiding a windfall payment to someone who had not been otherwise generously treated.

[81] [2010] All ER (D) 99 (Oct).

that the discriminatory Danish legislation was incompatible with the Equal Treatment Directive 2007/78. The measure deprived such workers entitlement to the severance allowance merely because they could, even if they did not, draw their pension.

The measure prohibited an entire category of workers defined on the basis of age from waiving **12.80** their immediate pension in exchange for the severance allowance, the latter being aimed at assisting them to find new employment. The measure thus forced them to accept an old-age pension from their employer. This was lower than the pension they would have been entitled to had they remained in employment, thus reducing their overall income in the long term. The measure therefore went beyond what was necessary to achieve any social policy aims.

D. Unfair Dismissal Law: Proceduralism Revisited

Finally, it should be added that redundancy agreements were particularly relevant to unfair **12.81** dismissal[82] until 1994 since, by virtue of s 59(1)(b) of the EPCA 1978, it was automatically unfair to dismiss an employee if the reason (or principal reason) for dismissal was redundancy and the redundancy applied equally to one or more other employees in the same undertaking who held similar positions but those employees were not dismissed and the dismissed employee was selected for redundancy in contravention of a customary arrangement or agreed procedure relating to redundancies, and there were no special reasons justifying a departure from that arrangement or procedure in the case of that employee. The Deregulation and Contracting Out Act 1994 repealed EPCA 1978, s 59(1)(b), and since 1994 it is no longer automatically unfair to dismiss an employee as redundant contrary to the terms of an existing collectively agreed redundancy procedure.[83]

Nevertheless, it is always open for an employee to argue that the dismissal is unfair under **12.82** general principles under s 98(4) of the ERA 1996 if it flouts an agreement between a union and the employer. Chapter 10 deals in more detail with the importance of proceduralism to the general law of unfair dismissal.

---

[82] See Chapter 10.

[83] One of the last cases under the provision to be heard on appeal was *Ball v Balfour Kilpatrick Ltd* [1997] ICR 740. It is now, on this point, only of historical interest.

APPENDICES

1. Redundancy Payment Ready Reckoner   269

2. Redundancy Selection Matrix   271

3. Specimen Letter: Informing Trade Unions and/or Employee
   Representatives and Initiating Consultation on Collective
   Redundancies Pursuant to TULRCA 1992, section 188   272

4. Specimen Letter: To Affected Employees Inviting Them to
   Elect Representatives   273

5. Specimen Letter/Notice: Informing all Employees of Redundancy Proposals   275

6. Specimen Letter: Informing Individual Employee of Proposed
   Selection for Redundancy   276

7. Specimen Letter: To Individual Employee Informing Him of Final
   Selection for Redundancy   277

8. Form HR1 (Advance Notification of Redundancies)   278

9. Form RP1 (Redundancy Payments: Claims From the
   National Insurance Fund)   280

APPENDIX 1

Redundancy Payment Ready Reckoner

Age	2	3	4	5	6	7	8	9	10	11	12	13	14	15	16	17	18	19	20
17	1																		
18	1	1½																	
19	1	1½	2																
20	1	1½	2	2½															
21	1	1½	2	2½	3														
22	1	1½	2	2½	3	3½													
23	1½	2	2½	3	3½	4	4½												
24	2	2½	3	3½	4	4½	5	5½											
25	2	3	3½	4	4½	5	5½	6	6½										
26	2	3	4	4½	5	5½	6	6½	7	7½									
27	2	3	4	5	5½	6	6½	7	7½	8	8½								
28	2	3	4	5	6	6½	7	7½	8	8½	9	9½							
29	2	3	4	5	6	7	7½	8	8½	9	9½	10	10½						
30	2	3	4	5	6	7	8	8½	9	9½	10	10½	11	11½					
31	2	3	4	5	6	7	8	9	9½	10	10½	11	11½	12	12½				
32	2	3	4	5	6	7	8	9	10	10½	11	11½	12	12½	13	13½			
33	2	3	4	5	6	7	8	9	10	11	11½	12	12½	13	13½	14	14½		
34	2	3	4	5	6	7	8	9	10	11	12	12½	13	13½	14	14½	15	15½	
35	2	3	4	5	6	7	8	9	10	11	12	13	13½	14	14½	15	15½	16	16½
36	2	3	4	5	6	7	8	9	10	11	12	13	14	14½	15	15½	16	16½	17
37	2	3	4	5	6	7	8	9	10	11	12	13	14	15	15½	16	16½	17	17½
38	2	3	4	5	6	7	8	9	10	11	12	13	14	15	16	16½	17	17½	18
39	2	3	4	5	6	7	8	9	10	11	12	13	14	15	16	17	17½	18	18½
40	2	3	4	5	6	7	8	9	10	11	12	13	14	15	16	17	18	18½	19
41	2	3	4	5	6	7	8	9	10	11	12	13	14	15	16	17	18	19	19½
42	2½	3½	4½	5½	6½	7½	8½	9½	10½	11½	12½	13½	14½	15½	16½	17½	18½	19½	20½
43	3	4	5	6	7	8	9	10	11	12	13	14	15	16	17	18	19	20	21
44	3	4½	5½	6½	7½	8½	9½	10½	11½	12½	13½	14½	15½	16½	17½	18½	19½	20½	21½
45	3	4½	6	7	8	9	10	11	12	13	14	15	16	17	18	19	20	21	22
46	3	4½	6	7½	8½	9½	10½	11½	12½	13½	14½	15½	16½	17½	18½	19½	20½	21½	22½
47	3	4½	6	7½	9	10	11	12	13	14	15	16	17	18	19	20	21	22	23
48	3	4½	6	7½	9	10½	11½	12½	13½	14½	15½	16½	17½	18½	19½	20½	21½	22½	23½
49	3	4½	6	7½	9	10½	12	13	14	15	16	17	18	19	20	21	22	23	24
50	3	4½	6	7½	9	10½	12	13½	14½	15½	16½	17½	18½	19½	20½	21½	22½	23½	24½
51	3	4½	6	7½	9	10½	12	13½	15	16	17	18	19	20	21	22	23	24	25
52	3	4½	6	7½	9	10½	12	13½	15	16½	17½	18½	19½	20½	21½	22½	23½	24½	25½
53	3	4½	6	7½	9	10½	12	13½	15	16½	18	19	20	21	22	23	24	25	26
54	3	4½	6	7½	9	10½	12	13½	15	16½	18	19½	20½	21½	22½	23½	24½	25½	26½
55	3	4½	6	7½	9	10½	12	13½	15	16½	18	19½	21	22	23	24	25	26	27
56	3	4½	6	7½	9	10½	12	13½	15	16½	18	19½	21	22½	23½	24½	25½	26½	27½
57	3	4½	6	7½	9	10½	12	13½	15	16½	18	19½	21	22½	24	25	26	27	28
58	3	4½	6	7½	9	10½	12	13½	15	16½	18	19½	21	22½	24	25½	26½	27½	28½
59	3	4½	6	7½	9	10½	12	13½	15	16½	18	19½	21	22½	24	25½	27	28	29
60	3	4½	6	7½	9	10½	12	13½	15	16½	18	19½	21	22½	24	25½	27	28½	29½
61+	3	4½	6	7½	9	10½	12	13½	15	16½	18	19½	21	22½	24	25½	27	28½	30

An annotated redundancy payment calculator is provided on the direct.gov.uk website, using the following link: <http://www.direct.gov.uk/redundancy.dsb>

Source: Department for Business, Innovation and Skills URN 11/508.

APPENDIX 2

Redundancy Selection Matrix

ABC Limited: ESSENTIAL JOB REQUIREMENTS
FOR THE ROLE OF [ADMINISTRATOR]
(Appropriate for use when there is a small pool for selection)

Essential Job Requirements	Employee A	Employee B	Employee C	Employee D
Computer / IT skills				
Organisational ability				
Ability to work in a team				
Flexible/co-operative				
Communication skills				
Attendance				
Punctuality				
Rating key				
4—Exceeds requirements				
3—Meets requirements				
2—Below requirements				
1—Needs training				
0—Unsatisfactory				

Note:

Extreme care is needed in the use of criteria.

1. They must not be based on the subjective interpretation of one manager.
2. They must be capable of being objectively applied.
3. Have the criteria been the subject of agreement, or at the very least consultation?
4. Use of the criteria must be objective. A caution of safety is to have a second blind marker, a review by a third party, and an appeal.
5. Above all, consult with the employee in relation to marks awarded and consider adjusting marks in the light of the employee's response.

APPENDIX 3

Specimen Letter

INFORMING TRADE UNIONS AND/OR EMPLOYEE
REPRESENTATIVES AND INITIATING CONSULTATION ON
COLLECTIVE REDUNDANCIES PURSUANT TO
TULRCA 1992, SECTION 188

[To be addressed to the relevant official at the head office of the recognised trade union or the designated agent for other elected representatives]

Dear [   ]

In accordance with section 188 of the Trade Union and Labour Relations (Consolidation) Act 1992, and further to the communication to all staff on [*date*] I am writing to inform you, as representative for [*insert category of employee represented*] of the Company's proposals to effect collective redundancies.

1. The Company proposes to make the redundancies at [*location*] and envisages that a total of [*number and description*] employees who are employed at [*location*] will be affected.
2. The reason for the proposed redundancies is [*insert reason*].
3. The proposed method of selection of redundancy is [*specify*] and subject to our discussions, the dismissals will be carried out in accordance with [*specify procedures e.g. by reference to a redundancy policy or procedure agreed with the union in any collective agreement*].
4. The Company intends to reduce the impact of the proposed redundancies by [*e.g. inviting volunteers for redundancy, offering relocation/redeployment, etc*].
5. It is anticipated that the redundancies will be made on [*specify date or period of time*]. Redundant employees will receive their statutory redundancy payment [*together with any entitlement to company-enhanced redundancy payments*] calculated as follows:

[*Specify method*]

I would welcome a meeting with you at the earliest opportunity with a view to reaching agreement about ways of avoiding the dismissals, or reducing the numbers involved, and mitigating the consequences.

Yours sincerely

[*signature of employer*]

APPENDIX 4

Specimen Letter

TO AFFECTED EMPLOYEES INVITING THEM TO ELECT REPRESENTATIVES

Dear [   ]

As you are aware from the Company's letter dated [*date*] the Company are proposing to make a number of redundancies and to make related changes to its operations at [*specify location*].

The Company has a legal obligation to consult with representatives of "affected employees", which means representatives of those employees affected by the proposed dismissals or by measures taken in connection with them.

The affected employees are as follows:

[*specify the categories of affected employees, with a brief explanation of why they are so affected*].

As a [*insert description of employee*]. You are an "affected employee" and the purpose of this letter is to invite you and your colleagues to elect representatives for the purposes of consultation. In the interests of ensuring sufficient representatives to represent the interests of all affected employees, the Company has decided that the number of representatives [*and their categories*] shall be as follows:

EITHER

[The affected employees shall elect [*specify number*] representatives]

OR

(i) the affected employees shall be divided into the following constituencies – [*insert details, by reference to category of employee, geographical location, department etc.*]
(ii) each constituency shall elect [*specify number*] representatives [*or detail the number of representatives to be elected from each constituency*], giving a total number of [*specify number*] representatives.

Each affected employee will have as many votes as to the number of representatives to be elected [*from his or her constituency, e.g. there are [2] representatives to be elected from the production department, and so each member of that department may vote for two candidates from their constituency*].

The election will be carried out on [*date*] by secret ballot and any affected employee [*from the relevant constituency*] as at the date of election shall be entitled to stand. The election will take place in [*specify location*] and ballot papers will be made available at that time.

The result of the ballot will be announced as soon as possible thereafter and the identity of the elected representatives will be confirmed in writing to all affected employees. The ballot papers will be counted by [*insert date*] and opened for verification by any affected employee until [*insert date*]. Any challenge to the result should be made by [*insert date*].

The duties and responsibilities of the elected representatives will be as follows:

(i) to attend meetings with the Company to receive and discuss information on the Company's proposals;
(ii) to consult with affected employees to explain and discuss the Company's proposals;
(iii) to respond to the Company on behalf of those affected employees he/she represents and conduct consultation with the Company with a view to reaching agreement on ways or means of avoiding the redundancies, reducing the numbers to be dismissed and mitigating the consequences of the redundancies.

In view of the Company's proposals, it is proposed that the term of office for those elected will be [*insert date*].

Should you wish to stand as a candidate please inform [*insert name*] in writing before [*specify time*] on [*date*].

If you have any queries on the election process or the duties of representatives, please contact [*insert delegated point of contact*]

Yours sincerely

[*signature of employer*]

APPENDIX 5

Specimen Letter/Notice

INFORMING ALL EMPLOYEES OF REDUNDANCY PROPOSALS

[To be addressed to all employees]

Dear [   ]

I am writing to inform you that the Company is currently considering a reorganisation programme which could involve a number of redundancies at [*insert geographical location of anticipated redundancies*] and related organisational changes within the business.

The Company's proposals are as follows:

(i) [*Describe the reason for the proposed redundancies—e.g. 'the closure of the Company's [   ] site', or 'the cessation of widget production at [site]' or 'a reduction in the number of production operatives at [site]', etc [set out details of the number of anticipated redundancies and categories and numbers of employees to be dismissed].*

(ii) [*Give details of any measures relating to the proposed redundancies, e.g. the transfer of production to another site, changes to shift working, restriction of overtime work, reduction in working hours, etc*].

The Company regrets the need to make these proposals, but considers that the steps outlined above are necessary to [*insert reasons for proposals*].

The company will make every effort to avoid compulsory redundancies and minimise the number of employees affected. The proposals set out above will be the subject of consultation with [*trade union*] [*elected*] representatives of affected employees [*and the Company will be contacting affected employees to invite them to elect representatives for the purposes of this consultation*].

Further information on, and details of, the Company's proposals will be provided to representatives of the affected employees in due course. All affected employees will be kept updated on the outcome of this consultation process and will be consulted about the proposals insofar as they affect them individually.

In the meantime, if you have any immediate queries regarding these proposals or any other issue raised in this letter, please feel free to contact [*insert delegated point of contact*].

Yours sincerely

[*signature of employer*]

APPENDIX 6

Specimen Letter

INFORMING INDIVIDUAL EMPLOYEE OF PROPOSED SELECTION FOR REDUNDANCY

[To be addressed to the individual employee]

Dear [   ]

You will be aware from our letter of [*date*] that the Company anticipates having to make redundancies in the near future. It is likely that your position in the Company will be one of those considered for redundancy.

The Company regrets that these measures are necessary but are unavoidable due to [*specify reason*]. It is proposed that over the next few weeks the Company will be consulting individually with all employees affected. The purpose will be to discuss ways of avoiding redundancy or mitigating its consequences and to consider whether alternative employment within the Company is possible.

I would therefore be grateful if you could attend a meeting on [*specify date and time*], at which I will discuss with you further the redundancy proposals and their potential effect on your position.

Yours sincerely

[*signature of employer*]

APPENDIX 7

Specimen Letter

TO INDIVIDUAL EMPLOYEE INFORMING HIM OF FINAL SELECTION FOR REDUNDANCY

[To be addressed to the individual employee]

Dear [   ]

Further to our meeting[s] on [*insert date*[s]] in which consultation about proposed redundancies took place, I am sorry to inform you that the Company has decided that your position as [*specify job role*] is redundant.

Every effort has been made to find you suitable alternative employment within the Company. However, no suitable vacancy exists and I must therefore inform you that your employment will terminate on [*date*]. Of course, if any suitable alternative position in the Company does arise before that date you will be considered for it and consulted about it.

In terms of redundancy payments, you are entitled to [*specify redundancy entitlement*]. This is calculated as follows [*set out calculations*].

If you feel that your selection for redundancy is unfair or inappropriate in some way, the Company is prepared to discuss this further with you by way of an appeal meeting. The decision to make your position redundant may be reviewed in the light of any relevant new factors. Please notify me in writing within seven days of this letter if you wish to pursue an appeal and of any points you wish to be considered.

The Company regrets that these measures are necessary and has done its best to avoid and minimise the adverse effect upon you. Thank you for your contribution to the Company over the past [*years*] and on behalf of the Company may I wish you the very best for the future.

You have the right of appeal against this decision and an appeal must be made in writing to [*name*] stating the grounds of the appeal.

Yours sincerely

[*signature of employer*]

Form HR1 (Advance Notification of Redundancies)

 THE INSOLVENCY SERVICE
www.insolvency.gov.uk

Restricted Commercial

HR1

Advance notification of redundancies
Trade Union and Labour Relations (Consolidation) Act 1992, Part IV, Chapter II

Note for employer

There is a statutory requirement for the Government to assist employees facing redundancy. In order to do this, advance notification of potential redundancies is required from you. Failure to comply with the statutory notification requirements below without good cause may result in prosecution and a fine, on summary conviction, of up to £5000, for the company and/or officer of the company.

The Redundancy Payments Service (RPS), acting on behalf of the Secretary of State for Business, Innovation and Skills, collects the information and distributes it to the appropriate Government Departments and Agencies who offer job brokering services and/or training services so that they can discharge their obligation to your employees. The information about your company is commercially confidential and may be used only for the purpose of assisting those facing redundancy. The other Government Departments and Agencies are bound by the same confidentiality terms as the RPS. You will be contacted directly by your local JobcentrePlus and other service providers in your local area with offers of assistance during this notification/consultation period.

Data Protection Act 1998 We will store the information you give us in a computer system, which will help us deal with it more efficiently. We may use the information for statistical purposes.

How to complete this form

1) Use a separate form for each establishment where 20 or more redundancies may occur within a 90-day period.

2) Use **black ink** and write your answers in CAPITALS, as this will make it easier for us to read.

3) Where tick boxes appear, please tick those that apply.

4) If there is not enough space for your answers, please use a separate sheet of paper and attach it to this form.

5) If the circumstances outlined in this form change, please notify us immediately.

6) Please return the completed form, by post to:
The Insolvency Service, Redundancy Payments Service, PO Box 15425, BIRMINGHAM, B16 6HP

or by fax on **0121 455 0531**

or by email:**HR1@.insolvency.gsi.gov.uk**. Please attach a read receipt to your e-mail if you require an acknowledgement.

NB. If you fax or email the form to us there is no need for you to send the original form by post.
Tel: 0121 456 4411 for assistance on completing the form.

Further information on assistance for employers

For more copies of the form you can down load one from our website on http://www.insolvency.gov.uk/forms/forms.htm

Guidance on redundancy handling and assistance for employers can be found on the following websites:

- Business Link http://www.businesslink.gov.uk
- BIS http://www.bis.gov.uk/whatwedo/employment/employment-legislation/ice/index.html
- Local Development Agency http://www.englandsrdas.com
- Local Skills Agency http://inourhands.lsc.gov.uk
- Wales http://wales.gov.uk/topics/businessandeconomy/?lang=en
- Scotland http://www.scottish-enterprise.com/grow-your-business

Your legal obligations

1) You are required by law to notify the RPS of a proposal to dismiss 20 or more employees as redundant at one establishment within a period of 90 days or less.

2) If you operate from more than one site, each one is treated separately for notification and consultation purposes. An **establishment** is the site where an employee is assigned to work. You must complete a form for each site where 20 or more redundancies are proposed.

3) Your **Minimum period** for notification and consultation for:

- between **20 to 99** redundancies at one of your establishments, is **at least 30 days before** the first dismissal.

- **100 or more** redundancies at one of your establishments, is **at least 90 days before** the first dismissal.

4) You must notify us **at least 30/90 days before the first dismissal and before you issue any individual notices of dismissal.**

5) You must **send a copy of this notification to the representatives** of the employees being consulted.

6) If you have already notified us about one group of redundancies and you need to make further redundancies you should treat them as separate events. You do not need to add the numbers in the two groups together to calculate the minimum period for either group.

7) The **notification date** is the date on which we **receive your completed form.**

8) If it is not reasonably practicable for you to comply with the minimum notification periods you must make every effort to do so as far as you are able. **You must give reasons why you could not provide the information on time.**

URN 09 / 1563-

1. Employer's details

Name:
Address:

Postcode:
Tel:
Email:

2. Employer's contact details (MUST be completed)

Name:
Address (if different to 1):

Postcode:
Tel:
Email:

3. Establishment where redundancies are proposed
(Please tick relevant boxes)

a) Address at 1; b) Address at 2; c) Different to 1 or 2
☐   ☐   ☐
Please write different address here:

Postcode:
Tel:
Email:

4. Timing of redundancies

a) Date of first proposed dismissal [ ]

b) Date of last proposed dismissal [ ]

c) If you have given less than the required 30/90-day notification period please give reason for late notification.

5. Method of selection for redundancy

6. Staff numbers/redundancies at this establishment

Occupational group	Total number of employees	Number of possible redundancies
Manual		
Clerical		
Professional		
Managerial		
Technical		
Apprentices/trainees		
Under 18		
Other		
Totals		

7. Nature of main business

8. Closure of business

Do you propose to close this establishment?

Yes ☐   No ☐

9. Reason for redundancies

Please tick one or more boxes to show the main reason(s) for the proposed redundancies.

A	Lower demand for products or services	
B	Completion of all or part of contract	
C	Transfer of work to another site or employer	
D	Introduction of new technology/plant/machinery	
E	Changes in work methods or organisation	
F	Other (please give brief details below)	
G	Insolvency	

10. Consultation

a)   Please provide the name(s) of

Recognised trade union	Name of Representative	Description of employee they represent

b) If you do not recognise trade unions for any groups of employees please give the name(s) of their elected representative below.

Name of elected representative	Description of employee they represent

c) Have you given a copy of this form to all the appropriate representatives?

Yes ☐   No ☐

d) Have you started the consultation process with the appropriate representatives?

Yes ☐   No ☐

e) If yes, please give the date consultation started.

[ ]

f) Have you given individual notices of dismissal to the employees?

Yes ☐   No ☐

11. Declaration

I certify that the information given on this form is, so far as I know, correct and complete.

Signature: Date:

Position:

Form RP1 (Redundancy Payments: Claims from the National Insurance Fund)

Data Protection Act 1998: We will put the information you give us onto a computer. It will help us to deal with your claim. We may also give this information to your last employer, their representative, and any other relevant government departments or agencies.

THE INSOLVENCY SERVICE
www.insolvency.gov.uk

Redundancy Payments—Claim for payments from the National Insurance Fund
Employment Rights Act 1996

Your personal details

1. National insurance number
We cannot pay you without this number. It will be on your P45 or P60. If you do not have one, you should contact your local Jobcentre Plus office immediately.

2. Sex   Male   Female

3. Title   Mr   Mrs   Miss   Other

If other, please enter here

4. First names

5. Surname

6. Date of birth (DD/MM/YYYY)

7. Full address

8. Postcode

9. E-mail address (if you wish to be contacted by e-mail)

10. Daytime telephone number (including dialling code)

11. Mobile number

12. Name and address of your bank or building society

13. Sort code (xx-xx-xx)

14. Bank account number

15. Building society roll number

16. Account holder's name

Note: We make payments directly to your bank account, as this is more secure. Please see paragraph 28 of the booklet.

Details of the employer who made you redundant

17. Name of employer

18. Employer's full address and postcode

Postcode

19. Employer's telephone number

20. Address where you worked if different from the one in question 18.

Postcode

21. Is your employer:
a) **Still trading?**   Yes [ ]   No [ ]
b) **Dead?**   Yes [ ]   No [ ]
c) **Insolvent?**   Yes [ ]   No [ ]
(This means a liquidator, receiver, administrator, trustee, or Official Receiver has been appointed to deal with your employer's affairs.)

Details of the insolvency practitioner/Official Receiver

22. Name of insolvency practitioner or official receiver (if insolvent)	**24. Full address of insolvency practitioner or official receiver**
23. Telephone number of insolvency practitioner or official receiver	Postcode

Your employment details

25. What was your job title?

26. What was your personnel roll number/staff number?

27. If you are one of the following categories of worker, we will send you another form for more information. (Please tick relevant box.)

a) Director ☐

b) Labour-only sub-contractor ☐

c) Freelance worker ☐

d) Agency worker ☐

e) Casual worker ☐

f) Fixed term contracts worker ☐

g) Homeworker ☐

28. When did you start work for this employer? (DD/MM/YYYY)

29. When was the last day you worked? (DD/MM/YYYY)

30. Date your employment ended if different from the date you last worked (DD/MM/YYYY)

31. Did your employer give you notice?

Yes ☐ No ☐

32. If yes, when did your employer give you notice? (DD/MM/YYYY)

33. What was your gross basic rate of pay (before taking off tax and national insurance and without overtime)?

£ [   ] every [hour / day / week / month / year]

34. Did your pay include any bonus or commission?

Yes ☐ No ☐

35. Give details of the amount and type of bonus or commission earned and when it was paid.

36. How many hours and days did you normally work each week? (Do not include overtime.)

[hours] [days]

37. If you did not work the same hours or days each week, please give details of your shift pattern (e.g. week 1 Monday to Wednesday, week 2 Thursday and Friday)

38. As part of your contract did your employer have to provide you with regular overtime?

Yes ☐ No ☐

39. In return, were you required to work overtime?

Yes ☐ No ☐

40. If you did have to work overtime as part of your contract, please give details.

[hours] every [week / month / year]

41. If there were any breaks in your employment with this employer, please give dates and reasons.

From	To	Reason

Your employment details continued

42. If you have ever been on strike during your employment with this employer, please give dates and reasons.	44. Did you pay UK class 1 national insurance contributions for the whole time you were abroad?

42. If you have ever been on strike during your employment with this employer, please give dates and reasons.

From	To	Reason

43. If you have ever worked abroad for this employer for periods of more than a month, please give dates and countries.

From	To	Country

44. Did you pay UK class 1 national insurance contributions for the whole time you were abroad?

Yes ☐   No ☐   Don't know ☐

45. If no, please give dates where you did not pay UK contributions below.

From	To

Business transfer details/new employment details

46. Have you had a new job since you were made redundant?

Yes ☐   No ☐   (if no go to Q54)

47. If you have started a new job since this employer made you redundant, please give details below. (This includes self-employment or setting up your own business from which you have not yet received money.)
a) Full address of new employer (or state if self employed)

Postcode

b) Telephone number of new employer

c) When did you start the new job? (DD/MM/YYYY)

48. Who offered you the job?

49. Was the change of ownership under the Transfer of Undertakings (Protection of Employment) Regulations 2006?

Yes ☐   No ☐

50. Has your job remained the same?

Yes ☐   No ☐

51. Are you dealing with the same customers?

Yes ☐   No ☐

52. Have your terms and conditions of employment changed?

Yes ☐   No ☐

53. If yes, please give details of changes below.

54. Have you refused an offer of work with the new employer?

Yes ☐   No ☐

Your claims for a redundancy payment from the National Insurance Fund

55. To qualify for a redundancy payment you must:
- have been made redundant; and
- have worked continuously for your employer for 2 years or more; and
- made a written claim to your employer for your redundancy payment, or made a complaint to an employment tribunal, within 6 months of your dismissal.

Are you claiming redundancy pay?

Yes ☐   No ☐

Note: you have not been dismissed as redundant if you transfer to a new employer under the Transfer of Undertakings (Protection of Employment) Regulations 2006.

56. If your employer has paid you part of your redundancy payment, please give details below:

Amount	Date

57. Please give us the date on which you wrote to your employer, or complained to an employment tribunal. (DD/MM/YYYY)

57. If you complained to an employment tribunal please send us a copy of the decision with this claim form.

Your claims for wages, holiday pay, notice pay, and a basic award for unfair dismissal from the National Insurance Fund

58. Are you owed any holiday pay? Yes ☐ No ☐ (If no, go to Q69)	**69. Are you owed any wages?** Yes ☐ No ☐

59. What is the start date of your holiday year? (DD/MM/YYYY)

☐☐☐☐☐☐☐☐

If yes, please give details of the dates and gross amounts you are owed. (See paragraph 15 of the booklet for details of what you can claim.)

From	To	Days	Amount

60. How many days' holiday per year (excluding bank holidays) were you entitled to?

61. Under your contract of employment, were you allowed to carry forward untaken holiday entitlement from your previous holiday year?

Yes ☐   No ☐

70. Did your employer give you your full statutory notice of your job ending? (See paragraph 19 for details of your statutory (legal) entitlement.)

Yes ☐   No ☐

62. If yes, how many days were you allowed to carry forward each year?

71. If no, do you want to claim compensation for loss of notice?

Yes ☐   No ☐

If yes, you are expected to keep your loss to a minimum by doing your best to find a new job or by claiming jobseeker's allowance. A claim form for notice pay will be sent to you at the end of your statutory notice period.

63. Have you carried forward any days this year?

Yes ☐   No ☐

64. If yes, how many days did you carry forward?

72. Do you wish to claim for a tribunal's unpaid basic award for unfair dismissal?

Yes ☐   No ☐

65. How many days' holiday have you taken this year?

If so, please enclose a copy of the tribunal award with your claim form. If you made a settlement through ACAS or a compromise agreement with your employer, please provide a copy of the agreement.

66. Of the days taken, how many have not been paid?

67. How many days are you owed up to your termination date?

73. Do you owe your employer any money? If so, it has to be taken into account before we can pay you. Please give details below.

Amount	Reason you owe your employer money

68. How many bank holidays have you taken but not been paid?

Declaration—Please read this carefully before signing.

- The information I have given on this form is correct as far as I know. You may check this information with my ex-employer, their representatives, government departments, and agencies.
- This is my only application for payment for this employment.
- I understand that you may take legal action against me if I have made a false statement on this form.

Your signature	Date

Now send the form to the Redundancy Payments Office (see Appendix 1 for address), or to the insolvency practitioner if instructed to do so.

INDEX

ACAS (Advisory, Conciliation and Arbitration Service) 8.*n2*, 10.38–42

age, discrimination on grounds of 8.13–15, 10.145, 10.151–153
  contractual redundancy schemes 12.70–80

agents, employment status 1.137

alternative employment 10.43–45, 10.176–184
  broadview 10.180–183
  duty to consult 10.117–118, 11.09
  failure to seek 10.176
  importance 10.177
  limited view 10.178–179
  opportunity of finding 10.88, 10.117–118
  time off to look for *see* time off
  unreasonable refusal 9.16–17

apprenticeships 1.119–122
  modern 1.120–122
  traditional 1.119

associated employers, offers from 4.19–21

attendance, as criterion for redundancy 10.157, 10.163

attitude to work, as criterion for redundancy 10.108–109, 10.144

automatically unfair dismissal 10.231–256
  circumstances giving rise to 10.232–233
  on grounds of union activities 10.234–247
  on grounds relating to pregnancy/ childbirth 10.248–256

bumping 3.94–106
  defined 3.95
  justification 3.102
  and redundancy payment entitlement 3.97–106, 3.107
  and unfair dismissal 3.96

casual workers 1.29–47
  absence of legal definition 1.29
  employee status 1.30–31, 1.37–41, 1.44–4
  mutuality of obligation test 1.32–47, 1.78

closure of business
  involuntary 9.08
  transfer/redundancy resulting from 3.09–11, 3.23–31

collective agreements 12.09–14
  (alleged) breaches 12.16, 12.18, 12.25
  aptness of terms for incorporation 12.15–17
  bridging 12.14
  enforceability 12.11–13
  fixed-term 12.16–17
  long-term planning 12.18–30
  redundancy pay 12.31–33

common law
  and lay-off/short-time work 6.03

trial re-employment periods 4.51–57

company handbooks 12.06–08

compensation (contractual redundancy schemes) 12.56–58

compensation (for unfair dismissal) 10.206–230
  additional award 10.228–230
  basic award 10.207–210
  calculation 10.207, 10.212, 10.226–227
  compensatory award 10.211–220
  deductions 10.208, 10.222
  discriminatory issues 10.221–227
  limitation 10.213–215
  for work time lost prior to re-employment 10.205

conciliation 9.39

consultation 10.78–118
  absence 10.90–92; employer's obligation to justify 10.93–94; need for exceptional reasons 10.99–104
  breakdown due to industrial action 10.105–107
  complaints to employment tribunal 11.63–66
  content/standards 10.95–96
  distinguished from early warning 10.85–89
  employee representation 11.34–40
  EU requirements 11.01–92
  futility of 10.97–98
  importance of 10.79–80, 10.92, 10.104, 10.108–109
  inadequate 10.110
  with individual employees 10.90–96, 11.91
  information requirements 11.54–55
  interrelation between regulations 11.92
  mitigation of responsibilities 11.60–62
  on multiple redundancies 11.01–92
  obligation to complete before notice of dismissal 11.41–46
  '*Polkey* exception' 10.94, 10.97–107
  premature 10.82, 10.91
  quality requirements 11.56–59
  on reasons for redundancies 11.47–53
  special circumstances 11.60–62, 11.67–72
  statutory minimum periods 11.27
  summary of principles 10.95, 10.111

continuous employment 1.01, 1.145–158
  breaks in continuity 1.149–157
  calculation 1.146–148
  non-standard workers 1.158
  one-year qualifying period (for unfair dismissal) 10.03–16
  two-year qualifying period (for redundancy payment) 1.145, 10.04

contract test
  favoured by courts 3.10–22, 3.107
  limits 3.23–29
  movement away from 3.30–31, 3.103–106, 3.107

contract test (*cont.*)
  vs geographical test 3.09–11, 3.32–34
  vs job function test 3.77–93
  see also mobility clauses
contracts of employment 1.07–09
  absence 1.31, 1.37–40, 1.59, 1.68–69, 1.72
  academic studies 1.05
  between agencies and workers 1.51–60
  breach 2.07, 2.11, 3.64, 4.51–55, 6.03,
      6.15, 9.02, 10.80
  defined 1.07
  disregarding of provisions 1.99–112
  distinguished from service contracts 1.08
  effect of lay-off/short-time work on 6.02
  express lay-off/short-time provisions 6.04–06
  factors inconsistent with 1.65
  fixed-term, non-renewal 2.06, 4.57, 11.10
  frustration of performance 2.08–09
  illegality 1.138–144
  implied 1.74
  implied terms 6.07–14
  between individual and client end user 1.61–90
  new, re-employment under 4.56–57
  non-standard workers 1.113–115
  (offers of) renewal 4.11–15
  redundancy schemes 12.05
  sham provisions 1.78, 1.92, 1.95, 1.99–112
  termination 2.01–27, 6.24–25; by mutual
      agreement 2.18–27, 10.18; notice of 2.12–17,
      6.24–25; by operation of law 2.08–09
  see also contractual redundancy schemes
contractual redundancy schemes 12.01–82
  age discrimination 12.70–80
  collective agreements 12.09–33
  company handbooks 12.06–08
  compensation 12.56–58
  contracts of employment 12.05
  custom and practice 12.34–53
  enforceability 12.11–13, 12.54–69
  injunctions 12.54–55
  range/diversity 12.*n1*
  sources of rules 12.04–14
  transfer of undertakings 12.59–69
  and unfair dismissal 12.81–82
  see also collective agreements

Danish law 11.25
death 5.01–06
  of employee 5.04–06, 8.11
  of employer 5.02–03, 5.*n8*
defences *see* reasonableness; special circumstances;
    unfair dismissal
definition of redundancy 3.01–04, 11.05, 11.07
  analysed 3.08–76
  see also diminution in requirements; location of
      employment
diminution in requirements 3.35–76
  anticipation 3.76
  hours of work 3.44–46
  number of employees 3.37–41, 3.68, 3.98
  work of a particular kind 3.42, 3.47–51

disability, discrimination in grounds of 4.*n8*, 10.156
discrimination
  age-based 8.13–15, 10.145, 10.151–153,
      12.70–80
  compensation for 10.221–227
  disability-based 4.*n8*, 10.156
  gender-based 10.05–16, 10.145, 10.157–158
  racial 10.159
  religious 10.147–149
  in selection criteria 10.145–160, 10.221–227
dismissal 2.01–27
  advance warning 2.10–11, 10.78–90
  alternatives to 10.43–45, 10.*n27*
  ambiguity of wording 2.03
  anticipation of expiry of notice 2.12–17
  consensual 10.17–23
  constructive 2.07, 2.11, 3.64, 10.81, 12.18
  contemplated 11.14–20
  death of employer as constituting 5.02
  defined 10.17
  and definition of redundancy 2.01, 3.01–04
  despite availability of work 3.47–51, 10.34–35
  distinguished from voluntary redundancy 2.18–27
  effective date 2.05, 8.03–11
  on grounds of misconduct/strike action 7.03–15
  by non-renewal of fixed-term contract 2.06
  notice of 2.10–11, 7.12–15
  during notice period 7.09, 7.11, 7.13–15
  reason for 10.24–26; establishing 10.28–36
  standard of reasonableness 10.37–77
  summary 8.08; employers' right of 7.06
  with/without notice 2.04–05
  see also unfair dismissal
downsizing 3.37–41

economic reality test 1.18–20
efficiency, as criterion for redundancy 10.164–166
eligibility 1.01–02
employee(s)
  cessation/diminution of requirements 3.35–76
  change of job function 3.52–58
  death 5.04–06, 8.11
  definitions 1.07, 1.15–20
  election of representatives 11.39–40, 11.61
  excluded categories 1.01
  expansion of categories 1.10–13
  failure to comply with reasonable requirements
      of employer 9.18
  qualification for redundancy payment 1.01
  recruitment in anticipation of diminishing
      need 3.76
  reduced hours 3.44–46
  reduced numbers 3.37–41, 3.68
  replacement by outside contractors 3.42–43
  representation 11.34–40, 11.63–66
  unique position within company 10.*n192*
employer(s)
  additional recourses in event of strike 7.13–15
  counter notice to redundancy payment
      claims 6.22–23
  death 5.02–03; Spanish law 5.*n8*

failure/inability to make redundancy
      payments 8.32–33
   mitigation of responsibilities 11.60–62, 11.67–72
   proceedings against, dismissal on
      grounds of 10.232–233
   reasonableness of conduct 10.46–66
   size/administrative resources 10.73–77
   unreasonable refusal of time off/
      remuneration 9.29–39
   see also consultation; reasonableness; special
      circumstances
employment, definitions 1.07, 1.10–13
   see also continuous employment; contracts of
      employment; employment relationships;
      employment status; location of employment
employment agency workers
   improvements to position 1.88–90
   status vis-à-vis agency 1.52–60
   status vis-à-vis client 1.61–90
   Temporary Worker Agreements 1.76
employment relationship(s)
   historical context 1.14–20
   statutory definitions 1.07–13
   types 1.03–06
employment status
   agents 1.137
   apprentices 1.119–122
   control test 1.15, 1.21–22, 1.25
   economic reality test 1.18–20
   expansion of scope 1.10–12
   freelance workers 1.116–117
   multi-factor approach 1.21–27
   mutual obligation test 1.25, 1.27, 1.28–90
   non-standard workers 1.113–115
   office holders 1.123–127
   organisational test 1.16–17, 1.25
   partners 1.135–136
   personal services test 1.23–24, 1.91–98
   risk allocation 1.*n19*
   shareholders 1.128–134
   tests for 1.02, 1.09, 1.14–20, 1.21–137;
      summarised 1.25
   see also employment relationships
employment tribunal, complaints to 11.63–66, 11.88
'establishment,' concept of (in EU law) 11.22–33
   definitions 11.22, 11.25, 11.30
   separate employers within 11.31
EU employment legislation 1.10
   contractual redundancy schemes 12.59–66
   information/consultation obligations 11.01–04,
      11.11–66
   proceedings against UK for breach of 11.11–13
   temporary workers 1.88–90
   unfair dismissal 10.05–14
extra-statutory arrangements *see* contractual
      redundancy schemes

flexibility clause 3.86–87
fraud *see* tax evasion
Freedland, Mark, Prof. 1.04–06
freelance workers 1.116–117

frustration 2.08–09
   by death 5.01

guarantee payments 9.01–23
   calculation 9.19–20
   exclusions 9.03, 9.14–18, 9.40
   failure to comply with reasonable
      requirements 9.18
   failure to pay 9.23
   and industrial action 9.15
   maximum number of days 9.20
   qualifying factors 9.01–06
   right to claim 9.09–13
   unreasonable refusal of alternative work 9.16–17
   workless days 9.07–08, 9.21

health and safety work, dismissal on grounds
      of 10.232
Hepple, Bob, Prof. 1.04
hours
   change of 3.65–67, 4.69
   reduction in 3.44–46

illegal contracts 1.138–144
   tax fraud 1.139–142
   where only one party is guilty 1.143–144
industrial action, breadth of definition 7.07–08
   see also strikes
information, disclosure requirements 11.54–55
injunctions 12.54–55
insolvency, as 'special circumstance' 11.67, 11.69–71
intent, role in contractual interpretation 1.25,
      1.40–41, 1.72, 1.99–112

job function
   change of attributes/qualifications for 3.59–62
   entire change of 3.52–58
   test, *vs.* contract test 3.77–93

'last in, first out' principle 10.145–154, 12.22
   discriminatory implications 10.146–149,
      10.151–153
   employers'/unions' preference for 10.150
   injunctions 12.54–55
lay-off 6.01–28
   common law 6.03
   contractual implications 6.02
   defined 6.01, 6.17
   employee's choices 6.14
   employer's right to impose 6.03, 9.02
   express contractual provisions 6.04–06
   and guarantee payments 9.22
   implied contractual terms 6.07–11
   redundancy payments 6.15–25; claim
      procedure 6.20–21; employer's
      counter-claim 6.22–23
   and 'relevant date' 8.07
   strikes/lock-outs 6.26–28, 7.12
   termination of employment 6.24–25
length of service, as criterion for redundancy *see also*
      contonuous employment; 'last in, first out' principle

location of employment 3.08–34
  and re-employment offers 4.67–68
  refusal to transfer 3.13–20
  see also contract test; mobility clauses
lock-outs 6.26–28

maternity leave 4.*n8*, 10.157, 10.248–256
misconduct 7.01–15
  dismissal on grounds of 7.03–08, 10.201–203
  during notice period 7.13–15
  and redundancy payments: EAT guidelines 7.02,
    7.Appendix; general scheme 7.03–05
mobility clauses 3.13–34, 3.77–78, 3.107
  implied 3.16–22
  limits on right to invoke 3.23–29
multiple redundancies 11.01–92
  successive batches 11.31–33
mutuality of obligation, as test of employment
    status 1.25, 1.27, 1.28–90
  casual workers 1.32–47
  employment agency workers 1.52–90
  outworkers 1.48–51

National Insurance Fund 8.33
natural disasters 9.08
non-standard workers 1.113–115
  continuous employment 1.158
notice, payment in lieu of 8.10
notice period
  death of employee during 5.04–06, 8.11
  dismissal during 7.09, 7.11
  paid time off during 9.24–40

offers of re-employment 4.16–31
  acceptance 4.32–57; time limits 4.58
  from associated employer 4.19–21
  collective 4.84
  communication 4.24–26
  contents 4.27–29
  death of employee prior to acceptance/rejection 5.05
  lateness/vagueness 4.74–76
  multiple 4.30
  oral/written 4.17–18
  requirement of genuineness 4.31, 4.*n29*
  timing 4.22–23
  see also reasonableness; suitability
office holders, employment status 1.123–127
organisational test 1.16–17
outsourcing 3.42–43
outworkers, employee status 1.48–51
overseas employees, eligibility for
    payments 1.160–161, 9.04
overtime bans 7.07–08

partners, employment status 1.135–136
pay rises, dismissal on grounds of claims for 10.232
pension schemes, dismissal on grounds
    connected with 10.232
personal service, as criterion of employee
    status 1.23–24, 1.91–98
'*Polkey* exception' 10.97–107

pregnancy/childbirth, dismissal on grounds relating
    to 10.248–256
  see also maternity leave
presumption of redundancy 3.05–07
'proposal to dismiss' 11.14–21
  distinguished from 'contemplated' 11.14–20
  distinguished from 'decision' 11.21
  successive batches 11.31–33
protective awards 11.72–88
  calculation 11.73–74
  commencement 11.85
  failure of payment 11.88
  penal effect 11.75–84
  procedure 11.72
  reduction 11.86–87

race, (alleged) discrimination on
    grounds of 10.159, 10.221
reasonableness (of dismissal/employer's
    conduct) 10.37–77, 10.106–107
  'band of reasonable responses' test 10.46–66
  consideration of alternatives 10.43–45
  as defence aginst unfairness 10.27
  key principles 10.48
  selections for redundancy 10.121
  size/administrative resources,
    relevance of 10.73–77, 10.102
reasonableness (of re-employment offer
    refusal) 4.58–59, 4.72–84
  alternative job prospects 4.83
  collective offers 4.84
  domestic problems 4.78–79
  financial uncertainty 4.82
  fringe benefits 4.73
  housing/schooling considerations 4.77
  lateness/vagueness of offer 4.74–76
  medical considerations 4.80–81
redundancy *see* continuous employment; contractual
    redundancy schemes; definition of redundancy;
    dismissal; multiple redundancies; presumption
    of redundancy; redundancy payments;
    voluntary redundancy
Redundancy Fund 8.32–33
redundancy payments
  age limits 1.162, 8.12–14
  calculation 8.08, 8.12–31; formula 8.16; repealed
    provisions 8.31; week's pay, as basis 8.17–30
  claim procedure 6.20–21
  collective agreements 12.31–33
  continuous employment, qualification
    period 1.145–158
  custom/practice 12.34–53
  disqualification from 7.03–08; exceptions 7.09
  exclusions from right to 1.159–161
  extensions of right to 1.163–164
  failure/inability to pay 8.32–33
  illegal contracts 1.144
  impact of misconduct/strike action 7.01–15
  qualifications for 1.145, 2.01, 3.01–04
  rebate payable on 8.32–33
  'relevant date' 8.03–11

statutory right to 6.15–28
'tapering' provisions, abolition 8.12
time limits 8.01–02
re-employment 4.01–84
    alternative job prospects 4.83
    distinction between renewal and
        re-engagement 4.07–15
    following childbirth/parental leave 10.248–256
    following death of employer 5.02
    following unfair dismissal 10.185, 10.191–205,
        10.248–256
    fringe benefits 4.73
    under new contract 4.56–57
    new start date 4.27–29
    priority categories of employee 4.n8
    statutory encouragement 4.01–02
    statutory trial period 4.03, 4.33, 4.38–57
    unreasonable refusal 4.58–84
    see also offers of re-employment; reasonableness;
        re-engagement; reinstatement; renewal;
        suitability; trial periods
re-engagement 10.185, 10.193–205
    distinguished from renewal 4.07–15
    obligations on tribunal 10.195–196
    orders for 10.193
    practicability 10.197–200
reinstatement 10.185
    defined 10.191
    orders for 10.192
renewal, distinguished from re-engagement 4.07–10
    significance of distinction 4.11–15
reorganisation (of buiness) 11.06
    changes to job description/requirements 3.69–72,
        3.88–92
    not necesarily giving rise to redundancy 3.51,
        3.63–75

Secretary of State, notification of 11.89–90
selection (for redundancy) 10.108–175
    appeals against 10.112–113, 10.175
    application of criteria 10.167–174
    collective agreements 12.19–30
    consultation over 10.68, 10.110–118
    employer's obligation to justify 10.122,
        10.170–174
    establishment of criteria 10.68, 10.142–166,
        12.19–30
    general principles 10.119–123
    and length of service 10.145–154
    personal considerations 10.161–162
    (potentially) discriminatory 10.145–160
    prohibited grounds 10.42, 10.144–160, 10.232
    selection pool 10.124–141
    subjective grounds 10.103, 10.119, 10.144
    unfair 10.02, 10.42, 10.108–109
self-employment 1.n19
service(s), contracts of/for, distinguished 1.08,
    1.25, 1.65
sham contractual provisions 1.78, 1.92, 1.95,
    1.99–112
    in re-employment offers 4.31, 4.n29

shareholders, employment status 1.128–134
short-time working 6.01–28
    common law 6.03
    contractual implications 6.02
    defined 6.01, 6.18–19
    employee's choices 6.14
    employer's right to impose 6.03
    express contractual provisions 6.04–06
    implied contractual terms 6.12–13
    redundancy payments 6.15–25; claim
        procedure 6.20–21; employer's
        counter claim 6.22–23
    and 'relevant date' 8.07
    strikes/lock-outs 6.26–28, 7.12
    termination of employment 6.24–25
sickness, absence from work on
    grounds of 1.150, 2.09
Spanish law 5.n8
special circumstances 11.60–62, 11.67–72
    applicability 11.67–71
    procedure 11.72
    see also protective awards
statutory rights, dismissal on grounds of
    claims for 10.232–233
strikes 6.26–28, 7.01–15
    defined 7.10
    EAT guidelines 7.02, 7.Appendix
    and guarantee payments 9.15
    impact on redundancy payments 7.01, 7.06–15
    during notice period 7.13–15
    in response to redundancy plans 10.105–107
substitutes, engagement of 1.23–24, 1.91–98
suitability (of re-employment offers) 4.58–71
    factors 4.65–71
    hours 4.69
    legal approach 4.61–64
    location 4.67–68
    pay/skills 4.70–71
    status 4.65–66
Sutcliffe, Gerry 8.13

tax evasion, illegality of contract on
    grounds of 1.139–142
temps see employment agency workers
time off, to look for work/training 9.24–40
    exemption orders 9.40, 9.n69
    procedure 9.27–28
    qualifying factors 9.24–26
    unreasonable refusal/non-remuneration 9.29–34;
        remedies 9.35–39
trade unions
    consultation with 10.68–69, 10.104–106,
        10.110–111, 10.116, 11.04, 11.34–36,
        12.75, 12.77
    membership/activities, dismissal on grounds
        of 10.25, 10.34, 10.232, 10.234–247
    non-members 11.36
    recognition 11.37–38
transfer of undertakings, in contractual redundancy
    schemes 12.59–69
transport (cessation of) provision 3.64

trial periods (for re-employment) 4.03, 4.33, 4.38–57
　'common law' 4.51–57
　death of employee during 5.05
　extension 4.41, 4.47, 4.50
　length 4.39–41, 4.51
　successive 4.48
　termination of employment during 4.42–47
　time limits 4.40, 4.47, 4.51
　working beyond 4.49–50

unfair dismissal 10.01–256, 11.91
　continuous employment qualification 10.03–16
　and contractual redundancy schemes 12.81–82
　defences 10.24–27
　defined 10.231
　key issues 10.42
　payment rules 8.09
　qualifying factors 10.03–23
　remedies 10.185–230 (*see also* compensation;
　　re-engagement; reinstatement); general
　　principles/types 10.185–190
　right to protection against 10.01
　see also automatically unfair dismissal; consultation;
　　reasonableness; warning

voluntary redundancy 2.18–27, 10.17–23,
　10.81, 11.08

warning (of impending redundancy) 10.78–89
　breach of contract 10.80–81
　distinguished from consultation 10.85–89
　premature 10.82, 10.91
week's pay, calculation 8.17–30
　date 8.29
　national average 8.*n19*
　no cap on (for protective purposes) 11.73–74
　no normal working hours 8.27–28
　normal working hours 8.18–23
　remuneration 8.24–26
　writen statements 8.30
women, (potential) discrimination against 10.05–16,
　10.145, 10.157–158, 10.224–225, 10.248–256
'workers', statuory definition/protection 1.10–13
　see also casual workers; employees; freelance workers;
　　non-standard workers
working time, dismissal on grounds
　connected with 10.232
working to rule 7.07
workless days, and guarantee payments 9.07–08, 9.21